Back Page Cricket

A CENTURY OF NEWSPAPER COVERAGE

Back Page Cricket

A CENTURY OF NEWSPAPER COVERAGE

E. W. SWANTON

Edited by George Plumptre

Macdonald
Queen Anne Press

A Queen Anne Press BOOK

First published in Great Britain in 1987 by
Queen Anne Press, a division of
Macdonald & Co (Publishers) Ltd
3rd Floor
Greater London House
Hampstead Road
London NW1 7QX

A BPCC plc Company

British Library Cataloguing in Publication Data

Swanton, E.W.
Back page cricket: a century of newspaper coverage.
1. Cricket – History – 20th century
I. Title
796.35'8'0904 GV913

ISBN 0 356 12774 5

Typeset by Angel Graphics Ltd
Printed and bound in Chichester, Sussex by R.J. Acford Ltd.

PICTURE CREDITS

The Aldus Archive 77, 99; W.E. Alleyne Associates 145; All-Sport 189,
192, 196, 198, 199, 200, 201, 202, 203, 204, 207, 208; BBC Hulton Picture
Library 11, 21, 22, 54, 55, 59; George Beldam 13,15, 18, 32, 33; *Daily Mail
(Manchester)* 36; Derbyshire C.C. 72; Patrick Eagar 149, 153, 160, 161,
163, 164, 167, 171, 172, 173, 174, 175, 179, 180, 181, 184, 188, 191, 194, 195,
197, 205, 206; H. Fishwick 57; Fox Photos Ltd. 77, 108; David Frith 10, 11,
17, 31, 46, 49, 56, 60; *Hastings and St. Leonard's Observer* 88; Ken Kelly 30,
91, 95, 112, 118, 165, 168; Kent C.C. 23, 38, 74; Lancashire C.C. 69; Mail
Newspapers PLC 120; Mansell Collection 14; MCC 12, 24, 27, 35, 36, 37,
41, 42, 44, 56, 131; Nottinghamshire C.C. 61; *Nottingham Evening Post* 28;
The Photosource Ltd. 39, 58, 62, 64, 67, 70, 75, 78, 79, 82, 83, 84, 89, 93, 97,
100, 101, 102, 107, 109, 124, 136, 140, 147, 151, 155, 156, 157, 159, 166;
Popperfoto 143; The Press Association 46, 148, 183; Sport and General
Press Agency Ltd. 66, 85, 86, 87, 96, 103, 104, 116, 117, 119, 122, 123, 127,
128, 129, 134, 137, 141, 150, 177; Surrey C.C. 34; *The Times* 48, 115, 176;
Topham Picture Library 73, 94, 105, 114; Unwin Hyman: *Archie* by Michael
Down 45; Winchester College 43.

Copyright extracts are reproduced by kind permission of the *Daily Mirror*,
the *Guardian*, the *Daily Telegraph*, the *Independent*, London Express News
and Feature Services, London News Service, Mail Newspapers PLC, the
Observer, Odhams Newspapers, Rex Features, Solo Syndication Ltd,
Times Newspapers Ltd, the *Sunday Telegraph*, the *Yorkshire Post*.

The publishers would like to thank the British Newspaper Library for
providing all copy for the newspaper articles in the book.

ACKNOWLEDGEMENTS

The principal acknowledgement in a book of this nature is obviously to all the newspapers and writers whose work appears in the various extracts. At the same time I would like to thank George Plumptre and those at Queen Anne Press responsible for the book's design – in particular Clare Forte – and production and for the photographic research. I am also grateful to C.W. Porter, editor of the Cricket Society Journal, for his helpful assistance.

CONTENTS

INTRODUCTION

I take it as one of the privileges of advanced years to be able to introduce later generations to happenings before their time. To prevent any misunderstanding, this is not to say I was about and taking notice when the opening item in this book occurred, the visit of the first West Indian team to England in 1900. I arrived in fact shortly before Colin Blythe of Kent, that romantic hero of his day, bowled South Africa to defeat in July 1907. The earliest events of which I can claim first-hand cognizance were those of the Australian tour of England fourteen years later. My professional involvement in cricket has covered then rather more than two-thirds of the period under review, dating from England's recovery of the Ashes at The Oval in 1926. I can see now Percy Chapman's happy team filing up the pavilion steps, and the crowd's excitement as they called for their heroes Jack Hobbs, Herbert Sutcliffe, and, not least, Wilfred Rhodes on to the dressing-room balcony.

What have we aimed for, it will be asked, in the presentation of these 150-odd stories spread over the 87 years of this century? To say that *Back Page Cricket* holds a mirror to history is to claim too much. Beneath the banner headlines a game evolves and changes in a way which may or may not be reflected in the high spots of a particular year. In any case we have been careful not to confine ourselves to the foremost occasions and the leading performers.

Our purpose has been rather to try and show the game as seen by English readers of their national newspapers in a wider framework, and just to relive and recapture a variety of happenings and a fairly representative selection of players – as it were in a kaleidoscope. A close look will show, I think, that few of the more notable cricketers of the century have escaped attention.

Within these guidelines we progress from the glamour of the Golden Age through the inter-war period – which for some was a second golden age or an extension of the first – and on to the boom years following the Second World War. Then came the slump in support for first-class cricket and its declining attraction, which led in turn to the arrival of the sponsor and the recruitment of overseas players to the county game. The Packer intrusion was confronted and survived, at the expense of the present heavy over-emphasis on Test and international one-day cricket played all the year round, in pursuit of ever-increasing financial reward. Thus we have seen what is basically the same game played in a manner and a spirit reflecting, as ever, the times in which we have lived. We have watched, and we have marvelled perhaps that the genius in cricket has sustained its survival in recognizable form.

But back to 1900: no cricket book with an historical bent could fail to make a reverential bow to the Old Man himself, and by a happy chance the first match of the first-ever West Indian tour was against a London County eleven managed and captained by Dr W.G. Grace. He was getting on for fifty-two, and more than a bit heavy of movement. Yet he had played his last game for England only a twelvemonth before, and he gave the ancestors of our most formidable antagonists an immediate taste of his skill and stamina. This was six years before, on his fifty-eighth birthday, he played at The Oval his 151st and last innings for the Gentlemen against the Players, made 74 good runs, then laid his bat on the dressing-room table and said that that would be all.

Great names of an altogether younger generation decorate the pages of the following pre-war years: Charles Fry, exemplar supreme of the *mens sana* ideal; G.L. Jessop, Hirst and Rhodes, F.S. Jackson, Sydney Barnes, 'Tip' Foster, Hobbs and Woolley. Immortals all. The Lord's Week, at the peak of its popularity, illuminates two heroes whose fame rests on one single match, P.R. Le Couteur and R.St.L. Fowler. Another such meteor flashes and fades, E.B. Alletson of Nottinghamshire and yet another, the Australian T.J. Matthews, who one fine day at Old Trafford helped himself to six South African wickets by the novel method of bagging a hat-trick in the first innings and another one in the second.

When the First World War brought cricket to a halt there were three Test countries, the original members of the Imperial Cricket Conference, England, Australia and South Africa. By the time the Second came along the number had doubled and the frequency of Test tours increased proportionately. No other Tests, though, caught public imagination to anything like the degree of the original battle of England v Australia.

Nor did any cricketer other than W.G. make such a startling impact on the scene as the prodigy from Bowral in the Australian outback, Don Bradman. On good pitches in both countries – and fate decreed he was very rarely asked to bat on any other – 'the Don' was immense alike in technical proficiency and single-minded dedication. There were other supremely good cricketers, both English and Australian, in action in those two decades. Run the eye down the names of the teams who played in the Lord's Test of 1930 where most will be found, and add a handful who for one reason or another were not then present: Macartney, Gregory, both just retired, and O'Reilly, waiting in the wings, among Australians; and of Englishmen Larwood, Sutcliffe, Verity and a pair soon to be acclaimed and mentioned in the same breath as Walter Hammond: Denis Compton and Len Hutton.

County cricket, with amateurs still taking a prominent role in all but the northernmost sides, was still the staple fare in England between the wars, Yorkshire being supreme for most of the time and never out of the limelight. The West Indians in this period showed glimpses of the power they might become in George Headley, of Jamaica, a magnificent player who was dubbed 'the black Bradman', and an all-rounder of high virtuosity in the Trinidadian, Learie Constantine.

During the last forty years, the cricketers from the Caribbean have brought glamour to fields throughout the world in the persons of 'the three Ws': Worrell, Weekes, and Walcott, and of *the* supreme all-rounder, Gary Sobers, all born and bred in the small island of Barbados. They have brought, too, menace in the form of their current battery of fast bowlers. Simultaneously India, Pakistan, and lately New Zealand have also enlarged the Test picture not only by vastly increasing the quantity of international cricket – an arguable benefit – but in contributing much to the quality. One thinks of the pleasure given by the great Indian spinners of the 1970s: Bedi, Chandrasekhar, Venkat and Prasanna. Not many batsmen in modern times have exhibited a technique equal to that of Sunil Gavaskar who has topped the 10,000-run mark in Tests (a summit unclimbable hitherto) or, for that matter, to compare with the ruthless power of a very different breed of batsman, Vivian Richards of West Indies. Can any country at the time of writing match the all-round virtues of Richard Hadlee of New Zealand or Imran Khan of Pakistan?

The trends in English cricket already mentioned can be seen surely in our selected items of the period from 1946-87. Increasing competition in the Test arena has been matched by a levelling of standards among the counties. Where in the old days Yorkshire, Surrey, Nottinghamshire, Middlesex, Lancashire and Kent (to list them according to the number of Championship wins) ruled the roost now there is not one of the 17 counties which has not won at least two of the several titles today on offer. There has been no parallel to Yorkshire's former eras of monopoly since Surrey's run of seven successive Championships in the 1950s.

It is perhaps a reflection of the more concentrated and diverse round of labour nowadays that over many years we have seen only one English all-rounder of top Test quality in Ian Botham. (By that I mean a man good enough to be chosen in either department irrespective of his credentials in the other.) There have been as many household names among bowlers as batsmen. On the one hand one must include Bedser, Trueman, Statham, Laker, Underwood and Willis, on the other the last amateur public school flowering of May, Cowdrey, and Dexter along with three products from the county staffs, Graveney, Barrington and Boycott. Of the current team let us add to this exalted company David Gower.

Inevitably the second half of the book contains episodes of friction in various guises, trouble over bowling methods, crowd misbehaviour, political upheaval, even a bomb scare. As ever the game is redolent of the age. It is useless to sigh for the cricket of the Pax Britannica. Let us just thank Heaven that, even with a few major reservations, there is enough to enjoy and admire in the cricket and cricketers of today.

1900

CRICKET, introduced, as in most colonial territories, by the British Army and Navy, had flourished in the West Indies for half a century or so, and three English teams had toured there, prior to this first venture to the mother country.

It followed the first tours to England of the Australians (1878) and the Philadelphians (1884). It was not, however, the West Indies' first trip overseas for in 1886 a team had been sent to the USA and Canada, the Americans paying a return visit to the Caribbean the following year. Missionary tours by English teams to South Africa had begun in 1888. Such, then, were the beginnings of international cricket.

From the succinct report in *The Times* of the West Indies' first match

several points may be noticed, not least the prodigious energies of W.G. With his fifty-second birthday coming up, he made 71 going in first, and then bowled 49 overs and took eight wickets. Their captain was R.S.A. Warner, a brother of Plum – afterwards Sir Pelham – Warner from Trinidad (where both were born). Lebrun Constantine was father of Learie (afterwards Lord) Constantine. He and Ollivierre, from St Vincent, were the best batsmen; Burton, from Demerara (now Guyana) the leading bowler. Barbados supplied four players, Trinidad and Demerara three each, Jamaica two and St Vincent and Grenada one each. The team improved as they acclimatized, finishing a strenuous tour with five wins, admittedly against weakened county sides, eight defeats and four draws.

Though fifty years were to elapse before the West Indies beat England in England their cricket never looked back following this 1900 tour. Today, as all the world knows, they are second to none.

THE WEST INDIANS v. LONDON COUNTY.

The West Indians were beaten at the Crystal Palace yesterday by an innings and 198 runs. In less than a couple of hours Dr. Grace and Mr. Mason got the side out a second time. The wicket helped the bowlers. The West Indians did their best within a week of their arrival in this country, and no doubt they will play much better cricket as they get used to English weather and the condition of the grounds.

At luncheon yesterday in the Crystal Palace pavilion Dr. Grace took the opportunity of publicly welcoming the West Indian team. Mr. A. Warner thanked the Englishmen for their reception, and said that they had come to learn cricket and he felt sure that whatever were their match results the trip would be beneficial to West Indian cricket. Mr. W. L. Murdoch pointed out in a very good speech that the same spirit of humility existed among the Australians when they first visited England in 1878. He was sure that the West Indians would as years went on develop their talent as Australia had done.

The Times, 14 June, 1900

WEST INDIANS v LONDON COUNTY
Played at Crystal Palace,
11, 12, 13 June, 1900.
Result: London County won by an innings and 198 runs.

London County: First innings

Mr. W.G. Grace b Burton	71
Mr. J. Gilman b Burton	63
L.C. Braund b Woods	4
Mr. J.R. Mason c Cox b Ollivierre	126
Mr. A.E. Lawton c Constantine b Cox	46
W. Storer b Cox	0
Mr. W.L. Murdoch c Woods b Mignon	23
Mr. H.R. Parkes not out	106
Mr. S.M. Tindall lbw b Ollivierre	7
Mr. E.H.S. Berridge st Constantine b Mignon	50
F.H. Huish b Sproston	2
Extras (b 24, lb 13, w 3)	40
Total	538

Bowling: Burton 35-5-127-2, Woods 26-4-100-1, Mignon 19-3-72-2, Cox 15-2-84-2, Goodman 13-1-52-0, Ollivierre 8-3-24-2, Constantine 5-1-24-0, Sproston 3-0-15-1.

West Indians: First innings

Mr S.W. Sproston c Storer b Grace	5
Mr. G.H. Learmond b Grace	5
Mr. C.A. Ollivierre run out	10
Mr. L. Constantine c Lawton b Grace	2
Mr. P.A. Goodman c Braund b Mason	74
Mr. P.J. Cox c Mason b Storer	53
W.J. Burton b Mason	10
Mr. L.S. D'Ade c Huish b Mason	4
Mr. A. Warner not out	29
Mr. W. Mignon b Mason	1
S. Woods c Gilman b Mason	36
Extras (b 4, lb 2, nb 2)	8
Total	237

Bowling: Grace 34-3-102-3, Braund 13-7-21-0, Tindall 4-1-14-0, Storer 10-2-42-1, Mason 13.2-5-50-5.

West Indians: Second innings

Mr. S.W. Sproston c and b Grace	2
Mr. G.H. Learmond b Mason	7
Mr. C.A. Ollivierre b Mason	20
Mr. L. Constantine c Tindall b Mason	5
Mr. P.A. Goodman b Grace	7
Mr. P.J. Cox st Huish b Grace	3
W.J. Burton c Tindall b Mason	18
Mr. L.S. D'Ade lbw b Grace	0
Mr. A. Warner c Huish b Mason	20
Mr. W. Mignon not out	8
S. Woods b Grace	5
Extras (b 2, lb 5, nb 1)	8
Total	103

Bowling: Grace 15.2-2-52-5, Mason 15-4-43-5.

LEFT Cumberbatch (SEATED) and Woods, founders of the West Indies' fast-bowling tradition. Cumberbatch was unaccountably left out of the 1900 side. Woods toured and took 72 wickets in all matches

NO TECHNICAL question in cricket history has occasioned more fervent or regular debate than the lbw law. At the MCC annual general meeting of May 1901 some influential members led by the Hon Alfred Lyttelton proposed a change in the law, which, despite attempts at reform, had remained unaltered since 1788. This stipulated that the ball must pitch straight and the leg that was hit had to be in line with the stumps. The Lyttelton proposal was that whereas the leg had to be in line with the stumps the ball might pitch wide of them, either on the off or the leg.

In addition to W.G.'s letter quoted – from which some sympathy with the proposal comes through – a much longer one, also opposing the reform, appeared on the day of the MCC meeting, signed by, among others, Lord Hawke, J.R. Mason, A.P. Lucas and P.F. Warner. Despite this weight of criticism the members of MCC carried the motion by seventy-one votes, though without the necessary two-thirds majority. Another forty sup-porters – fewer, surely, than might have been swayed by *The Times* letters – would have won the day, and so effected a major change in the evolution of the game.

As it was, the law remained unchanged until 1937, since which the ball pitching to the off, but not to the leg, could result in lbw – a modification which has since been widely regarded as a mistake.

Note that the chief object of the proposed reform of 1901 was to rectify the balance between bowler and batsman and so reduce the number of drawn matches. The following are percentages of draws in the County Championship:

1900	42 per cent
1985	62 per cent
1864-1986	33 per cent

Alfred Lyttelton was England's first Test wicket-keeper, the finest all-round sportsman of his generation, and a brilliant lawyer and statesman. Of the eleven pages covering the debate verbatim in the 1902 *Wisden* three and a half are devoted to his opening speech.

1901

BELOW Hon Alfred Lyttelton, here with his close friend, A.J. Balfour, in whose Cabinet he was Colonial Secretary

BELOW Lord Hawke: leading and influential opponent of Lyttelton's proposed changes to the lbw law.

1901

THE CHOICE of this occasion was dictated by the achievement of C.B. Fry in scoring a sixth successive first-class hundred. At that date a handful of cricketers including him had three successive hundreds to their credit, but no more. This innings of 105 against the champion county followed a sequence of 106 v Hampshire, 209 v Yorkshire, 149 v Middlesex, 105 v Surrey and 140 v Kent. In all Fry in 1901 made the then record number of 13 hundreds, *Wisden* remarking how, 'his present position among the batsmen of the day affords a wonderful illustration of what a man can accomplish by intelligence and application, for during the four years he was at Oxford there was nothing about his play to suggest that he would take really high rank ...' Compared with the natural genius of his friend and colleague, K.S. Ranjitsinhji for instance, he was a 'made' player.

The report holds, however, other points of interest, and not least an illustration of the style and high quality of *The Times* cricket reports which were then and for many following years unsigned. Note a double layer of canvas sheeting protected the Lord's pitch before the match, an isolated instance of covering more than half a century before it became officially allowable.

Note, too, that Charles Fry was thoroughly upstaged by Jessop who next day went on to score 233, and of whom Fry later wrote, 'no man has ever driven a cricket ball so hard, so high, and so often in so many different directions. No man has ever made cricket so dramatic an entertainment'.

Finally it is, of course, very unusual for a match to be played for the benefit of an amateur's widow and children. William Yardley, a famous all-round cricketer in his day (he was the first man to score a century in the University match), a playwright and drama critic, had died suddenly aged fifty-one the previous year.

YORKSHIRE v REST OF ENGLAND
Played at Lord's,
12, 13, 14 September, 1901.
Result: Rest of England won by an innings and 115 runs.

Rest of England: First innings

Mr A.O. Jones c Tunnicliffe b Smith	65
Mr P.F. Warner c Wainwright b Rhodes	29
Mr G.W. Beldam c Tunnicliffe b Rhodes	54
Mr C.B. Fry c Hirst b Rhodes	105
Mr G.L. Jessop b Hirst	233
J. Gunn b Whitehead	21
Mr J.H. Sinclair b Hirst	1
Mr H.D.G. Leveson-Gower b Hirst	0
A.E. Trott b Hirst	0
Wilson not out	4
Mr R.B. Brooks b Hirst	4
Extras (b 7, lb 3)	10
Total	526

Bowling: Hirst 26.3-5-92-5, Rhodes 43-6-179-3, Wainwright 9-2-49-0, Brown 9-0-53-0, Smith 19-4-75-1, Whitehead 14-1-68-1.

Yorkshire: First innings

J. Tunnicliffe b Jones	27
J.T. Brown st Brooks b Jones	12
D. Denton lbw b Trott	12
Mr T.L. Taylor lbw b Trott	1
Lord Hawke b Trott	28
G.H. Hirst c Brooks b Sinclair	48
Mr E. Smith b Trott	52
W. Rhodes c and b Sinclair	26
Lees not out	14
D. Hunter c Warner b Trott	1
E. Wainwright absent hurt	0
Extras (b 6, lb 2)	8
Total	229

Bowling: Wilson 18-2-50-0, Trott 27.5-4-86-5, Jones 6-1-29-2, Gunn 6-2-23-0, Sinclair 10-2-33-2.

Yorkshire: Second innings:

J. Tunnicliffe b Trott	9
J.T. Brown lbw b Trott	44
D. Denton c Wilson b Trott	2
Mr T.L. Taylor st Brooks b Trott	0
Lord Hawke lbw b Trott	1
G.H. Hirst b Trott	5
Mr E. Smith not out	59
W. Rhodes c and b Trott	15
Lees Whitehead b Wilson	6
D. Hunter c Warner b Trott	2
E. Wainwright b Sinclair	30
Extras (b 9, lb 2, w 1)	12
Total	182

Bowling: Wilson 16-5-24-1, Trott 29.5-8-84-8, Sinclair 13-3-62-1.

LEFT C.B. Fry with his England and Sussex friend and colleague, K.S. Ranjitsinhji.

RIGHT Fry demonstrates the straight drive for the camera of George Beldam, the father of modern cricket photography

1902

ENGLAND v. AUSTRALIA.

THE LAST TEST MATCH.

A MARVELLOUS VICTORY.

ENGLAND WIN BY ONE WICKET.

BRILLIANT BATTING BY JESSOP.

JACKSON, HIRST. AND RHODES SHARE IN THE HONOURS.

THE PRESTIGE OF ENGLISH CRICKET RESTORED.

Sporting Life, 14 August, 1902

THE TEST series of 1902 was a classic beyond compare contested by two of the strongest Test teams in history. This Test at The Oval still rates as the most exciting ever played by England, more extraordinary even than the preceding one at Old Trafford won by Australia by three runs.

The anonymous *Sporting Life* reporter maintains throughout his account of the last day's play the note of fine patriotic fervour that marks his introduction. When Jessop came in to play his great innings England, needing 263 to win on a difficult pitch, were 48 for 5, and *Wisden* thought the odds were fifty to one against them. The Australians had had 'a poor opinion of Jessop as a hitter' before he demolished their attack to the tune of 102 in 75 minutes. (This is still the fastest hundred in England-Australia matches).

At the climax when Rhodes joined Hirst with 15 runs needed neither assuredly said to the other, as legend has it, that they would get them in singles. They would in any case have called them 'ones'. Rhodes in fact began with four through the slips, but was 'not quite the master of the stroke'. In the tensest atmosphere imaginable there were narrow escapes, but the two Yorkshiremen safely and solidly reached the target, 'whereat the crowd yelled with delight . . . and cheered until they were hoarse'.

ENGLAND v AUSTRALIA

Played at The Oval, 11, 12, 13 August, 1902
Result: England won by one wicket

Australia: First innings

V.T. Trumper b Hirst	42
R.A. Duff c Lilley b Hirst	23
C. Hill b Hirst	11
J. Darling* c Lilley b Hirst	3
M.A. Noble c and b Jackson	52
S.E. Gregory b Hirst	23
W.W. Armstrong b Jackson	17
A.J.Y. Hopkins c MacLaren b Lockwood	40
H. Trumble not out	64
J.J. Kelly† c Rhodes b Braund	39
J.V. Saunders lbw b Braund	0
Extras (b 5, lb 3, nb 2)	10
Total	324

Fall of Wickets: 1/47, 2/63, 3/69, 4/82, 5/126, 6/174, 7/175, 8/256, 9/324, 10/324.
Bowling: Lockwood 24-2-85-1, Rhodes 28-9-46-0, Hirst 29-5-77-5, Braund 16.5-5-29-2, Jackson 20-4-66-2, Jessop 6-2-11-0.

England: First innings

A.C. MacLaren* c Armstrong b Trumble	10
L.C.H. Palairet b Trumble	20
J.T. Tyldesley b Trumble	33
T.W. Hayward b Trumble	0
Hon F.S. Jackson c Armstrong b Saunders	2
L.C. Braund c Hill b Trumble	22
G.L. Jessop b Trumble	13
G.H. Hirst c and b Trumble	43
W.H. Lockwood c Noble b Saunders	25
A.F.A. Lilley† c Trumper b Trumble	0
W. Rhodes not out	0
Extras (b 13, lb 2)	15
Total	183

Fall of Wickets: 1/31, 2/36, 3/62, 4/67, 5/67, 6/83, 7/137, 8/179, 9/183, 10/183.
Bowling: Trumble 31-13-65-8, Saunders 23-7-79-2, Noble 7-3-24-0.

Australia: Second innings

V.T. Trumper run out	2
R.A. Duff b Lockwood	6
C. Hill c MacLaren b Hirst	34
J. Darling* c MacLaren b Lockwood	15
M.A. Noble b Braund	13
S.E. Gregory b Braund	9
W.W. Armstrong b Lockwood	21
A.J.Y. Hopkins c Lilley b Lockwood	3
H. Trumble (10) not out	7
J.J. Kelly† (11) lbw b Lockwood	0
J.V. Saunders (9) c Tyldesley b Rhodes	2
Extras (b 7, lb 2)	9
Total	121

Fall of Wickets: 1/6, 2/9, 3/31, 4/71, 5/75, 6/91, 7/99, 8/114, 9/115, 10/121.
Bowling: Lockwood 20-6-45-5, Rhodes 22-7-38-1, Hirst 5-1-7-1, Braund 9-1-15-2, Jackson 4-3-7-0.

England: Second innings

A.C. MacLaren* b Saunders	2
L.C.H. Palairet b Saunders	6
J.T. Tyldesley b Saunders	0
T.W. Hayward c Kelly b Saunders	7
Hon. F.S. Jackson c and b Trumble	49
L.C. Braund c Kelly b Trumble	2
G.L. Jessop c Noble b Armstrong	104
G.H. Hirst not out	58
W.H. Lockwood lbw b Trumble	2
A.F.A. Lilley† c Darling b Trumble	16
W. Rhodes not out	6
Extras (b 5, lb 6)	11
Total (9 wickets)	263

Fall of Wickets: 1/5, 2/5, 3/10, 4/31, 5/48, 6/157, 7/187, 8/214, 9/248.
Bowling: Trumble 33.5-4-108-4, Saunders 24-3-105-4, Noble 5-0-11-0, Armstrong 4-0-28-1.

FAR LEFT 'The Croucher' in repose.

LEFT The end of the match – 'the most exciting ever played by England' – and The Oval crowd express their rapture

1903

ALL ENGLISH tours to Australia prior to that of 1903-04 had been the result of private enterprises, the teams collected by individuals. The Australian authority had been the Melbourne Cricket Club, which for some years had been urging MCC to undertake the responsibilities of selection and management.

This Sydney Test has the special significance that it was the first to be played under the aegis of MCC – which continued to run Test tours abroad for seventy-odd years, until they were taken over by the Test and County Cricket Board. The beginning could hardly have been more auspicious, England winning a game of extraordinary fluctuations by five wickets and going on to regain by the odd Test of five the Ashes retained by Australia in 1902.

The score-card records the then highest innings in Test cricket, R.E. Foster's 287, a wonderful virtuoso performance by the third of the famous Worcestershire brotherhood of seven. His effort depended on a masterful 53 by J.T. Tyldesley made while the pitch of Bulli soil was recovering after rain. Wilfred Rhodes, the number 11 who, two tours later, was opening the England innings, gave inklings of his promise by helping to add 130 for the last wicket.

The brilliant Victor Trumper, responding to Foster's challenge, carried his bat through Australia's second innings for 185, and England had many anxious moments before victory came. The match went into the sixth day and was watched by 95,000.

RIGHT R.E. Foster: his record-breaking 287 was his sole century in Test cricket

AUSTRALIA v ENGLAND
Played at Sydney, 11, 12, 14, 15, 16, 17 December, 1903.
Result: England won by five wickets.

Australia: First innings

R.A. Duff c Lilley b Arnold	3
V.T. Trumper c Foster b Arnold	1
C. Hill c Lilley b Hirst	5
M.A. Noble* c Foster b Arnold	133
W.W. Armstrong b Bosanquet	48
A.J.Y. Hopkins b Hirst	39
W.P. Howell c Relf b Arnold	5
S.E. Gregory b Bosanquet	23
F. Laver lbw b Rhodes	4
J.J. Kelly† b Braund b Rhodes	10
J.V. Saunders not out	11
Extras (nb 3)	3
Total	285

Fall of Wickets: 1/2, 2/9, 3/12, 4/118, 5/200, 6/207, 7/259, 8/263, 9/271, 10/285.
Bowling: Hirst 24-8-47-2, Arnold 32-7-76-4, Braund 26-9-39-0, Bosanquet 13-0-52-2, Rhodes 17.2-3-41-2, Relf 6-1-27-0.

England: First innings

T.W. Hayward b Howell	15
P.F. Warner* c Kelly b Laver	0
J.T. Tyldesley b Noble	53
E.G. Arnold c Laver b Armstrong	27
R.E. Foster c Noble b Saunders	287
L.C. Braund b Howell	102
G.H. Hirst b Howell	0
B.J.T. Bosanquet c Howell b Noble	2
A.F.A. Lilley† c Hill b Noble	4
A.E. Relf c Armstrong b Saunders	31
W. Rhodes not out	40
Extras (b 6, lb 7, w 1, nb 2)	16
Total	577

Fall of Wickets: 1/0, 2/49, 3/73, 4/117, 5/309, 6/311, 7/318, 8/332, 9/447, 10/577.
Bowling: Saunders 36.2-8-125-2, Laver 37-12-119-1, Howell 31-7-111-3, Noble 34-8-99-3, Armstrong 23-3-47-1, Hopkins 11-1-40-0, Trumper 7-2-12-0, Gregory 2-0-8-0.

Australia: Second innings

R.A. Duff (3) c Relf b Rhodes	84
V.T. Trumper (5) not out	185
C. Hill (4) run out	51
M.A. Noble* (6) st Lilley b Bosanquet	22
W.W. Armstrong (7) c Bosanquet b Rhodes	27
A.J.Y. Hopkins (8) c Arnold b Rhodes	20
W.P. Howell (10) c Lilley b Arnold	4
S.E. Gregory (1) c Lilley b Rhodes	43
F. Laver† c Relf b Rhodes	6
J.J. Kelly (2) b Arnold	13
J.V. Saunders run out	2
Extras (b 10, lb 15, w 2, nb 1)	28
Total	485

Fall of Wickets: 1/36, 2/108, 3/191, 4/254, 5/334, 6/393, 7/441, 8/468, 9/473, 10/485.
Bowling: Hirst 29-1-79-0, Arnold 28-2-93-2, Braund 12-2-56-0, Bosanquet 23-1-100-1, Rhodes 40.2-10-94-5, Relf 13-5-35-0.

England: Second innings

T.W. Hayward st Kelly b Saunders	91
P.F. Warner* b Howell	8
J.T. Tyldesley c Noble b Saunders	9
R.E. Foster (4) st Kelly b Armstrong	19
L.C. Braund (5) c Noble b Howell	0
G.H. Hirst (6) not out	60
B.J.T. Bosanquet (7) not out	1
E.G. Arnold	
A.F.A. Lilley†	did not bat
A.E. Relf	
W. Rhodes	
Extras (b 3, lb 1, w 2)	6
Total (5 wickets)	194

Fall of Wickets: 1/21, 2/39, 3/81, 4/82, 5/181.
Bowling: Saunders 18.5-3-51-2, Laver 16-4-37-0, Howell 31-18-35-2, Noble 12-2-37-0, Armstrong 18-6-28-1.

DERBY'S MARVELLOUS WIN.

All Cricket Records Beaten by Midlanders.

ESSEX BATTING FAILS.

The Derbyshire eleven gained an astounding victory over Essex at Chesterfield yesterday. To lose the toss, field out for an innings of nearly 600, and win at the finish by nine wickets, is a performance quite unprecedented in the annals of county cricket, the nearest approach to it in first-class matches being the memorable Test match in Australia nearly ten years ago, when the Colonials were beaten by ten wickets after making a dozen or so fewer than were credited to Essex in their first innings.

Such a result was quite unlooked for on Tuesday evening, when Derbyshire had replied to their opponents' gigantic total by making 446 for the loss of four wickets. Yesterday morning the innings closed in rather quiet fashion for an additional 102 runs, Cadman alone of the later batsmen playing really well.

Altogether Derbyshire were batting about six hours, and left off in a minority of 49. In three-quarters of an hour before lunch the game underwent a sensational change, Bestwick and Warren bowling so finely that six wickets went down for 27 runs. Subsequently Sewell and Douglas made a great effort to get the side out of trouble, and put on 57 in fifty minutes before they were separated. The end, however, came after an hour and fifty minutes' batting, Gillingham, who was suffering from lumbago, being unable to go in.

Derbyshire had two hours and five minutes in which to get 147 runs to win the match; and, after losing Wright at 11, they always looked like getting them. The wicket had certainly worn to some extent, but Buckenham and Reeves could not get as much aid from it as the famous Derbyshire pair had done.

Ollivierre and Storer scored with the utmost freedom and confidence. The result was that the runs were hit off in an hour and twenty minutes. Ollivierre, who had hard lines in not reaching three figures for the second time in the match, played brilliant and faultless cricket, hitting fifteen 4's and five 2's.

There were about 3,000 people on the ground, and there was naturally a great scene of enthusiasm when Derbyshire's brilliant victory was consummated. It was the first occasion on which they had ever beaten the eastern county in a championship match on Derbyshire soil.

Daily Mirror, 21 July, 1904

DERBYSHIRE v ESSEX
Played at Chesterfield, 18, 19, 20 July, 1904.
Result: Derbyshire won by nine wickets.

Essex: First innings

Mr F.L. Fane lbw b Curgenven	63
H. Carpenter b Bestwick	5
Mr P. Perrin not out	343
Mr C. McGahey b Warren	32
Rev F.H. Gillingham c and b Warren	43
E.H.D. Sewell b Warren	10
W. Reeves b Warren	0
Mr R.P. Keigwin lbw b Ashcroft	14
Mr J.W.H.T. Douglas b Ollivierre	47
E. Russell c Humphries b Cadman	23
C.P. Buckenham lbw b Bestwick	3
Extras (b 2, lb 5, w 3, nb 4)	14
Total	597

Bowling: Warren 29-3-143-3, Bestwick 42.1-8-160-3, Cadman 22-3-65-1, Storer 7-0-41-0, Curgenven 16-1-67-1, Ashcroft 7-1-38-1, Morton 8-1-39-0, Wright 4-0-15-0, Ollivierre 3-0-15-1.

Derbyshire: First innings

Mr L.G. Wright c Fane b Reeve	68
Mr C.A. Ollivierre b Reeves	229
W. Storer b Buckenham	44
Mr E.M. Ashcroft b Sewell	34
E. Needham b Reeves	47
Mr G. Curgenven b Buckenham	31
Morton b Reeves	16
A. Warren b Douglas	18
Cadman c Douglas b Reeves	34
J. Humphries not out	2
W. Bestwick lbw b Douglas	0
Extras (b 6, lb 18, w 1)	25
Total	548

Bowling: Buckenham 43-5-176-2, Keigwin 7-1-36-0, Reeves 51-7-192-5, Douglas 15.3-1-54-2, McGahey 11-2-34-0, Sewell 7-0-31-1.

'MARVELLOUS' and 'astounding' are words which scarcely overstate the happenings of this game wherein the batting of P.A. Perrin for Essex on the first day was matched by that of C.A. Ollivierre for Derbyshire on the second and third.

Perrin's 343 not out was made in five and three-quarter hours and contained 68 fours – which is still the world record for the number of boundaries in an innings. Yet it was all in a lost cause since Ollivierre – a St Vincentian, who had come to England with the first West Indian side in 1900 and stayed on to qualify for Derbyshire – led a brilliant counter-attack in their first innings, and, after Warren and Bestwick skittled Essex when they batted a second time, ran up an unbeaten 92 out of 149 for 2 in eighty minutes to clinch the eight-wicket victory. *Wisden* records that a crowd of 3,000 were there at the finish to cheer on their side at Queen's Park, that attractive ground beneath the crooked spire.

'Peter' Perrin was very much of a character in the cricket world. A Cockney who learned his game in Tottenham, he would probably have played for England if he had been less inadequate in the field. As it was, he was identified with Test cricket throughout the 1930s as a highly-respected selector. As a first-rate shot and earthy raconteur he also later earned the friendship of King George V.

Essex: Second innings

Mr F.L. Fane b Warren	2
H. Carpenter c Warren b Bestwick	2
Mr P. Perrin c and b Warren	8
Mr C. McGahey c Cadman b Bestwick	5
E.H.D. Sewell c Cadman b Curgenven	41
W. Reeves b Bestwick	0
Mr R.P. Keigwin c Needham b Warren	0
Mr J.W.H.T. Douglas not out	27
E. Russell b Curgenven	0
C.P. Buckenham b Warren	3
Rev F.H. Gillingham absent ill	–
Extras (w 2, nb 2)	4
Total	97

Bowling: Warren 16.1-5-42-4, Bestwick 16-4-34-3, Cadman 2-0-10-0, Curgenven 5-2-7-2.

Derbyshire: Second innings

Mr L.G. Wright c Carpenter b Buckenham	1
Mr C.A. Ollivierre not out	92
W. Storer not out	48
Extras (b 4, lb 2, w 1, nb 1)	8
Total	149

Mr E.M. Ashcroft, E. Needham, Mr G. Curgenven, Morton, A. Warren, Cadman, J. Humphries and W. Bestwick did not bat.

Bowling: Buckenham 13-0-78-1, Reeves 13-1-43-0, Douglas 2-0-14-0, McGahey 2-1-6-0.

TOP P.A. Perrin comes off the field having scored 343, despite which his side were beaten by eight wickets.

ABOVE Charles Ollivierre, prolific run-getter for Derbyshire between 1902 and 1907

1905

FOURTH TEST MATCH.

JACKSON SCORES HIS FIFTH CENTURY FOR ENGLAND.

STRONG POSITION.

The fourth test match, which opened at Manchester yesterday, was remarkable even if only for one feature—the wonderful success of F. S. Jackson, the English captain.

His performances in test matches are truly extraordinary. He has now no fewer than five centuries to his credit in these fixtures, while no other player, either English or Australian, can boast of more than two. The following is a list of Jackson's centuries for England:

103 at the Oval in 1893.
118 at the Oval in 1899.
128 at Manchester in 1902.
144 (not out) at Leeds in 1905.
103 (unfinished) at Manchester in 1905.

The present position of the English team is a particularly strong one. With only six wickets down they have scored 352.

Daily Express, 25 July, 1905

AUSTRALIANS COLLAPSE.

ENGLAND WINS RUBBER IN HOLLOW FASHION.

THE "ASHES" SAFE.

Daily Express, 27 July, 1905

RIGHT F.S. Jackson swinging the bat with characteristic panache.

THE TEST series of 1905 was a triumph for F.S. Jackson who was appointed in that year to the England captaincy after A.C. MacLaren had surrendered the two previous home series to Australia. Jackson won all five tosses and headed both batting and bowling averages with figures of 70 and 15 respectively. He made two hundreds, the second of which at Old Trafford in the Fourth Test helped England to secure the Ashes with her second victory. The other three matches were all drawn in England's favour.

Jackson was, by every contemporary estimation, a great cricketer, a stylish, free batsman of orthodox method and a lively bowler, fast-medium in pace and with a dangerous break-back. Above all he was a man of courage, always most dangerous in a crisis. In later life he became a minister and also Governor of Bengal. He died Colonel the Hon Sir Stanley Jackson PC, GCSI, GCIE, but known the cricket world over as 'Jacker'.

ENGLAND v AUSTRALIA

Played at Manchester, 24, 25, 26 July, 1905.
Result: England won by an innings and 80 runs.

England: First innings

A.C. MacLaren c Hill b McLeod	14
T.W. Hayward c Gehrs b McLeod	82
J.T. Tyldesley b Laver	24
C.B. Fry b Armstrong	17
Hon F.S. Jackson* c Cotter b McLeod	113
R.H. Spooner c and b McLeod	52
G.H. Hirst c Laver b McLeod	25
E.G. Arnold run out	25
W. Rhodes not out	27
A.F.A. Lilley† lbw b Noble	28
W. Brearley c Darling b Noble	0
Extras (b 17, lb 20, w 1, nb 1)	39
Total	446

Fall of Wickets: 1/24, 2/77, 3/136, 4/176, 5/301, 6/347, 7/382, 8/387, 9/446, 10/446.
Bowling: Cotter 26-4-83-0, McLeod 47-8-125-5, Armstrong 48-14-93-1, Laver 21-5-73-1, Noble 15.5-3-33-2.
Australia: First innings 197 (J. Darling 73; Brearley 4-72).
Australia: Second innings 169 (R.A. Duff 60; Brearley 4-54, Rhodes 3-36).

1906

W.G. HAD first taken the field for Gentlemen against Players as a slim lad of seventeen. Here he is, forty-one years later signing off, as it were, in heavy middle-age with an innings of 74, still retaining a large measure of his skill even if slowness between the wickets had reduced the full reward for his strokes. But for this, says the *Sporting Life* reporter, 'he would have passed the century easily'.

As he returned to The Oval dressing-room on his fifty-eighth birthday it is recorded that 'the Old Man' flung down his bat and declared, 'I shan't play any more'. So far as important cricket was concerned nor did he. The man who had personified cricket in the hearts and minds of Englishmen for so long – around whose deeds and personality it had grown from a country pastime to a national institution – had made his final bow to a fitting crescendo of applause.

The annual meeting of Gents and Players at The Oval never had the cachet of the great fixture at Lord's which, except when the Australians were visiting, was always the high point of the season. Nevertheless, it was a popular and competitive occasion, well supported by enthusiasts south of the river.

As it happened, W.G.'s average of 41 for his 62 innings at Lord's was almost identical with that for his 66 at The Oval. His record, towering over all others, for the Gentlemen was:

Inns. NotOut Runs Highest Aver.
151   10   6008   217   42.60

These runs included 15 hundreds: and he took 271 wickets in the matches at 18.72 each.

It is probable that 'the veteran' relished his appearance for the Gentlemen as much as any others during his long career. Certainly his was an unrivalled contribution in giving the matches against the Players the status and popularity which they enjoyed for so long. Before his advent the Players were far too strong. After he retired amateur victories were rare again. In his day they gave as good as they got. This is not the least measure of his influence on the game.

GENTLEMEN v PLAYERS

Played at The Oval
16, 17, 18 July, 1906
Result: Match drawn

Players: First innings

Hayward b May	16
Iremonger b Crawford	43
Hayes b Odell	34
Quaife c Colbeck b May	28
J. Gunn c Colbeck b May	27
King not out	89
Hardstaff lbw b Odell	44
Lees c Napier b Crawford	21
Trott b Jessop	24
Jayes b Crawford	7
Strudwick c May b Crawford	8
Extras (b 20, w 1, nb 3)	24
Total	365

Bowling: May 25-7-71-3, Odell 23-5-66-2, Crawford 31.3-5-105-4, Jessop 10-1-53-1, Napier 11-2-46-0.

Gentlemen: First innings

C.J.B. Wood b Trott	68
M.W. Payne b Gunn	3
J.N. Crawford c Gunn b Lees	26
A.E. Lawton c Gunn b Jayes	40
G.L. Jessop st Strudwick b Lees	38
L.G. Colbeck c Iremonger b Lees	54
W.G. Grace c Jayes b Lees	4
Lord Dalmeny b Trott	10
G.G. Napier b Trott	0
P.R. May b Lees	6
W.W. Odell not out	0
Extras (b 8, lb 1)	9
Total	258

Bowling: Lees 24.4-6-84-5, Gunn 17-3-55-1, Jayes 9-1-43-1, Trott 15-3-53-3, Hayes 5-1-14-0.

Players: Second innings

Hayward c Colbeck b May	10
Iremonger b Crawford	5
Hayes b May	9
Quaife run out	5
J. Gunn b May	1
King c Colbeck b Grace	88
Hardstaff c and b May	104
Lees c Payne b Napier	28
Trott not out	27
Jayes c Payne b Napier	6
Strudwick c Lawton b Crawford	22
Extras (b 25, lb 4, nb 1)	30
Total	335

Bowling: Crawford 29.5-8-84-2, May 21-2-89-4, Napier 13-2-73-2, Jessop 4-2-16-0, Grace 7-1-23-1, Lord Dalmeny 4-0-20-0.

Gentlemen: Second innings

C.J.B. Wood c Hayes b Gunn	49
M.W. Payne c Trott b Jayes	48
J.N. Crawford not out	71
A.E. Lawton c Hayward b King	11
G.L. Jessop c Hardstaff b King	0
L.G. Colbeck c Hayward b Quaife	8
W.G. Grace c Trott b Jayes	74
Lord Dalmeny b Quaife	2
G.G. Napier ⎫	
P.R. May ⎬ did not bat	
W.W. Odell ⎭	
Extras (b 8, lb 4, nb 2)	14
Total (7 wickets)	277

Bowling: Lees 10-3-26-0, Trott 13-3-38-0, Jayes 22-1-86-2, Gunn 10-1-41-1, Hayes 7-0-26-0, King 11-3-37-2, Quaife 2.3-0-9-2.

LEFT 'W.G.' dominated Gents v Players matches for nearly half a century. Here he takes his final bow with fitting dignity

1907

FOLLOWING the defeat in 1905-06 in South Africa of the first MCC side to tour there, P.W. Sherwell brought a side to meet the full strength of England for the first time. The visit was a pronounced success, despite a wet summer, the South Africans winning 17 first-class matches and coming with honour from the three-match Test series wherein England won the only game concluded by 53 runs.

South Africa brought no fewer than four practitioners of the newly-developing art of wrist-spin bowling: Faulkner, Vogler, Schwarz and White. Of these Faulkner became acknowledged as among the best all-rounders in the world. On a difficult, rain-affected pitch at Headingley in the Second Test he took 9 for 75. However it was the orthodox left-arm spin of Colin Blythe which proved decisive. His return of 15 wickets for 199 remains one of the outstanding analyses in Test history, and the best ever at Headingley.

Blythe was a highly-strung, violin-playing bowler of the classic type, an artist alike with the bow and the ball. He was the greatest cricketer among those killed in the First World War.

RIGHT Virtuoso spinner Colin Blythe, of whom Sydney Pardon wrote in his obituary 'To see him bowl to a brilliant hitter was a sheer delight'

THE SECOND TEST.

ENGLAND'S DECISIVE WIN.

COLONIALS DIE HARD.

BLYTHE'S BOWLING RECORD.

The "Dismal Jimmies" who at the close of Monday's play at Leeds made haste to blame England for having, on a most treacherous wicket, scored some 30 runs less than the South Africans will be at a loss for a text to-day. There is really nothing to croak about after all. A stubborn fight, in which the home side had some anxious moments, has ended—as, indeed, appeared probable on Tuesday evening—in a handsome victory for England by 53 runs. The first Test Match, as all will readily recall, was left drawn greatly in favour of the Mother Country, which has now won the second, despite a start so disastrous that it might well have meant defeat but for a good deal of resolute all-round play in the subsequent stages. There is no leveller like a thoroughly difficult wicket, to which the eminence the pitch at Leeds undoubtedly attained. But well as Faulkner, White, and others in the visiting team may have bowled, it is clear there is no one on the side capable of such deadly work as Blythe, of Kent, who in each innings was almost absolute master of the situation, as his memorable figures—15 wickets for 99 runs—conclusively show. Nor was there a South African batsman found equal to making a score in any way comparable to the 51 of the great Sussex player's runs were made while the bowlers had to use a slippery ball is, of course, true enough; but it must also be remembered that his innings was interrupted by several adjournments caused by rain, which means that he had to "get his eye in" not once only, but perhaps half a dozen times in the course of his splendid effort. In one respect our visitors showed superiority. It is definitely stated by those who saw the match throughout that the South Africans dropped not a single catch, whereas there were, it seems, several rather bad blunders in the field while they were batting, both on Monday and yesterday. Fortunately for England these errors made no serious difference—save that they mitigated in some measure the severity of the Colonial defeat. No: the jeremiads already half-written must be reserved for some fitter occasion. England—however unpalatable the fact may be to some of our critics—is still master of the cricket field. Meantime all sportsmen will join in the hope that the third Test, fixed for the Oval on the 19th of this month, may be played on a good, true wicket, with such luck as may be going apportioned quite equally. It is satisfactory to know that the game will be fought to a finish, irrespective of the number of days required to bring about a "consummation most devoutly to be wished."

Morning Post, 1 August, 1907

ENGLAND v SOUTH AFRICA

Played at Leeds,
29, 30, 31 July, 1907.
Result: England won by 53 runs.

England: First innings

T.W. Hayward st Sherwell b Faulkner	24
C.B. Fry b Vogler	2
J.T. Tyldesley b Faulkner	12
R.E. Foster* b Sinclair	0
L.C. Braund lbw b Faulkner	1
G.H. Hirst c Hathorn b Sinclair	17
G.L. Jessop c Sherwell b Faulkner	0
E.G. Arnold b Faulkner	0
A.F.A. Lilley† c Schwarz b Faulkner	3
C. Blythe not out	5
N.A. Knox c Faulkner b Sinclair	8
Extras (b 1, lb 2, nb 1)	4
Total	76

Fall of Wickets: 1/9, 2/41, 3/42, 4/42, 5/53, 6/53, 7/57, 8/63, 9/63, 10/76.
Bowling: Vogler 8-3-14-1, Schwarz 7-0-18-0, Faulkner 11-4-17-6, Sinclair 10.3-2-23-3.

England: Second innings

T.W. Hayward st Sherwell b Vogler	15
C.B. Fry lbw b White	54
J.T. Tyldesley c Snooke b Schwarz	30
R.E. Foster* lbw b Faulkner	22
L.C. Braund c Schwarz b White	0
G.H. Hirst b White	2
G.L. Jessop c Hathorn b Faulkner	10
E.G. Arnold c Schwarz b Faulkner	12
A.F.A. Lilley† lbw b White	0
C. Blythe not out	4
N.A. Knox run out	5
Extras (b 7, lb 1)	8
Total	162

Fall of Wickets: 1/37, 2/100, 3/106, 4/107, 5/115, 6/126, 7/151, 8/152, 9/154, 10/162.
Bowling: Vogler 4-0-18-1, Schwarz 5.4-0-18-1, Faulkner 20-3-58-3, Sinclair 4-0-13-0, White 16-3-47-4.

South Africa: First innings

L.J. Tancred st Lilley b Blythe	0
P.W. Sherwell*† lbw b Blythe	26
C.M.H. Hathorn c Lilley b Hirst	0
A.W. Nourse c Arnold b Blythe	18
G.C. White c Hirst b Blythe	3
J.H. Sinclair st Lilley b Blythe	2
G.A. Faulkner c Braund b Blythe	6
S.J. Snooke c Lilley b Knox	13
W.A. Shalders c Fry b Blythe	21
A.E.E. Vogler c Hayward b Blythe	11
R.O. Schwarz not out	5
Extras (b 3, lb 1, nb 1)	5
Total	110

Fall of Wickets: 1/6, 2/9, 3/34, 4/47, 5/49, 6/56, 7/59, 8/73, 9/102, 10/110.
Bowling: Hirst 9-3-22-1, Blythe 15.5-1-59-8, Arnold 4-1-11-0, Knox 3-0-13-1.

South Africa: Second innings

L.J. Tancred run out	0
P.W. Sherwell*† c Foster b Blythe	1
C.M.H. Hathorn b Arnold	7
A.W. Nourse lbw b Blythe	2
G.C. White c Arnold b Blythe	7
J.H. Sinclair (7) c Braund b Blythe	15
G.A. Faulkner (6) c Foster b Blythe	11
S.J. Snooke c Hirst b Blythe	14
W.A. Shalders lbw b Hirst	5
A.E.E. Vogler c Tyldesley b Blythe	9
R.O. Schwarz not out	0
Extras (b 3, nb 1)	4
Total	75

Fall of Wickets: 1/0, 2/3, 3/10, 4/16, 5/18, 6/38, 7/56, 8/66, 9/75, 10/75.
Bowling: Hirst 9-2-21-1, Blythe 22.4-9-40-7, Arnold 13-7-10-1.

IT USED TO be a truism that Lord Hawke, the seventh of that ilk, made Yorkshire cricket. When as a Cambridge undergraduate he took over the captaincy in 1883, aged twenty-two, he found an unruly, thirsty lot – professionally led – and gradually asserted his authority. He achieved this notably by the summary dismissals first of one leading slow left-arm bowler, Edmund Peate, and later of another even more distinguished player, Robert Peel. Around the turn of the century Yorkshire became pre-eminent, with the great Hirst and Rhodes in their prime and a team equipped at every point.

For the captain the summer of 1908 was one of special triumph. In July a public presentation was made to him at Leeds in recognition of his having completed 25 years as county captain – a duration approached by no other captain before or since. When the season ended with a match against Sussex ruined by rain Yorkshire emerged not only as champions but undefeated from 28 fixtures, 16 of which were won. It was Hawke's 8th championship and his last. *Wisden* marked the achievement by a departure from precedent in that instead of naming the customary Five Cricketers of the Year it specified 'Lord Hawke and Four'. It should be said that he was a decent, average player without aspiring to such eminence in his own right.

Yorkshire's historian J.M. Kilburn wrote that 'his good fortune in life was to pursue a pastime as a vocation'. He did this in Yorkshire to the extent of twenty-eight years as captain and forty (some overlapping) as President. At his death in 1938 aged seventy-eight he was both Yorkshire President and MCC Treasurer, a post he had taken up in 1932 on the death of his friend and rival, the equally firm yet benevolent autocrat, Lord Harris of Kent. For much of the time with Yorkshire it was a case of a coronet and ten pros. Nevertheless it was a cordial relationship for the captain bettered the lot of his players substantially, among other things instituting winter pay and an improved benefit system.

His lordship's own winters were frequently spent promoting the game overseas. In the heyday of Empire he took one team to Australia, two each to India, South Africa, Canada and the United States, and one to the West Indies and South America. Plum Warner called him 'the Odysseus of cricket', a title to which he himself had equal claim.

It has always been a criticism of Lord Hawke that at a Yorkshire AGM he said he hoped the day would never come when a professional would captain England. The explanation offered was that he meant he hoped the day would never come when no amateur would be good enough to be chosen.

This may well have been so, in which case he chose his words badly. It was an unfortunate remark in that it spotted a well-deserved reputation as a reforming and missionary force in the game fit to be mentioned in the same breath as Grace and Harris.

ABOVE Lord Hawke: pillar of Yorkshire cricket and architect of the county's great years. He was intimately connected with Yorkshire C.C. for 28 years as captain and 40 years as president

---

TWENTY-FIVE YEARS
CAPTAIN.

PRESENTATION TO LORD HAWKE.

The great services which Lord Hawke has rendered to the Yorkshire team and to the game of cricket all over the world were acknowledged in tangible form during an extended luncheon interval in the Yorkshire and Notts match at Leeds yesterday.

The Earl of Wharncliffe, on behalf of many thousands of subscribers, presented a number of articles of jewellery and old china to the Yorkshire captain, who had himself chosen this gift, representing the sum of £1,842 in subscriptions. It was a pleasant little function, though the speeches were somewhat too long for the large audience, who were anxious for the rigour of the game. Everything was, of course, in the happy note, and Lord Hawke must have blushed at the many panegyrics showered upon him had presentations been a novelty to him.

Perhaps the crowd were most pleased with the telegram from the Surrey Club offering heartiest congratulations on a well-deserved mark of appreciation not only for his work for Yorkshire cricket, but for cricket generally.

Lord Hawke, in thanking the public for their gift, asked why it was they had been so good to him. Was it not because he had tried to do his duty during his twenty-five years' captaincy? He had been supported by some of the very greatest cricketers, by some of the most charming fellows who had ever stepped on to a field. Without their loyal support, both on and off the field, he would not have been so honoured that day. After referring to the esprit de corps between amateurs and professionals, his lordship said Yorkshire had known no playing for self. They had played the hard and strenuous game, and had shown, he believed, keenness unequalled by any other side in England.

Daily Mail, 15 July, 1908

1909

TRIANGULAR TESTS.

SUGGESTION TO HOLD THEM IN 1912.

Representatives of England, Australia, and South Africa held a meeting at Lord's yesterday morning for the purpose of considering the rules governing Test matches and the interchange of visits.

The Earl of Chesterfield, president of the M.C.C., occupied the chair, Lord Harris and the Earl of Lichfield represented the M.C.C. committee, Mr. L. O. S. Poidevin alone represented Australia as Mr. P. A. McAlister was batting in the match, and Messrs. H. D. G. Leveson-Gower and G. W. Hillyard represented South Africa. Mr. F. E. Lacey, secretary of the M.C.C., was also present.

The rules of Test matches were first discussed. Rule I, which defines the Test matches as being between England and Australia or England and South Africa, with matches between Australia and South Africa, was approved, as also was Rule 3, which deals with qualification by birth, and says that, subject to Rule 2, a cricketer is always at liberty to represent the country of his birth.

On the proposal of Mr. G. W. Hillyard (South Africa), seconded by Mr. L. O. S. Poidevin (Australia), it was unanimously agreed:

"That the principle of triangular contests is approved,"

With the following rider, which was also unanimously carried:—

"That having regard to the following arrangements having been made—i.e., for England to visit South Africa in 1909-10 and South Africa to visit Australia in 1910-11, an effort should be made to have the first triangular cricket contest in England in 1912, subject to South Africa waiving its claim to come alone in that year, and to further this object England pledges itself to visit Australia in 1911-12."

Daily Mail, 16 June, 1909

THIS INAUGURAL meeting of the Imperial Cricket Conference on 15 June 1909 came about in response to a proposal by the South African, Sir Abe Bailey, for a Triangular Tournament. This was duly held in 1912. The character of the Conference was established at this first meeting. It would fix Test Match tours and legislate only on rules of qualification. Later it extended its scope to define first-class status. It has however never sought to impose other binding rules on member-countries: it has been a forum for debate rather than an executive body. The first word of the

ABOVE Sir Abe and Lady Bailey

title was changed to 'International' long after the British Empire dissolved into the Commonwealth.

Note that the main news item on the *Daily Mail* page of 16 June 1909 was a report of the Lord's Test between England and Australia. At the end of the report of more than three columns appeared the following:

Perrier Water is being supplied to the Australian Team for the Test Match.

Perrier Water with a slice of lemon is perfect

Are we seeing here the first instance of commercial team sponsorship?

THE PARTNERSHIP of 235 between Frank Woolley and Arthur Fielder for Kent at Stourbridge in 1909 remains an English record for the 10th wicket seventy-eight years later. When Fielder, the fast bowler, joined the 22-year-old Woolley on the second evening Kent's score stood at 320 for 9, 40 runs behind Worcestershire's 360. In the last hour they made 119 and next morning in one and a quarter hours a further 116, their side going on to win a highly dramatic and convincing victory by an innings and 33 runs with a mere quarter of an hour to spare.

A few weeks later Woolley, one of the greatest all-rounders in history made the first of fifty-two consecutive appearances for England. Fielder however had few pretensions as a batsman, his previous best score before this 112 not out being 39.

1909

WORCESTERSHIRE v KENT
Played at Stourbridge,
5, 6, 7 July, 1909.
Result: Kent won by an innings and 33 runs.

Worcestershire: First innings

Mr. H.G. Bache b Fielder	22
F. Bowley lbw b Fielder	37
F. Pearson c Huish b Fairservice	161
Mr. H.K. Foster run out	4
E. Arnold c Seymour b Fairservice	1
J.A. Cuffe b Blythe	57
Mr. M.K. Foster c Huish b Fielder	15
Mr. W.B. Burns b Seymour b Woolley	14
R.E. Turner c Seymour b Woolley	6
Mr. W.H. Taylor not out	13
G. Gaukrodger b Fairservice	10
Extras (b 5, lb 9, nb 6)	20
Total	360

Bowling: Fielder 26-4-95-3, Blythe 20-3-67-1, Fairservice 29.5-6-103-3, Woolley 23-5-75-2.

Kent: First innings

Mr. E.W. Dillon b Burns	0
E. Humphreys c Burns b Cuffe	37
James Seymour b Burns	4
Mr. K.L. Hutchings c Taylor b Cuffe	61
F.E. Woolley c H.K. Foster b Arnold	185
H.T.W. Hardinge lbw b Arnold	30
W.J. Fairservice b Cuffe	1
Mr. L.H.W. Troughton b Taylor	46
F.H. Huish b Taylor	23
C. Blythe c Cuffe b Taylor	0
A. Fielder not out	112
Extras (b 34, lb 14, w 8)	56
Total	555

Bowling: Burns 20-1-87-2, Cuffe 50-10-157-3, Pearson 14-0-82-0, Arnold 21-5-61-2, Taylor 20-0-93-3, Turner 3-0-19-0.

Worcestershire: Second innings

Mr. H.G. Bache b Blythe	10
F. Bowley c Huish b Blythe	1
F. Pearson b Blythe	43
Mr. H.K. Foster c Seymour b Blythe	8
E. Arnold b Blythe	12
J.A. Cuffe b Fielder	1
Mr. M.K. Foster c Huish b Fielder	30
Mr. W.B. Burns c Dillon b Blythe	3
R.E. Turner c Hutchings b Blythe	19
Mr. W.H. Taylor c Huish b Fielder	5
G. Gaukrodger not out	8
Extras (b 10, lb 1, w 1, nb 10)	22
Total	162

Bowling: Fielder 25-7-67-3, Blythe 24.5-10-44-7, Fairservice 6-1-19-0, Woolley 6-3-10-0.

WORCESTER v. KENT.

NEW LAST WICKET RECORD BY WOOLLEY & FIELDER.

KENT'S EMPHATIC VICTORY.

Result: Kent won by an innings and 33 runs.

WORCESTERSHIRE.	KENT.
First Innings 360	First Innings 555
Second Innings 162	

Last Season: A draw.

Ten years ago—to be precise, in June, 1899—R. W. Nicholls and Roche, playing at Lord's for Middlesex against Kent, put together 230 for the tenth wicket, and those figures stood intact until yesterday, when Woolley and Fielder set up a new record by scoring 235 for the last partnership of the Kent first innings. They came together at half-past five on Tuesday evening with the score at 320, and before play ceased had put on 119 runs and were still undefeated. Yesterday they took the score to 555, and when Woolley was caught at point they had beaten the previous record by five runs.

The figures set up by Nicholls and Roche, referred to above, were very closely approached at Melbourne, Australia, in January, 1903, when M. Ellis and T. Hastings, assisting Victoria against South Australia, hit up 211 before a separation was effected. The third best performance of this character was consummated so far back as July, 1885, when Briggs and Pilling, operating, of course, for Lancashire could not be parted by the Surrey bowlers until 173 runs had been made.

In matches below first-class, E. H. Kekewich and J. Matthews added the huge number of 298 for North Adelaide against Sturt, at Adelaide, Australia, in 1902, and there are several other instances of over 200 runs being added for the tenth wicket.

Woolley's share of the huge total scored by Kent yesterday was a magnificent 185, for which he batted five hours and three-quarters. He hit a 6, twenty-four 4's, one 3, and eleven 2's. It is his highest score in first-class cricket, his previous best being 152 against Northants at Gravesend. Fielder's not out 112 is by far his best batting effort, his previous highest score for Kent being 39, but he played an innings of 50 not out at Melbourne. He stayed for two hours and twenty minutes, and hit fourteen 4's, two 3's, and nine 2's.

Kent were batting nearly seven hours. In a minority of 195, Worcestershire batted again, and made a bad start, losing Bowley at 3, Bache at 21, H. K. Foster at 29, and Arnold at 50, while half the side were out for 60. Then came a useful stand by Pearson and M. K. Foster, who added 62 for the sixth wicket. However, Blythe and Fielder came on again, and both batsmen left at 122. Pearson batted two hours and a quarter for his 43. Burns was caught at short-leg, and Taylor did not stay long, but Turner showed good nerve. However, the innings closed at six o'clock for 162, Kent winning an exciting encounter with only a quarter of an hour to spare, by an innings and 33 runs.

Sporting Life, 8 July, 1909

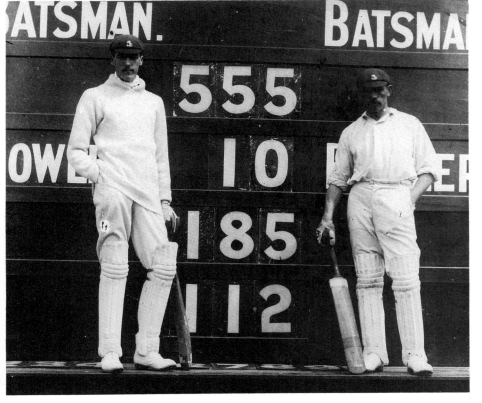

Frank Woolley (LEFT) and Arthur Fielder (RIGHT) flank the record scoreboard

1910

OXFORD'S EASY WIN

BRILLIANT DISPLAY BY LE COUTEUR.

160 RUNS AND 11 WICKETS

CAMBRIDGE COMPLETELY OUTPLAYED.

LE COUTEUR'S CENTURY.

A dull, grey sky and a slow and easy wicket ushered in the second day of the seventy-sixth 'Varsity match, with Oxford seven wickets down for 193 and Le Couteur and Pawson not out respectively 94 and 6. The interest of the resumption of the game was chiefly centred in the question—Would or would not Le Couteur add his name to the classic few who have gained three figures in the annual "Battle of the Blues?" As a matter of fact he did add his name without trouble, for before he was eventually caught at mid-off he had run up the big score of 160. While he was decidedly lucky regarding the fieldsmen, he none the less played admirable cricket. When he went in four wickets were down for 30 runs, and with Hooman he completely changed the situation. Mostly he played a hitting innings. But even with Hooman out five wickets were down for 134, and when stumps were drawn on Monday night seven men were out for 193.

Yesterday when Le Couteur and Pawson resumed their innings the Rhodes Scholar promptly ran into three figures by means of an on-drive for 2 and three singles. When Le Couteur reached his century his share was 100 out of a total of 160, and for those runs he had been batting no longer than two hours and a quarter. Naturally enough, his century was received with loud cheers, for a century in a 'Varsity match is sufficient of a rarity to be a matter for extreme congratulation.

Pawson had made 16 when he was taken at slip, but in the meantime he had stayed whilst the score was carried from 169 to 230, and his partnership with Le Couteur resulted in 61 runs being added in forty-five minutes. With Vidler in there came a further long stand. Half-an-hour produced 50 runs—indeed, with the bowling decidedly erratic, the batsmen were simply helping themselves. And all the time it was chiefly Le Couteur. He made his last 50 out of 80 scored in fifty minutes, and when he was eventually caught low down by Holloway at mid-off he had been batting three hours and twenty minutes for his 160 runs. He had stayed whilst the score of his side was raised from 30 to 291. Only J. F. Marsh and R. E. Foster have made a larger score in a 'Varsity match. But Le Couteur's innings was in every sense a lucky innings. He gave chances at 42, 89, 114, and 157, and in addition he made a number of bad strokes through the slips. His best hits were fifteen 4's, eleven 3's, and seventeen 2's. On the leg side he always hit hard and well. But he played a decidedly lucky innings.

Cambridge went in to bat against a surprisingly large score, and they met with an unexpected failure. Just as Oxford had begun badly, so did Cambridge open with a break-down. But whereas Oxford contrived to pull themselves together, so to say, half-way down their batting list, Cambridge continued to collapse until the latter end. Their first three wickets fell for 21 runs. Those who followed fared little better, and six wickets were down for 53. An awkward weakness for playing forward resulted in the whole side being dismissed for 76. Thus it came about that Cambridge followed on as many as 239 runs in arrears, and in less than two hours the Light Blues were dismissed again for 113 runs. No one appeared safe when facing Le Couteur, and no one played him properly. In the first innings the Australian took six wickets for 20 runs, and with five for 46 in the second he brought his aggregate for the match to eleven for 66.

Sporting Life, 6 July, 1910

THE EDWARDIAN AGE saw the apotheosis of amateur sport in general and cricket in particular. The Lord's Week in early July wherein the match between Oxford and Cambridge was followed by the oldest fixture in the calendar, Eton v Harrow, was not only a high point of the London season but an occasion each day of which commanded as much space in the press – both 'popular' and 'quality' – as a Test Match. Inverted snobbery, it would seem had not yet been invented.

In 1910 the Week began with one personal all-round achievement on paper never again equalled in the University Match, by P.R. Le Couteur of Oxford. It ended with another of transcendent merit on the part of R.StL. Fowler, of Eton, which moreover brought about a finish than which, according to *Wisden*, 'in the whole history of cricket there has been nothing more sensational.' It is for ever known as 'Fowler's Match'.

Le Couteur was an Australian Rhodes scholar from Victoria whose subsequent impact on the game was

minimal. His batting method was described as 'effective rather than graceful' as he punished bowlers who, after heavy rain at first, could not get a firm foothold on a treacherous surface. His 160 was more than half his side's score and it proved to be only 29 runs short of the aggregate of the Cambridge innings.

On a pitch now drying out Le Couteur then baffled his opponents with accurate, well-spun leg-breaks and googlies, a style of bowling which was still largely unfamiliar. With 11 wickets for 66 he finished off the match on the second evening. Thus fortified Philip Le Couteur retired to Bonn University to study psychology before settling to an academic life as a philosophy lecturer at the University of Western Australia.

A dozen of those engaged subsequently distinguished themselves in the game of cricket, including F.T. Mann, who captained Middlesex and England and A.J. Evans, who also won a Test cap for England and became captain of Kent.

OXFORD v CAMBRIDGE
Played at Lord's, 4, 5 July, 1910.
Result: Oxford won by an innings and 126 runs.

Oxford: First innings

Mr A.J. Evans c Nason b Cowie	0
Mr M.G. Salter c Ireland b Holloway	15
Mr R. Sale b Cowie	0
Mr C.V.L. Hooman c Mann b Holloway	61
Mr R.L.L. Braddell c Falcon b Holloway	0
Mr P.R. Le Couteur c Holloway b Cowie	160
Mr R.H. Twining st Tufnell b Lockhart	5
Mr R.O. Lagden c Holloway b Lockhart	0
Mr A.G. Pawson c Falcon b Ireland	16
Mr J.L.S. Vidler b Cowie	32
Mr F.N. Tuff not out	10
Extras (b 7, lb 5, w 2, nb 2)	16
Total	315

Bowling: Cowie 18-2-67-4, Lockhart 22-1-79-2, Holloway 27-4-106-3, Nason 2-0-18-0, Kidd 4-0-10-0, Ireland 12-4-19-1.

Cambridge: First innings

Mr N.C. Tufnell c and b Lagden	6
Mr J.W.W. Nason st Pawson b Le Couteur	9
Mr E.L. Kidd b Lagden	2
Mr J.F. Ireland c and b Lagden	4
Mr M. Falcon lbw b Le Couteur	11
Mr F.T. Mann lbw b Le Couteur	2
Mr D.C. Collins b Le Couteur	31
Mr O. Hughes st Pawson b Le Couteur	6
Mr N.J. Holloway b Le Couteur	2
Mr J.B.B. Lockhart c and b Vidler	0
Mr A.G. Cowie not out	3
Extras (b 5, nb 1)	6
Total	76

Bowling: Lagden 13-1-26-3, Vidler 10-1-24-1, Le Couteur 18.2-8-20-6.

Cambridge: Second innings

Mr N.C. Tufnell b Tuff	5
Mr J.W.W. Nason not out	10
Mr E.L. Kidd st Pawson b Le Couteur	26
Mr J.F. Ireland c Salter b Le Couteur	15
Mr N. Falcon b Evans	19
Mr F.T. Mann b Le Couteur	12
Mr D.C. Collins b Le Couteur	15
Mr O. Hughes b Evans	1
Mr N.J. Holloway c Hooman b Evans	1
Mr J.B.B. Lockhart c Vidler b Evans	0
Mr A.G. Cowie b Le Couteur	0
Extras (b 6, lb 1, w 1, nb 1)	9
Total	113

Bowling: Lagden 6-9-9-0, Vidler 11-1-21-0, Le Couteur 16-3-46-5, Tuff 7-1-21-1, Evans 4-2-7-4.

LEFT Le Couteur and BELOW the winning Oxford team: (BACK ROW) R. Sale, R.L.L. Braddell, F.N. Tuff, P.R. Le Couteur; (SEATED) M.G. Salter, A.J. Evans, A.G. Pawson, C.V.L. Hooman, R.O. Lagden; (FRONT ROW) J.L.S. Vidler, R.H. Twining.

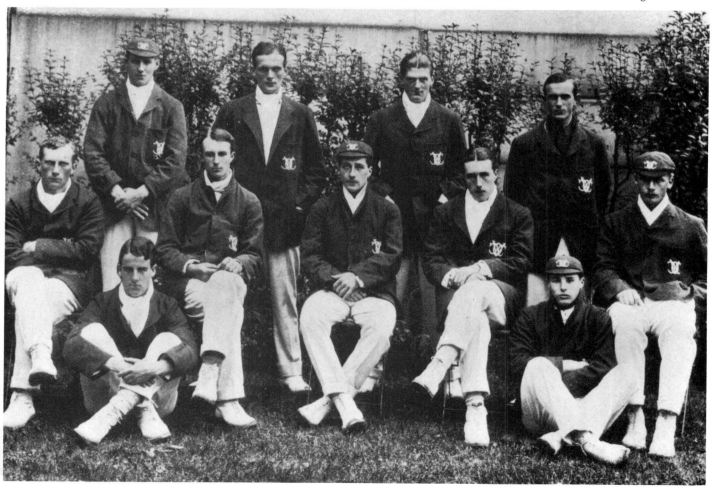

1910

WHATEVER the first match of the Week lacked in excitement and competitive challenge was amply made up for in the second. Harrow came to Lord's unbeaten, and until the second afternoon seemed assured of a hollow victory. At lunch Eton, having followed on, were still 127 behind with five second innings wickets left. Then Fowler with 64 put heart into his side helped by Wigan and Boswell (promoted from number 11). When the ninth wicket fell Eton were just four runs on. By this point though many had left the ground 10,000 still remained. Manners and Lister-Kaye with the courage of desperation now hit out, the former with great effect, every run being cheered – as is the way with last wicket stands the world over.

Earle, the Harrow captain, so the pundits said with hindsight, erred in ordering the heavy roller, so bringing up moisture which gave lift and turn to Fowler's medium-pace off-breaks. The Harrow innings was a catalogue of headlong disaster until T.O. Jameson who had gone in first was ninth out (bowled for two!) at 32: 23 needed... The future Earl Alexander of Tunis, who had taken five wickets in the match with his leg-breaks, now gave a sample of his quality. 'With the steeled and buoyant optimism which, thirty years later, turned defeat in the desert to victory,' as G.W. Lyttelton wrote, he and O.B. Graham in a tumult of emotion made 13 of them. Then 'Alex' edged a catch to slip, 'and the greatest hour in Eton's long cricket history had struck... No hero of fiction or film ever swayed events with more triumphant mastery than Fowler did on this day'.

Tommy Jameson's recollections in Sir Home Gordon's *Eton v Harrow at Lord's* record two items of perhaps sociological interest: when he and Bob Fowler played together as boys in

BELOW *The Eton team: (*BACK ROW*) A.B. Stock, D.G. Wigan, G.C.T. Giles, W.G.K. Boswell, K.A. Lister-Kaye;*
*(*SEATED*) C.W. Tufnell, R.H. Lubbock, R.St L. Fowler, A.I. Steel, W.T. Birchenough; (*FRONT ROW*) Hon J.N. Manners, W.T.F. Holland*

Ireland, Fowler 'would bowl for half an hour at a chalk-mark with the footman to throw the ball back to him' and when a telegram was sent merely to 'Fowler's mother, London' after her son's performance at Lord's, it was delivered to her at her hotel!

A melancholy footnote: eight of the twenty-two cricketers involved were soon to lose their lives in battle. Among their generation this was by no means an undue proportion. Of those who survived – Alexander apart – the Harrow wicket-keeper, Walter Monckton, 1st Viscount of Brenchley, as advocate, law officer and cabinet minister came to greatest fame.

BELOW Lord's Week, a highlight of the Edwardian Season. The Eton v Harrow fixture was regularly played to a packed house

ETON v HARROW

Played at Lord's, 9, 10 July, 1910.
Result: Eton won by 9 runs.

Harrow: First innings

Mr T.O. Jameson c Lubbock b Fowler	5
Mr T.B. Wilson b Kaye	53
Mr G.W.V. Hopley b Fowler	35
Mr T.L.G. Turnbull lbw b Fowler	2
Mr G.F. Earle c Wigan b Steel	20
Mr W.T. Monckton c Lubbock b Stock	20
Mr J.M. Hillyard st Lubbock b Fowler	62
Mr C.H.B Blount c Holland b Steel	4
Mr A.C. Straker c Holland b Steel	2
Mr O.B. Graham c and b Steel	6
Hon. R.H.L.G. Alexander not out	2
Extras (b 18, lb 2, nb 1)	21
Total	232

Bowling: Fowler 37.3-9-90-4, Steel 31-11-69-4, Kaye 12-5-23-1, Stock 7-2-12-1, Boswell 8-4-17-0.

Eton: First innings

Mr R.H. Lubbock lbw b Earle	9
Mr C.W. Tufnell b Hillyard	5
Mr W.T. Birchenough c Hopley b Graham	5
Mr W.T. Holland c Hopley b Hillyard	2
Mr R.St.L. Fowler c Graham b Jameson	21
Mr A.I. Steel b Graham	0
Mr D.G. Wigan c Turnbull b Jameson	8
Mr A.B. Stock lbw b Alexander	2
Hon. J.N. Manners c Graham b Alexander	4
Mr K. Lister Kaye b Straker b Alexander	0
Mr W.G.K. Boswell not out	0
Extras (b 10, w 1)	11
Total	67

Bowling: Earle 12-9-4-1, Hillyard 19-9-38-2, Graham 9-7-3-2, Jameson 4-1-4-2, Alexander 4.1-1-7-3.

Eton: Second innings

Mr R.H. Lubbock c Straker b Hillyard	9
Mr C.W. Tufnell lbw b Alexander	7
Mr W.T. Birchenough c Turnbull b Jameson	22
Mr W.T. Holland st Monckton b Alexander	5
Mr R.St.L. Fowler c Earle b Hillyard	64
Mr A.I. Steel c Hopley b Hillyard	6
Mr D.G. Wigan b Graham	16
Mr A.B. Stock b Earle	0
Hon. J.N. Manners not out	40
Mr K. Lister Kaye c Jameson b Earle	13
Mr W.G.K. Boswell b Earle	32
Extras (b 2, w 3)	5
Total	219

Bowling: Earle 17.3-3-57-3, Hillyard 23-7-65-3, Graham 8-12-33-1, Jameson 9-1-26-1, Alexander 11-4-33-2, Wilson 2-2-0-0.

Harrow: Second innings

Mr T.O. Jameson b Fowler	2
Mr T.B. Wilson b Fowler	0
Mr G.W.V. Hopley b Fowler	8
Mr T.L.G. Turnbull c Boswell b Fowler	0
Mr G.F. Earle c Wigan b Fowler	13
Mr W.T. Monckton b Fowler	0
Mr J.M. Hillyard c Kaye b Fowler	0
Mr C.H.B. Blount c and b Steel	5
Mr A.C. Straker b Fowler	1
Mr O.B. Graham not out	7
Hon. R.H.L.G. Alexander c Holland b Steel	8
Extras (b 1)	1
Total	45

Bowling: Fowler 10-2-23-8, Steel 6.4-1-12-2, Kaye 3-0-9-0.

1911

SUSSEX v NOTTINGHAMSHIRE
Played at Brighton, 18, 19, 20 May, 1911.
Result: Match drawn.

Nottinghamshire: First innings

Mr. A.O. Jones b Cox	57
J. Iremonger c and b A.E. Relf	0
G. Gunn st Butt b Cox	90
J. Hardstaff b Cox	8
J. Gunn c Relf b Killick	33
W. Payton c Heygate b Killick	20
W. Whysall b Killick	1
G.M. Lee c and b Killick	10
E. Alletson c Killick b A.E. Relf	7
T. Oates not out	3
W. Riley c Smith b Killick	3
Extras (b 5, nb 1)	6
Total	238

Bowling: A.E. Relf 19-5-40-2, Leach 11-2-53-0, Vincett 4-0-31-0, R. Relf 11-0-36-0, Cox 25-4-58-3, Killick 10.2-4-14-5.

Sussex: First innings

R. Relf b Jones	42
J. Vine b Jones	77
Mr. R.B. Heygate c Lee b Iremonger	32
G. Cox c Alletson b Riley	37
A.E. Relf c and b Jones	4
Mr. C.L. Tudor c Oates b Riley	23
E.H. Killick c Hardstaff b Lee	81
G. Leach b Lee	52
Mr. C.L.A. Smith not out	33
J.H. Vincett c Iremonger b Lee	9
H.R. Butt b Riley	13
Extras (b 4, lb 3, w 1, nb 3)	11
Total	414

Bowling: Iremonger 34-7-97-1, Riley 29.4-5-102-3, J. Gunn 29-2-87-0, Jones 22-2-69-3, Alletson 1-0-3-0, Lee 14-1-45-3.

Nottinghamshire: Second innings

Mr. A.O. Jones b Leach	0
J. Iremonger c Tudor b Killick	83
G. Gunn st Butt b Relf	66
J. Hardstaff c Butt b A.E. Relf	7
J. Gunn b R. Relf	19
W. Payton lbw b A.E. Relf	0
W. Whysall c Butt b A.E. Relf	3
G.M. Lee c Cox b Leach	26
E. Alletson c Smith b Cox	189
T. Oates b Leach	1
W. Riley not out	10
Extras (b 3, lb 2, w 2, nb 1)	8
Total	412

Bowling: A.E. Relf 33-13-92-3, Leach 19-2-91-3, Vincett 3-1-25-0, R. Relf 19-6-39-2, Cox 9.4-2-27-1, Killick 20-2-130-1.

Sussex: Second innings

R. Relf c Oates b Jones	71
J. Vine c Payton b Riley	54
Mr. R.B. Heygate b J. Gunn	13
G. Cox st Oates b Riley	5
A.E. Relf c Oates b Riley	0
Mr. C.L. Tudor b J. Gunn	4
E.H. Killick c Lee b Riley	21
G. Leach b J. Gunn	31
Mr. C.L.A. Smith not out	12
J.H. Vincett not out	1
H.R. Butt did not bat	
Extras (nb 1)	1
Total (8 wickets)	213

Bowling: Iremonger 14-2-34-0, Riley 33-9-82-4, J. Gunn 25-9-41-3, Jones 5-1-24-1, Lee 4-0-31-0.

RIGHT E.B. Alletson: hitter extraordinary

THERE IS no reason to doubt at the beginning of *The Times* report that no more remarkable hitting had ever been seen than that of Edwin Boaler Alletson for Nottinghamshire against Sussex at Hove on 20 May 1911. Equally for speed of scoring there is no subsequent record to compare with the second phase of his innings after lunch – at which stage he was 47 not out, made in 50 minutes. Thereafter with the last man, Riley, at the wicket he added another 142 runs in forty minutes.

At this point the intermediate afternoon timings are a matter for conjecture, the only impossibility being *The Times* statement repeated in *Wisden* that the final phase of the innings yielded 82 runs in fifteen minutes. In his admirable essay *Alletson's Innings*,

published in 1957, John Arlott gives this approximation made by Roy Webber from a study of the bowling analyses: Alleston went from 47 to 100 in about sixteen minutes and on to 189 in about twenty-four minutes more. Five of Alletson's eight sixes were hit during this last unbelievable onslaught, some out of the ground on to or over the roof of a skating rink beyond the wall at the south end, while it took time to prise one ball out of the soft wood-work of the new stand. It must have taken a minute or two to deliver either the ball struck or a replacement into the hands of the reluctant bowlers. According to Webber's reconstruction 11.2 overs plus two no-balls were bowled in the forty minutes. Alletson making 142 runs off 51 balls of them, W. Riley 10 in the remaining 19.

Considering that there was only one reporter present and that only one of the scorers, the elderly Nottingham-shire man, kept the bowling analysis it is fortunate that the individual and total scores tallied even if there was a slight discrepancy or two in the final analysis.

Before he went in Alletson – who had started the morning with a bathe as the men of Nottinghamshire were apt to do when playing at the seaside – had had leave of his captain to have a go, A.O. Jones having given up the match as lost. 'Then I'm not half going to give Tim Killick some stick,' he said. From his fourth and last over after lunch Alletson, helped by the two no-balls, hit 34, comprising three sixes and four fours, the record from one over until Sir Garfield Sobers hit M.A. Nash for six sixes many years later at Swansea.

'Ted' Alletson was a big fellow, over six foot and weighing fifteen and a half stone. He was chiefly a driver in the arc from mid-on to extra-cover. He had unusually long arms with which he swung a bat weighing (be it noted!) a little over two pounds three ounces including a second rubber grip on the handle.

Players on both sides agreed that they had never seen the ball hit so hard. A reported exchange between Robert

Relf and Joe Vine rings true enough. The former said 'Look out, he'll hit you one any minute now,' to which came the reply, '_____ him, I don't want it!' The bowlers were almost too nervous to bowl, the fielders scared they would suffer grievous bodily harm. When in the end the Sussex captain, C.L.A. Smith, (afterwards Sir Aubrey, the doyen of Hollywood cricket) held a catch which pinned him against the stand behind the bowler's arm, Sussex needed to make 237 in just over three hours and finished 24 short with eight men out.

The Duke of Portland, on whose estate at Welbeck the Alletson family lived and worked, gave Ted a gold watch and an inscribed medallion. His father, Arlott tells us, sent him a home-fed ham. Not the least extraordinary thing about this magnificent display of hitting was that, though he played several valuable, if much briefer, forcing innings afterwards. Alletson was scarcely more then a fringe member of the Nottinghamshire side. In his nine years at Trent Bridge he scored only 3,217 runs at an average of 18. This was his only hundred. John Gunn summed him up thus: 'He was a good chap, Ted, and a real trier; you would not call him a great player, but once or twice a season he would hit harder than anyone else I've ever seen.'

BELOW The remarkable match card

SUSSEX v. NOTTINGHAMSHIRE.
EXTRAORDINARY HITTING BY ALLETSON.
56 RUNS IN TWO OVERS.

Probably nothing has been accomplished either at Brighton or on any other enclosure more remark-able than the hitting seen in this match on Saturday. Alletson gave a most extraordinary exhibition of rapid and fierce scoring. He has always been known as a batsman with strong punishing powers, but on Saturday, going in when his side were apparently in a most hopeless position—Nottinghamshire with seven wickets down in their second innings being only nine runs on—he accomplished the extraordinary feat of scoring 189 runs out of 227 in 90 minutes.

He scored 47 runs in 50 minutes before luncheon, but this was just the beginning. Afterwards, when he had Riley, the last man, as his partner, the latter played the part of the quiet onlooker. Alletson took the game into his own hands and treated Killick and Leach as though they were a pair of school-boys. He began by scoring nine runs off each bowler in the first two overs, and then hit Killick for 22 in one over. Thirteen came from Leach's second over, and he reached his 100 in 75 minutes, having made his second 50 in 20 minutes.

He now proceeded to hit Killick for 11 in the following over and Leach for 17 in the succeeding one, and then came the crowning point—34 runs in one over from Killick, and that bowler sent down two no-balls, so that the hitter had eight balls to deal with. He scored from seven of them, hitting three 6's and four 4's. He had thus since lunch made 115 runs out of 120 from seven consecutive overs, and R. Relf was then put on for Leach, and was hit for 15 in his second over; and then Cox, after being twice sent to leg for four, got Alletson ex-tremely well caught by Smith standing with his back to the grand stand.

Some idea of the remarkable character of the closing stages of this wonderful innings was that Alletson scored his last 89 runs in 15 minutes, and with two or three exceptions all his runs came from tremendous drives. Twice he sent the ball over the grand stand, once into the pavilion seats, and on five other occasions he cleared the ring either to the on or off. His score was made up by eight 6's, 23 4's, four 3's, ten 2's, and 17 singles. He made 142 out of 152 in 40 minutes after lunch, the latter figures being the amount of the stand for the last wicket.

Sussex were left with 237 runs to get to win in three hours and a quarter, and were nearly beaten, though R. Relf and Vine gave their side a brilliant start. When they left wickets fell quickly and Sussex played to avert defeat. Killick and Leach stayed together for an hour, and the match ended in a draw, Sussex with only two wickets to fall being 24 runs short of the number required to win.

The Times, 22 May, 1911

Cricket Match.	Played at the Hove Gd, Brighton	Date May. 18. 19. 20. 1911			
	Nottinghamshire VERSUS Sussex Second INNINGS OF Nottinghamshire				
ORDER OF GOING IN	BATSMAN'S NAME	RUNS AS SCORED	HOW OUT	BOWLER'S NAME	TOTAL RUNS
1	A. O. Jones Esq			Leach	0
2	J. Iremonger	4111616123411112141122112166633444141	c Tudor	Killick	83
3	G. Gunn	4112521111151611111113166162121111	st Butt	R. Relf	66
4	J. Hardstaff	34	c Butt	A. E. Relf	7
5	J. Gunn	11131243114		R. Relf	19
6	H. Payton		l b w	A. E. Relf	0
7	W. Whysall	21	c Butt	A. E. Relf	3
8	G. Lee	54111344	c Cox	Leach	26
9	E. Alletson	42161136344343166444626 12112511111111124121	c Smith	J B	189
10	T. Oates	1hh		Leach	1
11	W. Riley	113431	not out		10
BYES |||	LEG BYES ||	WIDE BALLS ||		NO BALLS		8
RUNS AT THE FALL OF EACH WICKET.	1 for 5	2 for 129	3 for 139	4 for 181	5 for 152 6 for 184 7 for 155 8 for 258 9 for 200 10 for 412	TOTAL 412

1911

WARWICKSHIRE'S victory in the Championship of 1911 was the first since the 1870s by a side outside the magic circle of Yorkshire, Lancashire, Nottinghamshire, Surrey, Middlesex and Kent. There could scarcely have been a greater surprise since their position in the three preceding years had been 12th, 12th and 14th. The success was largely due to the brilliant emergence of F.R. Foster, who at the age of twenty-two was promoted to the captaincy and by the end of the summer, with his fastish left-arm bowling and forcing batting, was accounted – his leadership qualities apart – as the best all-rounder in England.

BELOW The victorious Warwickshire team captained by the talented Foster: (BACK ROW) W.C. Hands, E.J. Smith, J.H. Parsons, C. Charlesworth, S.P. Kinneir; (SEATED) S. Santall, F.G. Stephens, F.R. Foster, G.W. Stephens, E.F. Field; (FRONT ROW) W.G. Quaife, C.S. Baker

The Sporting Life.

WITH WHICH ARE INCORPORATED

"BELL'S LIFE IN LONDON."

AND THE "SPORTING TELEGRAPH."

[REGISTERED AT THE G.P.O. AS A NEWSPAPER.]   LONDON, WEDNESDAY, AUGUST 30, 1911.   [DAILY.]

NEW CHAMPIONS.

WARWICKSHIRE'S WELL WON HONOUR.

A WONDERFUL CHANGE.

By their victory over Northamptonshire yesterday Warwickshire made their position secure as champions. Even if Kent defeat Essex at Leyton this weekend they cannot now regain first place.

By LONG LEG.

It has been paradoxically said that cricket teaches you to expect the unexpected; but even those of us who drank in this great lesson years ago have not been able to behold without an astonished gasp the sudden rise of Warwickshire. From last place but three in 1910 to Championship in 1911; from grey despondency to brilliant achievement at a single bound. Even a full appreciation of cricket's uncertainties and topsy-turvyisms had not prepared us for such a sudden transformation, such a right-about-face of character and record, as this!

On the good old English principle of "Go it, little 'un," Warwickshire's success should be popular; on the principle that change broadens interest their success is gratifying.

It was only in recent seasons that Warwickshire actually sank to the depths and rubbed shoulders with the pigmies of the Championship. Until 1908 September rarely found them more than half-way down the table. They began to compete in the first-class competition in 1895, and their positions year by year from that time have been these:—1895, sixth; 1896, twelfth; 1897, seventh; 1898, ninth; 1899, seventh; 1900, sixth; 1901, fifth; 1902, sixth; 1903, seventh; 1904, eighth; 1905, seventh; 1906, sixth; 1907, ninth; 1908, twelfth; 1909, twelfth; 1910, fourteenth; 1911, first.

A moderately good record fairly consistently maintained, you observe. But even in their most successful seasons the general impression left by Warwickshire was that of a neutral-tinted team, possessing neither great vices nor great virtues; a team hard to beat, but a team incapable of brilliant achievement. In brief, an undemonstrative team, seldom in the limelight, lacking in personality and initiation—"hewers of wood and drawers of water."

All this has been changed in 1911.

A QUESTION OF PERSONALITY.

And yet in this season of their triumph Warwickshire have still been a little lacking in individuality. Few of the players have that clean-cut personality which gets over the ropes, as it were, causing the possessor thereof to be regarded by the man in the crowd in the light of a personal friend. The appearance of C. B. Fry, or Hirst, or K. L. Hutchings is almost as well known to the average follower of cricket as the appearance of his own brother; but ask the average follower of cricket what manner of man is Charlesworth or Baker, and unless he comes from Warwickshire he will probably be at a loss. When Kent or Yorkshire have been champions, even the casual follower of cricket could write down the names of the team without a pause; but set the casual follower of cricket to write down the names of the Warwickshire team, and it is very long odds that he will be biting his pencil with a puzzled frown before he has named

cess primarily to the fact that they possessed in Wass and Hallam two bowlers who were exactly suited by the rain-affected pitches which for the most part prevailed. Between them they could generally be trusted to dismiss the opposing team cheaply enough to give Notts a reasonable chance of victory. But a team must have many resources to finish top in a dry season. And although Foster has been always in the vanguard of battle, Warwickshire's success has been the success of the many.

A WELCOME SUCCESS.

Of course, a shriek will go up that Warwickshire are in a false position because they have not played some of the strongest counties—just as was the case when Middlesex were champions in 1903. Well, it is clearly very regrettable that all the teams do not meet each other, but so long as there are sixteen counties so long will such an ideal remain impossible. It is already being urged against Warwickshire that they have not met Kent. But, after all, it cuts both ways. Supposing Kent had won the Championship, would anyone have suggested that they were in a false position because

CHAMPIONS' WELCOME.

REMARKABLE SCENES IN BIRMINGHAM.

CAPTAIN'S TRIBUTE TO HIS MEN.

At the conclusion of the match between Warwickshire and Northants yesterday the victors received the congratulations of their opponents, Mr A. J. Darnell, hon. sec. of Northamptonshire, speaking on behalf of the club, and G. A. T. Vials and Thompson for the players.

Mr Foster, replying, said that Warwickshire had achieved success because everybody had pulled together, and Quaife, speaking on behalf of the professionals, paid a tribute to Mr Foster, not only for his fine captaincy, but for the close personal interest he took in his men.

SUSSEX FACING DEFEAT

HIRST'S GREAT EFFORT FOR YORKSHIRE.

Though not to be compared with that of the opening afternoon, yesterday's cricket at Hastings in the second stage of the match between Sussex and Yorkshire, proved thoroughly interesting. In facing such a big score as 522, Sussex had practically nothing to hope for, but with the pitch just as good as at the start of the game no reason existed why they should not make plenty of runs. Up to a point their batting presented few noteworthy features, but after lunch runs always came at an attractive pace.

In fifty minutes Yorkshire increased their overnight score of 445 for four by 77 for the loss of three more wickets, and at this point White declared the innings closed. Hirst, who had batted so brilliantly on Monday evening, was fifth to leave at 508, having in three hours and a half obtained his 218

SOMERSET FARE BADLY.

LANCASHIRE BOWLERS' GOOD WORK.

At Bath yesterday Lancashire gained the comfortable lead of 98 runs on the first innings as the result of rather feeble batting by Somerset, and at the close the visitors had pressed home their advantage to the extent of putting themselves 286 runs ahead with eight wickets in hand. All day the game went in favour of Lancashire, Somerset being hopelessly outplayed.

Overnight Lancashire had scored 238 for eight wickets, and they obtained another 20 runs in fifteen minutes before the innings closed. Last out, Macleod batted brightly for an hour and a half yesterday. He twice lifted Robson over the ring for 6, and his figures also included five 4's. Somerset lost their first two wickets for seven runs to awkward balls from Dean and Cook, but the effects of the roller soon disappeared, and they should have made more than 160.

THERE IS generally an element of luck in a hat-trick, and many a successful bowler has gone through a career without bagging one. J.A. Snow and J.H. Wardle, who took 3,000 wickets between them, never had a hat-trick. T.E. Bailey and F.J. Titmus, each with more than 2,000 wickets, claimed only one apiece. S.F. Barnes, perhaps the greatest of all bowlers, had only one hat-trick. (D.V.P. Wright, by contrast, has the world record of seven!)

What then of the feat of T.J. Matthews, a diminutive Victorian leg-spinner who goes down in history as the only man who achieved two hat-tricks in the same Test Match? Moreover they both happened on the same day, for Australia v South Africa at Old Trafford in the 1912 Triangular Tournament. As the *Daily Mail* observed, he took the last three wickets in South Africa's first innings and three in the middle of the second, the match being brought to an end in two days. His fifth and sixth wickets – the hat-tricks were the only wickets he took – came from excellent catches by himself off his own bowling.

Though he played only 67 first-class matches all told Matthews, a grounds-man by trade, achieved two other hat-tricks. Jack Pollard in *Australian Cricket* says: 'he was tough and persistent, his skin darkened by a lifetime in the sun, over coming his lack of height by sound technique.'

AUSTRALIA v SOUTH AFRICA
Played at Manchester, 27, 28 May, 1912.
Result: Australia won by an innings and 88 runs.

Australia: First innings

C.B. Jennings c Schwarz b Pegler		32
C. Kelleway c Ward b Pegler		114
C.G. Macartney b Pegler		21
W. Bardsley c and b White		121
S.E. Gregory* st Ward b Pegler		37
R.B. Minnett c and b Schwarz		12
T.J. Matthews not out		49
S.H. Emery b Schwarz		1
G.R. Hazlitt lbw b Schwarz		0
W. Carkeek† b Pegler		4
W.J. Whitty st Ward b Pegler		33
Extras (b 14, lb 9, w 1)		24
Total		448

Fall of Wickets: 1/62, 2/92, 3/294, 4/314, 5/328, 6/375, 7/376, 8/376, 9/385, 10/448.
Bowling: Faulkner 16-2-55-0, Nourse 14-1-62-0, Pegler 45.3-9-105-6, Schwarz 32-0-142-3, Hartigan 9-0-31-0, White 6-1-29-1.

South Africa: First innings

G.P.D. Hartigan c Carkeek b Emery		25
H.W. Taylor c Carkeek b Whitty		0
A.W. Nourse b Whitty		17
S.J. Snooke b Whitty		7
G.A. Faulkner not out		122
G.C. White lbw b Whitty		22
F. Mitchell* b Whitty		11
R.O. Schwarz b Hazlitt		19
R. Beaumont b Matthews		31
S.J. Pegler lbw b Matthews		0
T.A. Ward† lbw b Matthews		0
Extras (b 2, lb 5, w 1, nb 3)		11
Total		265

Fall of Wickets: 1/4, 2/30, 3/42, 4/54, 5/143, 6/167, 7/200, 8/265, 9/265, 10/265.
Bowling: Hazlitt 16-4-46-1, Whitty 34-12-55-5, Emery 37-10-94-1, Kelleway 11-3-27-0, Matthews 12-3-16-3, Minnett 6-2-16-0.

South Africa: Second innings

G.P.D. Hartigan b Kelleway		4
H.W. Taylor (5) b Matthews		21
A.W. Nourse c Bardsley b Whitty		18
S.J. Snooke b Whitty		9
G.A. Faulkner (2) b Kelleway		0
G.C. White c Carkeek b Kelleway		9
F. Mitchell* b Kelleway		0
R.O. Schwarz c and b Matthews		0
R. Beaumont (10) b Kelleway		17
S.J. Pegler (11) not out		8
T.A. Ward† (9) c and b Matthews		0
Extras (b 5, lb 1, nb 3)		9
Total		95

Fall of Wickets: 1/1, 2/22, 3/22, 4/43, 5/70, 6/70, 7/70, 8/70, 9/78, 10/95.
Bowling: Whitty 6-3-15-2, Kelleway 14.2-4-33-5, Matthews 8-1-38-3.

ABOVE T.J. Matthews: a unique Test record of a hat-trick in each innings and yet only a total of 16 Test wickets in his career

1912

WHILE THE one and only Triangular Tournament was being contested between England, Australia and South Africa in the English summer of 1912 news came from the South of France of the premature death at St Jean d'Arvey of Tom Richardson, aged 41, one of the legendary heroes of the Golden Age. Our cutting is taken from a main news page of the *Daily Mail* which also recorded the visit to London of Mr Borden, the Prime Minister of Canada with most of his cabinet, an attempt to assassinate Lord Kitchener in Cairo and an epidemic of cattle disease in the north of England!

The picture that has survived of the great Surrey fast bowler is an attractive one. A tall, handsome, cheerful black-moustached figure, strong and willing enough to keep up a formidable pace to the end of the longest day, he would reduce his speed after hitting a batsman and first rubbing the bruise. In the six seasons from 1893 to 1898 he took more wickets (1,347) than any fast bowler excluding the 123 obtained over two exhausting intervening tours of Australia. Though he was only a small boy when Richardson was in his prime Neville Cardus was no doubt romanticizing with a degree of poetic justice when he wrote of his action as being 'like a great wave of the sea about to break.' He never spared himself and by the age of thirty-three was quite burned out. On retirement he took a public-house at Richmond and had been in France with his family for the sake of his health. The circumstances of his death suggested the possibility of suicide, but it was subsequently firmly established that he died of a heart attack.

BELOW Tom Richardson in characteristic action. In just 14 Tests against Australia he took 88 wickets

DEATH OF TOM RICHARDSON.

TRAGIC END IN SOUTH OF FRANCE.

FROM OUR OWN CORRESPONDENT,
PARIS, Thursday, 1 a.m.

The *Journal* has received a telegram from Aix-les-Bains announcing that Tom Richardson, the famous Surrey fast bowler, was found dead yesterday morning at the foot of a hill by the village of St. Jean d'Arvey. Death was apparently due to cerebral congestion brought on by exposure.

On Tuesday night Richardson, according to the *Journal*, left his hotel, without being observed by the nurses or his family. He went out in his slippers and without a tie or collar.

THE GREAT FAST BOWLER.

Tom Richardson, the greatest fast bowler of his day, was forty-two years of age, and dropped out of first-class cricket in 1905. Every lover of the game will remember his long, powerful figure, his dark face and hair, and the terrific pace and power of his bowling. In county cricket between 1892 and 1901 he took 1,402 wickets at an average of 15 runs apiece.

In 1893 he went to the top of the bowling averages, and for five seasons remained at his very best. No fast bowler was ever so consistently successful as he was from 1893 to 1897 inclusive. Considering the excellence of the grounds on which he had to bowl, his records are nothing less than amazing. In first-class matches he took 174 wickets in 1893, 196 in 1894, 290 in 1895, 246 in 1896, and 273 in 1897.

This last season marked the culminating point of his career. He was never the same bowler after his second visit to Australia in the winter of 1897-8. There was a marked falling off in his form in 1898 and, increasing greatly in weight, he gradually lost his old pace and spin. He still took a good many wickets—as many as 159 fell to him in 1901—but he was no longer the bowler he had been in his prime. He took 115 wickets for Surrey in 1903, bowling very well in that wet summer, but a year later he dropped out of the eleven, only taking part in four matches. No county has ever had two such fast bowlers as Richardson and Lockwood at their best.

After retiring from the game Richardson took a public-house, the Prince's Head, at Richmond.

Daily Mail, 4 July, 1912

S.F. BARNES'S 17 wickets in the Second Test between England and South Africa at Johannesburg established a Test record which stood until surpassed by J.C. Laker's even more famous 19 wickets against Australia at Old Trafford in 1956.

Throughout the series, destined to be the last before the war and the last in which Barnes was to play, he displayed complete mastery of the South African batsmen. By the end of the Fourth Test in February 1914, which he took 14 wickets in the match, Barnes, aged nearly forty-one had taken his bag for the series to 49, a world record still. In all he took 189 wickets in Test cricket, 106 against Australia and 83 against South Africa. They were taken in 27 Tests At 16 runs apiece – figures unparalleled in this century both as regards economy and striking rate per match.

Complete mastery does, however, underestimate the performance of H.W. Taylor, a batsman of classic method and impressive accomplishment. Captain of his country at the early age of twenty-four 'Herbie' Taylor, scored 29 and 40 in this Second Test and throughout the series conducted a classic duel with Barnes on his country's matting wickets.

In *The World of Cricket* H.S. Altham gave a vivid picture of Barnes: 'The fine picture of Barnes which hangs at Lord's well reflects the formidable menace with which batsmen found themselves faced: long arms, and at the end of them a comprehensive hand with long, strong fingers, a tall, gaunt, erect and co-ordinated body, and above it a face of austere but composed hostility. A run, not long but full of life and spring, a high delivery, and the head leading a full and perfectly balanced follow-through – this was the basic machinery that commanded such control of length and direction; but the secret of his mastery lay in the supple steel of his fingers and hand. At appreciably more than medium pace he could, even in the finest weather and on the truest wickets in Australia, both swing and break the ball from off or leg. Most deadly of all

was the ball which he would deliver from rather wide on the crease, move in with a late swerve the width of the wickets, and then straighten back off the ground to hit the off stump.

Art, resolution, stamina, he commanded them all. Well might a man who saw him in his prime have found himself saying "Here was a Caesar, when comes such another?"'

As for Taylor, it is safe to place him among South African batsmen as the superior of all until one comes in recent times to Graeme Pollock and Barry Richards, who are worthy to stand with him.

SOUTH AFRICA v ENGLAND
Played at Johannesburg,
26, 27, 29, 30 December, 1913.
Result: England won by an innings and 12 runs.

South Africa: First innings

J.W. Zulch c Woolley b Barnes	14
H.W. Taylor* b Barnes	29
P.A.M. Hands c Rhodes b Barnes	0
R. Beaumont c Strudwick b Barnes	0
A.W. Nourse b Barnes	17
L.J. Tancred st Strudwick b Barnes	13
G.P.D. Hartigan c Smith b Rhodes	51
T.A. Ward† b Woolley	19
C.J. Newberry st Strudwick b Barnes	1
J.M. Blanckenberg not out	0
J.L. Cox c Strudwick b Barnes	0
Extras (b 10, lb 4, nb 2)	16
Total	160

Fall of Wickets: 1/22, 2/22, 3/24, 4/56, 5/63, 6/78, 7/155, 8/159, 9/160, 10/160.
Bowling: Douglas 2-0-11-0, Barnes 26.5-9-56-8, Relf 14-1-34-0, Woolley 3-1-5-1, Rhodes 13-5-23-1, Bird 4-1-15-0.

England: First innings

W. Rhodes c and b Blanckenberg	152
A.E. Relf b Blanckenberg	63
J.B. Hobbs lbw b Newberry	23
C.P. Mead c Beaumont b Blanckenberg	102
Hon. L.H. Tennyson lbw b Cox	13
J.W.H.T. Douglas* c Taylor b Blanckenberg	3
F.E. Woolley b Newberry	0
M.C. Bird c Ward b Newberry	1
E.J. Smith lbw b Cox	9
H. Strudwick† c Cox b Blanckenberg	14
S.F. Barnes not out	0
Extras (b 18, lb 4, w 1)	23
Total	403

Fall of Wickets: 1/141, 2/181, 3/333, 4/354, 5/373, 6/374, 7/376, 8/376, 9/395, 10/403.
Bowling: Cox 30-8-74-2, Nourse 21-2-62-0, Blanckenberg 38-13-83-5, Newberry 26-2-93-3, Hartigan 5-0-24-0, Hands 6-0-17-0, Taylor 8-0-27-0, Beaumont 1-1-0-0.

South Africa: Second innings

J.W. Zulch c Relf b Barnes	34
H.W. Taylor* c Rhodes b Barnes	40
P.A.M. Hands (6) c Rhodes b Barnes	40
R. Beaumont (3) c Strudwick b Relf	5
A.W. Nourse (4) c Strudwick b Barnes	56
L.J. Tancred (7) b Barnes	20
G.P.D. Hartigan (5) lbw b Barnes	2
T.A. Ward† b Barnes	0
C.J. Newberry st Strudwick b Barnes	5
J.M. Blanckenberg not out	12
J.L. Cox b Barnes	0
Extras (b 9, lb 6, nb 2)	17
Total	231

Fall of Wickets: 1/70, 2/77, 3/93, 4/106, 5/177, 6/194, 7/201, 8/212, 9/223, 10/231.
Bowling: Douglas 6-0-27-0, Barnes 38.4-7-103-9, Relf 9-3-19-1, Woolley 21-5-45-0, Rhodes 9-2-20-0.

ABOVE The great S.F. Barnes

1914

HOBBS' BENEFIT AT LORD'S TO-DAY.

A BATTING GENIUS AND HIS METHODS.

MILITARY AUTHORITIES AND THE OVAL.

By LONG LEG.

Those who are not too busy sympathising with themselves might spare a moment to sympathise with John Berry Hobbs, whose benefit is to take place at Lord's to-day. Seldom did a benefit promise better until the war cloud burst. Surrey stand at the head of the championship; Kent are their near rivals; and Hobbs himself has never before been in better form for his county. Now the match is to be played on an alien ground; and no matter what arrangements Hobbs may have made with his county, his benefit cannot be so substantial as in normal times.

There are probably a number of folk who consider that a man who devotes his manhood to the playing of games has wasted his existence. They will tell you that he does "nothing useful." As a matter of fact a professional stands among the most useful of mankind, because by the exhibition of his skill he gives pleasure to thousands upon thousands of his fellow creatures. He is at least as much service to the world as the music-hall comedian or the writer of light fiction. Yet his career is short, and his income comparatively small. To his benefit he must look for his old age pension.

Hobbs deserves well not only of Surrey, but of England. No other player ever did greater service in Test matches in so short a period. No one has surpassed him as a Test match player in point of average. It may be that he has been fortunate to meet the Australians and the South Africans in their lean years during recent seasons; it may be that his path has not been beset with nearly so many difficulties as was the road travelled by the batsmen of the generations before him. Yet it is worth while to remember that he conquered the googly in its prime on South African wickets, for Vogler and Faulkner were at their best when he averaged 67.37 in Test matches for H. D. G. Leveson-Gower's unsuccessful team in 1909-10—and his figures generally have been phenomenal. He made his debut as a Test match batsman in 1907 as a member of the M.C.C.'s team in Australia, captained by A. O. Jones, and in the representative games averaged 43.14. Against the Australians in this country in 1909 he appeared only in three of the big games, and averaged no more than 26.40; but ever since then he has stood in the forefront of Test match batsmen. After his big success during the first South African tour he again visited Australia in 1911-12, and averaged in Test matches 82.75; in the Triangular tournament two seasons ago he averaged 48.37—easily the best figures—while it is fresh in everyone's memory that in South Africa last winter his Test match average panned out at 63.28.

FIRST APPEARANCE FOR SURREY.

It does not seem like nine years since Hobbs, pale and slight, made his first appearance for Surrey. This was against the Gentlemen of England, captained by W. G. Grace, on April 24, 1905, and, after being dismissed for 18 in the first innings, he gathered 88 in the second in a couple of hours, against such bowlers as Brearley, G. W. Beldam, and W. W. Odell. Hobbs had come to the Oval a ready-made cricketer, for in the previous year he averaged 58.00 for Cambridgeshire; but he was not, in those early days, the electric, versatile batsman so familiar to-day. From the first he was very strong in on-side strokes, but the beautiful array of effervescing off-side shots were of later development.

It is popularly supposed that he modelled his game upon that of Tom Hayward, and no doubt he learned much from going in first so often with such a polished and correct exponent of batsmanship as Hayward is. Especially can he be regarded as a disciple of his first-wicket partner in the way he uses his feet. He is able to get himself in the best possible position to meet balls of any length. But, of course, he has been no slavish imitator. In many of its essentials his game is totally different from Hayward's. He is distinctly original. Through his batting there runs that rare something called genius.

In proportion to his Test match success his scores for his county have been moderate in any year save this. It was as if he needed a big occasion to bring out the best of him. A crisis came like a stimulant. Yet in the ten seasons for which he has held a bat for Surrey he has not failed to average more than 30 since his first year, when his figures were 25.82, while on only four occasions has his average been below 40. Sometimes he has appeared almost deliberately rash—he has been found cutting at the impossible off-ball in his first over—but for some time no one in the country has been more capable of "carrying a side." His big scores have often been made when all others in the team have failed. As an example, his 215 against Essex this year at Leyton was obtained in an innings when no other Surrey batsman reached 30. He is a scientific fast scorer who hits very hard. No stroke is beyond him. And because he has wrists remarkably flexible, his every stroke has beauty.

Good luck to him!

RIGHT Jack Hobbs in 1914

BELOW Surrey (BACK ROW) J.W. Hitch, H. Strudwick, A. Ducat, T. Rushby, E.G. Goatly, A. Sandham, W.J. Abel, (SEATED) P.G.H. Fender, E.G. Hayes, C.T.A. Wilkinson, J.B. Hobbs, W.C. Smith

WAR OFFICE AND THE OVAL.

In the consequences of a great war, with its mighty tragedies, the fate of a county cricket ground may appear a small thing. Many a fair garden, and many a noble building, and many a picturesque town must suffer destruction ere the guns are silent again. Yet I do not think that those of us who felt sharp regret, even something akin to pain, when we heard that the Oval was to be used for military purposes, are deserving of reproach. Sentiment sways most people to a point, and there would be many sentimental reasons for regret were gun-carriages and the hoofs of horses digging holes in the delicate turf upon which Hobbs might have been found scoring a charming hundred to-day in happier circumstances.

One Samuel Apted, I fancy, must have suffered a very real shock when he heard of the plan which broke cricket off with a jerk on the Surrey ground—the first open space to be selected by the War Office of all London's many open spaces. For he reverenced that stretch of velvet grass which under his care came to produce the best wickets in England. Humourists have suggested that he had a Christian name for every blade of grass. "Were Apted groundsman still," someone said, half playfully, half seriously, when the news was heard that necessity was to bring a regiment to the Oval, "he would have stood at the gate and declared that the soldiers should only take possession over his dead body."

Happily, I can assure those who have a sentimental regard for a classic cricket ground that until Saturday at least the Oval was very much the same as it had been before it came into the hands of the military. From personal inspection, I am able to say that all that has happened is this: Hurdles have been placed round the playing area some eight yards from the boundary line. Upon that narrow fringe of turf guns have been placed. Horses there are on the ground, but they have not placed a single hoof upon the grass. They are confined to the asphalt space at the Vauxhall end. So those who had visions of cavalry drill on "Apted's best" can sleep in peace again.

There are no doubt some well-meaning people who regard an indulgence in cricket at the present crisis of our history as a sin that approaches sacrilege. I have already heard murmurs of "flannelled fools at the wickets." Yet a little thought must show how wise was the statement made by the secretary of the M.C.C. to the effect that until some means was shown by which untrained men could help their country cricket should be carried on as usual in the common interest. Of course, an unrelieved diet of war news and nothing but war news, cannot be good for the country's health. Once lead the people to believe that the end of all things is at hand and disorder and riot must ensue.

Owing to the war, the cricket match between Somersetshire and Northamptonshire, which was to have commenced at Taunton to-day, has been abandoned.

Sporting Life, 10 August, 1914

THE DECLARATION of war on 4 August 1914 had little immediate impact on the county cricket season except that the Army at once occupied The Oval, thus necessitating the Surrey v Kent match for Hobbs's Benefit being transferred to Lord's. In announcing this 'Long Leg' in the *Sporting Life* of 10 August follows a heartfelt eulogy of the beneficiary with some equally sentimental words about the desecration of The Oval by the War Office and the supposed feelings of the famous groundsman, Sam Apted. However he can reassure his readers that guns are merely positioned round the boundary and horses confined to the asphalt. 'They have not placed a single hoof upon the grass.'

The cricket page of the *Sporting Life*, covering minor county, club cricket and the tour of the Merion CC of Philadelphia, contained an item about Worcestershire, indicating how some of the lesser counties existed on a shoe-string. I recall, incidentally, meeting Dick Burrows, a lovely fellow, scoring many years later for Sir Julien Cahn's team. The generous gesture mentioned was typical of the man – and indeed of that generation of professionals.

Hobbs's Benefit was a financial failure, and Surrey promised him another, which duly came his way in 1919. Later in the month W.G. Grace wrote to the newspapers urging cricketers to join the colours and for an end to public cricket, while Lord Roberts in a recruiting speech was critical of those who continued to play. Thereupon further fixtures were cancelled and Surrey were declared champions, It was their first win since 1899 – and due to be their last until 1950.

WORCESTERSHIRE TO CONTINUE.

At a special general meeting of the Worcestershire County Cricket Club, on Saturday, it was decided to continue the club for two years. Mr Paul Foley stated that Kent, Yorkshire, Hampshire, and Surrey had each promised £20 for two years, while other counties hoped to make donations. Burrows, on behalf of the professionals, said that they would play two matches free, or contribute £100 towards the fund. Viscount Deerhurst offered £20, and Sir George Hingley £50 for two years, and the guarantee fund of £1,100 is practically subscribed.

1914

THE EFFECT of W.G. Grace's stern letter to the *Sportsman* of 27 August, 1914, urging that cricket should be stopped and that cricketers should join up, brought the first-class season to an end within a few days. After the declaration of war on 4 August the county season had continued despite dwindling crowds and the prompt departure of a number of amateurs to join the colours. The great man's *fiat* was decisive. His letter is interesting in itself for the prediction – made at a time when many thought the war might be over by Christmas – that the fighting would probably be severe and prolonged. Club players also heeded the letter – for instance the St John's College, Cambridge team playing in Kent on reading it are on record as promptly abandoning their tour and taking the London train. By scratching their last two matches Surrey, then leading the Championship, technically forfeited the title; but Middlesex, the runners-up, obviously did not claim it.

Leo Munro's cartoon in the *Sportsman*, underlining W.G.'s message, no doubt caught the spirit of the moment.

THE STERNER GAME.

MANHOOD OF BRITAIN, OUR COUNTRY
IS CALLING.
PUT BY YOUR TOYS, FOR NO LONGER 'TIS
PLAY.
OURS BE NO SHIRKING WHILE COMRADES
ARE FALLING;
RALLY WE NOW, AND LET OURS BE
"THE DAY."

PROVE WE THE LESSONS OUR CLEAN SPORTS
HAVE TAUGHT US,
THE PLUCK THAT ENDURES AND THE SCORNING
TO YIELD,
NO MATTER THE STRENGTH OF THE FOEMEN
WHO FOUGHT US —
THAT WAS THE SPIRIT THAT WON US THE FIELD

THAT WAS THE OBJECT OF SPORT AS A
TRAINING,
EACH FOR HIS SIDE, NONE FOR PERSONAL
FAME.
PROVE NOW ITS VALUE, GIVE ALL
UNCOMPLAINING,
GIVE FOR YOUR COUNTRY, THOUGH STERNER
THE GAME.

Leo Munro 1914

RIGHT W.G. *with A.C. MacLaren and Ranji*

FAR RIGHT Gilbert Jessop *recruiting*

1915

NO PUBLIC figure symbolized the Victorian age so perfectly as W.G., not only transcendent in cricketing skills, but large alike in physique and personality. He was essentially a simple man in thought and speech, conscious of his dignity yet modest as to his own achievements. The official parish doctor in one of the less affluent parts of Bristol, he needed to employ two *locum tenens* when he was away playing. Bernard Darwin records how he nevertheless looked after his patients at week-ends, and that in a match in which he scored two hundreds he sat up all night with a poor woman whom he had promised to see through her confinement.

Stories critical of his sportsmanship are still current, many no doubt apocryphal. On this delicate subject Darwin, who knew him well and played golf with him in later years, wrote that 'He never did what he thought a dishonourable thing, but he had a different standard of honour from our own ... He had his own notions of what was right and permissable and I am convinced that he would never willingly have done anything contrary to them.' That he was apt to give umpires a hard time can be assumed from the observation of a friend who qualified 'an invariable kindness to those younger than himself' by adding, 'except that he tried to chisel them out lbw'. Against what may be accounted this amiable weakness must be set a whole catalogue of qualities.

The acute distress occasioned by the Great War and the loss of his friends and their children was proof if it were needed that his heart was in the right place.

Further detail of W.G.'s achievements must be sought in the record books, apart from the following figures spanning his career:

Innings	Runs	Not Out	H/score	Av.	H'dreds
1493	54,896	105	344	39.55	126

He took 2,876 wickets at 17.92 runs each: Only Wilfred Rhodes and Frank Woolley might be held to have matched these all-round feats.

RIGHT W.G. in July 1914 at the Rectory Field, Blackheath. With him is R.N.R. Blaker and the latter's son, K.G. Blaker

CRICKET.

AUSTRALIANS BEATEN.

AUSTRALIANS.. 1st inns., 81; 2nd inns., 296.
ENGLAND XI.. 1st inns., 187; 2nd inns., 191 (8 wkts.)

The closing match of the Scarborough Festival ended yesterday in a victory for the England XI., but the honours rested to a large extent with the Australians who, after being 106 runs behind on the first innings, only lost by two wickets.

Daily Telegraph, 11 September, 1919

1919

THE RESUMPTION of English cricket in 1919 was enlivened by an Australian Imperial Forces team which won 12 first-class matches, drew 12 and lost four. Their visit brought to prominence Jack Gregory, the great fast bowling all-rounder, H.L. Collins, subsequently captain of Australia and several more who formed a nucleus for the successful Test teams of the early 1920s. They ended the tour with a narrow and thoroughly honourable defeat against C.I. Thornton's powerful side at Scarborough.

The County Championship consisted in 1919 of two-day matches with long hours of play, it being considered that in the post-war world three-day cricket would not be able to hold its own. The experiment lasted only this one season – wherein Yorkshire won the Championship.

MR. C.I. THORNTON'S ENGLAND ELEVEN v AUSTRALIANS

Played at Scarborough, 8, 9, 10 September, 1919.
Result: Mr C.I. Thornton's XI won by two wickets.

Australians: First innings

Mr H.L. Collins b Hitch	4
Mr J.M. Gregory lbw b Douglas	7
Mr W.L. Trennery b Hitch	0
Mr C.E. Pellew c Dolphin b Hitch	12
Mr C.B. Willis b Hitch	2
Mr J.M. Taylor b Hitch	12
Mr J.T. Murray b Rhodes	18
Mr A.W. Lampard b Falcon	7
Mr W.S. Stirling run out	5
Mr W.A. Oldfield b Hitch	5
Mr C.S. Winning not out	4
Extras (b 4, lb 1)	5
Total	81

Bowling: Douglas 10-1-30-1, Hitch 12.1-5-24-6, Falcon 6-1-16-1, Rhodes 3-2-6-1.

Mr C.I. Thornton's England Eleven: First innings

J.B. Hobbs c Collins b Gregory	20
Mr D.J. Knight b Gregory	15
Mr R.H. Twining b Gregory	1
Mr J.W.H.T. Douglas c Taylor b Collins	3
Mr R.H. Spooner b Gregory	47
W. Rhodes lbw b Winning	24
G.H. Hirst lbw b Gregory	30
Mr G.T.S. Stevens not out	35
W. Hitch c Oldfield b Gregory	1
Mr M. Falcon c Oldfield b Gregory	3
A. Dolphin c Gregory b Collins	5
Extras (lb 3)	3
Total	187

Bowling: Gregory 29-6-83-7, Collins 23.4-8-55-2, Winning 11-1-30-1, Lampard 6-0-16-0.

Australians: Second innings

Mr H.L. Collins c Twining b Rhodes	35
Mr J.M. Gregory c Knight b Falcon	26
Mr W.L. Trennery c Rhodes b Douglas	0
Mr C.E. Pellew c Rhodes b Hitch	6
Mr C.B. Willis c Dolphin b Hirst	96
Mr J.M. Taylor c Knight b Hitch	71
Mr J.T. Murray b Hirst	1
Mr A.W. Lampard b Hitch	36
Mr W.S. Stirling c Dolphin b Hitch	11
Mr W.A. Oldfield b Hitch	5
Mr C.S. Winning not out	2
Extras (b 4, lb 2, nb 1)	7
Total	296

Bowling: Douglas 19-2-45-1, Hitch 30.2-4-102-5, Falcon 10-1-43-1, Rhodes 20-5-50-1, Stevens 2-0-16-0, Hirst 12-2-33-2.

Mr C.I. Thornton's England Eleven: Second innings

J.B. Hobbs c Oldfield b Winning	93
Mr D.J. Knight b Gregory	0
Mr R.H. Twining b Collins	14
Mr J.W.H.T. Douglas c Gregory b Collins	3
Mr R.H. Spooner c Taylor b Winning	23
W. Rhodes not out	23
G.H. Hirst c Winning b Gregory	9
Mr G.T.S. Stevens b Gregory	14
W. Hitch c Willis b Collins	1
Mr M. Falcon not out	0
A. Dolphin did not bat	
Extras (b 9, lb 2)	11
Total (8 wickets)	191

Bowling: Gregory 29.5-7-77-3, Collins 27-6-67-3, Winning 10-2-36-2.

LEFT J.M. Gregory, who first appeared in the Australian Imperial Forces XI

39

1920

"RECORD" AT NORTHAMPTON.

1,475 RUNS FOR 27 WICKETS.

Surrey beat Northamptonshire, at Northampton, yesterday, by eight wickets.

The match, which was remarkable for the wonderful hitting throughout, created a new "record," the aggregate number of runs scored—1,475 for the loss of 27 wickets—being larger than obtained in any previous inter-county match. The largest aggregate hitherto was 1,446 for 33 wickets at Southampton, when Kent opposed Hampshire.

Although beaten easily in the end, Northamptonshire deserved high praise for the splendid fight they made against their powerful opponents. Going in a second time 313 runs behind, they had lost two men for 59 on Thursday evening, and yesterday morning Haywood and Woolley, the not outs, added altogether 107. Haywood, caught at backward point, made his 96 in an hour and 50 minutes, hitting three 6's and 13 4's in a splendid innings. Woolley left soon afterwards, but Walden and Humphries put on 55 in 35 minutes, Walden getting 63 in 80 minutes, punishing the Surrey bowlers with great severity for the second time in the match. He hit 10 4's and was unlucky to play a ball from Hitch on to the wicket with the total 288. Wells, missed by Rushby when 40, hit hard, having 11 4's in his 71, which occupied only 83 minutes, and the plucky batting continued until the innings closed for 430, the highest score made by Northamptonshire this season.

Surrey wanted 118 runs for victory, and they got the runs in 80 minutes. Hobbs made 54 out of 93. He lost Sandham at 24, but the result was never in doubt, as play could have gone on for another half-hour if necessary. Hitch took his 100th wicket in the match.

The Times, 28 August, 1920

THE MATCH between Northampton-shire and Surrey at Northampton in 1920 was noteworthy in two ways. The time for P.G.H. Fender's hundred – thirty-five minutes – is the fastest ever recorded (though equalled in 1983 by S.J. O'Shaughnessy of Lancashire in farcical circumstances when Leicester-shire fed him a succession of long hops and full tosses in hope of hastening a declaration). Also the aggregate of 1,475 runs for 27 wickets was and remains a record for a county match.

Fender went in with the Surrey score 448 for 5, Andrew Ducat and Alan Peach having just added 288 in about two and a quarter hours, leaving the Northamptonshire attack in tatters. Fender in these circumstances hit freely from the start in the most carefree way, only pausing somewhat at the end to see young Peach safely to his double hundred before C.T.A. Wilkinson declared. Fender was a tall, strong man with extremely powerful wrists and (despite wearing spectacles) a wonder-fully keen eye. He hit five sixes and either 17 or 18 fours, the speed of scor-ing having led to discrepancies between the scorers and the match reports.

As to the press coverage, the next day's papers made no mention of this having been the fastest hundred, nor in those less statistically conscious days was Fender aware at the time that he had achieved a record.

ABOVE 'Percy George': an unmistakeable bespectacled figure who only ever wore one batting glove. In a first-class career spanning three decades he made nearly 20,000 runs and took 1,894 wickets. Fender's captaincy was frequently as inspired and daring as his batting

NORTHAMPTONSHIRE v SURREY
Played at Northampton,
25, 26, 27 August, 1920.
Result: Surrey won by eight wickets.

Northamptonshire: First innings 306 (F. Walden 128, C.N. Woolley 58; Fender 3-69).

Surrey: First innings

J.B. Hobbs c Bellamy b Murdin	3
A. Sandham c Hawtin b Woolley	92
Mr C.T.A. Wilkinson b Woolley	43
T. Shepherd c Bellamy b Woolley	9
H.A. Peach not out	200
A. Ducat c Bellamy b Thomas	149
Mr P.G.H. Fender not out	113
W. Hitch	
Mr J.H. Lockton } did not bat	
H. Strudwick	
T. Rushby	
Extras (b 9, lb 1)	10
Total (5 wickets declared)	619

Bowling: Wells 31-6-133-0, Murdin 22.4-0-162-1, Thomas 23-0-142-1, Woolley 26-3-116-3, Humphrey 4-0-36-0, Haywood 4-0-20-0.

Northamptonshire: Second innings 430 (R. Haywood 96, W. Wells 71, F. Walden 63).

Surrey: Second innings 120 for 2 (J.B. Hobbs 54).

40

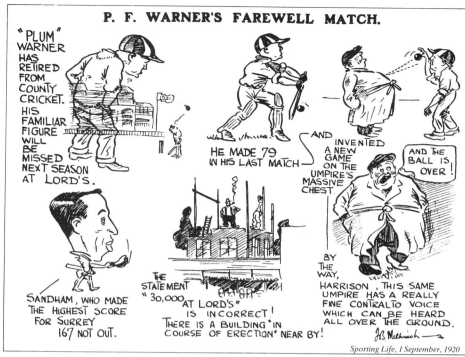

P. F. WARNER'S FAREWELL MATCH.

"PLUM" WARNER HAS RETIRED FROM COUNTY CRICKET. HIS FAMILIAR FIGURE WILL BE MISSED NEXT SEASON AT LORD'S.

HE MADE 79 IN HIS LAST MATCH

AND INVENTED A NEW GAME ON THE UMPIRE'S MASSIVE CHEST

AND THE BALL IS OVER!

SANDHAM, WHO MADE THE HIGHEST SCORE FOR SURREY 167 NOT OUT.

THE STATEMENT "30,000 AT LORD'S" IS INCORRECT! THERE IS A BUILDING IN COURSE OF ERECTION" NEAR BY!

BY THE WAY, HARRISON, THIS SAME UMPIRE HAS A REALLY FINE CONTRALTO VOICE WHICH CAN BE HEARD ALL OVER THE GROUND.

Sporting Life, 1 September, 1920

PLUM WARNER'S last match, wherein Middlesex won an extraordinary victory over Surrey at Lord's, so securing the County Championship, stands as one of the more sentimental moments of cricket history.

Warner's involvement with cricket was total all his life. Though often plagued by ill-health, he had played on until he was nearly forty-seven. He had led two MCC teams to Australia, bringing home the Ashes each time, one to South Africa, and had also toured the West Indies (where he was born), New Zealand and North America. After his retirement came more minor touring and the management (an unhappy

episode) of the Bodyline tour. He founded the *Cricketer,* wrote copiously about the game, served as a selector, and held almost every MCC office, including the Presidency.

As the scorecard shows it was a fine, fluctuating struggle with Middlesex having 'their necks against the collar' as the *Sporting Life* reporter put it, and Surrey accepting with spirit a generous challenge.

In the end they failed by 55 runs, whereupon 'there was a scene of wild excitement that has rarely been witnessed on the sedate and classic enclosure of the headquarters of the game'.

MIDDLESEX v SURREY
Played at Lord's, 28, 30, 31 August, 1920.
Result: Middlesex won by 55 runs.

Middlesex: First innings

Mr. C.H.L. Skeet c Ducat b Rushby	2
H.W. Lee c Hitch b Fender	12
J.W. Hearne c and b Hitch	15
E. Hendren b Reay	41
Mr. P.F. Warner b Rushby	79
Mr. F.T. Mann c and b Fender	12
Mr. N. Haig b Reay	18
Mr. G.T.S. Stevens b Fender	53
Mr. H.K. Longman b Fender	0
H.R. Murrell c Ducat b Hitch	9
T.J. Durston not out	0
Extras (b 12, lb 12, nb 3)	27
Total	268

Bowling: Hitch 32.1-10-66-2, Rushby 23-9-48-2, Fender 28-4-76-4, Reay 26-17-31-2, Ducat 3-1-10-0, Shepherd 6-3-10-0.

Surrey: First innings

J.B. Hobbs c Mann b Hearne	24
A. Sandham not out	167
Mr. M. Howell c Murrell b Durston	7
T. Shepherd c Murrell b Durston	0
H.A. Peach hit wicket b Stevens	18
A. Ducat st Murrell b Lee	49
Mr. P.G.H. Fender c Haig b Durston	30
W. Hitch b Durston	1
Mr. G.M. Reay c Haig b Lee	6
H. Strudwick b Hearne	9
T. Rushby not out	6
Extras (b 17, lb 5, nb 2)	24
Total (9 wickets declared)	341

Bowling: Durston 30-9-97-4, Haig 10-4-25-0, Stevens 16-0-72-1, Hearne 24-8-57-2, Lee 15-2-66-2.

Middlesex: Second innings

Mr. C.H.L. Skeet c Fender b Hitch	106
H.W. Lee b Hitch	108
J.W. Hearne c and b Rushby	26
E. Hendren c Sandham b Rushby	5
Mr. P.F. Warner not out	14
Mr. F.T. Mann c Peach b Fender	22
Mr. N. Haig b Rushby	1
Mr. G.T.S. Stevens not out	21
H.R. Murrell b Reay	0
Mr. H.K. Longman } did not bat	
T.J. Durston	
Extras (b 8, lb 4, w 1)	13
Total (7 wickets declared)	316

Bowling: Hitch 20-5-71-2, Rushby 22-7-73-3, Fender 16.5-2-70-1, Reay 18-1-61-1, Ducat 3-0-12-0, Shepherd 4-0-16-0.

Surrey: Second innings

J.B. Hobbs c Lee b Haig	10
A. Sandham c and b Hearne	68
Mr. M. Howell st Murrell b Stevens	25
T. Shepherd c Hendren b Stevens	26
H.A. Peach b Stevens	11
A. Ducat lbw b Hearne	7
Mr. P.G.H. Fender b Durston	1
W. Hitch b Stevens	6
Mr. G.M. Reay b Hearne	5
H. Strudwick b Stevens	10
T. Rushby not out	7
Extras (b 11, lb 1)	12
Total	188

Bowling: Durston 14-1-42-1, Haig 8-0-19-1, Stevens 13.4-0-61-5, Hearne 11-0-37-3, Lee 4-0-17-0.

LEFT 'Plum' Warner's finest hour

1921

MR. MACARTNEY'S 345.

AUSTRALIAN "RECORD" BEATEN AT TRENT BRIDGE.

The Australians had little difficulty in piling up the huge score of 608 for seven wickets on a perfect pitch at Trent Bridge, on Saturday. They certainly lost Mr. Bardsley for a cipher, but, afterwards, the Nottinghamshire bowlers had a dreadful time. The county, too, were unfortunate in losing, after the tea interval, the services of Barratt, who had injured a finger. Mr. Taylor scored exactly 50 and Mr. Pellew exactly 100, but it was, of course, the 345 of Mr. Macartney which made the total what it was.

Mr. Macartney's innings, in fact, was the highest ever played by an Australian in this country. Previously, Mr. W. W. Armstrong, who was not playing in this match, had held the distinction, for in 1905 he had scored 303 not out against Somerset, at Bath.

Mr. Macartney went in when Mr. Bardsley had been bowled by the first ball sent down by Richmond with only one run on the scoreboard. He made his runs in four hours, out of the 540 scored whilst he was in. Finally he was out leg-before-wicket to Hardstaff. When he had scored nine, he had a great piece of luck, being missed in the slips, and, at 213, he gave a hard chance to mid-on, but these were the only blemishes in a really dazzling innings, in which he revealed in the most brilliant fashion all his wonderful footwork, together with extraordinary accuracy in cutting and power in driving and leg hitting. His hits included four 6's, 47 4's, three 3's, and 30 2's. One remarkable feature of the innings was the pace at which the runs were obtained.

Apart from their terribly expensive mistakes in catching, the Nottinghamshire men fielded well, their ground work being excellent. There were about 10,000 spectators.

The Times, 27 June, 1921

NOTTINGHAMSHIRE v AUSTRALIANS
Played at Nottingham,
25, 27 June, 1921.
Result: Australians won by an innings and 517 runs.

Australians: First innings

W. Bardsley b Richmond	0
T.J.E. Andrews c Oates b Barratt	29
C.G. Macartney lbw b Hardstaff	345
J.M. Taylor c Whysall b Barratt	50
C.E. Pellew c Oates b Staples	100
J.M. Gregory c G. Gunn b Hardstaff	19
J. Ryder b Hardstaff	20
H.L. Hendry st Oates b Hardstaff	51
W.A. Oldfield b Staples	40
E.A. McDonald b Hardstaff	1
A.A. Mailey not out	0
Extras (b 8, lb 10, w 1, nb 1)	20
Total	675

Bowling: Barratt 23-4-89-2, Richmond 36-1-193-1, Staples 27-3-131-2, J. Gunn 9-1-71-0, Lee 2-0-14-0, Carr 1-0-24-0, Hardstaff 28.2-3-133-5, Whysall 1-1-0-0.

Nottinghamshire: First innings 58 (Gregory 4-23, McDonald 3-24).
Nottinghamshire: Second innings 100 (Mailey 4-36, Gregory 3-26).

RIGHT The pugnacious C.G. Macartney

SATURDAY 25 June 1921 was a day of great heat on which bowlers and fielders toiled and sweated as batsmen made hay; and nowhere did they do so as plentifully as at Trent Bridge and on Agar's Plough at Eton. On the one ground the famous C.G. Macartney for the Australians against Nottinghamshire cut, hooked and drove his way to 345, the highest individual number of runs ever scored in a single day. On the other young J.L. Guise for Winchester against Eton made 278, the highest innings ever played by a schoolboy in an inter-school game – notwithstanding which his side lost the match.

Macartney was sturdy, broad and well-knit, a shortish fellow with an in-born contempt for bowlers. R.C. Robertson-Glasgow wrote of him that 'no Australian batsman, not even Bradman, has approached him for insolence of attack. He made slaves of bowlers'. He was apt to take outrageous liberties, as much apparently for his own amusement as for the entertainment of the crowd; he was the very antithesis of the run-hungry accumulator.

Yet so fast did runs accrue to him on a flawless pitch that at some point in the afternoon he either conceived the idea – or it was suggested to him – that he might better the highest individual score ever made in England, A.C. MacLaren's 424 for Lancashire at Taunton in 1895. He went in within five minutes of the start, Bardsley having been bowled 'for a cypher' by the first ball of the second over. He scored almost from the beginning at a breathless pace and was going easily fast enough to have overhauled MacLaren before close of play when, having made 345 in just under four hours, he was adjudged lbw to the seventh bowler tried, 'Old Joe' Hardstaff. An excellent batsman, Hardstaff was a bowler so occasional that in his career he took only 58 very expensive wickets. Perhaps Charlie Macartney had let his concentration slip for a moment. Anyway he departed if not disgruntled (as the great P.G. Wodehouse might have put it), positively not gruntled.

WHILE A Nottinghamshire crowd of 10,000 saw their bowlers being put to the sword the usual select assemblage at Eton were watching a far more tense struggle. Winchester on the first day had been bowled out for 57 to which Eton replied with 255. When Winchester went in again Guise edged the first ball of the innings between keeper and slip for four. The keeper M.L. Hill left it to first slip because he was still pulling his gloves on. The future Prime Minister, now Lord Home of the Hirsel, made a vain, despairing dive. The bowler, Gubby Allen, registered only mild displeasure 'because they had batted so very poorly in the first innings', wherein, incidentally, he had taken 5 for 20. Allen's verdict – consistent over all the intervening years – is that both he and Hill were equally to blame for not seeing whether the other was ready!

By the close on the first day John Guise was 87 not out and Winchester were 130 for 3. Next day he simply plundered the bowling. The pitch was fast, the heat tropical, and Guise's leg-side play was tremendous. E.R. Wilson, the great coach and historian of Winchester cricket, wrote: 'he hit 45 fours and his hooking of the fast bowling was amazing'. Guise nursed the bowling skilfully, but no one else did anything – the second top score was 21 – and when he went at last, run out with number 11 at the wicket, Eton were left with 184 to get. In the circumstances anything might have happened, but Ronny Aird, a future Secretary of MCC, contributed an assured hundred to bring a phenomenal game to an end.

ETON v WINCHESTER
Played at Eton, 24, 25 June, 1921.
Result: Eton won by eight wickets.

Winchester: First innings

J.L. Guise c Sheldon b Bridgman	8
R.C. Huband c Hill b Allen	15
B. Pinney c Cox b Bridgman	4
T.B. Raikes c Barber b Allen	1
A.R.V. Barker c Sheldon b Allen	0
E.H.F. Fuller b Sheldon	5
M.N. Macmullen b Allen	1
G.C.W. Dicker b Allen	0
D.H. Macpherson c Aird b Sheldon	10
F.C. Mallett c Hill b Sheldon	2
G.E. Brown not out	8
Extras (b 3)	3
Total	57

Bowling: Allen 8-2-20-5, Sheldon 3-1-7-3, Bridgman 8-2-22-2, Brand 3-1-5-0.

ABOVE J.L. Guise, a Winchester legend

Eton: First innings

Hon. D.F. Brand c Barker b Macpherson	6
G.O. Allen b Macpherson	11
R. Aird c Guise b Raikes	5
P.E. Lawrie st Huband b Guise	92
T.C. Barber b Raikes	21
G.K. Cox c Brown b Raikes	64
M. Ll. Hill b Raikes	6
Lord Dunglass not out	25
Hon. J.B. Coventry c Fuller b Raikes	1
H.D. Sheldon lbw b Raikes	11
M.R. Bridgman c Brown b Raikes	0
Extras (b 3, lb 5, nb 5)	13
Total	255

Bowling: Raikes 27.2-5-92-7, Macpherson 11-2-44-2, Guise 17-3-63-1, Brown 7-0-31-0, Mallett 2-0-12-0.

Winchester: Second innings

J.L. Guise run out	278
R.C. Huband b Bridgman	0
B. Pinney b Coventry	21
T.B. Raikes b Sheldon	2
A.R.V. Barker c Brand b Dunglass	13
E.H.F. Fuller lbw b Allen	6
M.N. Macmullen c Bridgman b Allen	9
G.C.W. Dicker b Aird	5
D.H. Macpherson c Dunglass b Allen	9
F.C. Mallett b Allen	0
G.E. Brown not out	0
Extras (b 30, lb 5, w 3)	38
Total	381

Bowling: Allen 27-7-74-4, Sheldon 7-2-30-1, Bridgman 14-0-76-1, Brand 16-1-72-0, Coventry 8-1-32-1, Dunglass 3-2-8-1, Cox 7-0-37-0, Aird 3-1-14-1.

Eton: Second innings

Hon. D.F. Brand b Guise	12
R. Aird not out	112
P.E. Lawrie c Macmullen b Raikes	42
T.C. Barber not out	1
G.O. Allen	
G.K. Cox	
M. Ll. Hill	
Lord Dunglass	did not bat
Hon. J.B. Coventry	
H.D. Sheldon	
M.R. Bridgman	
Extras (b 11, lb 3, w 1, nb 2)	17
Total	184

Bowling: Raikes 19.5-5-58-1, Macpherson 8-1-45-0, Guise 11.4-2-50-1, Brown 5-2-14-0.

ETON V. WINCHESTER.

GREAT INNINGS BY J. L. GUISE.

Eton beat Winchester at Agar's Plough on Saturday by seven wickets. Winchester made a great effort in their second innings, but were unable to make up for the failure in the first.

The feature of the Winchester second innings was the magnificent batting of J. L. Guise, who went in first, and was the last man out. He hit up 278 out of a total score of 381, and was, unfortunately, run out in an effort to get the bowling. His display was one of the finest ever witnessed on the Eton Playing Fields. Some say he gave a difficult chance before he had scored, but this is disputed. He certainly hit the ball hard and cleanly, and it was noticeable that he very rarely missed a leg ball. His scoring strokes included over 40 to the boundary. Overnight he had made 87, and at the luncheon interval on Saturday he had raised his score to 243. The total was then 345 for nine. Afterwards, he made 35, at which point Barber threw his wicket down smartly from some distance out—half-way to the boundary on the leg side.

Guise received a great ovation on returning to the pavilion, his score of 278 generally being regarded as a "record" for the series of matches between the two schools. His innings occupied over four hours. With the exception of B. Pinney and A. R. V. Barker, none of the other Winchester batsmen reached double figures, their batting, in fact, being rather feeble.

G. O. Allen again was the best bowler on the Eton side, and by taking four wickets for 74 runs brought the match to nine for 94. He kept a good length, and bowled no fewer than 27 overs in the second innings. The other Eton bowlers were very moderate, but, taking into account the great heat and the long time they were out in the field, the Eton team fielded very well.

Eton were left to score 184 runs in order to win, and quickly lost G. K. Cox, who was run out badly before he had scored. R. Aird and the Hon. D. F. Brand then put on 71 runs before the latter was bowled by J. L. Guise for 12. Brand had played very carefully, Aird doing most of the scoring. P. E. Lawrie joined Aird, and both played brilliant cricket. Aird, although feeling far from well, played most attractive cricket, his strokes to leg being particularly brilliant. He gave a chance when he had made about 50, but he has seldom batted better, and he is undoubtedly the prettiest bat in the Eton eleven. His hits included 18 fours. Aird, who was still not out at the finish, was helped by Lawrie to make victory quite certain. Lawrie also hit very powerfully, and only two runs were required to win the match when he was out to a catch at cover-point. T. C. Barber joined Aird, and shortly afterwards made the winning hit, the game being over just before 5.30.

The Winchester bowling and fielding were excellent. Raikes probably was the best bowler in the two teams, and he captained his side splendidly. Macmillan again fielded magnificently at cover-point. The game was a most interesting one to watch. The wicket wore very well, and much credit was due to Austin, the groundsman, for its condition.

The Times, 27 June, 1921

1921

CRICKET.

ENGLAND'S PLUCKY RALLY.

A STRONG 'TAIL' AGAINST THE AUSTRALIANS.

TENNYSON'S BRILLIANCE.

Manchester Guardian, 5 July, 1921

THE THIRD TEST against Australia at Headingley in July 1921 had all the elements of high drama. England under J.W.H.T. Douglas having just lost seven successive Tests in the course of as many months, the selectors gave the captaincy to Lionel Tennyson, grandson of the poet. Within an hour of the start England's new leader, fielding at silly point, split the web between the thumb and forefinger of the left hand. No sooner was it stitched up than Jack Hobbs was suddenly taken to hospital with appendicitis (and played no more that summer).

On the second day, with the board

ABOVE Lionel Tennyson on the attack

showing 165 for 7 and England needing 91 more to save the follow-on, Tennyson went in, his hand bandaged, amidst much patriotic cheering to do or die. Who better to tell the romantic tale than a youthful Cardus in the *Manchester Guardian?*

Tennyson's last-minute rally today might have moved his poetic ancestor to lofty verse, though only the majestic cadences of his 'Ulysses' would do suitable honour. For Tennyson, with his left hand all bandages and coming to the wicket late in the innings just gave a happy cavalier smile at the enclosing gloom, and, to the joy, aye, and the bewilderment of the multitude, straightaway attacked the Australian fast bowlers, and his bat, all curves and thrusts, flashed the ball to the remote parts of the field ...

Tennyson in a ruinous hour for his side, to the accompaniment of stabs of pain from the wounded hand, yet played the happy wayfarer and again he blazoned the news to the land that a big heart will take one a long way against these Australians. Tennyson came in to bat when Douglas was 51 and the total score 166. He drove to the off and glided through the slips in such tune that he made 62 while Douglas made 24. He put Gregory and McDonald to flight by hitting eight fours from their fast bowling ...

The lessons of today's cricket will not be lost; we are slowly finding these Australians out! Let Tennyson only go along his dauntless way. And for his watchword there are fine words in his grandfather's volumes:

'Tho' much is taken, much abides; and tho'
We are not now that strength which in old days
Moved earth and heaven; that which we are, we are;
One equal temper of heroic hearts.'

Tennyson made 63, thus saving the follow-on, and 36 – also one-handed – in the second innings, albeit England again lost heavily. Did he use the left hand at all? In his book *Sticky Wickets*

the hero wrote that an exceptionally strong right hand did the job, and a photograph shows him slashing away one-handed. The probability is that Cardus's 'stabs of pain' can be regarded as poetic licence.

ENGLAND v AUSTRALIA
Played at Leeds, 2, 4, 5 July, 1921.
Result: Australia won by 219 runs.

Australia: First innings

W. Bardsley c Woolley b Douglas	6
T.J.E. Andrews c Woolley b Douglas	19
C.G. Macartney lbw b Parkin	115
C.E. Pellew c Hearne b Woolley	52
J.M. Taylor c Douglas b Jupp	50
J.M. Gregory b Parkin	1
W.W. Armstrong* c Brown b Douglas	77
H.S.T.L. Hendry b Parkin	0
H. Carter† b Jupp	34
E.A. McDonald not out	21
A.A. Mailey c and b Parkin	6
Extras (b 16, lb 7, nb 3)	26
Total	407

Fall of Wickets: 1/22, 2/45, 3/146, 4/255, 5/256, 6/271, 7/271, 8/333, 9/388, 10/407.
Bowling: Douglas 20-3-80-3, White 25-4-70-0, Parkin 20.1-0-106-4, Hearne 5-0-21-0, Jupp 18-2-70-2, Woolley 5-0-34-1.

England: First innings

F.E. Woolley b Gregory	0
H.T.W. Hardinge lbw b Armstrong	25
J.W. Hearne b Parkin	7
A. Ducat c Gregory b McDonald	3
J.W.H.T. Douglas b Armstrong	75
V.W.C. Jupp c Carter b Gregory	14
G. Brown† c Armstrong b Mailey	57
J.C. White b McDonald	1
Hon. L.H. Tennyson* c Gregory b McDonald	63
C.H. Parkin not out	5
J.B. Hobbs absent ill	–
Extras (lb 3, nb 6)	9
Total	259

Fall of Wickets: 1/0, 2/13, 3/30, 4/47, 5/67, 6/164, 7/165, 8/253, 9/159.
Bowling: Gregory 21-6-47-2, McDonald 26.1-0-105-4, Armstrong 19-4-44-2, Mailey 17-4-38-1, Hendry 10-4-16-0.

Australia: Second innings

W. Bardsley b Jupp	25
T.J.E. Andrews b Jupp	92
C.G. Macartney c and b Woolley	30
C.E. Pellew (5) c Ducat b White	16
J.M. Taylor (6) c Tennyson b White	4
J.M. Gregory (8) c Jupp b White	3
W.W. Armstrong* not out	28
H.S.T.L. Hendry (9) not out	11
H. Carter† (4) lbw b Parkin	47
E.A. McDonald	
A.A. Mailey	} did not bat
Extras (b 10, lb 4, nb 3)	17
Total (7 wickets declared)	273

Fall of Wickets: 1/71, 2/139, 3/193, 4/223, 5/227, 6/227, 7/230.
Bowling: Douglas 11-0-38-0, White 11-3-37-3, Parkin 20-0-91-1, Jupp 13-2-45-2, Woolley 18-4-45-1.

England: Second innings

F.E. Woolley (4) b Mailey	37
H.T.W. Hardinge c Gregory b McDonald	5
J.W. Hearne c Taylor b McDonald	27
A. Ducat (6) st Carter b Mailey	2
J.W.H.T. Douglas b Gregory	8
V.W.C. Jupp (7) c Carter b Armstrong	28
G. Brown† (1) lbw b Gregory	46
J.C. White (9) not out	6
Hon. L.H. Tennyson* (8) b Armstrong	36
C.H. Parkin b Mailey	4
J.B. Hobbs absent ill	–
Extras (b 3)	3
Total	202

Fall of Wickets: 1/15, 2/57, 3/98, 4/124, 5/126, 6/128, 7/190, 8/197, 9/202.
Bowling: Gregory 14-1-55-2, McDonald 15-2-67-2, Armstrong 3-0-6-2, Mailey 20.2-3-71-3.

AUSTRALIANS
LOSE £15,000
BY THEIR DEFEAT.

£1,000 EACH HAD THEY NOT LOST A MATCH.

28 RUNS MARGIN.

MACLAREN'S TRIUMPH IN HIS LAST BIG MATCH.

From the "Daily Chronicle" Special Correspondent.

EASTBOURNE, Tuesday.

The surprise victory gained by an England XI. by 28 runs at Eastbourne to-day has cost the Australian team £15,000.

Warwick Armstrong, their captain, said to G. E. C. Wood, to-night, that if the team had come through the tour unbeaten each member would have been presented with £1,000.

Armstrong warmly acknowledged the genuineness of this surprise defeat by "a better side on the play in the match."

A. C. MacLaren, the famous old Test match skipper, led a team composed largely of young players, most of whom have not been considered for international honours. But these men succeeded where elevens reputed to be the strongest in England have failed.

Their victory was all the more noteworthy because in the first innings the total was only 43, and they began the second venture 131 behind.

AUSTRALIAN REVERSES.

In spite of a great effort by England's batsmen in their last knock, the odds always appeared to be in favour of the Colonials until their batting failure yesterday.

England's bowlers, particularly Gibson, were assisted by a rain-soaked wicket. Early on, however, Gibson had 16 runs scored off two overs, and this suggested that the 195 runs needed for an Australian victory would be easily obtained. But as Bardsley at 52, Carter at the same total, and Macartney at 73 went back to the pavilion the home men's hopes were raised.

Reverse followed reverse for the Australians. Although their score gradually drew near to that of their opponents, wickets fell regularly.

Daily Chronicle, 31 August, 1921

ABOVE A. C. MacLaren leaving the field at Eastbourne after his amateur side had inflicted the first defeat on Warwick Armstrong's Australians

1921

A.C. MACLAREN'S ENGLAND XI
v THE AUSTRALIANS
Played at Eastbourne,
30, 31 August, 1921.

A.C. MacLaren's XI: First innings

Mr G.N. Foster c Gregory b McDonald	5
Mr G.A. Faulkner b Armstrong	3
Mr G. Ashton lbw b Armstrong	6
Mr H. Ashton b McDonald	0
Mr A.P.F. Chapman b McDonald	16
Mr C.T. Ashton c Ryder b Armstrong	1
Mr M. Falcon b McDonald	8
Mr G.E.C. Wood lbw b Armstrong	1
Mr A.C. MacLaren b McDonald	0
Mr C.H. Gibson not out	1
Mr W. Brearley b Armstrong	1
Extras (nb 1)	1
Total	43

Bowling: Gregory 2-0-6-0, McDonald 10-2-21-5, Armstrong 8.1-4-15-5.

Australians: First innings

H.L. Collins b Falcon	19
W. Bardsley lbw b Armstrong	70
C.G. Macartney b Faulkner	24
T.J.E. Andrews b Faulkner	0
C.E. Pellew c H. Ashton b Falcon	1
J. Ryder b Falcon	10
W.W. Armstrong b Falcon	13
H. Carter c H. Ashton b Faulkner	10
J.M. Gregory not out	16
E.A. McDonald b Falcon	4
A.A. Mailey b Falcon	4
Extras (b 1, lb 2)	3
Total	174

Bowling: Falcon 18.4-2-67-6, Gibson 14-2-54-0, Faulkner 16-1-50-4.

A.C. MacLaren's XI: Second innings

Mr G.N. Foster c and b McDonald	11
Mr G.A. Faulkner c Mailey b Armstrong	153
Mr G. Ashton lbw b Armstrong	36
Mr H. Ashton lbw b Armstrong	75
Mr A.P.F. Chapman b McDonald	11
Mr C.T. Ashton b McDonald	0
Mr M. Falcon c and b McDonald	17
Mr G.E.C. Wood b Armstrong	2
Mr A.C. MacLaren b McDonald	5
Mr C.H. Gibson not out	0
Mr W. Brearley run out	0
Extras (b 10, lb 1, nb 5)	10
Total	326

Bowling: Gregory 9-0-51-0, McDonald 31-3-98-6, Armstrong 24.5-6-74-3, Ryder 5-1-11-0, Mailey 22-3-76-0.

Australians: Second innings

H.L. Collins c H. Ashton b Gibson	12
W. Bardsley b Gibson	22
C.G. Macartney b Falcon	14
T.J.E. Andrews b Faulkner	31
C.E. Pellew c H. Ashton b Gibson	16
J. Ryder c G. Ashton b Gibson	28
W.W. Armstrong lbw b Faulkner	11
H. Carter c C.T. Ashton b Falcon	16
J.M. Gregory lbw b Gibson	0
E.A. McDonald not out	9
A.A. Mailey b Gibson	0
Extras (lb 3, nb 5)	8
Total	167

Bowling: Falcon 18-2-82-2, Gibson 22.4-6-64-6, Faulkner 5-1-13-2.

THE *DAILY CHRONICLE*, a sober journal of Liberal persuasion, gave front-page coverage to this classic of the unexpected, and added an exclusive touch in the revelation that defeat in the match deprived each member of the hitherto all-conquering Australians of a bonus of £1,000 each. It was never in the Australian character to take a game lightly, and any suggestion that Warwick Armstrong's team might have done so here is disposed of by this financial consideration.

The background to the occasion and the play had all the ingredients of fiction. MacLaren, whose fame had largely been achieved in the period 1890-1914, now in his fiftieth year and long retired from the first-class game, declared earlier in the summer when England were going down to wholesale defeat, that he would produce an amateur team to beat the Australians. The boast by the arch-pundit seemed grotesque when on the first morning his selected side were bowled out before lunch for 43.

MacLaren had based his choice on the highly successful Cambridge side of 1921, the Ashton brotherhood of Gilbert, Hubert and Claude, Chapman and Gibson, with two earlier light blues in Falcon and Wood. He also played

Walter Brearley, his old fast bowler, who had not played first-class cricket for ten years and who never bowled a ball because he pulled a muscle when batting!

His key all-rounder, who had last played in a Test Match nine years earlier, was, however, Aubrey Faulkner, the South African, one of the googly quartet of 1907 who was also a high-class bat. He and Hubert Ashton (who in general estimation should have been picked for England that summer) provided the backbone of the second innings, while the whole of the bowling in both Australian innings, backed by superlative fielding, was done by three men, Gibson, Falcon and Faulkner. Such was the tension as the crisis rose to a climax that, according to Arthur Mailey, his vast captain Warwick Armstrong was shaking like a jelly as he left the dressing-room. However that may be, his comment at the end was generous enough.

The score-card looks as fascinating today as it did to readers on that late August morning not far off seventy years ago.

1922

WARWICKSHIRE v HAMPSHIRE

Played at Birmingham,
14, 15, 16 June, 1922.
Result: Hampshire won by 155 runs.

Warwickshire: First innings

L.A. Bates c Shirley b Newman	3
E.J. Smith c Mead b Newman	24
Mr F.R. Santall c McIntyre b Boyes	84
W.G. Quaife b Newman	1
Hon. F.S.G. Calthorpe c Boyes b Kennedy	70
Rev. E.F. Waddy c Mead b Boyes	0
Mr B.W. Quaife b Boyes	0
J. Fox b Kennedy	4
J. Smart b Newman	20
C. Smart c Mead b Boyes	14
H. Howell not out	1
Extras (lb 2)	2
Total	**223**

Bowling: Kennedy 24-7-74-2, Newman 12.3-0-70-4, Boyes 16-5-56-4, Shirley 3-0-21-0.

Hampshire: First innings

A. Bowell b Howell	0
A. Kennedy c Smith b Calthorpe	0
Mr H.L.V. Day b Calthorpe	0
C.P. Mead not out	6
Hon. L.H. Tennyson c Calthorpe b Howell	4
G. Brown b Howell	0
J. Newman c Smart b Howell	0
Mr W.R. Shirley c J. Smart b Calthorpe	1
Mr A.S. McIntyre lbw b Calthorpe	0
W.H. Livsey b Howell	0
G.S. Boyes lbw b Howell	0
Extras (b 4)	4
Total	**15**

Bowling: Howell 4.5-2-7-6, Calthorpe 4-3-4-4.

Hampshire: Second innings

A. Bowell c Howell b W.G. Quaife	45
A. Kennedy b Calthorpe	7
Mr H.L.V. Day c Bates b W.G. Quaife	15
C.P. Mead b Howell	24
Hon. L.H. Tennyson c C. Smart b Calthorpe	45
G. Brown b C. Smart	172
J. Newman c and b W.G. Quaife	12
Mr W.R. Shirley lbw b Fox	30
Mr A.S. McIntyre lbw b Howell	5
W.H. Livsey not out	110
G.S. Boyes b Howell	29
Extras (b 14, lb 11, w 1, nb 1)	27
Total	**521**

Bowling: Howell 63-10-156-3, Calthorpe 33-7-97-2, W.G. Quaife 49-8-154-3, Fox 7-0-30-1, J. Smart 13-2-37-0, Santall 5-0-15-0, C. Smart 1-0-5-1.

Warwickshire: Second innings

L.A. Bates c Mead b Kennedy	1
E.J. Smith c Shirley b Kennedy	41
Mr F.R. Santall b Newman	0
W.G. Quaife not out	40
Hon. F.S.G. Calthorpe b Newman	30
Rev. E.F. Waddy b Newman	0
Mr B.W. Quaife c and b Kennedy	7
J. Fox b Kennedy	0
J. Smart b Newman	3
C. Smart c and b Boyes	15
H. Howell c Kennedy b Newman	11
Extras (b 6, lb 4)	10
Total	**158**

Bowling: Kennedy 26-12-47-4, Newman 26.3-12-53-5, Boyes 11-4-34-1, Brown 5-0-14-0.

RIGHT Hon F.S.G. Calthorpe, captain of the losing side in an extraordinary match

---

COUNTY CRICKET SUMMARY.

YORKSHIRE'S DEFEAT OF THE CHAMPIONS.

MAGNIFICENT TRIUMPH FOR HAMPSHIRE.

Sporting Life, 17 June, 1922

THE MATCH between Warwickshire and Hampshire at Edgbaston produced perhaps the most extravagant change of fortune in the history of county cricket. The evidence given by players involved does not go far towards a rational explanation, at least in respect of Hampshire's dismissal for 15 (only three lower scores have been recorded in the Championship). Their second innings recovery owed something, however, to Warwickshire's conscious easing of the pressure when victory seemed round the corner while their own collapse in the fourth innings was surely, psychologically speaking, not improbable. Here are a few relevant facts and opinions, some taken from the late Leslie Duckworth's admirable *The Story of Warwickshire Cricket*.

Rain before the start led one Honourable captain, Tennyson, on winning the toss to ask the other one, Calthorpe, to bat. The Hampshire bowlers got some help, and dismissed their opponents for 223. When Warwickshire went out to field the pitch was rated as almost perfect. 'Tiger' Smith said he had never seen Harry Howell bowl so fast. H.L.V. Day talked of Freddy Calthorpe's prodigious swing. Philip Mead (6 not out) however was unperturbed, 'No one bowled me anything that I couldn't play in the middle.' When Warwickshire's captain suggested on the first evening that after the match was over the amateurs should play one another at golf his opposite number's reply in Anglo-Saxon vernacular ended with a £10 bet that Hampshire would win. Calthorpe did not give the new ball in the second innings to Howell, nor take the second one when due at 200 for 6 with Hampshire

---

HAMPSHIRE'S REMARKABLE VICTORY.

COMPLETE REVERSAL OF FORM AT EDGBASTON.

Overnight Scores: Warwickshire, 223; Hampshire, 15 and 475 for nine.

One of the most remarkable games in the annals of cricket ended at Edgbaston yesterday in a victory for Hampshire by 155 runs.

For a side to be dismissed for 15 and then make 521 and finally win by such a margin represents indeed a marvellous reversal of form, and Hampshire are to be warmly congratulated upon their triumph. The Hampshire innings was finished off for 521, Livsey taking out his bat for a faultless 110, his first century in county cricket. He batted three hours and a quarter, and hit ten 4's.

Set to get 314, Warwickshire made a fairly good start, Smith and Calthorpe batting well, but later Newman bowled with marked success and had creditable figures. Quaife took out his bat for a patient 40, but many of the side shaped very lamely, the team possessing a modicum of grit.

Sporting Life, 17 June, 1922

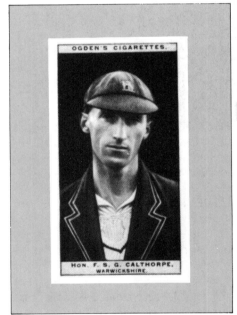

still a few runs behind. However the redoubtable George Brown was settled in, and he and Walter Livsey, who fulfilled the taxing double duty of keeping wicket for his county and serving as valet to its captain, combined in a prodigious partnership of 177 for the ninth wicket. The last wicket added 70 and Livsey reached 110 not out, the highest score of his life. After fielding out to a score of 521 Warwickshire's second innings showing was not perhaps wholly surprising. The margin of victory was 155 runs.

GREAT WIN FOR WEST INDIES.

SURREY DEFEATED BY TEN WICKETS.

CHALLENOR'S MATCH : D. R. JARDINE'S 100.

At the Oval (Third Day).

Overnight Scores: Surrey, 87 and 233 for four; West Indies, 305.

The West Indies team gained a notable triumph over Surrey yesterday at the Oval by ten wickets. They were set only 119 to win when they went to the wicket a second time, and so light-heartedly did they set to work that the runs were obtained in sixty-seven minutes without loss.

Surrey were 15 runs on with six wickets in hand when play was resumed yesterday morning before an excellent attendance, looking at the position of affairs, but the hopes that were cherished that the remaining batsmen would put on a lot of runs were not fulfilled. Abel added only five to his overnight total, when he put a ball from Francis into the slips, where it was safely held by Small.

Abel's partnership with Jardine had been of inestimable value from Surrey's point of view. They came together when four wickets had been lost for 125, and 93 runs were required to avoid the innings defeat, and before they were separated they carried the total to 260, the partnership thus yielding 135, put together in five minutes over two hours. Abel hit five 4's in his innings of 63, resourceful defence and powerful driving being its outstanding features.

Sporting Life, 4 August, 1923

THE THIRD West Indian tour of England in 1923 was the penultimate stepping-stone to Test status, which followed directly on the MCC visit of 1925-26. The high spot was the wholesale defeat of Surrey at The Oval, a result due to the excellence of George Challenor's batting and the fast bowling of George Francis, both from Barbados, one white, one black. The latter was the forerunner, with George John and the 21-year-old Learie Constantine, of the succession of West Indian men of speed with which most of their subsequent teams have been well supplied.

But whereas in 1923 Francis led a successful all-round attack Challenor had to shoulder the batting largely on his own. He was third in the English batting averages to Hendren and Mead with 51 – the next best being 34: he made 1,556 runs, double as many as anyone else. *Wisden* says of him that 'he had everything – style, hitting power and strength of defence.' C.L.R.

James, the prime West Indian cricket authority of all time, wrote that 'he was the originator of the great tradition of Barbados, i.e. of West Indian batting... The history of West Indies maturity is unintelligible unless it begins with the batting of George Challenor.'

Francis and John gave notice of events to come at Scarborough in the last match against a C.I. Thornton's XI of Test strength. The latter needed only 31 in the last innings, whereupon this formidable pair shot out five of them for 19. Somehow Douglas and Fender scrambled those last 12 runs.

Another portentous performance will have been noted, incidentally, in the score of the Surrey match. Young D.R. Jardine, fresh into the county side from Oxford, made his second hundred within a week. The *Sporting Life* reported that 'he gave a display of resourcefulness in defence, and clean, hard driving that stamped him as a batsman of parts.'

1923

SURREY v WEST INDIES
Played at The Oval, 1, 2, 3, August, 1923.
Result: West Indies won by ten wickets.

Surrey: First innings

H.S. Harrison c Francis b Browne	1
A. Sandham c Dewhurst b Francis	29
A. Ducat lbw b Francis	0
T. Shepherd run out	25
Mr. D.R. Jardine c Francis b Browne	16
W.J. Abel b Browne	9
Mr. P.G.H. Fender c and b Francis	0
H.A. Peach b Francis	0
W. Sadler b Francis	0
H. Strudwick c Francis b Browne	0
R.F. Lowe not out	2
Extras (lb 5)	5
Total	87

Bowling: Francis 21-6-31-5, Browne 24.1-14-41-4, Constantine 4-2-10-0.

West Indies: First innings

G. Challenor not out	155
P.H. Tarilton b Sadler	3
H.W. Ince b Peach	27
C.R. Browne lbw b Fender	0
J. Small c Harrison b Fender	0
R.K. Nunes c Abel b Fender	0
H.B.G. Austin lbw b Abel	19
V. Pascall b Sadler	22
L. Constantine lbw b Shepherd	2
G. Dewhurst b Shepherd	7
G. Francis b Fender	41
Extras (b 13, lb 15, nb 1)	29
Total	305

Bowling: Sadler 20-3-60-2, Lowe 10-2-34-0, Peach 24-10-48-1, Fender 25.1-2-71-4, Abel 8-1-29-1, Shepherd 14-5-34-2.

Surrey: Second innings

H.S. Harrison b Small	27
A. Sandham lbw b Francis	0
A. Ducat st Dewhurst b Browne	12
T. Shepherd b Constantine	53
Mr. D.R. Jardine c Dewhurst b Pascall	104
W.J. Abel c Small b Francis	63
Mr. P.G.H. Fender b Pascall	30
H.A. Peach b Francis	17
W. Sadler b Francis	1
H. Strudwick not out	2
R.F. Lowe b Francis	1
Extras (b 16, lb 9, nb 1)	26
Total	336

Bowling: Francis 24.4-4-45-5, Browne 45-11-94-1, Constantine 14-1-49-1, Pascall 26-4-61-2, Small 17-2-61-1.

West Indies: Second innings

G. Challenor not out	66
P.H. Tarilton not out	36
H.W. Ince	
C.R. Browne	
J. Small	
R.K. Nunes	
H.B.G. Austin	did not bat
V. Pascall	
L. Constantine	
G. Dewhurst	
G. Francis	
Extras (b 12, lb 3, w 4)	19
Total	121

Bowling: Sadler 6-1-25-0, Lowe 3-0-16-0, Peach 4-1-18-0, Fender 5-0-20-0, Abel 9-2-28-0.

ABOVE LEFT George Challenor

47

1924

ENGLAND v SOUTH AFRICA
Played at Birmingham,
14, 16, 17 June, 1924.
Result: England won by an innings and 18 runs.

England: First innings

J.B. Hobbs lbw b Blanckenberg		76
H. Sutcliffe b Parker		64
F.E. Woolley c Ward b Parker		64
E.H. Hendren c Nourse b Parker		74
A.P.F. Chapman b Parker		8
P.G.H. Fender c Taylor b Blanckenberg		36
R. Kilner c and b Pegler		59
M.W. Tate c Taylor b Parker		19
A.E.R. Gilligan* b Pegler		13
G.E.C. Wood† b Parker		1
C.H. Parkin not out		8
Extras (b 4, lb 11, nb 1)		16
Total		438

Fall of Wickets: 1/136, 2/164, 3/247, 4/255, 5/315, 6/356, 7/386, 8/407, 9/410, 10/438.
Bowling: Parker 37-2-152-6, Pegler 36-8-106-2, Blanckenberg 32-5-95-2, Nupen 18-2-66-0, Nourse 1-0-3-0.

South Africa: First innings

H.W. Taylor* b Tate		7
R.H. Catterall b Gilligan		0
M.J. Susskind c Kilner b Tate		3
A.W. Nourse lbw b Gilligan		1
J.M.M. Commaille not out		1
J.M. Blanckenberg b Tate		4
H.G. Deane b Gilligan		2
E.P. Nupen b Gilligan		0
S.J. Pegler b Tate		0
T.A. Ward† b Gilligan		1
G.M. Parker lbw b Gilligan		0
Extras (b 1, lb 7, nb 3)		11
Total		30

Fall of Wickets: 1/1, 2/4, 3/6, 4/14, 5/20, 6/23, 7/23, 8/24, 9/30, 10/30.
Bowling: Gilligan 6.3-4-7-6, Tate 6-1-12-4.

South Africa: Second innings

H.W. Taylor* c and b Tate		34
R.H. Catterall (5) c Hobbs b Tate		120
M.J. Susskind b Gilligan		51
A.W. Nourse c Wood b Gilligan		34
J.M.M. Commaille (2) c Hendren b Tate		29
J.M. Blanckenberg c Chapman b Gilligan		56
H.G. Deane run out		5
E.P. Nupen lbw b Tate		5
S.J. Pegler (10) c Hobbs b Gilligan		6
T.A. Ward† (9) b Gilligan		19
G.M. Parker not out		2
Extras (b 4, lb 18, w 1, nb 6)		29
Total		390

Fall of Wickets: 1/54, 2/101, 3/152, 4/161, 5/275, 6/284, 7/295, 8/350, 9/371, 10/390.
Bowling: Gilligan 28-6-83-5, Tate 50.4-19-103-4, Parkin 16-5-38-0, Kilner 22-10-40-0, Fender 17-5-56-0, Woolley 10-2-41-0.

RIGHT England take the field: (Left to right) R. Kilner, H. Sutcliffe, M.W. Tate, C.H. Parkin, J.B. Hobbs, E. Hendren, A.P.F. Chapman, A.E.R. Gilligan (captain), P.G.H. Fender. F.E. Woolley and G.E.C. Wood are obscured. FAR RIGHT The captain and his Sussex partner: Gilligan and Tate who with six and four wickets respectively were responsible for South Africa's sorry demise

THE THIRD South African Test team to England were bowled out in the First Test at Edgbaston in 1924 for the lowest score made in a Test Match in this country. They had run England close on their own matting wickets two winters before, and they recovered their form and morale to put up a better fight as this series developed.

Connoisseurs both of cricket and of Fleet Street may be interested to note that the *Daily Express* employed a famous old England captain as its reporter, and that Archie MacLaren addressed his readers as followers whom he expected to know the game.

The bowlers who destroyed South Africa were the Sussex pair, Maurice Tate, playing in his first Test, and Arthur Gilligan, captain both of Sussex and now of England. Tate, initially employed by Sussex as a batsman, had broken through as a magnificent fast-medium bowler for the county two years earlier. How he did so was by way of a fluke involving Gilligan, who in the nets asked Tate, up to then a slow bowler, to send him down some quicker ones. Tate accordingly got those great shoulders working and gave his captain more than he had bargained for. By those few balls Tate's future was

SENSATIONAL PLAY IN THE TEST MATCH.

COLLAPSE AND RECOVERY OF THE SOUTH AFRICANS.

By A. C. MACLAREN.

Daily Express, 17 June, 1924

charted. Of his type there has never been a better bowler. For a few months in 1924 Gilligan's sheer speed and Tate's swing and life off the pitch were irresistible. Then, however, Gilligan suffered a severe blow over the heart when batting, and, though he took MCC to Australia the following winter he was never the same cricketer afterwards. This in fact was his finest hour. As for Tate he was on the threshold of fame.

SOUTH AFRICA OUT FOR 30.

FINE-RECOVERY IN THE SECOND INNINGS.

The South Africans collapsed in astonishing fashion in the Test match at Birmingham yesterday. They were dismissed for 30 runs —the lowest score ever made in a Test match in this country.

A. E. R. Gilligan, England's captain, captured six wickets for 7 runs, and Tate four for 12.

England's innings had been completed earlier for 498. This was the highest total ever made against South Africa in a Test match in this country.

When the South Africans followed on, 468 runs behind, they gave a much better batting display, and at the close of the day they had scored 274 for four wickets.

Daily Express, 17 June, 1924

49

SOMERSET v SURREY

Played at Taunton, 15, 17, 18 August, 1925.
Result: Surrey won by ten wickets.

Somerset: First innings

Mr J.C.W. MacBryan b Holmes	6
A. Young c Sadler b Lockton	58
Mr T.E.S. Francis b Sadler	0
Mr J.C. White b Sadler	1
Mr P.R. Johnson c and b Lockton	30
Mr E.F. Longrigg b Sadler	5
Mr R.A. Ingle b Fender	22
G. Hunt b Lockton	4
Mr R.C. Robertson-Glasgow c Jardine b Lockton	4
Mr J.J. Bridges c and b Shepherd	25
Mr M.L. Hill not out	0
Extras (lb 8, w 4)	12
Total	167

Bowling: Sadler 16-4-28-3, Holmes 6-2-12-1, Fender 13-3-39-1, Lockton 16-4-36-4, Peach 9-2-21-0, Shepherd 6.3-1-19-1.

Surrey: First innings

J.B. Hobbs c Hill b Bridges	101
A. Sandham c Longrigg b Bridges	13
Mr D.J. Knight run out	34
T. Shepherd b White	0
Mr D.R. Jardine run out	47
Mr E.R.T. Holmes c Hill b R-Glasgow	24
Mr P.G.H. Fender st Hill b Young	59
H.A. Peach b Young	20
W. Sadler c Johnson b Young	25
H. Strudwick not out	10
Mr J.H. Lockton absent	0
Extras (b 15, lb 8, nb 3)	26
Total	359

Bowling: Robertson-Glasgow 26-1-144-1, Bridges 37-5-115-2, White 29-13-51-1, Hunt 4-1-14-0, Young 5.3-1-9-3.

Somerset: Second innings

Mr J.C.W. MacBryan b Fender	109
A. Young c Strudwick b Sadler	71
Mr T.E.S. Francis c Strudwick b Lockton	12
Mr J.C. White c Strudwick b Sadler	30
Mr P.R. Johnson c Peach b Fender	16
Mr E.F. Longrigg run out	4
Mr R.A. Ingle c Shepherd b Peach	23
G. Hunt b Fender	59
Mr R.C. Robertson-Glasgow c Sadler b Fender	5
Mr J.J. Bridges b Fender	26
Mr M.L. Hill not out	1
Extras (b 9, lb 5, nb 4)	18
Total	374

Bowling: Sadler 21-5-59-2, Holmes 17-0-56-0, Fender 35.5-8-120-5, Lockton 9-2-15-1, Peach 20-7-46-1, Shepherd 21-5-60-0.

Surrey: Second innings

J.B. Hobbs not out	101
A. Sandham not out	74
Mr D.J. Knight	
T. Shepherd	
Mr D.R. Jardine	
Mr E.R.T. Holmes	
Mr P.G.H. Fender	did not bat
H.A. Peach	
W. Sadler	
H. Strudwick	
Mr J.H. Lockton	
Extras (b 6, lb 1, nb 1)	8
Total (0 wickets)	183

Bowling: Robertson-Glasgow 6-0-42-0, Bridges 11-3-27-0, White 14-6-34-0, Hunt 8-4-15-0, Young 15.5-1-39-0, Longrigg 3-0-18-0.

Hobbs's moment of glory: TOP RIGHT scoring the run that equals Grace's record, RIGHT being congratulated and FAR RIGHT being cheered into the pavilion.

THE EQUALLING and next day bettering of W.G.'s tally of 126 hundreds by J.B. Hobbs was a major milestone in cricket history. Comparison is more than usually futile as between cricketers of different generations. W.G. was unique – the Champion. Jack, in all critical estimation, was the greatest English batsman of his era (1905-1934). Having seen much of him in his last playing decade and all the best batsmen since his retirement I would maintain he has had no equal since. Perfection of technique and temperament went hand in hand. Nor could anyone have worn fame with a more endearing modesty.

My *Daily Telegraph* predecessor and old friend Philip Trevor, who here records the stirring happenings at Taunton in August 1925, always had a soft spot for Jack, whom he managed on the first of his five MCC tours to Australia, in 1907-08. Hobbs being 91 not out over the week-end, the Great Western Railway ran a special train

from Paddington to Taunton where the Monday crowd was estimated at 10,000.

And who can today read Trevor's report of the moment of triumph without a sigh for times past.

…It was acclamation of the right sort that they gave – good, hearty, unrestrained English cheers. There was none of that sentimentality run mad which, degenerating into excess, makes a big event either ugly or ridiculous or both.

Hobbs had made his 100th 100 at the age of forty early in the summer of 1923. He made his 197th and last in George Duckworth's Benefit at Old Trafford at Whitsuntide 1934 aged fifty-one. Between 1912 and that last summer he had only once ended a season with an average below 50. He was never an accumulator for the sake of it, yet his aggregate of 61,237 tops them all and is unlikely ever to be exceeded.

CRICKET.

HOBBS EQUALS RECORD.

SCENES AT TAUNTON.

By COLONEL PHILIP TREVOR, C.B.E.

Last Season: MATCH DRAWN.
SOMERSET .. 1st inns., 167; 2nd, 256 (3 wkts.)
SURREY .. .. 1st inns., 359

Yesterday morning, at Taunton, Hobbs got the hundredth run of his 126th hundred, and by so doing equalled the record of W. G. Grace. He did this amid great enthusiasm.

Daily Telegraph, 18 August, 1925

HOBBS EXCELS
THE
W. G. GRACE RECORD.

THE 127TH HUNDRED.

FOURTEEN IN A SEASON.

J. B. Hobbs set up a wonderful new cricket record at Taunton yesterday.

With a score of 101 not out in the second innings of the match with Somerset he passed Dr. W. G. Grace's record of 126 centuries in first-class cricket—a feat which was hailed with rapturous enthusiasm by the spectators.

Nor was this record the only one which Hobbs created. Yesterday was the first occasion on which a batsman has completed fourteen centuries in one season.

ONE OF HIS BEST.
THE CAUTIOUS NINETIES.

By COLONEL PHILIP TREVOR, C.B.E.
TAUNTON, Tuesday.

This afternoon, when Surrey beat Somerset by ten wickets, Hobbs made the 127th hundred of his career, and so broke the record long ago established by W. G. Grace. It will, of course, be remembered that the Grand Old Man, in his long playing career of forty-three years, made 126 hundreds. Only the day previously Hobbs had completed his 126th hundred, and so equalled the performance of the champion. That performance, and the scene which followed its accomplishment, were fully dealt with and described in to-day's *Daily Telegraph*, and so were the respective careers of Hobbs and his great predecessor.

To-day, when Grace's record was made a record no longer, fewer than 2,000 persons were on the ground. But they made up by the heartiness of their applause for their lack of numbers when Hobbs got his 100th run. The cheering continued for a minute and a half, and it seemed to grow in volume. The great batsman, who was evidently as delighted as everyone else, repeatedly waved his acknowledgments, and, indeed, hoisted his cap on the bat, which he lifted in the air.

Daily Telegraph, 19 August, 1925

1925

HAMMOND & DIPPER
PUT ON 330.

Manchester Guardian, 20 August, 1925

HAMMOND'S TRIUMPH.

AN ENGLAND CRICKETER OF TO-MORROW.

By Cricketer.

Yesterday was the gladdest I have spent on a cricket field for many years. The cricketers of Grace's lovely county —O the orchards of Gloucestershire and the ancient peacefulness of the Cotswolds!—came to dour Old Trafford and brought with them tidings of comfort and joy. The summer game is not dead, but is alive and returning to us, still the prodigal bearer of handsome sons who will grow up in the likeness of the men of old—the MacLarens and the Trumpers.

"Young fellow," said W. G. Grace, many times and oft, "you must put the bat to the ball." Yesterday Hammond, of Gloucestershire, put the bat most beautifully to the ball from morning till evening. Against the attack of Lancashire he played one of the finest innings that can ever have been accomplished by a boy of his age, which is twenty-two years. To be present at the rise of a new star in the sky and to know that it is going to be glorious—here is a moment thrilling indeed to men who live their lives imaginatively. It was as plain yesterday as the nose on Bardolph's face that Hammond is an England batsman of to-morrow; we could see the splendour of his cricket blossoming before us hour by hour. In years to come we shall remember August 19, 1925, at Old Trafford, for when in good time Hammond carves history out of Australian bowlers here and over the seas we shall be proud to say that we understood well enough that he was born for the company of master batsmen even in seasons that saw him at the wicket smooth and un-razored of cheek and apparently rather outside the consideration of the Wise Men of Lord's.

Manchester Guardian, 20 August, 1925

RIGHT The youthful Walter Hammond, whose good looks only enhanced his reputation as a batsman. 1925 saw the first signs of his future greatness and from then he never looked back

WITHIN A few days of Jack Hobbs achieving the second of his milestones a master batsman of the next generation was being proclaimed at Old Trafford, by Neville Cardus. On Wednesday, 19 August 1925 Walter Reginald Hammond played an innings against Lancashire in general and E.A. McDonald in particular which drew a eulogistic prophecy from the *Manchester Guardian's* Cricket Correspondent.

This is a revealing passage in respect of both author and subject. Hammond had made 1,000 runs for Gloucestershire in the two summers preceding this, though with a modest average in each case. He was rated 'promising' along with several other contemporaries. Cardus, however, on the strength of this innings – which was the major element in a third wicket partnership of 330 with A.E. Dipper that set a new Old Trafford record – was prepared, as they say, to stick his neck out, and the fact is that after this innings, apart from having to miss the 1926 season owing to illness, Hammond never looked back. He was chosen shortly afterwards to go to the West Indies with MCC, He had an auspicious tour, but contracted the illness referred to, and finally burst upon the world in May 1927.

LANCASHIRE v GLOUCESTERSHIRE
Played at Manchester,
19, 20, 21 August 1925.
Result: Match drawn.

Gloucestershire: First innings
Lt Col D.C. Robinson c Tyldesley b McDonald....... 18
A.G. Dipper c Parkin b Watson 144
R.A. Sinfield lbw b McDonald............................ 0
W.R. Hammond not out 250
B.S. Bloodworth c Tyldesley b Watson 1
R. Horton c Duckworth b McDonald 7
C. Parker c McDonald b Sibbles 10
Mr G.A. Wedel lbw b Sibbles 0
J.G. Bessant b McDonald 6
T.W. Goddard c Duckworth b McDonald 0
P. Mills b Tyldesley....................................... 5
Extras (b 13, lb 2)....................................... 15
Total 456

Bowling: McDonald 29-3-128-5, Sibbles 17-5-40-2, Tyldesley 34.1-6-106-1, Parkin 14-2-62-0, Watson 22-2-73-2, Iddon 7-0-32-0.

Lancashire: First innings 323 (F. Watson 93, Mr J. Sharp 75; Parker 5-120).

Gloucestershire: Second innings 53 for 1 (A.G. Dipper 28*).

IT IS CERTAIN that no subsequent writer on cricket matched either the authority of Sydney H. Pardon or his influence on the game – which dated from his undertaking the editorship of *Wisden* in 1890 to his sudden death in harness, aged seventy, in 1925. Pardon's interests were not confined to cricket. He was not only *The Times* cricket correspondent: he wrote special articles for the paper also on racing, music and drama.

As a young man I had the privilege of being briefly introduced to him outside the press box at The Oval. Though never a member of MCC he enjoyed the friendship and complete confidence of the hierarchy of his day, notably of Francis Lacey, secretary of MCC and their Lordships Harris and Hawke.

BELOW Sydney Pardon: Wisden's *most influential editor*

DEATH OF MR. PARDON.

CRICKET JOURNALIST.

SPORT AND THE DRAMA.

We regret to announce the death of Mr. Sydney H. Pardon, which occurred yesterday morning at St. Bartholomew's Hospital following a stroke at his office in Fleet-street late on Thursday night. Mr. Pardon was for many years the Cricket Correspondent of *The Times*, and was famous throughout the world as the editor of " Wisden's Almanack."

Sydney Pardon was one of those people who in these days become more and more rare. He was a distinct character. There was no one else who was quite like him. He was distinctive in appearance. In his body he was a small, frail man, with small feet, small hands, and long tapering fingers, which were never still. But the most arresting thing about him was his head, with its high domed forehead, its sensitive mouth, and rather small twinkling, restless eyes. He looked what he was, a very distinctive and in his own way, a very distinguished man. And true to his appearance it was his mental capacity and not his physical powers which made him—Sydney Pardon.

Sydney Pardon was never merely a reporter of cricket matches. He was a keen student of the game, and many years ago rightly came to be regarded as the greatest living authority on the game which, so far as is known, he had never played seriously. He wrote delightfully on the game and was a marvellous judge of a young player. The first occasion on which he saw the great Victor Trumper that batsman was out sixth ball, bowled by Young, the Essex and England bowler. Yet in that short innings Pardon was convinced that here was the greatest bat Australia had yet produced. Again, when Hobbs made his first appearance for Surrey Pardon stated in " Wisden's " that here was a new player " from whom a great deal can be expected, and who can be regarded as the best batsman brought forward for years." No further proof is surely needed as to his knowledge of the game and his judgment as to a player's promise.

The Times, 21 November, 1925

1926

BY THE middle of the 1920s sport, and cricket not least, was commanding much increased attention in the popular press. Even so the *Daily Express* coverage of England's Ashes victory at The Oval surely struck a new high. A banner headline across the width of the front page; a two-column lead report continued on page two, and two pictures; Wilfred Rhodes's (obviously ghosted) impressions; the leader itself; Strube's cartoon; and opening comment by the great humorous columnist 'Beachcomber' all added up to over seventy-five inches. Somebody must have told Lord Beaverbrook, the all-powerful owner, something about cricket!

As I so clearly recall, the excitement as the Fifth Test unfolded was enormous. There were, after all, so many humiliations to avenge, five defeats in Australia in 1920-21, three more in England in 1921, four more, as against a single victory in 1924-25. Four draws in that 1926 summer meant that the last match was to be played without limit of time. England appointed A.P.F. Chapman captain, in place of A.W. Carr, and recalled Rhodes at the age of forty-eight.

With Hobbs and Sutcliffe together in the second innings at close of play on the second day with 49 runs on the board the scales were evenly balanced but a severe thunderstorm overnight meant that play would continue on a sticky wicket: the heights of skill would be needed against the turning, lifting ball. It was forthcoming to a degree

Daily Express

DAILY EXPRESS, Thursday, August 19, 1926.

TO-DAY'S WEATHER. Sunny Intervals.

NO. 8,211.   LONDON, THURSDAY, AUGUST 19, 1926.   ONE PENNY.

ENGLAND'S THRILLING TEST MATCH VICTORY.

AUSTRALIA LOSE BY 289 RUNS.

EMOTIONAL SCENE AT THE OVAL.

TRIUMPH FOR RHODES.

WHOLE SIDE OUT IN THREE HOURS FOR 125.

THERE were unparalleled scenes of excitement and enthusiasm at the Oval yesterday, when England won the Test match by 289 runs.

England's second innings closed for 436—the highest third innings score made against Australia in this country. The Australians were set 415 to win, but were all out in three hours for 125. Rhodes took four wickets for 44 runs, Larwood three for 34, and Tate, Geary, and Stevens one each.

England last won a Test series at the Oval in August 1912. The "ashes" were regained by Australia in this country in 1921, and since then England had only won a single match.

I wonder which of the earnest statisticians is counting the number of words written about this Test Match. It must be another of the records they love so well. An amusing effect of the general excitement is that everybody you meet takes it for granted that there is nothing but the cricket in your mind. Paper-sellers tell you the score before you ask for the paper, and if you say to a man, "What's the time?" he replies mechanically "432 for nine." If you ask a barber for a shave, he says, "I don't know. He was still in when I last heard."

BEACHCOMBER.

HOW WE WON THE ASHES.

ENGLAND'S FINEST BATSMEN.

FILLIP TO CRICKET.

By WILFRED RHODES.

I never remember a game played in a better sporting spirit or one that I enjoyed more.

I have been on the English side in forty-one Test matches, and naturally I feel particularly gratified that in what is my last match for the Old Country we have won the "Ashes."

RIGHT Hobbs sweeps Mailey on his way to a famous hundred

that has made this stand one of the classic episodes of Test history. The score-board read 172 for 1, last man 100, when Jack Hobbs was bowled by Gregory with a ball that just tickled the off-bail. Herbert Sutcliffe went imperturbably on with succeeding partners until in the last over of the third day Mailey bowled him with a googly. That made it 375 for 6, last man 161, and the game, barring miracles, lost and won. Further rain in the night completely sealed Australia's fate. To this teenager the closing stages of their innings, and, at the end, the throng of many thousands calling for their heroes one by one is still a lively memory sixty years on.

WELL PLAYED, SIR !!
'I'M GLAD I CAME BACK IN TIME'

HOBBS SUTCLIFFE

ASHES

STRUBE

ENGLAND v AUSTRALIA
Played at The Oval, 14, 16, 17, 18 August, 1926.
Result: England won by 289 runs.

England: First innings

J.B. Hobbs b Mailey	37
H. Sutcliffe b Mailey	76
F.E. Woolley b Mailey	18
E.H. Hendren b Gregory	8
A.P.F. Chapman* st Oldfield b Mailey	49
G.T.S. Stevens c Andrews b Mailey	17
W. Rhodes c Oldfield b Mailey	28
G. Geary run out	9
M.W. Tate b Grimmett	23
H. Larwood c Andrews b Grimmett	0
H. Strudwick† not out	4
Extras (b 6, lb 5)	11
Total	280

Fall of Wickets: 1/53, 2/91, 3/108, 4/189, 5/213, 6/214, 7/231, 8/266, 9/266, 10/280.
Bowling: Gregory 15-4-31-1, Grimmett 33-12-74-2, Mailey 33.5-3-138-6, Macartney 7-4-16-0, Richardson 7-2-10-0.

Australia: First innings

W.M. Woodfull b Rhodes	35
W. Bardsley c Strudwick b Larwood	2
C.G. Macartney b Stevens	25
W.H. Ponsford run out	2
T.J.E. Andrews b Larwood	3
H.L. Collins* c Stevens b Larwood	61
A.J. Richardson c Geary b Rhodes	16
J.M. Gregory c Stevens b Tate	73
W.A.S. Oldfield† not out	33
C.V. Grimmett b Tate	35
A.A. Mailey c Strudwick b Tate	0
Extras (b 5, lb 12)	17
Total	302

Fall of Wickets: 1/9, 2/44, 3/51, 4/59, 5/90, 6/122, 7/229, 8/231, 9/298, 10/302.
Bowling: Tate 37.1-17-40-3, Larwood 34-11-82-3, Geary 27-8-43-0, Stevens 29-3-85-1, Rhodes 25-15-35-2.

England: Second innings

J.B. Hobbs b Gregory	100
H. Sutcliffe b Mailey	161
F.E. Woolley lbw b Richardson	27
E.H. Hendren c Oldfield b Grimmett	15
A.P.F. Chapman* b Richardson	19
G.T.S. Stevens c Mailey b Grimmett	22
W. Rhodes lbw b Grimmett	14
G. Geary c Oldfield b Gregory	1
M.W. Tate not out	33
H. Larwood b Mailey	5
H. Strudwick† c Andrews b Mailey	2
Extras (b 19, lb 18)	37
Total	436

Fall of Wickets: 1/172, 2/220, 3/277, 4/316, 5/373, 6/375, 7/382, 8/425, 9/430, 10/436.
Bowling: Gregory 18-1-58-2, Grimmett 55-17-108-3, Mailey 42.5-6-128-3, Macartney 26-16-24-0, Richardson 41-21-81-2.

Australia: Second innings

W.M. Woodfull c Geary b Larwood	0
W. Bardsley (4) c Woolley b Rhodes	21
C.G. Macartney c Geary b Larwood	16
W.H. Ponsford (2) c Larwood b Rhodes	12
T.J.E. Andrews (6) c Tate b Larwood	15
H.L. Collins* (5) c Woolley b Rhodes	4
A.J. Richardson (8) b Rhodes	4
J.M. Gregory (7) c Sutcliffe b Tate	9
W.A.S. Oldfield† b Stevens	23
C.V. Grimmett not out	8
A.A. Mailey b Geary	6
Extras (lb 7)	7
Total	125

Fall of Wickets: 1/1, 2/31, 3/31, 4/35, 5/63, 6/83, 7/83, 8/87, 9/114, 10/125.
Bowling: Tate 9-4-12-1, Larwood 14-3-34-3, Geary 6.3-2-15-1, Stevens 3-1-13-1, Rhodes 20-9-44-4.

BELOW Wilfred Rhodes – veteran hero of the match – drives boldly

55

1927

THE PROMISE of W.R. Hammond as an attractive stroke-player as well as a useful medium-pace bowler and a magnificent all-round fielder had been apparent for several seasons before 1927. Cardus had rhapsodized over a marvellous innings of 250 not out for Gloucestershire v. Lancashire at Old Trafford two years earlier. However an illness contracted on the MCC West Indies tour of 1925-26 kept him off the field all the English summer of 1926. It needed this achievement of 1,000 runs in May to foresee the young man just coming up to his twenty-fourth birth-day moving into the forefront at a time when English professional batting – with names like Hobbs, Woolley, Hendren, Mead, Sutcliffe, Ernest Tyldesley and others to conjure with – had never perhaps been so strong.

Thoughts of reaching a target hitherto only achieved by W.G. and by Tom Hayward of Surrey (who however batted first in April) seems not to have weighed Hammond down. On a day wherein the next highest score was 44 he made 192 out of 227 in two hours twenty-eight minutes. There were six sixes, 27 fours – and five chances.

Though few men could hit harder, as these figures suggest, Hammond proceeded to discipline himself to what he conceived as the needs of Test cricket when his chance came in South Africa the following winter. In 85 Tests he made 22 hundreds (the same number as Boycott and Cowdrey) his aggregate of 7,249 a little below theirs, his average of 58 distinctly higher.

Hammond was a man of magnificent physique and a stylist in all he did. One felt he could have excelled at any game he took up. In fact he briefly played professional football and was a high-class golfer.

BELOW W.R. Hammond, the classic picture, ABOVE spectating with admirers. Cardus wrote of Hammond in his obituary 'With his end a light and glow on cricket seemed to go out'

HAMMOND'S TRIUMPH.

GLOUCESTER MAN SCORES 1,000 RUNS IN MAY.

News of the World, 29 May, 1927

THE FIRST Test ever played at Brisbane was notable in several ways as well as being extraordinary in result. Although England had won back the Ashes at The Oval in 1926 Australia's record on their own pitches was quelling in the extreme, all Tests there being played to a finish (time-limited matches were only introduced after the Second World War). Australia had won nine Tests on the preceding two tours and lost only one, and that after the rubber had been decided.

It was in the light of recent history that A.P.F. Chapman's decision not to enforce the follow-on must be seen – this despite a first-innings lead of 399 and the break-down by that time of the great all-rounder J.M. Gregory. With C. Kelleway, Gregory's new ball bowling partner, also out of action through illness, England took their time to amass a gigantic lead of 741 before Chapman made his declaration (an unprecedented event in Australia) with eight wickets down. As if the situation were not sufficiently grotesque rain on the fourth night produced what *The Times* described as 'a very nasty wicket'. Australia's depleted side capitulated headlong. Nevertheless the phrase 'feeble batting' in the headline seems rather to be rubbing it in.

England's splendid all-round cricket in their first innings on the second day dictated the result. Hendren (169) was helped by Chapman (50) Tate (26) and Larwood (70) to add a further 249 for the last five wickets, thus bringing the score to 521. Thereupon before close of play Larwood (3 for 9) and Tate had reduced Australia to 44 for 4. An almost incredible catch by Chapman, throwing himself yards to his left in the gully to Bill Woodfull, set the standard for the series, it being claimed that not

a chance went down until after the Ashes were retained.

This was Don Bradman's first appearance for Australia, and it has often been suggested that his philosophy of Test cricket owed something to this rigorous experience: 675 is the largest winning margin of runs in Test history.

1928

AUSTRALIA v ENGLAND
Played at Brisbane,
30 November, 1, 3, 4, 5 December, 1928.
Result: England won by 675 runs.

England: First innings
J.B. Hobbs run out	49
H. Sutcliffe c Ponsford b Gregory	38
C.P. Mead lbw b Grimmett	8
W.R. Hammond c Woodfull b Gregory	44
D.R. Jardine c Woodfull b Ironmonger	35
E.H. Hendren c Ponsford b Ironmonger	169
A.P.F. Chapman* c Kelleway b Gregory	50
M.W. Tate c Ryder b Grimmett	26
H. Larwood lbw b Hendry	70
J.C. White lbw b Grimmett	14
G. Duckworth† not out	5
Extras (lb 10, nb 3)	13
Total	521

Fall of Wickets: 1/85, 2/95, 3/108, 4/161, 5/217, 6/291, 7/319, 8/443, 9/495, 10/521.
Bowling: Gregory 41-3-142-3, Kelleway 34-9-77-0, Grimmett 40-2-167-3, Ironmonger 44.3-18-79-2, Ryder 6-2-23-0, Hendry 10-1-20-1.

Australia: First innings
W.M. Woodfull c Chapman b Larwood	0
W.H. Ponsford b Larwood	2
A.F. Kippax c and b Tate	16
H.S.T.L. Hendry lbw b Larwood	30
C. Kelleway b Larwood	8
J. Ryder* c Jardine b Larwood	33
D.G. Bradman lbw b Tate	18
W.A.S. Oldfield† lbw b Tate	2
C.V. Grimmett not out	7
H. Ironmonger b Larwood	4
J.M. Gregory absent hurt	–
Extras (b 1, lb 1)	2
Total	122

Fall of Wickets: 1/0, 2/7, 3/24, 4/40, 5/71, 6/101, 7/105, 8/116, 9/122.
Bowling: Larwood 14.4-4-32-6, Tate 21-6-50-3, Hammond 15-5-38-0.

England: Second innings
J.B. Hobbs lbw b Grimmett	11
H. Sutcliffe c sub b Ironmonger	32
C.P. Mead lbw b Grimmett	73
W.R. Hammond c sub b Ironmonger	28
D.R. Jardine not out	65
E.H. Hendren c Ponsford b Grimmett	45
A.P.F. Chapman* c Oldfield b Grimmett	27
M.W. Tate c Bradman b Grimmett	20
H. Larwood c Ponsford b Grimmett	37
J.C. White } G. Duckworth† } did not bat	
Extras (lb 3, nb 1)	4
Total (8 wickets declared)	342

Fall of Wickets: 1/25, 2/69, 3/117, 4/165, 5/228, 6/263, 7/285, 8/342.
Bowling: Grimmett 44.1-9-131-6, Ironmonger 50-20-85-2, Ryder 14-3-43-0, Hendry 26-6-79-0.

Australia: Second innings
W.M. Woodfull not out	30
W.H. Ponsford c Duckworth b Larwood	6
A.F. Kippax c and b Larwood	15
H.S.T.L. Hendry c Larwood b White	6
C. Kelleway absent ill	–
J. Ryder* (5) c Larwood b Tate	1
D.G. Bradman (6) c Chapman b White	1
W.A.S. Oldfield (7) c Larwood b Tate	5
C.V. Grimmett (8) c Chapman b White	1
H. Ironmonger (9) c Chapman b White	0
J.M. Gregory absent hurt	–
Extras (nb 1)	1
Total	66

Fall of Wickets: 1/6, 2/33, 3/46, 4/47, 5/49, 6/62, 7/66, 8/66.
Bowling: Larwood 7-0-30-2, Tate 11-3-26-2, Hammond 1-0-2-0, White 6.3-2-7-4.

BELOW Patsy Hendren batting during his innings of 169. It was the top score in England's mighty first-innings total of 521 and was a masterful piece of concentration

1929

TO TAKE all 10 wickets is one of the rarer feats of cricket history. It has been done only some fifty times in first-class cricket worldwide since the turn of the century. It has happened only twice at Lord's within that span, once by Arthur Fielder of Kent, for the Players against the Gentlemen in 1906, and again in 1929 when G.O. Allen took 10 for 40 for Middlesex against Lancashire. It is the only instance ever at Lord's in a county match.

Gubby Allen was not – as there were plenty of in those days – a regular amateur who played county cricket the summer through. He could generally manage only some half a dozen appearances for Middlesex, thus eking out his annual holiday. In fact when urged to play in this match against Lancashire, the county champions of the three preceding years, he had to stipulate that as he was due to be working (at Debenham's, the department store) that Saturday morning, he could not get to Lord's until after the match had started.

Thus the ball had lost much of its shine by the time Allen appeared and was put on to bowl down the breeze from the pavilion end. He had Hallows's wicket straight away, and after lunch two more, before Ernest Tyldesley found a sturdy partner in Hopwood. Tyldesley completed a faultless hundred, whereupon he became Allen's fourth wicket, all bowled. Afterwards Allen's speed was altogether too much for the tail, the last four wickets falling in five balls.

Just short of his twenty-seventh birthday Allen at this time was reaching his peak as an all-rounder. His pace was probably second only to Larwood, he was a dependable bat and an excellent close fielder. A successful Test career as all-rounder and England captain lay just ahead.

B. Bennison, by the way, was the second-string cricket man for the *Daily Telegraph* and, candidly, rather more an authority on boxing. Philip Trevor, the chief cricket correspondent, was engaged in the First Test against South Africa at Birmingham to which Middlesex had contributed Patsy Hendren and Lancashire George Duckworth.

ALLEN BOWLS OUT LANCASHIRE.

ALL TEN WICKETS.

TYLDESLEY'S EFFORT AT LORD'S.

By B. BENNISON.

G. O. Allen, at Lord's on Saturday, for Middlesex against Lancashire, the champion county, had the rare distinction of taking all ten wickets, eight clean bowled, the last four with five balls without a run being scored from him. And a crowd of some 8,000 people, as he spread-eagled the stumps of Hodgson, Liverpool's footballer, to finish the innings, rose to him as one man; they cheered the old Cantab loud and long. Herewith his analysis:

O.	M.	R.	W.
25.3	10	40	10

Daily Telegraph, 17 June, 1929

MIDDLESEX v LANCASHIRE
Played at Lord's,
15, 17, 18 June, 1929.
Result: Match drawn.

Lancashire: First innings

C. Hallows b Allen	12
F. Watson b Allen	47
E. Tyldesley b Allen	102
J. Iddon b Allen	0
C. Hopwood c Price b Allen	48
T.M. Halliday b Allen	0
W. Farrimond b Allen	6
Mr P.T. Eckersley not out	8
R. Tyldesley b Allen	0
E.A. McDonald st Price b Allen	1
G. Hodgson b Allen	0
Extras (b 11, lb 5, nb 1)	17
Total	241

Bowling: Haig 29-8-48-0, Durston 10-3-17-0, Allen 25.3-10-40-10, Robins 22-1-54-0, Peebles 12-2-26-0, Hearne 8-1-28-0, Guise 5-1-11-0.

Middlesex: First innings 228 (H.W. Lee 124; R. Tyldesley 5-40).

Lancashire: Second innings 310 for 9 declared (C. Hopwood 106*, R. Tyldesley 53).

Middlesex: Second innings 170 for 5 (H.W. Lee 105*; Watson 4-37).

LEFT G.O. Allen: every inch a fast bowler

ENGLAND FACED WITH A STERN TASK

HOBBS AND WOOLLEY OUT : 206 NEEDED TO AVOID INNINGS DEFEAT

BRADMAN'S MAGNIFICENT BATTING

Daily Telegraph, 1 July, 1930

IT WAS perhaps on the third day of the Second Test at Lord's in 1930 that the full menace of Don Bradman's batting, supported as it was by four such men as Woodfull, Ponsford, Kippax and McCabe, became as abundantly clear to the British public as it had been progressively ever more apparent to A.P.F. Chapman and his fellows for a while past. On the first day of the game Duleepsinhji made a glorious century and England scored a highly respectable 425. Bradman, however, soon put their performance into perspective.

Not out 155 over the week-end – a peerless piece of batting in the last two hours and forty minutes of a sunlit Saturday – Bradman played himself in this Monday morning with ominous care before unleashing once again his complete repertoire. He and Kippax, starting at 404 for 2, took the score to 585 before the finest of all his innings ended at 254 with a superb catch by Chapman at silly (but not very silly) mid-off. It was the first stroke the Don had lifted off the floor.

Then came a final plunder of England's bowling and the comedy of an improvised '7' having to be fixed in the hundreds column of the Tavern scoreboard for the highest total ever made by Australia (as it still is), 729 for 6.

The heroics were far from over, as England on the last day staged a sparkling second innings recovery before one of the classic Test Matches – the first I ever reported and the best I ever saw – ended in a deserved win for Australia after tea on the fourth evening.

RIGHT Lord's 1930: the R101 hovers over the scene of one of the greatest of all Test Matches

ENGLAND v AUSTRALIA
Played at Lord's, 27, 28, 30 June, 1 July, 1930.
Result: Australia won by seven wickets.

England: First innings

J.B. Hobbs c Oldfield b Fairfax	1
F.E. Woolley c Wall b Fairfax	41
W.R. Hammond b Grimmett	38
K.S. Duleepsinhji c Bradman b Grimmett	173
E.H. Hendren c McCabe b Fairfax	48
A.P.F. Chapman* c Oldfield b Wall	11
G.O.B. Allen b Fairfax	3
M.W. Tate c McCabe b Wall	54
R.W.V. Robins c Oldfield b Hornibrook	5
J.C. White not out	23
G. Duckworth† c Oldfield b Wall	18
Extras (b 2, lb 7, nb 1)	10
Total	425

Fall of Wickets: 1/13, 2/53, 3/105, 4/209, 5/236, 6/239, 7/337, 8/363, 9/387, 10/425.
Bowling: Wall 29.4-2-118-3, Fairfax 31-6-101-4, Grimmett 33-4-105-2, Hornibrook 26-6-62-1, McCabe 9-1-29-0.

Australia: First innings

W.M. Woodfull* st Duckworth b Robins	155
W.H. Ponsford c Hammond b White	81
D.G. Bradman c Chapman b White	254
A.F. Kippax b White	83
S.J. McCabe c Woolley b Hammond	44
V.Y. Richardson c Hobbs b Tate	30
W.A.S. Oldfield† not out	43
A.G. Fairfax not out	20
C.V. Grimmett	
P.M. Hornibrook } did not bat	
T.W. Wall	
Extras (b 6, lb 8, w 5)	19
Total (6 wickets declared)	729

Fall of Wickets: 1/162, 2/393, 3/585, 4/588, 5/643, 6/672.
Bowling: Allen 34-7-115-0, Tate 64-16-148-1, White 51-7-158-3, Robins 42-1-172-1, Hammond 35-8-82-1, Woolley 6-0-35-0.

England: Second innings

J.B. Hobbs b Grimmett	19
F.E. Woolley hit wkt b Grimmett	28
W.R. Hammond c Fairfax b Grimmett	32
K.S. Duleepsinhji c Oldfield b Hornibrook	48
E.H. Hendren c Richardson b Grimmett	9
A.P.F. Chapman* c Oldfield b Fairfax	121
G.O.B. Allen lbw b Grimmett	57
M.W. Tate c Ponsford b Grimmett	10
R.W.V. Robins not out	11
J.C. White run out	10
G. Duckworth† lbw b Fairfax	0
Extras (b 16, lb 13, w 1)	30
Total	375

Fall of Wickets: 1/45, 2/58, 3/129, 4/141, 5/147, 6/272, 7/329, 8/354, 9/372, 10/375.
Bowling: Wall 25-2-80-0, Fairfax 12.4-2-37-2, Grimmett 53-13-167-6, Hornibrook 22-6-49-1, McCabe 3-1-11-0, Bradman 1-0-1-0.

Australia: Second innings

W.M. Woodfull* not out	26
W.H. Ponsford b Robins	14
D.G. Bradman c Chapman b Tate	1
A.F. Kippax c Duckworth b Robins	3
S.J. McCabe not out	25
V.Y. Richardson	
W.A.S. Oldfield†	
A.G. Fairfax } did not bat	
C.V. Grimmett	
P.M. Hornibrook	
T.W. Wall	
Extras (b 1, lb 2)	3
Total (3 wickets)	72

Fall of Wickets: 1/16, 2/17, 3/22.
Bowling: Tate 13-6-21-1, White 2-0-8-0, Robins 9-1-34-2, Hammond 4.2-1-6-0.

1930

DON BRADMAN'S innings of 309 not out against England at Headingley on 11 July 1930, increased next day to 334, was, arithmetically at least, the most remarkable of them all. Not only was it the highest ever, at the time, as between England and Australia: no one had ever made anywhere near so many in a Test Match in a single day. Of this 309 there came 105 before lunch, 115 more before tea, and in the third session of play a further 89. As an effort of prolonged technical excellence Sir Donald has always rated more highly his 254 in the preceding Test at Lord's. Who could quarrel with the assessment of the man himself? Assuredly not I who was lucky enough to have seen both innings. The pitches in each case were true and wonderfully easy in pace, the outfields fast. Such a speed of scoring would not otherwise have been possible. Granted these things, the impeccable judgement of length, the concentration that allowed hour after hour to pass without hint of human error against an attack comprising Larwood, Tate, Geary, Richard Tyldesley and Hammond, seem almost as extraordinary nearly sixty years on as they seemed at the time.

The day's cricket was one for Neville Cardus to rhapsodize over – and, as can be seen here, he did full justice to it. Australia's score at close of play was 458 for 3.

ENGLAND v AUSTRALIA
Played at Leeds, 11, 12, 14, 15 July, 1930.
Result: Match drawn.

Australia: First innings

W.M. Woodfull* b Hammond	50
A.A. Jackson c Larwood b Tate	1
D.G. Bradman c Duckworth b Tate	334
A.F. Kippax c Chapman b Tate	77
S.J. McCabe b Larwood	30
V.Y. Richardson c Larwood b Tate	1
E.L. A'Beckett c Chapman b Geary	29
W.A.S. Oldfield† c Hobbs b Tate	2
C.V. Grimmett c Duckworth b Tyldesley	24
T.W. Wall b Tyldesley	3
P.M. Hornibrook not out	1
Extras (b 5, lb 8, w 1)	14
Total	566

Fall of Wickets: 1/2, 2/194, 3/423, 4/486, 5/491, 6/508, 7/519, 8/544, 9/565, 10/566.
Bowling: Larwood 33-3-139-1, Tate 39-9-124-5, Geary 35-10-95-1, Tyldesley 33-5-104-2, Hammond 17-3-46-1, Leyland 11-0-44-0.

England: First innings

J.B. Hobbs c A'Beckett b Grimmett	29
H. Sutcliffe c Hornibrook b Grimmett	32
W.R. Hammond c Oldfield b McCabe	113
K.S. Duleepsinhji b Hornibrook	35
M. Leyland c Kippax b Wall	44
G. Geary run out	0
G. Duckworth† c Oldfield b A'Beckett	33
A.P.F. Chapman* b Grimmett	45
M.W. Tate c Jackson b Grimmett	22
H. Larwood not out	10
R.K. Tyldesley c Hornibrook b Grimmett	6
Extras (b 9, lb 10, nb 3)	22
Total	391

Fall of Wickets: 1/53, 2/64, 3/123, 4/206, 5/206, 6/289, 7/319, 8/370, 9/375, 10/391.
Bowling: Wall 40-12-70-1, A'Beckett 28-8-47-1, Grimmett 56.2-16-135-5, Hornibrook 41-7-94-1, McCabe 10-4-23-1.

England: Second innings

J.B. Hobbs run out	13
H. Sutcliffe not out	28
W.R. Hammond c Oldfield b Grimmett	35
K.S. Duleepsinhji c Grimmett b Hornibrook	10
M. Leyland not out	1
G. Geary	
G. Duckworth†	
A.P.F. Chapman*	did not bat
M.W. Tate	
H. Larwood	
R.K. Tyldesley	
Extras (lb 8)	8
Total (3 wickets)	95

Fall of Wickets: 1/24, 2/72, 3/94.
Bowling: Wall 10-3-20-0, A'Beckett 11-4-19-0, Grimmett 17-3-33-1, Hornibrook 11.5-5-14-1, McCabe 2-1-1-0.

Bradman Breaks All Records with Brilliant 309 Not Out.
ENGLAND'S BOWLING WEAKNESS.

Nature, they say, breaks the mould when she has made a masterpiece. It is not true: nor is it true that history repeats only her humdrum pages. Beauty changes her modes and aspects, but the substance, the ultimate vision, is the same. Nature is never tired of her good things: every year she repeats the miracle of the spring-time's rapture and the summer's fulfilment. To-day in a game of cricket Nature has lived again in a bygone experience, lived it as though with greater intensity because the genius of it all had once before thrilled her sensibilities.

Four years ago on this very same field of Headingley the Australians began an innings disastrously: they lost the wicket of Bardsley for none, then Macartney came forth and scored a hundred before lunch. To-day Australia lost Jackson with only one run made: then Bradman before lunch made a hundred also. Woodfull, who was Macartney's good companion and audience, was Bradman's. But whereas Macartney gave a chance when he was only two, Bradman sent no catch at all before lunch and was guilty of but a solitary mishit, when he was 35 and a high cut flashed yards wide of Chapman at backward point.

Manchester Guardian, 12 July, 1930

BELOW Bradman batting at Headingley

Remarkable Batting Feat By Notts.

GREAT WARWICK TOTAL PASSED.

George Gunn And His Son Make Hundreds—Only Ten Wickets Fall For 1,032 Runs.

Daily Express, 25 July, 1931

THE MATCH at Edgbaston between Warwickshire and Nottinghamshire in July 1931 was notable as the only time in history when father and son have made hundreds in the same match. George Gunn, nephew of William, younger brother of John and father of George Vivian was the genius of the famous Gunn family. For seventy years, between 1880 and 1950, there was always at least one Gunn playing for Nottinghamshire. For many years there were two and sometimes between 1902 and 1904 as many as three. Between them they made 164 first-class hundreds, and the eldest three played thirty-two times for England. Historians are unanimous that in father George's case he should have been called upon more often.

George Gunn was a unique character immortalized by Cardus, inimitable and much loved. He batted as the mood seized him, sometimes brilliant to a degree, sometimes almost as though his mind was miles away. His son, G.V., inherited part at least of his father's talent without quite living up to the family name. George was fifty-two in his penultimate year with the County when, with nothing but first innings points to play for, he batted just over seven hours for 183. Nottinghamshire

1931

had just reached their goal, with seven wickets down, on the third evening when Bob Wyatt kept his side on the field for an extra over or so to enable young G.V. to reach three figures.

This is a situation which could scarcely happen today when bonus points are restricted to the first hundred overs of an innings and there is no reward for the lead on first innings. But something like it was not all that uncommon in the 1930s. It is perhaps worth mentioning that the only comparable 'family' record was achieved by the Chappell brothers, Ian and Greg, forty-one years later when they both scored hundreds in the same innings of the Fifth Test between England and Australia in 1972.

WARWICKSHIRE v NOTTINGHAMSHIRE
Played at Birmingham,
22, 23, 24 July, 1931.
Result: Match drawn.

Warwickshire: First innings

Mr. G.D. Kemp-Welch c and b Harris	60
A.J. Croom c Staples b Oates	159
L.A. Bates c Lilley b Oates	105
Rev. J.H. Parsons not out	84
N. Kilner not out	81
Mr. R.E.S. Wyatt	
F.R. Santall	
J. Smart	did not bat
W. Sanders	
J.H. Mayer	
G. Paine	
Extras (b 10, lb 9, w 1, nb 2)	22
Total (3 wickets declared)	511

Bowling: Barratt 35-6-76-0, Carr 16-2-71-0, Harris 33-5-99-1, G.V. Gunn 34-4-115-0, G. Gunn 8-1-39-0, Oates 28-3-89-2.

Nottinghamshire: First innings

G. Gunn c Paine b Santall	183
W.W. Keeton c Sanders b Paine	72
W. Walker b Mayer	29
Mr. A.W. Carr c Parsons b Sanders	38
W. Payton lbw b Wyatt	6
A. Staples c Mayer b Wyatt	8
B. Lilley b Paine	30
G.V. Gunn not out	100
C.B. Harris not out	41
T.A.W. Oates	did not bat
P. Barratt	
Extras (b 10, lb 3, w 1)	14
Total	521

Bowling: Mayer 46-18-106-1, Wyatt 51-12-134-2, Paine 74-24-125-2, Sanders 34-11-62-1, Santall 24-4-72-1, Parsons 4-2-5-0, Bates 1-0-3-0.

George Gunn (CENTRE) with his two sons
J.S. Gunn (LEFT) and G.V. Gunn (RIGHT)

1932

PERCY HOLMES and Herbert Sutcliffe, the famous Yorkshire opening pair, against Essex at Leyton in June 1932 bettered by one run the first wicket record partnership of 554 established by their predecessors, J.T. Brown and J. Tunnicliffe, thirty-four years earlier.

The confusion headlined by the *Evening Standard* might well have grown to some bitterness had not the scorers, C.P. McGahey and W. Ringrose, after some delay conveniently discovered a no-ball uncounted after the 555 on the scoreboard had been adjusted to 554 following Sutcliffe's dismissal and Yorkshire's declaration the ball after the record had been apparently broken. The true explanation tacitly accepted at the time was probably that the scoreboard during the latter stages of the partnership had been one run ahead of the scorebooks. There were those indeed who claimed to have seen a run for a no-ball tick up on the board followed by a run scored from it. Since Sutcliffe had patently thrown his wicket away as soon as he saw 555 on the board the adjustment was mutually agreed. A lesser curiosity was the fact that Holmes, usually the faster scorer of the two, lagged behind on this occasion, being hampered throughout by lumbago.

Another 'record' of a kind might well have belonged to Essex in that on the day preceding the Yorkshire match they had been beaten by 9 wickets by Surrey at The Oval, J.B. Hobbs and R.J. Gregory scoring 232 against them in an unbroken stand for the second wicket. Thus Essex had fielded out for 787 runs in consecutive periods of play covering nine hours fifty minutes without taking a wicket until Sutcliffe gave them his. It so happened I reported both matches. Charles Bray, who afterwards became cricket correspondent of the *Daily Herald*, captained Essex in both – a fact of which his subsequent colleagues occasionally reminded him. The Holmes-Sutcliffe partnership remained a record for forty-four years until exceeded by Waheed Mirza and Mansoor Akhtar who in 1976-77 made 561 together for the Karachi Whites v Quetta at Karachi.

ESSEX v YORKSHIRE
Played at Leyton,
15, 16, 17 June, 1932.
Result: Yorkshire won by an innings and 313 runs.

Yorkshire: First innings

P. Holmes not out	224
H. Sutcliffe b Eastman	313
Extras (b 13, lb 3, nb 2)	18
Total (1 wicket declared)	555

A. Mitchell, M. Leyland, W. Barber, Mr A.B. Sellers, A. Wood, A.C. Rhodes, C.G. Macaulay, H. Verity and W.E. Bowes did not bat.

Bowling: Nicholas 31-4-105-0, Daer 40-5-106-0, Smith 46-10-128-0, O'Connor 23-5-73-0, Eastman 22.4-2-97-1, Crawley 3-0-7-0, Taylor 4-0-14-0, Bray 1-0-7-0.

Essex: First innings 78 (Verity 5-8, Bowes 4-38).
Essex: Second innings 164 (M.S. Nichols 59*; Verity 5-45, Bowes 5-47).

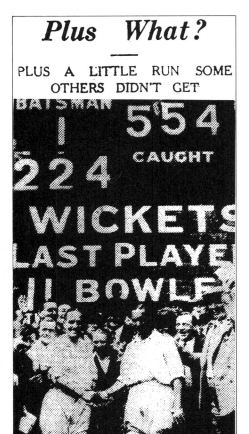

Plus What?

PLUS A LITTLE RUN SOME OTHERS DIDN'T GET

HOLMES and SUTCLIFFE receiving congratulations before the score-board when it read 554.

This is the story of a no-ball that got lost and nearly upset a new world cricket record. Holmes and Sutcliffe, the Yorkshire batsmen, started out at Leyton, Essex, to-day needing 132 to beat the record first-wicket stand of Brown and Tunnicliffe, also Yorkshiremen, made 34 years ago.

Holmes and Sutcliffe batted steadily on. At last Sutcliffe hit a four to leg, the scoreboard clicked and showed 555!

With his next stroke Sutcliffe dragged the ball on to his wicket and was out. The pair walked across and stood under the scoreboard to be photographed. Then it was seen that the score had clicked back to 554—equalling record. Under that score the batsmen actually were photographed.

Evening Standard, 16 June, 1932

RIGHT The scoreboard at Leyton, showing the record after the initial confusion. The Essex bowlers were seasoned stoics in the 1930s

THE THIRD TEST MATCH

ENGLAND'S LEAD

FINE INNINGS BY PONSFORD

FROM OUR OWN CORRESPONDENT

ADELAIDE, SOUTH AUSTRALIA, JAN. 16

England, as a result of the third day's play in the Test Match here, are in a winning position. They are now 204 runs ahead with nine wickets to fall, and as Australia will have to bat last victory seems assured for England. Although Sutcliffe is out, a big score is probable for England, and the Australians will have to face a substantial deficit. The wicket is wearing well, and the Australian spin bowlers are unlikely to receive any assistance from it. It is evident that Larwood is at present master of the situation, and Allen has proved himself to be a formidable second string. There had been mild demonstrations early to-day when Ponsford was hit on the body, but when Oldfield was struck on the head by a ball from Larwood the crowd of over 35,000 gave vent to their feelings. Larwood was then bowling to an orthodox off field, and Oldfield swung at a rising ball which seemed to fly off the edge of the bat on to Oldfield's temple. Oldfield staggered away and collapsed, and after receiving treatment had to retire. The indignant crowd abused Larwood and Jardine, and continued their wild shouting when England opened their innings. Oldfield is suffering from concussion and shock, but is expected to play to-morrow.

The Times, 17 January, 1933

"LEG-THEORY" BOWLING

AUSTRALIAN PROTEST

FROM OUR OWN CORRESPONDENT

ADELAIDE, JAN. 18

The Australian Cricket Board of Control has sent the following telegram to the M.C.C.:—

Body-line bowling has assumed such proportions as to menace the best interests of the game, making the protection of his body by a batsman his main consideration. It is causing intensely bitter feeling between the players as well as injury to them. In our opinion it is unsportsmanlike. Unless it is stopped at once it is likely to upset the friendly relations existing between Australia and England.

At the close of play in the Third Test Match here to-day Australia required 412 runs in order to win, with only six wickets in hand.

❦ The M.C.C. received the telegram sent by the Australian Cricket Board of Control on the subject of leg-theory bowling shortly before noon yesterday. It is not yet known when the matter will be discussed.

ADELAIDE, Jan. 19.—At a meeting of the English party to-day D. R. Jardine issued the following statement:—

Members of the M.C.C. and the England team do not desire to enter into public controversy, for they deplore the introduction of any personal feelings into the records of a great game.

In view, however, of statements which have been given space in some of the Press to the effect that there has been dissension and disloyalty in their team, they desire to deny this definitely and absolutely while assuring the public of England and Australia that they are, and always have been, utterly loyal to their captain, under whose leadership they hope to achieve an honourable victory.—*Reuter.*

The Times, 19 January, 1933

1933

AUSTRALIA v ENGLAND

Played at Adelaide,
13, 14, 16, 17, 18, 19 January, 1933.
Result: England won by 338 runs.

England: First innings 341 (M. Leyland 83, R.E.S. Wyatt 78, E. Paynter 77; Wall 5-72).

Australia: First innings 222 (W.H. Ponsford 85, W.A.S. Oldfield 41; Allen 4-71, Larwood 3-55).

England: Second innings 412 (W.R. Hammond 85, L.E.G. Ames 69, D.R. Jardine 56; O'Reilly 4-79).

Australia: Second innings 193 (W.M. Woodfull 73*, D.G. Bradman 66; Allen 4-50, Larwood 4-71).

BELOW Opening of hostilities: Woodfull is hit by a ball from Larwood

OF THE Third Test between Australia and England at Adelaide in January 1933 the editor of *Wisden* S.J. Southerton wrote that 'altogether the whole atmosphere was a disgrace to cricket'. Yet however lurid were the reports and comments printed elsewhere *The Times* was not going to add to the clamour to the extent of even a single headline. England indeed led at the end of this turbulent third day and Ponsford certainly played a fine innings. And the reader is given some idea in the body of the story of the hostile attitude of the crowd when Oldfield was hit on the head by Larwood and obliged to retire. It was left to other newspapers to put the ugly scene into fuller perspective, and to illustrate the situation by disclosing, for instance, that a strong force of mounted police stood by behind the grandstand in case

the crowd jumped the pickets and invaded the field to molest D.R. Jardine and members of his team.

The Australians sent their famous cable of protest against England's bowling methods to MCC the following day, 18 January. There followed the now well-known exchange of cables between the two countries. As will be seen they officially coined the word 'Bodyline'. They also questioned the sportsmanship of the team using it. It must be appreciated that the MCC Committee – before the days of easy telephone contact across the world and all but half a century before television via satellite – were somewhat in the dark regarding the tactics of which Bodyline was a fair description in so far as it went. The physical threat posed by fast bowling pitched persistently short on the line of the body was compoun-

ded by the additional technical risk of fending off the ball with the bat into the hands of five or sometimes even six short-leg fielders in a close crescent.

In their reply MCC deplored this cable and fastened upon the word 'unsportsmanlike'. They said that if the good relations between the two countries were at risk they would reluctantly consent to the cancellation of the remainder of the tour.

The MCC team after the match issued a statement denying reports of dissension and confirming complete loyalty to their captain. There was no truth in Australian press rumours of dissension, for those members who were already opposed to it were scrupulous in keeping their feelings to themselves. To close ranks in the circumstances was both natural and proper.

1933

WITHIN A FORTNIGHT of the momentous Adelaide Test Match the dispute over Bodyline bowling had become not only a sporting but a political issue. On the same day as MCC sent the fourth cable in the exchange with the Australian Board the Dominion's Secretary, J.H. Thomas called representatives of the club to Downing Street. The 'informal talk' that took place has a position in history as the first occasion on which cricket – or perhaps any game or sport – had occupied the attention of Government.

Whether Mr Thomas was much wiser at the end of it is open to doubt, though he certainly became so in the months following. The *Daily Mail* not only recorded the event in a banner headline

GOOD FELLOWSHIP AT STAKE

By R. H. BETTINGTON,

Oxford University, Middlesex, and New South Wales all-round cricketer, who is now a doctor in Australia

I feel it is a pity that England did not attempt to win the Tests by orthodox bowling in the first place. In my view they would have been good enough. Their bowling strength is very great, and Allen's success has been most surprising in view of English critics' fears that he was not good enough.

It is time sense was talked on body-line bowling. The whole question is: Is it worth winning Tests at the expense of good fellowship between the sides. An atmosphere of war rather than of sport prevails.

The Australian Board's cable to the M.C.C. was the worst thing in the history of cricket. They were stampeded by the Press. And Woodfull's protest to Warner, made in the heat of the moment, should have been withdrawn.

The board had no proper meeting: they could not have realised the momentous nature of their action. They asked for a good snub, and got it.

They could have put themselves in a strong position if, on requesting the English management to put an end to body-line bowling and being refused, they had publicly stated that they think the practice against the best interests of the game.

I think the English captain should stop this form of attack, though no question of fairness arises. If it is continued, some method of playing it will probably come — American football armour is the obvious costume.

There is a report that Jardine may modify leg-theory at Brisbane, but no official statement has been made.

Daily Mail, 2 February, 1933

but published a reasoned view of the situation by Reg Bettington, an anglophile Australian who was a triple Oxford blue, and who captained D.R. Jardine in the University match.

Nothing did so much to influence public opinion on the Bodyline issue as this unequivocal article, coinciding with the team's return, by Jack Hobbs who had covered the MCC tour for the

DOWNING-ST. TALK ON BODY-LINE BOWLING

M.C.C. LEADERS AT THE DOMINIONS OFFICE

ATTORNEY-GENERAL ALSO PRESENT

Mr. J. H. Thomas.

Lord Lewisham.

TEST MATCH INCIDENTS

INSIDE INFORMATION FOR MR. THOMAS

SPECIAL "DAILY MAIL" NEWS

LEADING MEMBERS OF THE M.C.C. VISITED THE DOMINIONS OFFICE, DOWNING-STREET, YESTERDAY, AND MET MR. J. H. THOMAS, SECRETARY FOR THE DOMINIONS.

I understand, writes our Political Correspondent, that Mr. Thomas had expressed a desire to be fully informed regarding the exchange of communications between the Australian Board of Cricket Control and the M.C.C. relating

"KAFFIR" SHARES AGAIN BOOMING

2 HOURS' HECTIC STREET DEALS

GOLD PROFITS LEAP

By Our City Editor

THE first batch of Rand gold mining returns showing the effect of the gold premium was announced yesterday and caused a fresh blaze-up in the market for "Kaffirs."

Dealings were fast and furious and were continued in the Street for more than two hours after the official close, later than on Monday, when the crowd was the largest seen for years.

BIGGER THAN 1895

Old-timers in this market recalled the days of the famous 1895 "Kaffir boom," one of them remarking that at the height of that period of great activity he did not go home from the City in the evenings.

The view was expressed, however, that yesterday's turnover of shares in this market, which ran into hundreds of thousands, probably exceeded that turnover of 1895, when companies' capitals were smaller and leading shares were higher-priced, their quotations being in two figures. Now

HITLER DISSOLVES REICHSTAG

NEW GERMAN ELECTIONS

POLLING ON MARCH 5

From Our Own Correspondent

BERLIN, Wednesday.

THE Reichstag, which was elected in November and in which no Chancellor has ever appeared, has been dissolved. A new Reichstag will be elected on March 5. On the same day a new Prussian Parliament is to be elected.

The Chancellor, Herr Hitler, launched the Government's election campaign to-night in a flaming broadcast speech in which he denounced the founders of the Republic as traitors.

The decree of President von Hindenburg for the dissolution of the Reichstag was signed this morning at the request of the Chancellor and of Herr von Papen, Deputy Chancellor, speaking for the whole Cabinet, and was published to-night.

HINDENBURG'S DECREE

It runs as follows:

COMPETITIONS FOR ALL

£4,400 IN PRIZES

"Daily Mail" competitions are providing endless amusement for readers old and young in all parts of the country.

Keen filmgoers are Spotting the Stars. This is the most popular film contest ever devised. 36 stars of the screen to spot during the week—and £1,000 which must be won. The fourth group of pictures in this week's contest will be found in Page 16.

Crossworders have a daily free to enter puzzle with a prize of £100. In addition there is a consolation prize of £100 for the next best entries in the weekly series that do not share in any of the five daily awards. This is the best news crosswords have had for years. To-day's puzzle is in Page 6, and on Saturday there will be the week-end puzzle with a must be won prize of £1,000.

Home Knitters are offered more than £300 in prizes in a simple knitting contest. Full details are in Page 13, and entrants for this simple contest may begin sending in their entries to-morrow.

"CO-OPS'" PROFITS RECOMMENDED TO BE TAXED

By Our Political Correspondent

The report of the committee appointed last year by the Chancellor of the Exchequer (Mr. Neville Chamberlain) to inquire into the

SECRETS OF POISONED WOMAN'S LIFE

A BROKEN LOVE AFFAIR?

HER STAY IN PARIS BEFORE HER DEATH

A Daily Mail picture of Mme. Zeinep Vlora which was telegraphed from Paris last night.

OFFICIALS SWORN TO SILENCE

Star but had come home when they went on from Australia to New Zealand.

Hobbs's reason for withholding his opinion while the tour was in progress is understandable in that he was still in the game. Several of the players were his close friends, while Jardine was his own county captain. After the players returned home, however, and the great inquest had begun, most of the team expressed their dislike of the tactics employed. The players spoke privately but Hobbs, the most famous English cricketer of the day, published his condemnation publicly in Fleet Street.

A journalistic note: the radical *Star*'s now definite line was directly opposite to that of its London evening paper rival, the right-wing *Evening Standard*, whose correspondent, Bruce Harris, backed Jardine completely. Jardine subsequently covered the 1934 Australian tour to England for the *Evening Standard*.

ABOVE An eclectic page from the Daily Mail: *perhaps the only time news of Adolf Hitler took second place to cricket?*

LEFT The full Bodyline field: Woodfull ducks another bouncer

The Star 6.30

No. 14022　LONDON, SATURDAY, MAY 6, 1933.　ONE PENNY.

CHEDLET CHEESE — Write for Booklet, "West Country 'Meals' Wool, Dept. F., Aplin & Barrett, etc., Ltd., Yeovil, Somerset

WHITE HORSE WHISKY EQUAL TO A FINE LIQUEUR　Small Flasks on sale

HOBBS CONDEMNS 'BODY-LINE.'

CONTRARY to SPIRIT OF CRICKET.

Body-line Bowling Dangerous And Not Good For The Game.

RISK IN MINOR MATCHES.

Why Hobbs Did Not Attack Leg-Theory Tactics In Test Cables.

"*Body-Line bowling is contrary to the spirit of cricket.*"

WITH these downright words Jack Hobbs reveals on the day the M.C.C. team lands in Britain his opinion on a controversy that has divided the cricket public of England almost as much as that of Australia, and is only now coming to a real crisis with the Australian ban via the no-ball.

Points Hobbs emphasises in the article given below are :—

Body-line bowling is not good for cricket.

There are undoubtedly elements of danger about it.

If used generally in first-class games it is sure to be adopted on club or park pitches, where the risk of accident is much greater.

Readers of Hobbs's graphic cables to " The Star " during the Test matches must have wondered why he did not take up a stand for or against " leg-theory." He now explains :—

" I did not wish to embarrass Mr. Jardine or the team. They had quite enough anxiety, and had I expressed a definite opinion it would have given the Australian critics a lever further to harass our team and stir up strife."

JACK DURSTON, TOO.

Hobbs's article is exclusive to " The Star." It is the first of a weekly series which the famous batsman will write for this paper throughout the summer.

Hobbs's condemnation of leg-theory bowling is supported by the Middlesex fast bowler, Jack Durston. B. J. Evans's interview with Durston is on Page 18.

A NOTE ON BARRACKING.

By JACK HOBBS

OUR boys who regained the Ashes so splendidly in Australia a few months ago arrived home to-day, and for the first time a team returning from Australia stepped ashore in Scotland.

This is, of course, due to the fact that

and those they left behind and who no doubt followed their fortunes so closely from the cabled reports will all be mighty glad to see them. After all, seven or eight months is a long time for a man to be away from his family.

In many respects it was a fine trip, but in its broader features it was not really so pleasant as many of those in which I took

Jack Hobbs dealing with a ball on the leg side.

Bagpipes Greet Test Team

"HIGHLAND FLING" IN HONOUR OF ENGLAND VICTORS.

SCOTLAND gave England's victorious Test cricketers a fine welcome home to-day. When their liner, the Duchess of Atholl, reached Glasgow from Montreal—

" Bagpipe bands gave of their best ; An enormous crowd tried to rush them ! Ship sirens blared ; Factory sirens blared.

Replying to the welcome, Mr. D. R. Jardine said that the men " made themselves a great side in the face of difficulties which might quite excusably have broken up most sides, and would undoubtedly have broken almost any side."

" We went out a happy band, and we return a happy and united band. It was a great privilege for me to lead the side."

DIVORCE BILL.

Insanity Not To Be Grounds For Decree

Mr. Hulford Knight's Bill, which sought to make five years' insanity ground for divorce, was " counted out " in the House of Commons.

It was opposed by Dr. O'Donovan (Con., Mile End), who said that all those who were insane were not by any means insensitive.

Many were conscious of all that was going on around them, and a husband or wife in an institution who knew that a partner whom he or she still loved was taking another mate would be grievously wronged.

There were also the children to be considered. All our customs were based on the assumption that the family was a unit. The Bill is now dead.

GERMAN AIR MANOEUVRES

The German naval port of Cuxhaven was completely enveloped in an artificial fog in the course of air defence manoeuvres against an attack by enemy planes. The cruiser

ON PARADE AT BOW-ST.

90 Men Arrested During Club Raid.

BIG BIND OVER.

Story Of Crown And Anchor At Long Acre.

NINETY men were " on parade " at Bow-street to-day.

They had been arrested by police who made a raid on the Acre Luncheon and Billiards Club, Long Acre, and were bound over before the court to answer charges under the Betting Act.

A large roped-off dock had recently been erected in the court, and into this the march of the ninety men began.

It took more than five minutes to get the men on parade before Mr. Dummett, the magistrate.

SHOULDER TO SHOULDER.

They stood shoulder to shoulder, some smiling, some looking very uncomfortable.

The seven principals in the case stood like captains at the head of the Long-acre battalion.

Then began the court gaoler's big task for the day—the roll call.

That took another ten minutes.

Very remaining-like were some of the replies to the call of names.

" Right, you are ! " called some of the men.

" Yes, yes," said others.

" Not guilty," cried another.

Some hesitated and did not reply until their names were called a second time.

At last the roll call was over, and only one absentee was reported.

" Doubtless he will appear later," remarked Mr. Dummett.

Addressing the " parade " he said that if they would not oppose the charge that they were frequenters of a betting house he would bind all of them over for one year on condition that they did not enter betting houses.

" Do you oppose this ? " he asked.

ALL IN FAVOUR.

" No, sir," came a chorus of replies from the men.

The warrant officer then said : " Anybody not willing to be bound over, put his hand up."

Nobody did.

The retreat from the court began to orders of " Come along, please," and " Hurry along, please."

PILE OF MONEY.

Only the seven principals were left. They were described as Francis Cullen, aged 51 (secretary) ; Pa Devlin, aged 52 ; Ernest Williams, aged 38 ; David Gagan, aged 32 ; Henry Randell, aged 32 ; John Stoger, aged 42 ; and Charles Frogwell, aged 38.

Mr. Barker, prosecuting, said that when the police raided the club they found a " Crown and Anchor " board in use, and before one of the principals was a pile of paper money and silver amounting to about £15.

Mr. Dummett said that none of the men

1934

VERITY WINS TEST FOR ENGLAND

14 Wickets For 80 Yesterday

BY SHORT SLIP

FOURTEEN wickets for 80 runs! This amazing analysis of Hedley Verity, the Yorkshire left-handed bowler, brought victory to England by an innings and 38 runs in the second Test match at Lord's yesterday.

Sporting Life, 26 June, 1934

'VERITY'S MATCH' at Lord's in June 1934 must still be clear in the memories of survivors who saw Monday's cricket after the weekend thunderstorm. I would not altogether go along with the *Sporting Life* writer who thought that the wicket 'would have beaten any side in the world'. In the absence of sun *Wisden* strengthens one's recollection that it was not genuinely 'sticky' except for one period after lunch. Nevertheless the turf took spin, slowly for the most part, and the Australians were therefore automatically at a disadvantage.

Their fate was decided by their failure, by seven runs, to save the follow-on, a possibility that scarcely occurred to them when on this third morning they continued their innings at 192 for 2. Only 99 runs more were needed for sanctuary. However the last eight wickets fell for 92, the only brief respite coming when the teams were presented to King George V.

The conclusive moment in the follow-on was when Bradman, endeavouring to knock Verity off his length, hit the ball vertically to an enormous height, wicket-keeper Ames making the catch. In an hour after tea Verity took 6 for 15, thus bringing the match to an end. In the day he had taken 14 wickets for 80 runs, in the match 15 for 104 – figures not bettered in an England v Australia Test until Jim Laker's phenomenal bag of 19 at Old Trafford many years later.

This England victory squared the rubber, Australia having won the First Test handsomely at Trent Bridge. If Verity's record in England v Australia was eventually overhauled it is worth noting that his astounding analysis of 10 for 10 in an innings for Yorkshire against Nottinghamshire in 1932 has never been approached.

ENGLAND v AUSTRALIA
Played at Lord's, 22, 23, 25 June, 1934.
Result: England won by an innings and 38 runs.

England: First innings

C.F. Walters c Bromley b O'Reilly	82
H. Sutcliffe lbw b Chipperfield	20
W.R. Hammond c and b Chipperfield	2
E.H. Hendren c McCabe b Wall	13
R.E.S. Wyatt* c Oldfield b Chipperfield	33
M. Leyland b Wall	109
L.E.G. Ames† c Oldfield b McCabe	120
G. Geary c Chipperfield b Wall	9
H. Verity st Oldfield b Grimmett	29
K. Farnes b Wall	1
W.E. Bowes not out	10
Extras (lb 12)	12
Total	440

Fall of Wickets: 1/70, 2/78, 3/99, 4/130, 5/182, 6/311, 7/359, 8/409, 9/410, 10/440.
Bowling: Wall 49-7-108-4, McCabe 18-3-38-1, Grimmett 53.3-13-102-1, O'Reilly 38-15-70-1, Chipperfield 34-10-91-3, Darling 6-2-19-0.

Australia: First innings

W.M. Woodfull* b Bowes	22
W.A. Brown c Ames b Bowes	105
D.G. Bradman c and b Verity	36
S.J. McCabe c Hammond b Verity	34
L.S. Darling c Sutcliffe b Verity	0
A.G. Chipperfield not out	37
E.H. Bromley c Geary b Verity	4
W.A.S. Oldfield† c Sutcliffe b Verity	23
C.V. Grimmett b Bowes	9
W.J. O'Reilly b Verity	4
T.W. Wall lbw b Verity	0
Extras (b 1, lb 9)	10
Total	284

Fall of Wickets: 1/68, 2/141, 3/203, 4/204, 5/205, 6/218, 7/258, 8/273, 9/284, 10/284.
Bowling: Farnes 12-3-43-0, Bowes 31-5-98-3, Geary 22-4-56-0, Verity 36-15-61-7, Hammond 4-1-6-0, Leyland 4-1-10-0.

Australia: Second innings

W.M. Woodfull* c Hammond b Verity	43
W.A. Brown c Walters b Bowes	2
D.G. Bradman (4) c Ames b Verity	13
S.J. McCabe (3) c Hendren b Verity	19
L.S. Darling b Hammond	10
A.G. Chipperfield c Geary b Verity	14
E.H. Bromley c and b Verity	1
W.A.S. Oldfield† lbw b Verity	0
C.V. Grimmett c Hammond b Verity	0
W.J. O'Reilly not out	8
T.W. Wall c Hendren b Verity	1
Extras (b 6, nb 1)	7
Total	118

Fall of Wickets: 1/10, 2/43, 3/57, 4/94, 5/94, 6/95, 7/95, 8/95, 9/112, 10/118.
Bowling: Farnes 4-2-6-0, Bowes 14-4-24-1, Verity 22.3-8-43-8, Hammond 13-0-38-1.

BELOW The vital wicket: Bradman, about to be caught by Ames for 13 in Australia's follow-on. Verity's performance was made doubly sweet in that it gave England their first victory over Australia at Lord's since 1896.

FOUR DAYS SUFFICE FOR FINAL TEST

CONGRATULATIONS TO WOODFULL

Bill Bowes The Hero Of Last Day's Play

By SHORT SLIP

Sporting Life, 23 August, 1934

1934

IN GAINING the largest margin of victory in runs ever recorded by them Australia, in the last Test of 1934 at The Oval, avenged the Bodyline Test series of 1932-33 and regained the Ashes for, as it transpired, a span of nineteen years.

The match was virtually decided on the first day when Ponsford (205 not out) and Bradman (244) made 451 for the second wicket (a Test record that still stands). The selectors were widely blamed for England's performance, for they picked three fast bowlers but, Hammond apart, gave them inadequate close catching support. Ponsford was said to have given five chances. They also chose Frank Woolley, aged forty-seven, who had been out of Test cricket for four years. Still a great county player, he was no longer mobile in the field. He conceded a record 37 byes when he was forced to deputize behind the stumps after Leslie Ames retired with cramp early in Australia's second innings.

ABOVE Frank Woolley keeping wicket

LEFT Ponsford on the way to his double-century at The Oval

ENGLAND v AUSTRALIA
Played at The Oval,18, 20, 21, 22 August, 1934.
Result: Australia won by 562 runs.

Australia: First innings 701 (W.H. Ponsford 266, D.G. Bradman 244).

England: First innings 321 (M. Leyland 110, C.F. Walters 64; Ebeling 3-74).

Australia: Second innings 327 (D.G. Bradman 77, S.J. McCabe 70; Bowes 5-55, Clark 5-98).

England: Second innings 145 (W.R. Hammond 43; Grimmett 5-64).

1934

SUSSEX v LANCASHIRE
Played at Eastbourne, 22, 23, 24 August 1934.
Result: Match drawn.

Lancashire: First innings

F. Watson c John Langridge b Tate	11
J.L. Hopwood c Eaton b Tate	28
J. Iddon b Tate	4
E. Tyldesley c H. Parks b J. Parks	84
E. Paynter lbw b Tate	24
Mr W.H.L. Lister c John Langridge b Pearce	8
L.W. Parkinson b Tate	18
Mr P.T. Eckersley b Tate	4
G. Duckworth c John Langridge b J. Parks	3
F.S. Booth c Jas. Langridge b J. Parks	0
R. Pollard not out	0
Extras (b 2, b 9, nb 1)	12
Total	196

Bowling: Tate 35-11-50-6, Hammond 16-4-41-0, J. Parks 31.5-11-48-3, Bowley 7-2-22-0, Pearce 12-3-23-1.

Sussex: First innings

J.H. Parks st Duckworth b Booth	0
John Langridge c Iddon b Hopwood	16
Mr A. Melville b Hopwood	18
T. Cook c Duckworth b Booth	0
Jas Langridge c Tyldesley b Hopwood	5
H.W. Parks not out	47
J. Eaton c and b Pollard	23
E.H. Bowley run out	2
H.E. Hammond b Pollard	0
G. Pearce c Hopwood b Pollard	4
M.W. Tate lbw b Pollard	21
Extras (nb 7)	7
Total	143

Bowling: Booth 18-5-25-2, Pollard 15.1-5-43-4, Hopwood 18-7-45-3, Iddon 4-2-7-0, Parkinson 6-2-16-0.

Lancashire: Second innings

F. Watson c Melville b Tate	28
J.L. Hopwood c Melville b Hammond	78
J. Iddon b Hammond	66
E. Tyldesley c Bowley b Pearce	52
E. Paynter st Eaton b Pearce	40
Mr W.H.L. Lister c John Langridge b Pearce	2
L.W. Parkinson b Pearce	11
Mr P.T. Eckersley b Pearce	10
G. Duckworth not out	5
F.S. Booth, R. Pollard — did not bat	
Extras (b 20, lb 5, w 1, nb 3)	29
Total (8 wickets declared)	321

Bowling: Tate 23-10-26-1, Hammond 22-6-67-2, J. Parks 37-17-82-0, Bowley 13-3-34-0, Pearce 18.5-4-61-5, Jas Langridge 16-5-22-0.

Sussex: Second innings

J.H. Parks not out	53
John Langridge b Hopwood	40
Mr A. Melville b Iddon	11
T. Cook not out	17
Jas Langridge, H.W. Parks, J. Eaton, E.H. Bowley, H.E. Hammond, G. Pearce, M.W. Tate — did not bat	
Extras (lb 4, nb 1)	5
Total (2 wickets)	126

Bowling: Booth 7-2-15-0, Pollard 8-2-16-0, Hopwood 9-1-17-1, Iddon 6-0-24-1, Parkinson 13-2-33-0, Paynter 3-0-16-0.

The Lancashire team: (STANDING) C. Washbrook, J.L. Hopwood, J. Iddon, F.S. Booth, R. Pollard, L.W. Parkinson, N. Oldfield; (SEATED) E. Paynter, E. Tyldesley, P.T. Eckersley (Captain), W.H.L. Lister, G. Duckworth

LANCASHIRE GO FOR THE RUNS TOO LATE

From E. W. SWANTON

At EASTBOURNE: Third day.

THE Lancashire innings, which had lived for two tedious hours and a quarter at Eastbourne last night, continued this morning to desecrate a lovely cricket ground on a perfect summer day. Lancashire began the proceedings with a lead of 133 runs and nine wickets in hand. Remembering the complete lack of enterprise which Lancashire showed yesterday, it was surprising that so many people deserted the pleasures of the seashore. The Saffrons ground, of course, is a pleasant place, and some may perhaps have thought Lancashire would attempt amends for their performance.

If that were so they were very speedily disillusioned. In point of fact the first hour's play this morning produced exactly 32 runs and the attitude of the batsmen even more obviously than the score board's evidence, proclaimed they were quite satisfied with the performance. Tate bowled a few overs, after which Melville spared him his energies and concentrated on Hammond and Pearce at one end, and James Parks and Bowley at the other. Hopwood's innings was quite indescribable, since he rarely if ever made

CHAMPIONSHIP TABLE TO-NIGHT IF SUSSEX DRAW

	Pts. Poss.	Pts. Obt.	Av.
Lancashire	435	252	57.93
Sussex	435	238	54.71

Sussex must win last match and Lancashire lose for Sussex to win Championship.

any stroke for the purpose of scoring—his runs arising by occasional deflections on either side of the wicket.

Iddon, after an hour and a quarter, went berserk, hitting a straight drive and hook for fours in successive overs. Shortly afterwards he lost his head, but unfortunately not his wicket, cover-point just failing to reach a sliced drive off Bowley's bowling. When Iddon reached his 50 he had batted two hours. The total was then 151, of which Hopwood had made 67 in three hours and three-quarters. Thereafter Sussex ceased to bother very much about keeping down the runs. Their bowling became loose, and the field was so close that mere prods and pushes trickled down the hill for fours. Seemingly Sussex thought that more Lancashire had on the board by luncheon the less long would they be afterwards in delaying their formal declaration.

At long last Hopwood, in playing a ball off his legs, gave backward short leg a catch, and that was 182—2—78. Tyldesley occupied the quarter of an hour before luncheon usefully, enough, and even appeared to influence Iddon to a less lethargic frame of mind. But contrition was too late by now, and it was a mercy when the interval arrived. Lancashire were then 258 ahead.

The first ball after luncheon mercifully disposed of Iddon. Paynter and Tyldesley then began to flog the ball over the field, so that the first half-hour produced 58 runs. Paynter hit Parks for two sixes in an over. The summit of illogicality by now had been reached. Lancashire seemed to be trying to win a match that had died a pre-destined draw three hours before.

Ultimately wickets fell fairly rapidly. Upon his dismissal Eckersley declared, leaving Sussex the impossible task of scoring 375 in a maximum of two hours and three-quarters. Thus was good cricket sacrificed on the altar of the championship!

Evening Standard, 24 August, 1934

WHEN LANCASHIRE went to Eastbourne towards the end of August, 1934 they held a narrow lead in the Championship (decided then by percentages because the counties played a differing number of matches), with Sussex – who had never won the title, and still have not – breathing down their necks in second place. Each side

had one match left after this one. In these circumstances Lancashire made it their business to secure a first innings lead (five points) and then to deprive Sussex of any prospect of winning, for which the prize was fifteen points. The slow batting on the second day – according to *Wisden* – was not to the liking of a good-sized crowd of 5,000.

Nor did their cricket on the third day please the young correspondent of the *Evening Standard*.

I well recall however Peter Eckersley, the Lancashire captain, justifying his tactics over dinner at the Grand Hotel on that second evening. He said that the winter pay of his professionals could well depend on their winning the

Championship: 'Do you think I'm going to risk that to please a lot of people on holiday?' It is perhaps easier for the 27-year-old reporter to see his point today than it was fifty-odd years ago.

Both Lancashire and Sussex won first innings points in their remaining match, so finishing in that order.

1935

FEWER THAN twenty-five batsmen in a century and more of County Championship cricket have scored a hundred on first appearance, and none is recorded as having done so in sixty-three minutes, as Harold Gimblett did on a fresh May day for Somerset against Essex at Frome in 1935.

The feat of the farmer's boy from Watchet in the west of the county was something of a seven-day wonder. Aged twenty (not eighteen as in the headline) Gimblett had had a pre-season trial at Taunton without greatly impressing the authorities. Called on at the last minute to make the cross-country journey over to Frome he missed a vital bus, we learned, which necessitated a long walk with his cricket bag. Going in at an inauspicious 107 for 6 'he raced to 50 in twenty-eight minutes, got his century in sixty-three minutes and reached 123 in eighty minutes'. He hit three sixes and 17 fours by strong, clean stroke-play and at once provoked the question – had another Jessop arrived?

Without quite living up to such a comparison Gimblett achieved the difficult and unusual distinction of becoming a dangerous, hard-hitting opening bat. Over his career he scored the Somerset record aggregate of 21,142 runs and hit 265 sixes, surely the most ever by a number one batsman. He is a Somerset legend still.

BELOW Harold Gimblett, who once hit three sixes in an over during which his partner appealed against the light!

SOMERSET v ESSEX
Played at Frome, 18, 20, 21 May, 1935.
Result: Somerset won by an innings and 49 runs.

Somerset: First innings

J.W. Lee c Pearce b Nichols	3
F.S. Lee lbw b Nichols	41
Mr R.A. Ingle c Eastman b Nichols	12
Mr J.C. White c Eastman b Nichols	4
Mr C.C. Case b P. Smith	35
Mr H.D. Burrough b Nichols	2
A.W. Wellard st Wade b Evans	21
H. Gimblett c and b Eastman	123
W.T. Luckes b Nichols	7
W.H.R. Andrews c O'Connor b Evans	71
H.L. Hazell not out	7
Extras (b 5, lb 5, w 1)	11
Total	337

Bowling: Nichols 23-3-87-6, R. Smith 13-2-43-0, Eastman 13-4-38-1, Evans 14.5-1-69-2; P. Smith 13-1-89-1.

Essex: First innings 141 (F. Rist 41; Wellard 5-66, J.W. Lee 4-26).

Essex: Second innings 147 (J.W. Lee 5-67).

Unknown Batsman's Hundred In 63 Minutes

DEBUT IN COUNTY CRICKET

18-YEAR-OLD SOMERSET DISCOVERY

SURPRISE FOR ESSEX

ANOTHER Jessop looms on the western horizon. This time the 18-year-old son of a Somerset farmer—a youth unknown in big cricket—has taken a quick leap to fame with a whirlwind century in his first county match.

Harold Gimblett flashed across the Frome scene with a hundred in 63 minutes. Played by Somerset for his medium-pace bowling in this game with Essex, he smashed his way to three figures with a string of seventeen 4's and three 6's.

It is too early to know whether Gimblett can maintain this lightning-like cricket. Yet there is the authentic stamp about him; he played the Essex attack as if he had been facing county bowling all his life—and liked it.

Six Somerset men were out for 107 runs when Gimblett arrived. Things looked bad; but the youth, whose only previous experience had been for Watchet in club games, settled down at once. He raced to fifty in 28 minutes, got his century in 63 minutes and reached 123 in 80 minutes.

There was nothing hit-or-miss about his display. It was fluent batsmanship—drives, cuts and leg hits came with style and certainty. In getting 123, he became the only Somerset player to equal B. L. Bisgood's 1907 record of a century in his first county game.

Daily Telegraph, 20 May, 1935

WELLARD'S FIVE SIXES

Somerset Player's Hurricane Hitting Against Kent at Taunton

Somerset nearly always fight best when their backs are against the wall. This they did at Taunton against Kent, who were kept in the field 4¾ hours, and still need 93 runs to win with nine wickets in hand, in spite of their first innings lead of 154.

Wellard set a gallant example for Somerset by scoring 75 in 58 minutes. His glorious innings contained five 6's and five 4's, and at one period he scored 44 runs in 20 minutes. With Frank Lee he helped to add 94 for the fifth wicket.

Somerset saved the innings defeat with six wickets in hand, and Frank Lee went on to complete his first century of the season in a little over four hours. He hit eight boundaries.

Kent, set to get 128 runs to win, lost Ashdown with 10 scored, the third Kent batsman dismissed by young Gimblett. Fagg and Woolley then played out time.

Daily Sketch, 25 June, 1935

WITHIN A few weeks of Harold Gimblett's sensational beginning for Somerset there came two highly remarkable pieces of hitting on the same day. As if to show the youngster that two could play at that game, Somerset's splendid all-rounder, Arthur Wellard hit 75, including five sixes, in fifty-eight minutes against Kent at Taunton. Simultaneously Horace Cameron, the South African, against Yorkshire at Bramall Lane, Sheffield also hit five sixes in his 103 not out. He reached 81 in an hour including this sequence in an over from Verity: 4, 4, 4, 6, 6, 6, making a total of 30.

This was the occasion of the well-known quip by the wicket-keeper, Arthur Wood: 'You've got him in two minds, Hedley – he doesn't know whether to hit you for four or six.' Poor Cameron died of enteric fever a few months after getting home from the tour. Wellard in his career hit a record 500 sixes, including 66 in a season, which was a record until in 1984 I.T. Botham achieved 80.

BELOW Arthur Wellard, a famous big-hitter.

BELOW RIGHT Horace Cameron, evidently enjoying his fame and autographing a bat

CAMERON HITS 30 IN ONE OVER

Three Successive Sixes Off Verity

THE South Africans look certain to keep their unbeaten record in this game with Yorkshire, and they may win.

At all events both Yorkshire's batting and bowling were made to look very ordinary indeed, with the result that at the close South Africa, with five wickets in hand, were 320 runs ahead.

Late in the day, when the Tourists were taking the upper hand, Cameron sent the crowd wild with some magnificent hitting. He scored 81 not out, and in one over he hit Verity for 30 runs! Three fours came off the first three balls, and three majestic sixes off the other three. It was hitting of the most exultant character, and at the end he had included four 6's and ten 4's in his brilliant display.

Daily Sketch, 25 June, 1935

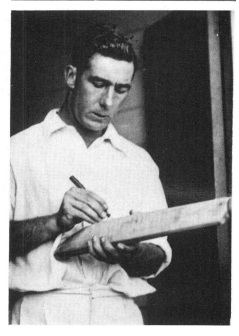

YORKSHIRE v SOUTH AFRICANS
Played at Sheffield,
22, 24, 25 June, 1935.
Result: South Africans won by 128 runs.

South Africans: First innings 263 (I.J. Siedle 51, H.B. Cameron 45; Fisher 4-52).

Yorkshire: First innings 201 (A. Mitchell 61; Balaskas 4-55, Bell 4-65).

South Africans: Second innings 301 for 7 declared (H.B. Cameron 103*, E.A. Rowan 76; Bowes 3-70).

Yorkshire: Second innings 235 (Mitchell 41; Balaskas 8-99).

1936

DERBYSHIRE CRICKET CHAMPIONS
AFTER 62 YEARS

DERBYSHIRE, one of the weaker counties throughout cricket history until this time, deservedly won their one and only Championship in 1936. The moment when the title became theirs was undramatic in that they were beaten by one wicket in a close-fought game against Somerset at Wells.

Their capture of first innings points however clinched the matter, and no one could dispute their right to finish at the top. They won 13 matches, three more than their nearest rivals, Middlesex, Yorkshire and Gloucestershire, and they possessed a well-knit side, sympathetically led by A.W. Richardson, especially strong in bowling. W. Copson bowled fast and T.B. Mitchell leg-breaks for England. The three leading batsmen, T.S. Worthington, D. Smith and L.F. Townsend, all achieved Test caps also, as did the wicket-keeper, H. Elliott, without winning regular places. In the years of economic depression most of the side came out of the pits – the traditional nursery for the hardy cricketers of Nottinghamshire and Derbyshire.

Wellard's Record of Five 6's in Over

By RONALD T. SYMOND

DERBYSHIRE, though beaten by one wicket by Somerset in the match that finished yesterday at Wells, won the County Cricket Championship for the first time for 62 years.

Several matches have yet to be played in the championship series, but as they failed to beat Sussex yesterday at Hove, Yorkshire cannot catch up with Derbyshire and have lost the championship they won last season.

Derbyshire well deserve the honour, gained by the ability of a well varied attack and keen fielding to dismiss their opponents cheaply, rather than by batting.

Two of their most successful players, Worthington, a batsman, and Copson, bowler, have been chosen to go to Australia with the M.C.C. during the winter.

When Derbyshire last won the championship, in 1874, they played three matches only, and were awarded it because they were the only county who escaped defeat.

Their match yesterday ended with one of the big thrills of the season, provided by the mighty hitting of Wellard, the Somerset fast bowler, who scored 86.

In one over he hit five successive 6's off Armstrong, a record for first-class cricket.

Alletson, of Nottinghamshire, hit 34 in 1911 against Sussex in one over, which contained two no balls, but his hits were three 6's and four 4's.

Daily Mail, 29 August, 1936

The Derbyshire team: (standing) H. Elliott, L.F. Townsend, W.H. Copson, H. Parker (scorer), A.V. Pope, D. Smith, C.S. Elliott (seated) H. Storer, T.S. Worthington, A.W. Richardson, T.B. Mitchell, A.E. Alderman

HAMMOND TAMES NORTH BOWLERS

INNINGS THAT WILL GO DOWN IN CRICKET HISTORY

North Beaten By Six Wickets At Lord's : Farnes' Great Bowling

By HOWARD MARSHALL

Daily Telegraph, 26 May, 1937

THE OCCASION of this unusual fixture was the celebration of MCC's 150th anniversary, which was marked by three successive matches at Lord's. North v South had been the special event marking the club's Jubilee; the matches following were between the MCC Australian team, recently returned, and the Rest, and finally Middlesex v Essex, the last-named being Middlesex's opponents in the first match ever played on Thomas Lord's original ground exactly 150 years before.

Howard Marshall, the first Test Match commentator (though more of an authority on Rugby football) and later a celebrated BBC war correspondent, was briefly the number one cricket man on the *Daily Telegraph*. He writes of Walter Hammond's 'glorious' hundred, and mentions what must have been 'a prodigious hit' into what was then the press-box and is now the offices of the MCC secretaries. (I must have remembered it if I had been in the box at the time!) 'No one,' he wrote, 'can deny Hammond his place among the immortals.'

His name is indeed secure there, as also are others engaged that day whose fame lay ahead of them. For Len Hutton, aged twenty, and Denis Compton, in his second summer and just nineteen, it was their first appearance in such exalted company. Hutton impressed all with his 102 for the North, while Compton scored an auspicious 70 for the South. Each was due to make a successful introduction to Test cricket when England took on the New Zealand touring team later in the summer.

NORTH v SOUTH
Played at Lord's, 22, 24, 25 May, 1937.
Result: The South won by six wickets.

North: First innings

E. Paynter b Gover	3
L. Hutton c Robins b Langridge	102
J. Hardstaff c Ames b Robins	71
M. Leyland c Barnett b Todd	31
Mr R.E.S. Wyatt c Ames b Gover	23
H.E. Dollery b Farnes	11
Mr C.R. Maxwell b Farnes	5
A.V. Pope c Compton b Robins	15
H. Verity st Ames b Robins	2
W. Voce not out	0
E. Hollies lbw b Robins	0
Extras (b 5, lb 1, nb 2)	8
Total	271

Bowling: Gover 20-6-49-2, Farnes 21-6-35-2, Todd 15-4-48-1, Hammond 10-4-17-0, Langridge 15-4-37-1, Robins 16-2-54-4, Compton 5-0-23-0.

South: First innings

C.J. Barnett c Hollies b Verity	22
H. Gimblett b Hollies	20
W.R. Hammond c Voce b Pope	86
L.E.G. Ames st Maxwell b Hollies	24
L.J. Todd c Maxwell b Verity	3
D.C.S. Compton b Verity	70
W.J. Edrich c Dollery b Voce	19
Jas Langridge lbw b Pope	0
Mr R.W.V. Robins lbw b Verity	38
A.R. Gover not out	1
Mr K. Farnes c Verity b Hollies	0
Extras (b 9, lb 7, nb 1)	17
Total	300

Bowling: Voce 19-3-43-1, Pope 22-4-59-2, Hollies 23.2-3-73-3, Wyatt 2-1-5-0, Verity 24-5-66-4, Hutton 6-0-37-0.

North: Second innings

E. Paynter b Robins	51
L. Hutton b Farnes	15
J. Hardstaff c Robins b Farnes	4
M. Leyland c Ames b Farnes	5
Mr R.E.S. Wyatt lbw b Farnes	49
H.E. Dollery b Farnes	4
Mr C.R. Maxwell b Gover	30
A.V. Pope b Robins	10
H. Verity not out	4
W. Voce c Ames b Gover	1
E. Hollies b Gover	0
Extras (b 6, lb 2, nb 3)	11
Total	184

Bowling: Gover 15-5-40-3, Farnes 17-8-43-5, Todd 5-0-28-0, Langridge 5-1-7-0, Robins 13-4-47-2, Barnett 3-1-8-0.

South: Second innings

C.J. Barnett c Maxwell b Hollies	22
H. Gimblett c Maxwell b Voce	10
W.R. Hammond not out	100
L.E.G. Ames b Verity	2
L.J. Todd b Verity	5
D.C.S. Compton not out	14
W.J. Edrich	
Jas Langridge	
Mr R.W.V. Robins } did not bat	
A.R. Gover	
Mr K. Farnes	
Extras (lb 5)	5
Total (4 wickets)	158

Bowling: Voce 10-1-43-1, Pope 11-2-24-0, Hollies 10-0-47-1, Verity 14-4-23-2, Hutton 2.2-0-16-0.

LEFT Hammond in full cry: on his day his batting was simply peerless

1937

Kent's Hurricane Hitting In Amazing Cricket Finish

219 IN 71 MINUTES TO BEAT GLOUCESTERSHIRE

Feat Without Parallel In History of the Game

Morning Post, 21 August, 1937

KENT'S SECOND innings against Gloucestershire at Dover in August 1937 is recognized as the fastest genuine example of rapid scoring measured both by time and by runs per 100 balls. They made 219 for 2 in 71 minutes, during which, be it noted, Gloucestershire, despite the punishment, bowled 23 overs. The run rate was 156 per 100 balls, which was 24 runs per 100 more than the next best.

The Crabble is a ground of average size, but it must have seemed far too small as the four batsmen concerned cracked away at the medium to slow bowling. In such circumstances the off-spinner is particularly vulnerable to a man using his feet in the manner of Leslie Ames – as poor Goddard's analysis shows. Frank Woolley liked going in first in his later years – he said he could see the new ball better. Bill Ashdown was a good-looking player of orthodox method, an ideal junior partner in the performance. The opening bowler, Alan Watt, promoted from number 10, could hit as hard as most in a simple, rustic way.

Kent needed to make 217 in five minutes under two hours: thus at the finish they had thirty-nine minutes to spare.

The *Morning Post* match report like all the others on the page was unsigned – in other words it was supplied by an agency. These were the declining days of the oldest English newspaper. A few weeks later it was bought by and absorbed into the *Daily Telegraph*.

KENT v GLOUCESTERSHIRE
Played at Dover, 18, 19, 20 August, 1937.
Result: Kent won by eight wickets.

Gloucestershire: First innings

C.J. Barnett b Watt	70
Mr G.W. Parker b Watt	210
Mr B.O. Allen c Spencer b Watt	21
W.R. Hammond c Ashdown b Woolley	3
J.F. Crapp c Ashdown b Watt	2
R.A. Sinfield not out	74
Mr B.H. Lyon c Pearce b Watt	0
W.L. Neale lbw b Watt	0
E.J. Stephens c Ashdown b Woolley	4
T.W. Goddard c Ames b Woolley	6
B.L. Watkins b Harding	25
Extras (b 9, lb 9, nb 1)	19
Total	434

Bowling: Harding 24.1-2-104-1, Watt 29-2-129-6, Todd 8-0-22-0, Wright 25-7-78-0, Woolley 24-6-82-3.

Kent: First innings

W.H. Ashdown c Hammond b Parker	45
F.E. Woolley c and b Sinfield	100
Mr F.G.H. Chalk b Neale	34
L.E.G. Ames b Neale	1
L.J. Todd b Parker	12
Mr B.H. Valentine c Hammond b Parker	30
Mr T.A. Pearce b Sinfield	59
T. Spencer b Sinfield	53
D.V.P. Wright c Watkins b Goddard	29
A.E. Watt c Barnett b Sinfield	0
N.W. Harding not out	14
Extras (b 22)	22
Total	399

Bowling: Barnett 16-2-45-0, Lyon 8-0-39-0, Sinfield 31-5-83-4, Goddard 23.1-2-77-1, Parker 24-5-78-3, Neale 11-0-55-2.

Gloucestershire: Second innings

C.J. Barnett c Valentine b Harding	0
Mr G.W. Parker b Watt	20
Mr B.O. Allen c Woolley b Todd	9
W.R. Hammond c Woolley b Wright	52
J.F. Crapp b Watt	1
R.A. Sinfield b Watt	26
Mr B.H. Lyon b Watt	21
W.L. Neale c Chalk b Todd	3
E.J. Stephens run out	15
T.W. Goddard b Harding	9
B.L. Watkins not out	11
Extras (b 7, lb 4, nb 4)	15
Total	182

Bowling: Harding 14.1-2-43-2, Watt 26-7-69-4, Todd 18-8-26-2, Wright 12-4-29-1.

Kent: Second innings

W.H. Ashdown not out	62
F.E. Woolley c Barnett b Sinfield	44
L.E.G. Ames c Barnett b Sinfield	70
A.E. Watt not out	39

Mr F.G.H. Chalk
L.J. Todd
Mr B.H. Valentine
Mr T.A. Pearce } did not bat
T. Spencer
D.V.P. Wright
N.W. Harding

Extras (b 2, lb 2)	4
Total (2 wickets)	219

Bowling: Barnett 3-0-23-0, Sinfield 9-0-69-2, Goddard 8.2-0-98-0, Parker 3-0-25-0.

BELOW The Crabble, Dover, scene of Kent's whirlwind record. Frank Woolley's hitting that day was as murderous as any in his long and distinguished career which spanned thirty-three seasons

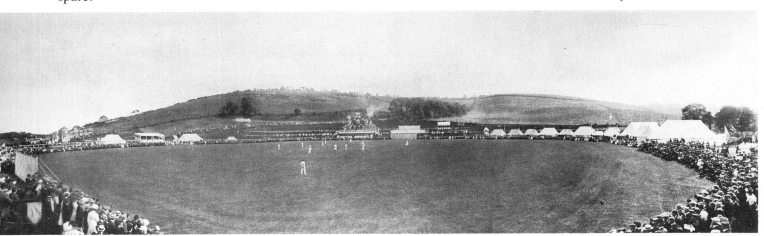

JIM SMITH HITS 50 IN 11 MINUTES

Eight 6's Against Gloucester

Daily Sketch, 17 June, 1938

BELOW Jim Smith: his hitting matched his physique. His sole century in first-class cricket took a sedate 81 minutes!

C.I.J. SMITH of Middlesex, universally known as Jim, was the most basic, the most rudimentary hitter of his day – which is to say the six summers from 1934 to 1939 inclusive. He was such a large man, tall and broad-chested, that as he marched to the wicket amid a hum of expectation he seemed to be carrying a ridiculously under-sized bat. If the scene was Lord's the Tavern emptied automatically. It would not – could not – last long, but it would be richly humorous. I never knew another cricketer whose efforts with the bat were marked by continued bursts of laughter.

Jim's method was to advance the front foot slightly, and roughly towards the line of the ball, before addressing the same stroke to everything. He swung the bat not too grossly across the line in a full arc which, if the connection was a true one, sent the ball whistling down to or over long-on. If he really 'middled it' woe betide the unlucky fielder who found himself in the way. More often than not the ball hit one of the bat's edges as it cleaved the air, and then it flew absolutely anywhere.

Bowlers were apt to make the mistake of pitching short to Smith. But long-hops were driven indiscriminately, often to a vast height. The ball that caused most bother – and a hurried attempt at a readjustment of the feet – was a long half-volley or a yorker. It was all hilarious fun, except sometimes for the fielding side who, if the game were in a critical state, were apt to become completely demoralized. His captain, Walter Robins, used sometimes to send him in when crisis threatened. Ten minutes of Jim was guaranteed to transfer the tension from his side to the opposition.

On the occasion at Bristol here recorded things were otherwise. Indeed the score was 499 for 8 on his arrival at the crease. Yet quick runs were still of value, as may be seen from the fact that Gloucestershire on the third day made 364 at their second attempt and still lost by an innings. After eighteen minutes he was bowled for 66 aiming to hit his ninth six! His 50 in eleven minutes is the fastest ever recorded except for one of those spurious modern efforts when a succession of full pitches was bowled in order to hasten a declaration.

This was also a notable day for a certain P.C. (John) Arlott – 'Harlott' indeed!

GLOUCESTERSHIRE v MIDDLESEX
Played at Bristol, 15, 16, 17 June 1938.
Result: Middlesex won by an innings and 42 runs.

Gloucestershire: First innings 209 (W.L. Neale 54*; Robins 3-91).

Middlesex: First innings

W.J. Edrich c Crapp b Sinfield	118
J. Robertson run out	43
S.M. Brown b Sinfield	4
D.C.S. Compton lbw b Haynes	45
J. Hulme b Sinfield	143
Mr R.W.V. Robins c Barnett b Monks	78
G.E. Hart b Sinfield	6
L. Muncer c Emmett b Sinfield	26
W.F. Price not out	26
J. Smith b Emmett	66
L.H. Gray b Sinfield	0
Extras (b 10, lb 8)	18
Total	573

Bowling: Scott 17-1-79-0, Barnett 4-1-4-0, Sinfield 63.4-9-184-6, Cranfield 7-0-29-0, Emmett 15-0-100-1, Haynes 36-4-123-1, Monks 3-0-24-1, Neale 2-0-12-0.

Gloucestershire: Second innings 322 (Mr B.O. Allen 104, W.L. Neale 94; Muncer 3-44).

POLICEMAN TURNS OUT FOR HANTS
So Does Harry Bedford, the Derby Masseur

Hants 313 and 163 for 6. Derby 356

A POLICE CONSTABLE and the Derby masseur were called upon to field as substitutes for Hampshire at Portsmouth yesterday.

P.-c. Harlott, a member of the Southampton constabulary, was a spectator at the match and he had to borrow flannels to take the field. He is a member of the Hants club.

Daily Sketch, 17 June, 1938

1938

THE LAST pre-Second World War Test between ancient rivals, wherein England's mammoth victory squared the series, albeit Australia having already retained the Ashes, was a grotesque game in several respects – as had been its predecessors of 1930 and 1934, both won by extravagant margins by Australia. As happened in 1934 a vast score by the side batting first took all heart and meaning from the contest, the situation this time being the more hopeless for the Australians in that two of the first three in the order, Fingleton and Bradman himself, had suffered injuries in the field and were unable to bat.

The course of subsequent events however did not detract – and should not in retrospect – from Len Hutton's masterpiece of unwearying concentration and stamina which stretched over the first two days and most of the morning of the third: 364 he made, bettering by 30 Don Bradman's record Test score. It had taken him thirteen hours twenty minutes. He had scored run for run with his successive partners, and a stumping chance two playing days earlier with his score at 40 had been his only visible error. It was a phenomenal innings played on a pitch of unnatural ease, concocted for the purpose. Indeed the only Englishman disappointed by England's declaration at 903 for 7 was 'Bosser' Martin, the groundsman. Having prepared pitches in 1930 and 1934 on which Australia had made 695 and 701 he was looking for four figures! Furthermore, but for the guaranteed absence of Bradman, Hammond would probably have allowed the innings to run its full course.

It was the fear of Bradman which chiefly dictated England's tactics. Consider: in the Oval Test of 1930 he had

HUTTON AND ENGLAND SMASH RECORDS

Injury to Bradman a Crushing Blow; Brown Stands Alone in the Last Ditch

A MATCH TAKEN OUT OF THE REALM OF CRICKET

By Neville Cardus (Cricketer)

Manchester Guardian, 24 August, 1938

made 232 (before leaving to a catch behind, for which mid-on was the only appealer!); in 1934 it had been 244. His appetite transcended that of ordinary mortals. Granted the dispositions of Hutton and his captain the course of

ENGLAND v AUSTRALIA
Played at The Oval, 20, 22, 23, 24 August, 1938.
Result: England won by an innings and 579 runs.

England: First innings

L. Hutton c Hassett b O'Reilly		364
W.J. Edrich lbw b O'Reilly		12
M. Leyland run out		187
W.R. Hammond* lbw b Fleetwood-Smith		59
E. Paynter lbw b O'Reilly		0
D.C.S. Compton b Waite		1
J. Hardstaff, jr not out		169
A. Wood† c and b Barnes		53
H. Verity not out		8
K. Farnes	did not bat	
W.E. Bowes	did not bat	
Extras (b 22, lb 19, w 1, nb 8)		50
Total (7 wickets declared)		903

Fall of Wickets: 1/29, 2/411, 3/546, 4/547, 5/555, 6/770, 7/876.
Bowling: Waite 72-16-150-1, McCabe 38-8-85-0, O'Reilly 85-26-178-3, Fleetwood-Smith 87-11-298-1, Barnes 38-3-84-1, Hassett 13-2-52-0, Bradman 2.2-1-6-0.

Australia: First innings

W.A. Brown c Hammond b Leyland	69
C.L. Badcock c Hardstaff b Bowes	0
S.J. McCabe c Edrich b Farnes	14
A.L. Hassett c Compton b Edrich	42
S.G. Barnes b Bowes	41
B.A. Barnett† c Wood b Bowes	2
M.G. Waite b Bowes	8
W.J. O'Reilly c Wood b Bowes	0
L.O'B. Fleetwood-Smith not out	16
D.G. Bradman* absent hurt	
J.H.W. Fingleton absent hurt	
Extras (b 4, lb 2, nb 3)	9
Total	201

Fall of Wickets: 1/0, 2/19, 3/70, 4/145, 5/147, 6/160, 7/160, 8/201.
Bowling: Farnes 13-2-54-1, Bowes 19-3-49-5, Edrich 10-2-55-1, Verity 5-1-15-0, Leyland 3.1-0-11-1, Hammond 2-0-8-0.

Australia: Second innings

W.A. Brown c Edrich b Farnes	15
C.L. Badcock b Bowes	9
S.J. McCabe c Wood b Farnes	2
A.L. Hassett lbw b Bowes	10
S.G. Barnes lbw b Verity	33
B.A. Barnett† b Farnes	46
M.G. Waite c Edrich b Verity	0
W.J. O'Reilly not out	7
L.O'B. Fleetwood-Smith c Leyland b Barnes	0
D.G. Bradman absent hurt	
J.H.W. Fingleton absent hurt	
Extras (b 1)	1
Total	123

Fall of Wickets: 1/15, 2/18, 3/35, 4/41, 5/115, 6/115, 7/117, 8/123.
Bowling: Farnes 12.1-1-63-4, Bowes 10-3-25-2, Verity 7-3-15-2, Leyland 5-0-19-0.

the England innings was logical enough.

Hutton broke the Don's record of 334 with a delicate late cut for four off O'Reilly. This is how Neville Cardus described what followed:

> The scene which now occurred moved even the hardened critics. Thousands of happy people stood up and cheered. Somebody with a cornet began to play " For he's a jolly good fellow " and the crowd took up the refrain in that evangelical tone which the British public invariably adopts when it lifts up its heart to rejoice in song. Moreover, the voices and the cornet did not keep together—but in the circumstances I admit that to say so is a piece of pedantic musical criticism. Bradman shook hands with the hero, all the Australians shook hands with him, journeying to the wicket from the remoter parts of the Oval—all except tired Bill O'Reilly, who lay prone on the grass until he saw a man coming out with drinks, when he got up at once and made for him, in a hurry. The cheers broke out again as soon as Hutton went beyond 336 and exceeded Hammond's innings against New Zealand in New Zealand. Hutton took the occasion with a charming modesty. He raised his cap in acknowledgment of the honours done to him, and bent his head. But what a moment for him!—the moment of his life.
>
> As the ground became resonant with the cheering the thought occurred to me that it was being heard far and wide, all over the Empire, not only all over this country. People walking down Collins Street in Melbourne would hear it, and it would roar and echo in Kandy, Calcutta, Allahabad, Penang : they would hear it in the Cocos Islands and join in, and on liners going patiently their ways over the seven seas they would hear it too, and drink Hutton's health. Possibly in some club in Pall Mall a permanent member would wake up and go to the lunch-room and have to be informed who was Hutton.

NO 1 TOTAL NO 7
336 711 78
WICKETS 5
BOWLER 11   BOWLER 10
CAUGHT
LAST PLAYER 1
LAST WICKET FELL 5 5 5

The Oval scoreboard records Hutton's passing of Bradman's record of 334 and England well on the way to their massive 903

Hutton, triumphant and weary, returns to the pavilion

1938

GODDARD PERFORMS HAT-TRICK

Daily Express, 27 December, 1938

MCC'S VISIT to South Africa in 1938-39 was notable in that for the first time the full strength of English cricket was mustered for the tour. South Africa had won the rubber of five three-day Tests in England three years earlier. Despite this the media was represented only by William Pollock of the *Daily Express*, their cricket correspondent and drama critic, and myself, engaged to broadcast the series for the BBC and the South African Broadcasting Corporation.

On Boxing Day afternoon, the second day of the match, South Africa made a steady reply to England's 422 and with twenty minutes to go had reached 160 for 2 when Tom Goddard, the off-spinner, took in those vast hands of his a return catch, offered by Nourse. N. Gordon, sent in as nightwatchman, dragged his back leg and was stumped first ball. Of all the Englishmen among the record crowd on the old Wanderers' ground at Johannesburg no one was more delighted than the lone figure perched in a small commentary box high above the crowd and behind the bowler's arm. (There was no room for a scorer, even if there had been one.) Hat-tricks in Test cricket are rare events – in almost a thousand Tests contested in this century there have been only a dozen. So as Gordon trooped back to the pavilion and South Africa's number six, Billy Wade, the wicket-keeper, made his reluctant way to the crease I had ample chance to alert listeners to the situation. One could imagine followers at home slumbering over the Yule log waking up and taking notice. And sure enough it happened. Wade went back, playing perhaps for the turn, and was clean bowled.

Any commentator worth his salt can make a good story out of a hat-trick.

ABOVE Tom Goddard: a bowler whose enormous hands disguised his teasing off-spin

My luck was to be on the air at the right time the first time I covered a Test match – as I also was, it so happened, to describe the next one, by Peter Loader against West Indies at Headingley in 1957.

The tone of Pollock's report brings back agreeable echoes: 'Batting bareheaded in the sunshine, Valentine took me back to Canterbury Week. He took the crowd by storm. Fielding was brilliant. Melville and Langton made some marvellous stops. The whole atmosphere of the game was delightful.' What happy, innocent days!

SOUTH AFRICA v ENGLAND
Played at Johannesburg,
24, 26, 27, 28 December, 1938.
Result: Match drawn.

England: First innings 422 (E. Paynter 117, B.H. Valentine 97, P.A. Gibb 93; Gordon 5-103).

South Africa: First innings

B. Mitchell b Farnes	73
P.G.V. van der Bijl lbw b Verity	4
A. Melville* c and b Verity	0
A.D. Nourse c and b Goddard	73
N. Gordon st Ames b Goddard	0
W.W. Wade† b Goddard	0
K.G. Viljoen b Wilkinson	50
E.L. Dalton c Edrich b Verity	102
G.E. Bond lbw b Wilkinson	0
A.B.C. Langton not out	64
E.Q. Davies b Verity	0
Extras (b 5, lb 18, nb 1)	24
Total	390

Fall of Wickets: 1/42, 2/44, 3/160, 4/160, 5/160, 6/173, 7/281, 8/281, 9/378, 10/390.
Bowling: Farnes 23-1-87-1, Edrich 9-0-44-0, Verity 44.1-16-61-4, Hammond 10-3-27-0, Wilkinson 22-0-93-2, Goddard 27-5-54-3.

England: Second innings 291 for 4 declared (P.A. Gibb 106, E. Paynter 100, W.R. Hammond 58).

South Africa: Second innings 108 for 1 (B. Mitchell 48*).

78

ENGLAND WIN TEST BY 8 WICKETS

Second Century for Headley

By RONALD T. SYMOND

Lord's (Third Day).—England beat West Indies by eight wickets.

Magnificent batting by magician Headley, with modest support from his colleagues, kept England in the field until 4.30, after Hammond's bold declaration, but even this praiseworthy resistance did not prevent England from reaching victory in comparative comfort at 5.55.

Daily Mail, 28 June, 1939

THE LAST Lord's Test before the Second World War was remarkable for the performance of George Headley, who became only the second man in history (after Herbert Sutcliffe) to twice score hundreds in each innings of a Test Match. Despite his efforts England won the three-day match by eight wickets with half an hour to spare. This was the first Test which the BBC broadcast ball-by-ball throughout – as I recall, having been the junior commentator of three, with Howard Marshall and Michael Standing. The *Daily Mail* cricket correspondent, R.T. Symonds, wrote that Headley's play 'confirmed once more his well-earned status as one of the best three batsmen in the world. He has the complete armoury, physical, technical and moral of a true champion'.

The scorecard illustrates Headley's superiority over his fellows. Whereas none of the others reached 1,000 runs on the tour or averaged more than 30 he scored 1,745 with an average of 72. Well might he be dubbed, as he was,

"ONE" FOR THE LOSERS
By TOM WEBSTER

the Black Bradman. (Though West Indians referred to the Don as the White Headley!) George was a delightful fellow, a model to his countrymen of modesty and sportsmanship.

Tom Webster was the leading sporting cartoonist of the day. This is a typical example of his work – to which the *Daily Mail* gave rather more space than to the report of the match.

BELOW The masterful George Headley

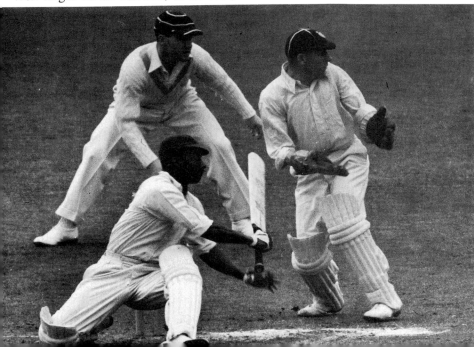

1939

ENGLAND v WEST INDIES

Played at Lord's, 24, 26, 27 June, 1939.
Result: England won by eight wickets.

West Indies: First innings

R.S. Grant*	c Compton b Copson	22
J.B. Stollmeyer b Bowes		59
G.A. Headley c Wood b Copson		106
J.E.D. Sealy c Wood b Wright		13
K.H. Weekes c Gimblett b Copson		20
L.N. Constantine lbw b Copson		14
J.H. Cameron c Hutton b Bowes		1
I. Barrow† lbw b Copson		2
E.A. Martindale lbw b Wright		22
L.G. Hylton not out		2
C.B. Clarke b Bowes		1
Extras (b 3, lb 9, nb 3)		15
Total		277

Fall of Wickets: 1/29, 2/147, 3/180, 4/226, 5/245, 6/250, 7/250, 8/261, 9/276, 10/277.
Bowling: Bowes 28.4-5-86-3, Copson 24-2-85-5, Wright 13-1-57-2, Verity 16-3-34-0.

England: First innings

L. Hutton c Grant b Hylton		196
H. Gimblett b Cameron		22
E. Paynter c Barrow b Cameron		34
W.R. Hammond* c Grant b Cameron		14
D.C.S. Compton c Stollmeyer b Clarke		120
J. Hardstaff, jr not out		3
A. Wood† not out		0
D.V.P. Wright		
H. Verity	did not bat	
W.H. Copson		
W.E. Bowes		
Extras (b 8, lb 6, w 1)		15
Total (5 wickets declared)		404

Fall of Wickets: 1/49, 2/119, 3/147, 4/395, 5/402.
Bowling: Martindale 20-2-86-0, Hylton 24-4-98-1, Constantine 13-0-67-0, Cameron 26-6-66-3, Clarke 6-0-28-1, Sealy 3-0-21-0, Grant 3-0-23-0.

West Indies: Second innings

R.S. Grant* b Bowes		23
J.B. Stollmeyer c Verity b Copson		0
G.A. Headley c Hutton b Wright		107
J.E.D. Sealy c Wood b Copson		29
K.H. Weekes c Wood b Verity		16
L.N. Constantine c Hammond b Verity		17
J.H. Cameron c and b Wright		0
I. Barrow† not out		6
E.A. Martindale c Bowes b Wright		3
L.G. Hylton c Hardstaff b Copson		13
C.B. Clarke c and b Copson		0
Extras (b 6, lb 4, w 1)		11
Total		225

Fall of Wickets: 1/0, 2/42, 3/105, 4/154, 5/190, 6/199, 7/200, 8/204, 9/225, 10/225.
Bowling: Bowes 19-7-44-1, Copson 16.4-2-67-4, Wright 17-0-75-3, Verity 14-4-20-2, Compton 3-0-8-0.

England: Second innings

L. Hutton b Hylton		16
H. Gimblett b Martindale		20
E. Paynter not out		32
W.R. Hammond* not out		30
D.C.S. Compton		
J. Hardstaff, jr		
A. Wood†		
D.V.P. Wright	did not bat	
H. Verity		
W.H. Copson		
W.E. Bowes		
Extras (lb 2)		2
Total (2 wickets)		100

Fall of Wickets: 1/35, 2/39.
Bowling: Martindale 7.7-0-51-1, Hylton 7-1-36-1, Constantine 3-0-11-0.

The Yorkshire Post
and Leeds Mercury

LEEDS, MONDAY, SEPTEMBER 4, 1944

Hedley Verity Memorial Match at Roundhay Park

NEWS OF the death of Hedley Verity was received in England on 1 September 1943, four years to the day since he came off the field for the last time, having won the match for Yorkshire at Hove by taking seven Sussex wickets for nine runs. He died as a prisoner of war in Italy from wounds received when leading his company in an assault on a German strong-point at Catania in Sicily. R.C. Robertson-Glasgow in the 1944 *Wisden* tells the story which ended thus:

> The strongest point appeared to be a farm-house, to the left of the ridge; so Verity sent one platoon round to take the farm-house, while the other gave covering fire. The enemy fire increased, and, as they crept forward, Verity was hit in the chest, 'Keep going,' he said, 'and get them out of that farm-house.' When it was decided to withdraw, they last saw Verity lying on the ground, in front of the burning corn, his head supported by his batman, Pte Thomas Reynoldson, of Bridlington. So, in the last grim game, Verity showed, as he was so sure to do, that rare courage which both calculates and inspires.

At the end of the following summer a Memorial Match was played at Roundhay Park, Leeds between Herbert Sutcliffe's Yorkshire team and one composed mostly of Verity's Test contemporaries collected by Jack Appleyard and captained by Walter Hammond. The proceedings were curtailed by rain, but not before the crowd of 10,000 had seen Len Hutton and Sutcliffe taking part in one last partnership and Hutton going on to make a brilliant 82.

The object of the game was achieved, that of raising funds to perpetuate the memory of Captain Hedley Verity by endowing a bed at Leeds General Infirmary. There is no name more revered in Yorkshire's cricket history than that of this quiet, dedicated man.

BELOW Hedley Verity: in uniform as an officer in the Green Howards

H. SUTCLIFFE'S YORKSHIRE XII
v J. APPLEYARD'S XII
Played at Roundhay Park, 3 September, 1944.
Result: Match abandoned.

H. Sutcliffe's Yorkshire XII

H. Sutcliffe st Duckworth b Bailey	14
L. Hutton c Smith b Bailey	82
A. Mitchell not out	26
M. Leyland not out	6
Extras	1
Total (2 wickets)	129

W. Barber, W. Watson, H. Fisher, F. Dennis, C. Turner, A. Wood, K. Fiddling and E.P. Robinson did not bat.
Bowling: Bailey took two wickets for 27.

J. Appleyard's XII
W.R. Hammond, E. Paynter, G. Duckworth, L.F. Townsend, T.B. Mitchell, J. Smith, C.S. Dempster, R. Stanford, G.V. Gunn, J. Bailey, L.G. Berry, J. Crapp.

THE VICTORY matches of 1945 were the climax of extensive cricket programmes which throughout the Second World War, as opposed to the complete shut-down during the First, helped to sustain morale and give relief from civilian strain. At no ground was there greater activity than at Lord's where three of the five 'Victory Tests' were played. The series got away to a rousing start with the first match over the Whitsun holiday which attracted 67,660 customers over the three days (at a shilling each!) and ended, as described by Charles Buchan in the *News Chronicle*, with a win for Australia in the last over.

The great find of the series was Flying-Officer Keith Miller, a night fighter pilot, who through the latter part of the war managed to get to Lord's whenever duties allowed. His hundred here set Australia on the road to a big score, as did another one in a later Lord's 'Test'. Warrant-Officer Lindsay Hassett, a youthful member of the 1938 Australian side in England, was captain.

The position some way down page three of the lead sports story of the day is a reminder of the rationing of newsprint which continued for the early years of peace. Buchan was the famous Sunderland and Arsenal footballer who took to sports reporting after his retirement.

1945

ENGLAND v AUSTRALIA
Played at Lord's, 19, 21, 22 May, 1945.
Result: Australia won by six wickets.

England: First innings
L. Hutton c Simsey b Williams	1
Flt-Sgt C. Washbrook st Simsey b Ellis	28
Capt J.D. Robertson lbw b Ellis	53
W.R. Hammond b Williams	29
Sqn-Ldr L.E.G. Ames c Price b Cheetham	57
Sqn-Ldr W.J. Edrich b Miller	45
Sqn-Ldr R.W.V. Robins b Cheetham	5
Lt-Col J.W.A. Stephenson c Simsey b Price	31
Lt-Col S.C. Griffith c Simsey b Cheetham	9
Lt D.V.P. Wright b Price	0
A.R. Gover not out	0
Extras (b 1, lb 6, w 1, nb 1)	9
Total	267

Fall of Wickets: 1/1, 2/54, 3/97, 4/130, 5/205, 6/213, 7/233, 8/267, 9/267.
Bowling: Cheetham 13.1-1-49-3, Williams 19-2-56-2, Pepper 19-2-59-0, Ellis 31-8-59-2, Miller 9-2-11-1, Price 9-1-24-2.

Australia: First innings
Flt-Sgt J.A. Workman b Gover	1
Capt R.S. Whitington c Griffith b Wright	36
W/O A.L. Hassett b Stephenson	77
Sqn-Ldr S.G. Simsey c Wright b Edrich	37
P/O K.R. Miller c Ames b Stephenson	105
F/O R.M. Stanford st Griffith b Stephenson	49
Sgt C.G. Pepper c Griffith b Stephenson	40
Capt A.G. Cheetham c Hammond b Wright	0
W/O R.G. Williams c Griffith b Wright	53
Sgt C.F. Price c Robertson b Stephenson	35
F/O R.S. Ellis not out	1
Extras (b 9, lb 10, nb 2)	21
Total	455

Fall of Wickets: 1/11, 2/52, 3/136, 4/171, 5/270, 6/357, 7/358, 8/366, 9/454.
Bowling: Gover 25-3-90-1, Stephenson 36-4-116-5, Edrich 17-2-61-1, Wright 37.3-9-122-3, Robins 10-0-45-0.

England: Second innings
L. Hutton b Pepper	21
Flt-Sgt C. Washbrook lbw b Pepper	32
Capt J.D. Robertson c Sismey b Cheetham	84
W.R. Hammond lbw b Ellis	33
Sqn-Ldr L.E.G. Ames b Ellis	7
Sqn-Ldr W.J. Edrich c Workman b Price	50
Sqn-Ldr R.W.V. Robins c Hassett b Pepper	33
Lt-Col J.W.A. Stephenson b Price	1
Lt-Col S.C. Griffith not out	4
Lt D.V.P. Wright run out	1
A.R. Gover st Simsey b Pepper	1
Extras (b 18, lb 8, nb 1)	27
Total	294

Fall of Wickets: 1/52, 2/75, 3/149, 4/175, 5/218, 6/286, 7/286, 8/289, 9/292.
Bowling: Cheetham 17-2-44-1, Williams 21-7-47-0, Pepper 32.4-7-80-4, Ellis 17-3-33-2, Miller 9-1-23-0, Price 19-3-40-2.

Australia: Second innings
Capt R.S. Whitington lbw b Stephenson	0
W/O A.L. Hassett c Hammond b Gover	37
P/O K.R. Miller run out	1
Sgt C.G. Pepper not out	54
Capt A.G. Cheetham run out	0
Sgt C.F. Price not out	10
Flt-Sgt J.A. Workman	
Sqn-Ldr S.G. Simsey	
F/O R.M. Stanford } did not bat	
W/O R.G. Williams	
F/O R.S. Ellis	
Extras (b 4, lb 1)	5
Total (4 wickets)	107

Fall of Wickets: 1/9, 2/11, 3/63, 4/76.
Bowling: Gover 11.4-1-51-1, Stephenson 11-0-51-1.

Australia's great win in last over—By CHARLES BUCHAN
England 267 and 294, Australia 455 and 107 for 4 wkts.

OFF the fourth ball of the last over of extra time, Pepper, the burly New South Wales batsman, pulled a ball from Gover to leg for two and gave Australia a fighting victory by six wickets which they richly deserved by their all-round superior play.

Pepper's winning stroke was a fitting climax to a great effort, and received a wonderful ovation from the 16,000 spectators who saw as exciting a finish as ever witnessed on the famous Lord's enclosure.

Left with 107 runs to get in 70 minutes, Australia made a bad start, but Hassett gave them a fighting chance by an innings which stamped him as one of the best batsmen in the game. Then came Pepper.

When Hassett left 42 runs were wanted with only 15 minutes to go. Still Pepper hit away undauntedly, taking all sorts of risks, but with two overs to go 15 runs were still wanted.

Then Pepper on-drove Stephenson gloriously for six in the last over but one and, despite Gover's strenuous efforts to check his furious hitting in the last over, the Australian never faltered.

While paying tribute to Australia's great triumph, a word of praise must also be given to Gover and Stephenson, who made heroic efforts to save England from defeat.

ROBERTSON THE STAR
England's batting, on a pitch which for an hour or so before lunch played queer tricks, was dour and determined against an Australian attack which, much superior to ours, maintained a high standard all day.

News Chronicle, 23 May, 1945.

The England team for the fifth 'Victory Test': H. Eliott, L.B. Fishlock, Sgt R. Pollard, Major F.A. Sloan, Pte G.H. Pope, Flt-Sgt W.E. Phillipson, Lieut J.D. Robertson, Lt-Col G.O Allen, F. Chester; Flt-sgt C. Washbrook, Sgt L. Hutton, Major-Gen T.F.N. Wilson, Flt-Lieut W.R. Hammond (Captain), Wing Cmdr W.H.N. Shakespeare, Lt-Col S.C. Griffith, Lieut D.V.P. Wright; Sqd Ldr W.J. Edrich, Sgt W.B. Roberts

1946

INDIAN PAIR BREAK LAST WICKET RECORD

Sarwate & Banerjee in Stand of 249

By E. M. WELLINGS

Evening News, 13 May, 1946

SURREY v INDIA

Played at The Oval,
11, 13, 14 May, 1946.
Result: India won by nine wickets.

India: First innings

V.M. Merchant b Squires	53
V.S. Hazare lbw b A.V. Bedser	0
R.S. Modi b A.V. Bedser	0
Gul Mahomed b A.V. Bedser	89
R.B. Nimbalkar c Mobey b Parker	18
Mushtaq Ali lbw b Parker	6
S.W. Sohoni lbw b Watts	6
V. Mankad c Mobey b A.V. Bedser	16
C.S. Nayudu c Bennett b A.V. Bedser	9
C.T. Sarwate not out	124
S. Banerjee b Parker	121
Extras (b 7, lb 4, nb 1)	12
Total	454

Bowling: Gover 7-2-18-0, A.V. Bedser 47-8-135-5, Watts 38-7-122-1, Parker 27.2-7-64-3, Squires 12-1-36-1, E.A. Bedser 8-0-25-0, Gregory 5-1-23-0, Fishlock 3-0-19-0.

Surrey: First innings

R.J. Gregory lbw b Sohoni	16
L.B. Fishlock hit wkt b Nayudu	62
H.S. Squires c Nimbalkar b Hazare	4
T.H. Barling b Hazare	8
J.F. Parker c Merchant b Banerjee	20
E.A. Bedser lbw b Mankad	6
E.A. Watts b Mankad	2
N.H. Bennett c Mustaq Ali b Nayudu	0
A.V. Bedser b Nayudu	0
A.R. Gover lbw b Banerjee	7
G.S. Mobey not out	6
Extras (b 1, lb 1, nb 2)	4
Total	135

Bowling: Hazare 16-9-20-2, Sohoni 9-1-31-1, Banerjee 9-0-42-2, Nayudu 12-3-30-3, Mankad 5-1-8-2.

Surrey: Second innings

R.J. Gregory lbw b Mankad	100
L.B. Fishlock c Merchant b Hazare	83
H.S. Squires st Nimbalkar b Nayudu	21
T.H. Barling b Mankad	16
J.F. Parker b Sarwate	20
E.A. Bedser lbw b Sarwate	21
E.A. Watts st Nimbalkar b Sarwate	2
N.H. Bennett c Mankad b Sarwate	24
A.V. Bedser not out	31
A.R. Gover lbw b Sarwate	0
G.S. Mobey lbw b Mankad	5
Extras (b 5, lb 9, w 1)	15
Total	338

Bowling: Hazare 16-5-36-1, Sohoni 6-0-15-0, Banerjee 11-1-45-0, Nayudu 25-4-93-1, Mankad 25-7-80-3, Sarwate 16-5-54-5.

India: Second innings

V.M. Merchant not out	15
C.T. Sarwate c Watts b A.V. Bedser	1
R.S. Modi not out	4
V.S. Hazare	
Gul Mahomed	
R.B. Nimbalkar	
Mushtaq Ali	} did not bat
S.W. Sohoni	
V. Mankad	
C.S. Nayudu	
S. Banerjee	
Total (1 wicket)	20

Bowling: A.V. Bedser 3-0-14-1, Watts 2.5-0-6-0.

RIGHT Sarwate and Banerjee: two bowlers who achieved a rare batting feat

THE FIRST post-war season was only a few days old when two memorable events took place at The Oval. In the first of them two members of the touring Indian team hit the headlines by breaking one of the more interesting and amusing records. C.T. Sarwate and S. Banerjee, two bowlers neither of whom achieved very much thereafter, batting at numbers 10 and 11 respectively, scored 249 together for the last wicket against Surrey. (The record of Woolley and Fielder of 235 had lasted since 1909).

Both Sarwate and Banerjee made hundreds. They came together after tea on the first day and lasted an hour on the second morning. They gave no chances for 190 minutes and moved E.M. Wellings, not the easiest of critics to please, to a rare eulogy:

So ended a stand which was more than historic. It was also a magnificent exhibition of brilliant stroke-play and a lesson in aggression sensibly applied to batting.

The extraordinary thing was that their subsequent careers were so undistinguished: two glorious flashes in the pan!

The King Sees Woolley's Swan-song

By L. V. MANNING

THE young gentlemen of Old England, age 606 (735 if you add umpires Hobbs and Strudwick), turned back the history pages and gave the biggest cricket crowd of the season (15,000) a rich feast at the Oval yesterday.

It wasn't only because they kept their hats on that Percy George Fender's team of old masters looked from the ring just as they used to look. Their strokes were ageless; the eye keen to see the short one which calls for the hook and, if warning notices from the lumbar region at times turned Surrey singles into twos or threes, they fielded with noble fortitude and bowled with lion hearts.

Daily Sketch, 24 May, 1946

1946

THE SECOND occasion was the one-day game between Surrey and Old England held in delayed celebration of the centenary of the County Club which in fact was founded, and The Oval first played on, in 1845. It was a function that might have gone sadly wrong. Wednesday 23 May might have been chilly or wet or both. Just as likely, the old heroes brought out of retirement, try as they would, might not have measured up. After all, the average age of those who batted was 53; of the bowlers it was 50. Moreover few of them had played much or any cricket since the war started.

As it turned out the day was a brilliant success. The weather was warm and sunny, and 15,000 came, including King George VI. They saw a game wherein 480 runs were scored and in which the old 'uns, with a little subtle indulgence by Surrey, acquitted themselves admirably. The Oval bore scars still of the ravages of war but the groundsman, Bert Lock, had miraculously restored the renowned excellence of the pitch which, covered beforehand, played perfectly.

One could shut one's eyes – my part in the proceedings was to man the public address system – and hardly believe it was all true. To see Frank Woolley and Pat Hendren in the flesh once again, bringing out the old familiar strokes with scarcely a hint of time's passing. Playing from memory, one might call it, I suppose, but in all games the technique of the truly great is apt to defy the years.

Surrey, mind you, played like gentlemen in that, after the early dismissal of Sutcliffe and Sandham, they desisted from lbw appeals at least until the third wicket pair were established. If that civility had been operative from the start of the innings poor Sutcliffe might have been spared to remind us of his Ashes triumph on this same pitch twenty years before. Jack Hobbs and Herbert Strudwick did the umpiring, and the other Herbert did not look exactly delighted when 'Struddy' adjudged him leg-before – a small cloud only in an otherwise clear blue sky.

SURREY v OLD ENGLAND

Played at The Oval, 23 May, 1946.
Result: Match drawn.

Surrey: First innings

R.J. Gregory b Fender	62
L.B. Fishlock c Fender b Freeman	25
H.S. Squires b Holmes	68
T.H. Baring lbw b Fender	0
J.F. Parker c and b Allom	12
A.J. McIntyre not out	39
E.A. Bedser c Brooks b Allom	23
E.A. Watts not out	13
N.H. Bennett	
G.J. Whittaker } did not bat	
G.S. Mobey	
Extras (b 5, lb 1)	6
Total (6 wickets declared)	248

Bowling: Tate 8-1-26-0, Allom 17-2-76-2, Freeman 15-3-58-1, Holmes 8-1-36-1, Fender 8-0-46-2.

Old England: First innings

H. Sutcliffe lbw b Watts	1
A. Sandham c A.V. Bedser b Watts	1
F.E. Woolley c McIntyre b A.V. Bedser	62
E. Hendren c Barling b A.V. Bedser	94
D.R. Jardine b Parker	54
P.G.H. Fender not out	12
D.J. Knight not out	2
M.W. Tate	
E.R.T. Holmes } did not bat	
M.J.C. Allom	
E.W.J. Brooks	
Extras (b 3, lb 2, nb 1)	6
Total (five wickets)	232

Bowling: A.V. Bedser 21-3-45-2, Watts 18-3-83-2, Parker 15-0-51-1, Squires 7-0-29-0, E.A. Bedser 4-2-3-0, McIntyre 2-0-11-0, Gregory 1-0-4-0.

LEFT Six of Old England take the field: A. Sandham, E. Hendren, A.P. Freeman, M.W. Tate, M.J.C. Allom, P.G.H. Fender

ENGLAND v INDIA

Played at Lord's, 22, 24, 25 June, 1946.
Result: England won by ten wickets.

India: First innings

V.M. Merchant	c Gibb b Bedser	12
M.H. Mankad	b Wright	14
L. Amarnath	lbw b Bedser	0
V.S. Hazare	b Bedser	31
R.S. Modi	not out	57
Nawab of Pataudi, sr*	c Ikin b Bedser	9
Gul Mahomed	b Wright	1
A.H. Kardar	b Bowes	43
D.D. Hindlekar†	lbw b Bedser	3
C.S. Nayudu	st Gibb b Bedser	4
S.G. Shinde	b Bedser	10
Extras (b 10, lb 6)		16
Total		200

Fall of Wickets: 1/15, 2/15, 3/44, 4/74, 5/86, 6/87, 7/144, 8/147, 9/157, 10/200.
Bowling: Bowes 25-7-64-1, Bedser 29.1-11-49-7, Smailes 5-1-18-0, Wright 17-4-53-2.

England: First innings

L. Hutton	c Nayudu b Amarnath	7
C. Washbrook	c Mankad b Amarnath	27
D.C.S. Compton	b Amarnath	0
W.R. Hammond*	b Amarnath	33
J. Hardstaff, jr	not out	205
P.A. Gibb†	c Hazare b Mankad	60
J.T. Ikin	c Hindlekar b Shinde	16
T.F. Smailes	c Mankad b Amarnath	25
A.V. Bedser	b Hazare	30
D.V.P. Wright	b Mankad	3
W.E. Bowes	lbw b Hazare	2
Extras (b 11, lb 8, nb 1)		20
Total		428

Fall of Wickets: 1/16, 2/16, 3/61, 4/70, 5/252, 6/284, 7/344, 8/416, 9/421, 10/428.
Bowling: Hazare 34.4-4-100-2, Amarnath 57-18-118-5, Gul Mahomed 2-0-2-0, Mankad 48-11-107-2, Shinde 23-2-66-1, Nayudu 5-1-15-0.

India: Second innings

V.M. Merchant	lbw b Ikin	27
M.H. Mankad	c Hammond b Smailes	63
L. Amarnath (8)	b Smailes	50
V.S. Hazare	c Hammond b Bedser	34
R.S. Modi (3)	lbw b Smailes	21
Nawab of Pataudi, sr*	b Wright	22
Gul Mahomed	lbw b Wright	9
A.H. Kardar (5)	b Bedser	0
D.D. Hindlekar†	c Ikin b Bedser	17
C.S. Nayudu	b Bedser	13
S.G. Shinde	not out	4
Extras (b 10, lb 2, nb 3)		15
Total		275

Fall of Wickets: 1/67, 2/117, 3/126, 4/129, 5/174, 6/185, 7/190, 8/249, 9/263, 10/275.
Bowling: Bowes 4-1-9-0, Bedser 32.1-3-96-4, Smailes 15-2-44-3, Wright 20-3-68-2, Ikin 10-1-43-1.

England: Second innings

L. Hutton	not out	22
C. Washbrook	not out	24
D.C.S. Compton		
W.R. Hammond*		
J. Hardstaff, jr		
P.A. Gibb†	did not bat	
J.T. Ikin		
T.F. Smailes		
A.V. Bedser		
D.V.P. Wright		
W.E. Bowes		
Extras (lb 1, w 1)		2
Total (0 wickets)		48

Bowling: Hazare 4-2-7-0, Amarnath 4-0-15-0, Mankad 4.5-1-11-0, Nayudu 4-0-13-0.

RIGHT Alec Bedser: England's post-war bowling find

BEDSER CRASHES INTO TEST CRICKET

Seven India Wickets for 49: England Shocks, Too

By LORD TENNYSON,
Former England and Hampshire Captain

News of the World, 23 June, 1946

IN THE FIRST post-war Test, at Lord's against India, Alec Bedser, who in 1939 with his twin brother Eric had played just a couple of games for Surrey against the Universities, took 7 for 49 in his first spell for England and 11 for 145 in the match. Following the seven-year gap the crying need was for bowlers. Of the leading pre-war bowlers of Test class or thereabouts Hedley Verity and Kenneth Farnes had been killed, Voce, Gover, Copson, Bowes and Perks were in their late thirties, while such men as Goddard, Nicholls, Sims, Robins, Mitchell and Wellard, though still getting wickets for their counties, had turned 40. Only Doug Wright, a wrist-spinner highly dangerous on his day but not the man around whom to build a Test attack, could be described as in his prime.

The strong, burly Bedser, just coming up to his twenty-eighth birthday, was therefore hailed with rapture – and inevitably overworked accordingly both by England and Surrey. He was quickly compared to Maurice Tate whom he resembled in pace – medium-fast with plenty of life off the pitch. He was hampered by having to learn, as the leading England bowler, the basics of his craft. The period of his true greatness indeed lay four years ahead.

It was as much an exploratory tour for India as for England. In a wet summer they beat eight of the counties and lost to only three. England won the rubber by their Lord's victory. The tour marked the start of successful Test careers for Mankad, Modi, Hazare, and (subsequently for Pakistan) Kardar.

THE MCC TEAM of 1946-47 were greeted with the utmost warmth as they made their traditional progress round the Australian coast from Perth eastwards to Brisbane, but nowhere was the welcome quite so marked as in the premier sports-loving city of Melbourne. On All Saints Day 1946 – a Friday – around 30,000 people came to see the first English visitors for ten years, and especially to take a first look at the pair who had made such a mark against their side in the far-away English summer of 1938, Denis Compton and Len Hutton. Both obliged handsomely, Denis with a brilliant 143 in the first innings and Len with a masterly 151 not out on a wearing pitch in the second.

Though we had little reason to suppose so at the time this was in a way the high point of the tour. It was in fact the only first-class victory. From this point – largely because of a discrepancy in the quality of leadership between Hammond and Bradman – things began to go wrong. Walter Hammond, it will be seen, stood down from this match, MCC being led by Norman Yardley, the vice-captain, who was one of the successes of the tour.

COMPTON TO THE RESCUE

CENTURY OF SUPERB QUALITY

From E. W. SWANTON
MELBOURNE, Thursday.

There are some occasions which recur frequently in one's thoughts with undiminished clarity when most else is forgotten or only half-remembered and I know that, for me, to-day will be one of them, though when the Tests come along the match against Victoria will not seem specially important.

On this magnificent ground and in bright sunshine Compton played an innings of superb quality and the charm that is all his own.

Daily Telegraph, 1 November, 1946

1946

M.C.C. v VICTORIA
Played at Melbourne,
31 October, 1, 2, 4 November, 1946.
Result: M.C.C. won by 244 runs.

M.C.C. First innings

L. Hutton b Johnson	15
C. Washbrook c Barnett b Johnston	0
P.A. Gibb b Ring	22
D.C.S. Compton c Harvey b Ring	143
J. Hardstaff lbw b Freer	15
N.W.D. Yardley c and b Tribe	70
J.T. Ikin not out	31
J. Langridge lbw b Tribe	0
W. Voce c and b Johnson	21
A.V. Bedser run out	22
D.V.P. Wright b Tribe	0
Extras (b 11, lb 7, nb 1)	19
Total	358

Bowling: Johnston 18-1-68-1, Freer 19-3-62-1, Johnson 18-2-79-2, Tribe 25.7-4-88-3, Ring 9-1-42-2.

Victoria: First innings

G.E. Tamblyn c and b Wright	5
K. Meuleman c Yardley b Voce	2
M. Harvey c and b Wright	21
K.R. Miller c Hutton b Wright	32
A.L. Hassett c Bedser b Ikin	57
I.W. Johnson c Gibb b Voce	31
B.A. Barnett not out	17
F. Freer c Ikin b Voce	0
D. Ring c Gibb b Wright	1
G. Tribe lbw b Wright	4
W. Johnston b Wright	0
Extras (b 5, lb 10, nb 4)	19
Total	189

Bowling: Voce 17-4-48-3, Bedser 8-3-19-0, Wright 14.4-1-48-6, Langridge 10-0-37-0, Ikin 4-0-18-1.

M.C.C.: Second innings

L. Hutton not out	151
C. Washbrook b Tribe	17
P.A. Gibb c Tribe b Ring	16
D.C.S. Compton c Tribe b Ring	18
J. Hardstaff lbw b Johnson	21
N.W.D. Yardley lbw b Johnson	20
J.T. Ikin st Barnett b Johnson	21
W. Voce c Freer b Johnson	7
J. Langridge	
A.V. Bedser } did not bat	
D.V.P. Wright	
Extras (b 2, lb 6)	8
Total (7 wickets declared)	279

Bowling: Johnston 11-1-66-0, Freer 10-0-45-0, Johnson 15.4-4-38-4, Tribe 14-0-70-1, Ring 10-0-52-2.

Victoria: Second innings

G.E. Tamblyn b Hutton	24
K. Meuleman run out	14
M. Harvey c Ikin b Bedser	57
K.R. Miller b Langridge	8
A.L. Hassett b Compton b Wright	57
I.W. Johnson c Ikin b Wright	0
B.A. Barnett c Ikin b Bedser	3
F. Freer c Hardstaff b Bedser	14
D. Ring b Wright	0
G. Tribe c Hutton b Wright	13
W. Johnston not out	7
Extras (b 5, lb 2)	7
Total	204

Bowling: Voce 5-0-14-0, Bedser 11-3-40-3, Wright 16.4-2-73-4, Langridge 11-1-33-1, Ikin 4-1-12-0, Compton 5-0-17-0, Hutton 1-0-8-1.

LEFT The Compton sweep

1947

THE FINAL TEST MATCH

ENGLAND LOSE A GOOD GAME

FROM OUR SPECIAL CORRESPONDENT
SYDNEY, MARCH 5

On paper England has lost the final Test match easily, but it was not as easy as all that. Australia had to struggle, and the decision has so much been on a thread that, but for a shocking mishap that curtailed Compton's innings and a missed catch that gave Bradman a second chance, England surely must have come very close to a well deserved victory. And a popular one.

Compton batted with ease at the day's beginning, and with the most stylish control while Smith hung on against unpleasant spin from McCool. Smith also performed one or two strokes, including a belligerent drive from a full toss of Tribe, who bowled rather aimlessly in conditions which should have suited him.

The Times, 6 March, 1947

AUSTRALIA, by victories in the first two Tests and drawn matches in the Third and Fourth, had already retained the Ashes when the Fifth Test was contested at Sydney. A Test however is an end in itself, and England (led for the first time by Yardley since Hammond was incapacitated by lumbago) put up a valiant fight which would probably have been crowned with success had Bradman not been badly missed by Edrich at slip when he had made only two. As an evenly-contested game reached its climax the pitch grew progressively more helpful to spin. Australia needed 214 in the fourth innings, and Bradman's 63, made out of 98 in partnership with Hassett, proved decisive.

The Times report – as always until 1967 – was unsigned, but it bears the unmistakeable stamp of Neville Cardus, who had gone to Australia at the start of the war and was still there.

The 'shocking mishap' that disposed of Denis Compton was no more than an attempted sweep which edged the ball to the wicket-keeper's pads and thence into short-leg's hands.

The Test averages illustrate with stark clarity the bowling weakness which, together with the contrast in leadership, was the chief difference between the sides.

AUSTRALIA v ENGLAND
Played at Sydney, 28 February,
1 (no play), 3, 4, 5, March, 1947.
Result: Australia won by five wickets.

England: First innings

L. Hutton retired ill	122
C. Washbrook b Lindwall	0
W.J. Edrich c Tallon b Lindwall	60
L.B. Fishlock b McCool	14
D.C.S. Compton hit wkt b Lindwall	17
N.W.D. Yardley* c Miller b Lindwall	2
J.T. Ikin b Lindwall	0
T.G. Evans† b Lindwall	29
T.P.B. Smith b Lindwall	2
A.V. Bedser not out	10
D.V.P. Wright c Tallon b Miller	7
Extras (b 7, lb 8, w 1, nb 1)	17
Total	280

Fall of Wickets: 1/1, 2/151, 3/188, 4/215, 5/225, 6/225, 7/244, 8/269, 9/280.

Bowling: Lindwall 22-3-63-7, Miller 15.3-2-31-1, Tribe 28-2-95-0, Toshack 16-4-40-0, McCool 13-0-34-1.

Australia: First innings

S.G. Barnes c Evans b Bedser	71
A.R. Morris lbw b Bedser	57
D.G. Bradman* b Wright	12
A.L. Hassett c Ikin b Wright	24
K.R. Miller c Ikin b Wright	23
R.A. Hamence not out	30
C.L. McCool c Yardley b Wright	3
D. Tallon† c Compton b Wright	0
R.R. Lindwall c Smith b Wright	0
G.E. Tribe c Fishlock b Wright	9
E.R.H. Toshack run out	5
Extras (b 7, lb 6, nb 6)	19
Total	253

Fall of Wickets: 1/126, 2/146, 3/146, 4/187, 5/218, 6/230, 7/230, 8/233, 9/245, 10/253.

Bowling: Bedser 27-7-49-2, Edrich 7-0-34-0, Smith 8-0-38-0, Wright 29-4-105-7, Yardley 5-2-8-0.

England: Second innings

C. Washbrook b McCool	24
W.J. Edrich st Tallon b McCool	24
L.B. Fishlock (1) lbw b Lindwall	0
D.C.S. Compton (4) c Miller b Toshack	76
N.W.D. Yardley* b McCool	11
J.T. Ikin (5) st Tallon b McCool	0
T.G. Evans† (7) b Miller	20
T.P.B. Smith (8) c Tallon b Lindwall	24
A.V. Bedser st Tallon b McCool	4
D.V.P. Wright (10) not out	1
L. Hutton absent ill	–
Extras (b 1, lb 1)	2
Total	186

Fall of Wickets: 1/0, 2/42, 3/65, 4/65, 5/85, 6/120, 7/157, 8/184, 9/186.

Bowling: Lindwall 12-1-46-2, Miller 6-1-11-1, Tribe 14-0-58-0, Toshack 4-1-14-1, McCool 21.4-5-44-5, Barnes 3-0-11-0.

Australia: Second innings

S.G. Barnes c Evans b Bedser	30
A.R. Morris run out	17
D.G. Bradman* c Compton b Bedser	63
A.L. Hassett c Ikin b Wright	47
K.R. Miller not out	34
R.A. Hamence c Edrich b Wright	1
C.L. McCool not out	13

D. Tallon†
R.R. Lindwall
G.E. Tribe — did not bat
E.R.H. Toshack

Extras (b 4, lb 1, nb 4)	9
Total (5 wickets)	214

Fall of Wickets: 1/45, 2/51, 3/149, 4/173, 5/180.

Bowling: Bedser 22-4-75-2, Edrich 2-0-14-0, Smith 2-0-8-0, Wright 22-1-93-2, Yardley 3-1-7-0, Compton 1.2-0-8-0.

TEST MATCH AVERAGES
AUSTRALIA
BATTING.

	Innings	Not out	Runs	Highest score	Avge.
D. G. Bradman	8	1	680	234	97.14
K. Miller	7	2	384	141*	76.80
S. Barnes	6	0	443	234	73.83
A. Morris	8	1	503	155	71.85
C. McCool	7	2	272	104*	54.40
A. L. Hassett	7	0	332	128	47.42
R. Lindwall	5	0	160	100	32.00
R. Hamence	2	1	31	30*	31.00
D. Tallon	6	0	174	92	29.00
M. Harvey	2	0	43	31	21.50
I. Johnson	5	0	106	52	21.20
G. Tribe	3	1	35	25*	17.50
B. Dooland	3	0	49	29	16.33
E. Toshack	5	2	14	6	4.66
F. Freer	1	1	28	28*	—

* Not out.

BOWLING.

	Overs	Maidens	Runs	Wickets	Avge.
R. Lindwall	122.1	20	367	18	20.38
K. Miller	122.3	15	334	16	20.87
F. Freer	20	3	74	3	24.66
E. Toshack	178.4	49	437	17	25.70
C. McCool	182	27	491	18	27.27
I. Johnson	124.6	35	306	10	30.60
B. Dooland	98	9	351	8	43.87
G. Tribe	95	9	330	2	165.00
S. Barnes	7	0	23	0	—

* Not out.

ENGLAND
BATTING

	Innings	Not out	Runs	Highest Score	Avge.
L. Hutton	9	1	417	122*	52.12
D. Compton	10	1	459	147	51.00
W. J. Edrich	10	0	462	119	46.20
J. Hardstaff	2	0	76	67	38.00
C. Washbrook	10	0	363	112	36.30
N. W. D. Yardley	10	2	252	61	31.50
W. R. Hammond	8	0	168	37	21.00
J. T. Ikin	10	0	184	60	18.40
A. V. Bedser	10	3	106	27*	15.14
T. G. Evans	8	2	90	29	15.00
P. A. Gibb	2*	0	24	13	12.00
W. Voce	3	1	19	18	9.50
D. V. P. Wright	8	3	47	15*	9.40
P. Smith	4	0	32	24	8.00
L. B. Fishlock	2	0	14	14	7.00

BOWLING

	Overs	Maidens	Runs	Wickets	Avge.
N. W. D. Yardley	114	15	372	10	37.20
D. V. P. Wright	240.2	23	990	23	43.04
W. J. Edrich	115.3	12	483	9	53.66
A. V. Bedser	246.3	37	876	16	54.75
P. Smith	47	1	218	2	109.00
W. Voce	44	12	161	0	—
D. Compton	16.2	0	78	0	—
J. T. Ikin	7	0	48	0	—
L. Hutton	3	0	28	0	—

* Not out.

M.C.C. AVERAGES
(First class matches, including Test Matches)
BATTING

	Innings	Not out	Runs	Highest score	Avge.
L. Hutton	21	3	1,267	151*	70.38
D. Compton	25	3	1,432	163	65.09
J. Langridge	3	1	130	100	65.00
W. J. Edrich	21	2	881	119	46.36
W. R. Hammond	14	0	633	208	45.21
J. Hardstaff	13	1	471	155	39.25
C. Washbrook	25	0	891	124	35.64
N. W. D. Yardley	23	4	614	70	32.31
J. T. Ikin	24	3	590	71	28.09
L. B. Fishlock	12	1	299	57	27.18
T. G. Evans	16	5	224	41*	20.36
P. Smith	8	0	154	46	19.25
P. A. Gibb	14	1	199	37*	15.30
A. V. Bedser	17	3	214	51	15.28
W. Voce	9	1	116	28	14.50
R. Pollard	7	3	45	12*	11.25
D. V. P. Wright	16	5	76	20	6.90

BOWLING

	Overs	Maidens	Runs	Wkts.	Avge
J. Hardstaff	14	1	50	3	16.66
N. W. D. Yardley	134.7	16	443	15	29.53
P. Smith	235.6	14	993	30	33.10
D. V. P. Wright	395.4	39	1,699	51	33.31
J. T. Ikin	107	9	481	13	37.00
J. Langridge	100	15	297	7	42.42
W. J. Edrich	235	26	949	22	43.13
A. V. Bedser	392.3	57	1,359	28	48.53
D. Compton	86.2	11	327	6	54.50
R. Pollard	233	45	735	13	56.53
L. Hutton	18	1	116	2	58.00
W. Voce	179.7	33	660	11	60.00
W. R. Hammond	3	0	8	0	—
L. B. Fishlock	1	0	3	0	—
P. A. Gibb	1	0	14	0	—

* Not out.

OPPOSITE Doug Wright: he had Bradman missed on 2 in Australia's second innings

LEFT Bradman square drives: Evans is in perfect position behind the stumps.

1947

ENGLAND v SOUTH AFRICA

Played at Lord's, 21, 23, 24, 25 June, 1947.
Result: England won by ten wickets.

England: First innings

L. Hutton b Rowan		18
C. Washbrook c Tuckett b Dawson		65
W.J. Edrich b Mann		189
D.C.S. Compton c Rowan b Tuckett		208
C.J. Barnett b Tuckett		33
N.W.D. Yardley* c Rowan b Tuckett		5
T.G. Evans† b Tuckett		16
G.H. Pope not out		8
A.V. Bedser b Tuckett		0
D.V.P. Wright } did not bat		
W.E. Hollies		
Extras (b 2, lb 10)		12
Total (8 wickets declared)		554

Fall of Wickets: 1/75, 2/96, 3/466, 4/515, 5/526, 6/541, 7/554, 8/554.
Bowling: Tuckett 47-8-115-5, Dawson 33-11-81-1, Mann 53-16-99-1, Rowan 65-11-174-1, Smith 17-2-73-0.

South Africa: First innings

B. Mitchell st Evans b Compton		46
A. Melville* c Bedser b Hollies		117
K.G. Viljoen b Wright		1
A.D. Nourse lbw b Wright		61
O.C. Dawson c Barnett b Hollies		36
T.A. Harris st Evans b Compton		30
A.M.B. Rowan b Wright		8
L. Tuckett b Wright		5
N.B.F. Mann b Wright		4
J.D. Lindsay† not out		7
V.I. Smith c Edrich b Pope		11
Extras (lb 1)		1
Total		327

Fall of Wickets: 1/95, 2/104, 3/222, 4/230, 5/290, 6/300, 7/302, 8/308, 9/309, 10/327.
Bowling: Edrich 9-1-22-0, Bedser 26-1-76-0, Pope 19.2-5-49-1, Wright 39-10-95-5, Hollies 28-10-52-2, Compton 21-11-32-2.

South Africa: Second innings

B. Mitchell c Edrich b Wright		80
A. Melville* b Edrich		8
K.G. Viljoen b Edrich		6
A.D. Nourse b Edrich		58
O.C. Dawson c Edrich b Compton		33
T.A. Harris c Yardley b Compton		3
A.M.B. Rowan not out		38
L. Tuckett lbw b Wright		9
N.B.F. Mann b Wright		5
J.D. Lindsay† c Yardley b Wright		5
V.I. Smith c Edrich b Wright		0
Extras (b 3, lb 4)		7
Total		252

Fall of Wickets: 1/16, 2/28, 3/120, 4/192, 5/192, 6/201, 7/224, 8/236, 9/252, 10/252.
Bowling: Edrich 13-5-31-3, Bedser 14-6-20-0, Pope 17-7-36-0, Wright 32.2-6-80-5, Hollies 20-7-32-0, Compton 32-10-46-2.

England: Second innings

L. Hutton not out		13
C. Washbrook not out		13
W.J. Edrich		
D.C.S. Compton		
C.J. Barnett		
N.W.D. Yardley*		
T.G. Evans† } did not bat		
G.H. Pope		
A.V. Bedser		
D.V.P. Wright		
W.E. Hollies		
Total (0 wickets)		26

Bowling: Tuckett 3-0-4-0, Dawson 6-2-6-0, Mann 3.1-1-16-0.

554 for 8 declared

EDRICH BOWLED AT 189, COMPTON CAUGHT AT 208

Flash from Lords: England 554 for 8 declared.

From BRUCE HARRIS: Lord's, Monday

Seventeen runs—four 4s and a single—were hit off five successive balls by W. J. Edrich off V. I. Smith, South African slow bowler, at Lord's to-day.

It happened immediately after Smith came on, the fifth bowler of the morning, to try to break the Edrich-Compton stand which broke record after record.

The bowler's length was sadly at fault during that hurricane minute, and Edrich slammed his fours hard round to the on boundary.

It looked as if one of them would have been a chance if any human fieldsman could have captured a ball travelling at such velocity.

No records exist of feats like that of Edrich, but I should say that these 17 runs were unique in Test cricket.

The pair went on to smash three records before Edrich was bowled at 189. Then Compton was caught when he had hit 208, his first double century in any Test.

The score then was 515 for four.

Successive records

In the two hours before lunch the two Middlesex batsmen, who on Saturday scored 216 together, added another 131.

This unfinished partnership at lunch-time, with its 347 runs, broke in succession the

Wyatt-Woolley record of 245 for third wicket against the South Africans in 1929;

English record of 264 for that wicket for all Tests—previously held by Hammond and Hutton (264 against West Indies, at the Oval, 1939; and finally the

South African 319 record—by Melville and Nourse, at Nottingham a fortnight ago.

All the bowling came alike to Edrich and Compton to-day.

Evening Standard, 23 June, 1947.

THE NAMES of Compton and Edrich, coupled in partnership for Middlesex and England, are as well-known as any of the great pairings in cricket history. Denis Compton had made his bow at Lord's, aged just eighteen, in 1936, Bill Edrich, after qualifying from Norfolk, aged twenty-two, a year later. Their association at number three and four in the Middlesex order, interrupted by six years of war and by operations on Denis's knee, lasted from 1937 to 1957. It reached its most productive peak in 1947 when they broke many records.

In the August of that lovely hot summer Denis bettered Tom Hayward's record aggregate, Bill following shortly afterwards: Compton 3,816, average 90; Edrich 3,539, average 80. They also found the energy to bowl between them 1,200 overs, taking respectively 73 and 67 wickets.

The South African tourists suffered grievously. Compton scored four Test hundreds, and made 1,000 runs against them off his own bat. They had a joint Test average of 100. As England's opening bowler Edrich also took 16 wickets.

The high spot of all this plunder was their partnership of 370 for the third wicket – still easily an England record and only twice bettered for any wicket – in the Second Test at Lord's. The background to this performance is worth mentioning. England, after losing the rubber in Australia 3-0 in the preceding winter, had been obliged to follow on in the First Test at Trent Bridge, and were only saved by time from heavy defeat. Coming together at 96 for 2 on the first day the pair laid the foundations of victory and ultimate success in the series. With the gates closed on a crowd

of 30,000 the partnership lasted until shortly after lunch on the second day – in good time for the later editions of the *Evening Standard*. A record Test stand by two local boys on their home ground: what better could a sports editor ask for? The *Standard* went to town. For a war-weary country anxious to relax and forget, the tone for the summer was set.

There has probably never been such a universal sporting hero – remember that he was also the victorious Arsenal's outside left – as the debonair, disarming Denis Compton in those years of the late 1940s.

BELOW LEFT The 'debonair' Compton, in need of the well-advertised Brylcreem

BELOW Bill Edrich on the way to his 189: in the summer of 1947 Compton and he broke all records.

1948

DID BRADMAN SNUB LORD TENNYSON? ACCUSED OF RUDENESS

By PETER WILSON

Sunday Pictorial, 30 May, 1948

LORD TENNYSON.
He wanted to ask Bradman to dinner.

DON BRADMAN.
He hasn't yet phoned to apologise.

ABOVE The main protagonists in the Sunday Pictorial's *'scoop'*

THIS ILLUSTRATION of the seamy side of sporting journalism is included as an example of the sort of story that has made famous personalities habitually wary of the press. The victim was Don Bradman, who was publicly and unjustly maligned in circumstances which gave him no possibility of redress. Note that Peter Wilson's story in the *Sunday Pictorial* of 30 May 1948 was a follow-up of one by an Australian columnist David McNicoll which made big headlines in Sydney and was duly cabled back. Wilson in his report quoted McNicoll thus:

> "Lord Tennyson is very browned-off with Bradman, and doesn't hesitate to say so. After Bradman's innings at Lord's on Saturday Lord Tennyson went to the Australian dressing-room and requested an attendant to ask Bradman if he could spare a moment.
>
> "According to what Tennyson told me at Lord's yesterday the attendant came back and said: 'Sorry, my Lord, Mr. Bradman says he's too busy to see you.'
>
> "Tennyson told me he was so furious with this treatment that he immediately wrote to Bradman telling him that he did not consider his behaviour very commendable.
>
> "Tennyson said: 'I told him I thought that as a former captain of England and a son of a former Governor-General of Australia he might have seen fit to spare me a moment. I also told him that I had merely wanted to congratulate him and to ask him and Hassett, Brown and Miller to dine with me at White's

Club. I was so furious that I added that good manners cost nothing.'"

McNicoll says that the Tennyson affair is one of a growing list of examples of needless brusqueness and lack of tact on Bradman's part, and adds:

"It would be a great pity if he were to spoil what could be his triumphal visit to England by displays of tactlessness and rudeness."

The facts of the story were correct – so far as they went. But to complete the picture it was also true that Lord Tennyson had previously that afternoon visited the MCC dressing-room where it was all too clear that he had lunched not wisely but too well and was far better kept out of the way of young cricketers, whether English or Australian. One of the England selectors and a warm friend of Bradman's had earlier encountered him in the MCC dressing-room and happened to be with Bradman in the Australian room when Tennyson's message was brought to him. It was on this friend's firm advice that the Australian captain made his reply.

Lionel Tennyson was a jovial and popular fellow, whom I knew well. He was apt to overdo it on occasion, as everyone knew. It is hard to think that everyone did not include the socially-inclined McNicoll. Whether or not he was aware of the full background to his story he undoubtedly did Bradman an injury. For what comment could the victim make other than to answer enquiries as he did: 'I am sorry but I can't say anything about it.'

AUSTRALIA ON the first four days of this Fourth Test at Headingley were held by England who entered the last day 400 runs ahead, apparently secure from defeat and, with the pitch dusting and taking plenty of spin, strongly scenting victory. The complete failure to grasp the opportunity made this one of the more depressing episodes within my watching experience. If chances had been taken Compton's wrist-spin could have won the match easily. As it was, Morris offered two chances and Bradman three, four of these at the expense of Compton, who should have had both batsmen stumped. Evans had a bad day.

At an early stage of his innings Bradman decided it might be easier to win the match than to save it, and as England's out-cricket deteriorated the play confirmed his judgement.

By winning by seven wickets with fifteen minutes to spare Australia made the most runs ever to score a Test victory. As for Bradman he ended his sequence of Test innings at Headingley by making 173 not out. This brought his Test aggregate on the ground to 963, average 192.6! Neil Harvey at the age of nineteen and three quarters marked his first Test innings against England by making 112. Although Archie Jackson remained the youngest centurion in England v Australia Tests, having been junior by four months when in 1928-29 he made 164 at Adelaide, Harvey was already the youngest Australian Test centurion (153 v India earlier in the year).

The crowd of more than 158,000 still ranks as the highest to have watched a match in England. Jack Fingleton, the best of Australian cricket writers, whose journalism was too seldom seen either in England or his own country, laments that England failed to rise to a great opportunity. What made the last day's cricket the more galling was the fact that after losing the first two Tests by heavy margins England had recovered to the extent of having all the better of the Third at Old Trafford until they were robbed of their chance by the weather. At the close of the third day

ABOVE Harvey returns after his hundred

England led by 316 with seven second innings wickets in hand – a cast-iron position if ever there was one. Rain then prevented play until after lunch on the fifth day. Now at Headingley for the first four days the English counter-attack had continued. But then came Bradman...

A black day for English cricket

By J. H. FINGLETON, former Australian Test player.

I T'S all over at Headingley bar the lamenting—and after seeing the Englishmen, particularly Evans behind the stumps, miss chance after chance yesterday, I dare say there will be plenty of that.

Yorkshire Post, 28 July, 1948

ENGLAND v AUSTRALIA
Played at Leeds, 22, 23, 24, 27 July, 1948.
Result: Australia won by seven wickets.

England: First innings
L. Hutton b Lindwall	81
C. Washbrook c Lindwall b Johnston	143
W.J. Edrich c Morris b Johnson	111
A.V. Bedser c and b Johnson	79
D.C.S. Compton c Saggers b Lindwall	23
J.F. Crapp b Toshack	5
N.W.D. Yardley* b Miller	25
K. Cranston b Loxton	10
T.G. Evans† c Hassett b Loxton	3
J.C. Laker c Saggers b Loxton	4
R. Pollard not out	0
Extras (b 2, lb 8, w 1, nb 1)	12
Total	496

Fall of Wickets: 1/168, 2/268, 3/423, 4/426, 5/447, 6/473, 7/486, 8/490, 9/496, 10/496.
Bowling: Lindwall 38-10-79-2, Miller 17.1-2-43-1, Johnston 38-12-86-1, Toshack 35-6-112-1, Loxton 26-4-55-3, Johnson 33-9-89-2, Morris 5-0-20-0.

Australia: First innings
A.R. Morris c Cranston b Bedser	6
A.L. Hassett c Crapp b Pollard	13
D.G. Bradman* b Pollard	33
K.R. Miller c Edrich b Yardley	58
R.N. Harvey b Laker	112
S.J.E. Loxton b Yardley	93
I.W. Johnson c Cranston b Laker	10
R.R. Lindwall c Crapp b Bedser	77
R.A. Saggers† st Evans b Laker	5
W.A. Johnston c Edrich b Bedser	13
E.R.H. Toshack not out	12
Extras (b 9, lb 14, nb 3)	26
Total	458

Fall of Wickets: 1/13, 2/65, 3/68, 4/189, 5/294, 6/329, 7/344, 8/355, 9/403, 10/458.
Bowling: Bedser 31.2-4-92-3, Pollard 38-6-104-2, Cranston 14-1-51-0, Edrich 3-0-19-0, Laker 30-8-113-3, Yardley 17-6-38-2, Compton 3-0-15-0.

England: Second innings
L. Hutton c Bradman b Johnson	57
C. Washbrook c Harvey b Johnston	65
W.J. Edrich lbw b Lindwall	54
A.V. Bedser (9) c Hassett b Miller	17
D.C.S. Compton (4) c Miller b Johnston	66
J.F. Crapp (5) b Lindwall	18
N.W.D. Yardley* (6) c Harvey b Johnston	7
K. Cranston (7) c Saggers b Johnston	0
T.G. Evans† (8) not out	47
J.C. Laker not out	15
R. Pollard did not bat	
Extras (b 4, lb 12, nb 3)	19
Total (8 wickets declared)	365

Fall of Wickets: 1/129, 2/129, 3/232, 4/260, 5/277, 6/278, 7/293, 8/330.
Bowling: Lindwall 26-6-84-2, Miller 21-5-53-1, Johnston 29-5-95-4, Loxton 10-2-29-0, Johnson 21-2-85-1.

Australia: Second innings
A.R. Morris c Pollard b Yardley	182
A.L. Hassett c and b Compton	17
D.G. Bradman* not out	173
K.R. Miller lbw b Cranston	12
R.N. Harvey not out	4
Extras (b 6, lb 9, nb 1)	16
Total (3 wickets)	404

S.J.E. Loxton, I.W. Johnson, R.R. Lindwall, R.A. Saggers†, W.A. Johnston and E.R.H. Toshack did not bat.

Fall of Wickets: 1/57, 2/358, 3/396.
Bowling: Bedser 21-2-56-0, Pollard 22-6-55-0, Cranston 7.1-0-28-1, Laker 32-11-93-0, Yardley 13-1-44-1, Compton 15-3-82-1, Hutton 4-1-30-0.

1948

AFTER THE damage to England's morale inflicted at Headingley the débâcle on the first day of the Fifth Test at The Oval was surprising only in its totality. In humid weather Lindwall bowled superbly and the Australians caught everything that flew above ground. Hutton, relatively untroubled, was last out for 30. England's score of 52 was their lowest in Tests bar one.

When Bradman came in to bat in his last Test the Australian reply stood at 117 for 1. As a contest the result was all but foregone. Yet it was of its nature a highly emotional moment. The crowd stood, and Yardley, with the England team gathered round, called for three cheers. Bradman then took guard, played Hollies's first ball, went forward to the second, which was a googly, and was bowled between bat and pad. Was there ever such an anti-climax? Just four runs would have given him an aggregate of 7,000 in Tests and an average of 100. As it is his 99.64 is more than half as high again as the figures of those who come next. (At the moment of writing only R.G. Pollock, G.A. Headley and H. Sutcliffe finished their careers with an average of 60.)

Yet, this chance statistic apart, for Bradman the last tour achieved all he could have hoped for. His team departed with an unbeaten record – as no other side has ever done. They left in an aura of goodwill and with a record profit of £75,000. The captain signalled his fortieth birthday soon after the last Test with hundreds in his last three innings, making 11 in all, and an average for the summer of 89.

It was indeed the end of an era in England v Australia Tests – an era of all but twenty years dominated (apart from one interruption) by one transcendent batsman. In the New Year's Honours of 1949 'the Don' became 'Sir Donald'. Simultaneously the administrator took over from the cricketer, and for the next thirty years continued to leave his mark on the game.

OPPOSITE Bradman is cheered by the England players as he arrives for his last Test innings. Two balls later he is bowled for 0

ENGLAND v AUSTRALIA
Played at The Oval, 14, 16, 17, 18 August, 1948.
Result: Australia won by an innings and 149 runs.

England: First innings
L. Hutton c Tallon b Lindwall	30
J.G. Dewes b Miller	1
W.J. Edrich c Hassett b Johnston	3
D.C.S. Compton c Morris b Lindwall	4
J.F. Crapp c Tallon b Miller	0
N.W.D. Yardley* b Lindwall	7
A.J. Watkins lbw b Johnston	0
T.G. Evans† b Lindwall	1
A.V. Bedser b Lindwall	0
J.A. Young b Lindwall	0
W.E. Hollies not out	0
Extras (b 6)	6
Total	52

Fall of Wickets: 1/2, 2/10, 3/17, 4/23, 5/35, 6/42, 7/45, 8/45, 9/47, 10/52.
Bowling: Lindwall 16.1-5-20-6, Miller 8-5-5-2, Johnston 16-4-20-2, Loxton 2-1-1-0.

Australia: First innings
S.G. Barnes c Evans b Hollies	61
A.R. Morris run out	196
D.G. Bradman* b Hollies	0
A.L. Hassett lbw b Young	37
K.R. Miller st Evans b Hollies	5
R.N. Harvey c Young b Hollies	17
S.J.E. Loxton c Evans b Edrich	15
R.R. Lindwall c Edrich b Young	9
D. Tallon† c Crapp b Hollies	31
D.T. Ring c Crapp b Bedser	9
W.A. Johnston not out	0
Extras (b 4, lb 2, nb 3)	9
Total	389

Fall of Wickets: 1/117, 2/117, 3/226, 4/243, 5/265, 6/304, 7/332, 8/359, 9/389, 10/389.
Bowling: Bedser 31.2-9-61-1, Watkins 4-1-19-0, Young 51-16-118-2, Hollies 56-14-131-5, Compton 2-0-6-0, Edrich 9-1-38-1, Yardley 5-1-7-0.

England: Second innings
L. Hutton c Tallon b Miller	64
J.G. Dewes b Lindwall	10
W.J. Edrich b Lindwall	28
D.C.S. Compton c Lindwall b Johnston	39
J.F. Crapp b Miller	9
N.W.D. Yardley* c Miller b Johnston	9
A.J. Watkins c Hassett b Ring	2
T.G. Evans† b Lindwall	8
A.V. Bedser b Johnston	0
J.A. Young not out	3
W.E. Hollies c Morris b Johnston	0
Extras (b 9, lb 4, nb 3)	16
Total	188

Fall of Wickets: 1/20, 2/64, 3/125, 4/153, 5/164, 6/167, 7/178, 8/181, 9/188, 10/188.
Bowling: Lindwall 25-3-50-3, Miller 15-6-22-2, Johnston 27.3-12-40-4, Loxton 10-2-16-0, Ring 28-13-44-1.

THANKS FOR THE MEMORY MR. BRADMAN!

But *YOU* Will Remember This Test Match, Too

By VIVIAN JENKINS

ENGLAND'S fifth Test match of 1948 will be remembered not for Don Bradman's farewell alone. As though determined to give him the send-off he deserved, the Australian team went berserk with the most astonishing bowling and fielding performance for 60 years.

In two and a half hazy, crazy hours they shot out the cream of England's batting for a paltry 52 runs, our second lowest score since Tests between the two countries started and the lowest-ever score in a Home Test match. "The Don" was like an excited schoolboy in the field, startled by the success which even he could hardly have expected, but when he came in to bat the unbelievable happened: he was out for a "duck."

To watching eyes, accustomed as they are to seeing England's cricketers in the doldrums, the whole thing took on the appearance of some fantastic ballet.

Magnified Australian cricketers, with huge yellow eyes in the middle of their green caps, cavorted and whirled in a frenzy of destruction.

Wickets hurtled through the air like flailing boomerangs, gargantuan arms stretched out to take unimagined catches. Round and round the mad vortex went, while in the centre the England batsmen did a pitiful halting little dance of death.

News of the World, 15 August, 1948

1949

Robertson hits 331 not out in a day

Sunday Pictorial, 24 July, 1949

IN 1949 WORCESTERSHIRE, so often the chopping-block of the stronger counties, made a spirited challenge for the Championship, in the end finishing in third place behind Middlesex and Yorkshire, who shared the honours.

Worcestershire met with contrasting fortunes in the two matches shown here wherein occurred two remarkable personal feats.

On a flawless Worcester pitch late in July, J.D. Robertson on the first day made an undefeated 331 for Middlesex out of a total of 623 for 5. Only two men, Macartney and Duleepsinhji, ever scored more runs in an English day's play and only three counties have ever tallied more. Robertson shared successive century partnerships with J.G. Dewes, F.G. Mann, G.O. Allen and R.W.V. Robins, the last three captains of England – probably another record!

Jack Robertson was a delightful batsman – and, for that matter, is a delightful man – whose fate it was to perform rather in the shadow of Compton and Edrich. There was an easy elegance about his batting that recalled another admirable Lord's batsman whom he would have seen as a youngster on the groundstaff, J.W. Hearne. Earlier in the summer, deputizing for Cyril Washbrook, he made 26 and 121 against New Zealand in the Lord's Test. It was his second and last appearance for England at home, for Washbrook promptly returned.

MIDDLESEX v WORCESTERSHIRE
Played at Worcester, 23, 25, 26 July, 1949.
Result: Middlesex won by an innings and 54 runs.

Middlesex: First innings

J.D. Robertson not out	331
S.M. Brown b Palmer	3
J.G. Dewes b Perks	45
J.G. Mann c Bird b Palmer	65
G.O. Allen b Palmer	98
R.M.V. Robins c Cooper b Bird	95
H. Sharp L. Compton J. Sims } did not bat J.A. Young L. Gray	
Extras (b 14, lb 5, nb 3)................................	22
Total (5 wickets declared)	623

Bowling: Perks 24-7-92-1, Palmer 30-8-119-3, Jenkins 30-4-153-0, Howorth 24-5-99-0, Jackson 23-1-104-0, Bird 4.3-0-34-1.

Worcestershire: First innings 188 (R.E. Bird 44*; Sims 5-54).
Worcestershire: Second innings 381 (L. Outschoorn 94*, E. Cooper 68, H. Yarnold 61; Gray 3-26, Young 3-75).

LEFT The talented Jack Robertson: only two men have bettered his 331 in a day in England

ROLY JENKINS AT IT AGAIN
Hat-trick in each innings against Surrey

Daily Herald, 31 August, 1949

ENTER NOW 'Roly' Jenkins, one of the the characters of his time, bandy-legged and with a rocking gait who purveyed leg-breaks of enticing trajectory and dangerous spin, often with wryly humorous accompaniment. With 183 wickets at 21 runs each he was the leading wicket-taker of 1950. It was one of the properties of wrist-spin that tail-enders were apt to surrender to it fairly quickly though often only after a few good cracks. On this occasion against Surrey he polished off the tail without resistance in each innings, picking off

Alec Bedser and Stuart Surridge for 'pairs'. A. Shaw and C.W.L. Parker are the only other cricketers in the history of county cricket to achieve a hat-trick in each innings. (By extraordinary coincidence Jenkins had also taken a hat-trick against Surrey in the preceding summer.)

Note that Jenkins took 11 wickets in this match, the same number that fell in 'Robertson's Match' to Sims and Robins. On good pitches no side in those days was complete without at least one leg-spinner.

WORCESTERSHIRE v SURREY
Played at Worcester, 27, 29, 30 August, 1949.
Result: Worcestershire won by 109 runs.

Worcestershire: First innings

E. Cooper b Surridge	10
D. Kenyon b Surridge	3
L. Outschoorn b Surridge	1
C.H. Palmer run out	59
M.L.Y. Ainsworth b Surridge	0
R.E. Bird c McIntyre b A.V. Bedser	4
R.E.S. Wyatt c McIntyre b Surridge	40
R.O. Jenkins c Parker b A.V. Bedser	9
R. Howorth b A.V. Bedser	0
H. Yarnold b A.V. Bedser	5
R.T.D. Perks not out	10
Extras (w 1)	1
Total	142

Bowling: A.V. Bedser 14-4-23-4, Surridge 16-1-53-5, Parker 6-3-4-0, Laker 17-4-42-0, Lock 14-9-15-0, E.A. Bedser 4-2-4-0.

Surrey: First innings

L.B. Fishlock c Cooper b Jenkins	43
E.A. Bedser b Perks	25
H.S. Squires b Jenkins	24
B. Constable b Perks	0
J.F. Parker c Yarnold b Jenkins	57
M.R. Barton lbw b Howorth	4
A.J. McIntyre c Outschoorn b Jenkins	13
J.C. Laker c Jenkins b Howorth	7
A.V. Bedser b Jenkins	0
W.S. Surridge c Perks b Jenkins	0
G.A.R. Lock not out	4
Extras (b 1, lb 2)	3
Total	180

Bowling: Perks 24-11-38-2, Wyatt 7-2-22-0, Jenkins 27-4-112-6, Howorth 10.1-7-5-2.

Worcestershire: Second innings

E. Cooper c Squires b Lock	60
D. Kenyon b E.A. Bedser	51
L. Outschoorn b E.A. Bedser	7
C.H. Palmer b A.V. Bedser	35
M.L.Y. Ainsworth c McIntyre b Lock	0
R.E. Bird b Lock	0
R.E.S. Wyatt c Lock b A.V. Bedser	48
R.O. Jenkins c McIntyre b A.V. Bedser	11
R. Howorth c Surridge b Laker	31
H. Yarnold not out	0
R.T.D. Perks c Parker b A.V. Bedser	0
Extras (b 8, lb 1, nb 2)	11
Total	254

Bowling: A.V. Bedser 25-6-52-4, Surridge 17-3-47-0, Parker 4-1-10-0, Laker 20-12-21-1, Lock 35-15-65-3, E.A. Bedser 24-9-48-2.

Surrey: Second innings

L.B. Fishlock c Bird b Jenkins	43
E.A. Bedser lbw b Wyatt	9
H.S. Squires b Perks	7
B. Constable c Yarnold b Perks	13
J.F. Parker c Outschoorn b Howorth	31
M.R. Barton c and b Jenkins	1
A.J. McIntyre st Yarnold b Jenkins	0
J.C. Laker c Outschoorn b Howorth	0
A.V. Bedser c and b Jenkins	0
W.S. Surridge c and b Jenkins	0
G.A.R. Lock not out	0
Extras (lb 3)	3
Total	107

Bowling: Perks 13-5-18-2, Wyatt 9-4-16-1, Jenkins 15.3-2-54-5, Howorth 14-7-16-2.

LEFT Roly Jenkins: two hat-tricks and eleven wickets in the match

1949

THE NEW ZEALAND side under W.A. Hadlee did much to enliven the fine English summer of 1949. Their batting was far stronger than their bowling, as was England's. It was not surprising then that all four Tests were drawn. In other matches their thirteen wins included eight against counties, and they were beaten only once, by the University on a difficult pitch at Oxford.

Two left-handers, M.P. Donnelly and B. Sutcliffe, were their star batsmen among no fewer than eight who topped 1,000 runs. Martin Donnelly scored 2,287, average 61, Bert Sutcliffe 2,626, average 59. Of the two Donnelly was the stylist, but Sutcliffe, too, had a free, pleasing method which served his country admirably for the first two decades after the war. At Southend against Essex he got into trim for the last Test by making 243 and 100 not out – well over half the runs scored by his side.

Sutcliffe makes more records

BERT SUTCLIFFE set up two more **New Zealand** records in the match with **Essex** at Southend yesterday.

In scoring a not out 100 he became the first member of a New Zealand touring side to make two separate hundreds in a match in England and also the first to complete 2,000 runs in a season. His 243 in the first innings was the highest score ever made here by a member of a New Zealand touring side.

News Chronicle, 13 August, 1949

No Test series was contested in a better spirit than that of 1949. The New Zealanders were shrewdly led and managed by Walter Hadlee and J.H. Phillipps respectively. They brought to the mother-country, still rationed, a plentiful supply of food parcels – a gesture which naturally made them more than ordinarily welcome!

ESSEX v NEW ZEALANDERS
Played at Southend, 10, 11, 12 August, 1949.
Result: Match drawn.

New Zealanders: First innings

B. Sutcliffe c Pearce b Vigar		243
V.J. Scott b P. Smith		29
J.R. Reid b R. Smith		4
W.A. Hadlee b P. Smith		55
M.P. Donnelly c Vigar b R. Smith		20
F.B. Smith c Vigar b R. Smith		0
F.L.H. Mooney c Wade b R. Smith		4
T.B. Burtt b P. Smith		18
C.C. Burke not out		27
H.B. Cave c P. Smith b Vigar		2
G.F. Cresswell c Wade b P. Smith		1
Extras (b 8, lb 7, w 2)		17
Total		420

Bowling: R. Smith 36-9-93-4, Pullinger 30-3-113-0, P. Smith 43.4-4-148-4, Vigar 12-0-49-2.

Essex: First innings

T.C. Dodds lbw b Burtt		82
S.J. Cray c Donnelly b Burtt		29
F.H. Vigar c Sutcliffe b Cave		89
S.C. Eve c Scott b Cresswell		40
D.J. Insole c Mooney b Cave		23
R. Horsfall c and b Cresswell		9
T.N. Pearce run out		6
R. Smith b Cresswell		12
T.P.B. Smith b Cave		0
T.H. Wade not out		2
G.R. Pullinger b Cave		0
Extras (b 9, lb 1, nb 2)		12
Total		304

Bowling: Cave 24.5-2-82-4, Cresswell 29-7-63-3, Burtt 23-6-65-2, Burke 14-0-52-0, Sutcliffe 6-0-30-0.

New Zealanders: Second innings

B. Sutcliffe not out		100
V.J. Scott c Wade b Pullinger		25
J.R. Reid lbw b R. Smith		7
W.A. Hadlee b R. Smith		57
M.P. Donnelly lbw b Vigar		1
F.B. Smith c Wade b Pullinger		7
F.L.H. Mooney c Vigar b Pullinger		4
T.B. Burtt c and b Vigar		7
C.C. Burke lbw b Vigar		5
H.B. Cave } did not bat		
C.F. Cresswell }		
Extras (b 1, lb 4)		5
Total (8 wickets declared)		218

Bowling: R. Smith 24-1-68-2, Pullinger 19-3-58-3, P. Smith 8-0-46-0, Vigar 7-0-41-3.

Essex: Second innings

T.C. Dodds c Sutcliffe b Cave		7
S.J. Cray c Sutcliffe b Burtt		60
F.H. Vigar st Reid b Burke		46
S.C. Eve b Cave		69
D.J. Insole not out		25
R. Horsfall }		
T.N. Pearce }		
R. Smith } did not bat		
T.P.B. Smith }		
T.H. Wade }		
G.R. Pullinger }		
Extras (b 4, lb 5)		9
Total (4 wickets)		216

Bowling: Cave 15-1-39-2, Cresswell 16-3-32-0, Burtt 16-5-47-1, Burke 11-1-66-1, Sutcliffe 3-0-23-0.

RIGHT Walter Hadlee: captain of a successful and popular New Zealand side.

OPPOSITE The forceful Bert Sutcliffe

TEAMWORK GAINED WEST INDIES WIN BY 326 RUNS

Great Bowling Feat By Two Men

By E. W. SWANTON

LORD'S. Thursday.

SOON after lunch to-day West Indies gained the victory that had seemed theirs from the time on Monday afternoon when England's batting failed against Ramadhin and Valentine. The difference was 326 runs. Thus West Indies follow South Africa, who not only chose Lord's as the scene of their first and only success in a Test in England 15 years ago, but also won by a handsome and conclusive margin.

Daily Telegraph, 30 June, 1950

ENGLAND v WEST INDIES

Played at Lord's, 24, 26, 27, 28, 29 June, 1950.
Result: West Indies won by 326 runs.

West Indies: First innings

A.F. Rae c and b Jenkins	106
J.B. Stollmeyer lbw b Wardle	20
F.M.M. Worrell b Bedser	52
E. de C. Weekes b Bedser	63
C.L. Walcott† st Evans b Jenkins	14
G.E. Gomez st Evans b Jenkins	1
R.J. Christiani b Bedser	33
J.D.C. Goddard* b Wardle	14
P.E. Jones c Evans b Jenkins	0
S. Ramadhin not out	1
A.L. Valentine c Hutton b Jenkins	5
Extras (b 10, lb 5, w 1, nb 1)	17
Total	326

Fall of Wickets: 1/37, 2/128, 3/233, 4/262, 5/273, 6/274, 7/320, 8/320, 9/320, 10/326.
Bowling: Bedser 40-14-60-3, Edrich 16-4-30-0, Jenkins 35.2-6-116-5, Wardle 17-6-46-2, Berry 19-7-45-0, Yardley 4-1-12-0.

England: First innings

L. Hutton st Walcott b Valentine	35
C. Washbrook st Walcott b Ramadhin	36
W.J. Edrich c Walcott b Ramadhin	8
G.H.G. Doggart lbw b Ramadhin	0
W.G.A. Parkhouse b Valentine	0
N.W.D. Yardley* b Valentine	16
T.G. Evans† b Ramadhin	8
R.O. Jenkins c Walcott b Valentine	4
J.H. Wardle not out	33
A.V. Bedser b Ramadhin	5
R. Berry c Goddard b Jones	2
Extras (b 2, lb 1, w 1)	4
Total	151

Fall of Wickets: 1/62, 2/74, 3/74, 4/75, 5/86, 6/102, 7/110, 8/113, 9/122, 10/151.
Bowling: Jones 8.4-2-13-1, Worrell 10-4-20-0, Valentine 45-28-48-4, Ramadhin 43-27-66-5.

West Indies: Second innings

A.E. Rae b Jenkins	24
J.B. Stollmeyer b Jenkins	30
F.M.M. Worrell c Doggart b Jenkins	45
E. de C. Weekes run out	63
C.L. Walcott† (6) not out	168
G.E. Gomez (7) c Edrich b Bedser	70
R.J. Christiani (8) not out	5
J.D.C. Goddard* (5) c Evans b Jenkins	11
Extras (lb 8, nb 1)	9
Total (6 wickets declared)	425

P.E. Jones, S. Ramadhin and A.L. Valentine did not bat.

Fall of Wickets: 1/48, 2/75, 3/108, 4/146, 5/199, 6/410.
Bowling: Bedser 44-16-80-1, Edrich 13-2-37-0, Jenkins 59-13-174-4, Wardle 30-10-58-0, Berry 32-15-67-0.

England: Second innings

L. Hutton b Valentine	10
C. Washbrook b Ramadhin	114
W.J. Edrich c Jones b Ramadhin	8
G.H.G. Doggart b Ramadhin	25
W.G.A. Parkhouse c Goddard b Valentine	48
N.W.D. Yardley* c Weekes b Valentine	19
T.G. Evans† c Rae b Ramadhin	2
R.O. Jenkins b Ramadhin	4
J.H. Wardle lbw b Worrell	21
A.V. Bedser b Ramadhin	0
R. Berry not out	0
Extras (b 16, lb 7)	23
Total	274

Fall of Wickets: 1/28, 2/57, 3/140, 4/218, 5/228, 6/238, 7/245, 8/248, 9/258, 10/274.
Bowling: Jones 7-1-22-0, Worrell 22.3-9-39-1, Valentine 71-47-79-3, Ramadhin 72-43-86-6, Gomez 13-1-25-0, Goddard 6-6-0-0.

IT TOOK the West Indies 11 Tests, spread over more than twenty years, to beat England on an English pitch. When they did so, at Lord's in June 1950, nothing could have been more complete or clear-cut. They batted to the delight of all on the first day and on the second reduced England's batsmen to a state of embarrassing immobility. The respective first innings performances were broadly repeated in the

BELOW LEFT 'Sonny' Ramadhin: England's tormentor displays his supple action

BELOW The Lord's calypso band serenade in celebration

second, bringing runaway victory by 326 runs.

The quality of the new generation of West Indian batsmen was well enough appreciated. What came as such an overwhelming surprise was the mesmerizing effect of two young spin bowlers who had been brought over, with absolutely no experience, on brilliant selectorial hunches. 'Sonny' Ramadhin bowled both off- and leg-break, finger-spin from the front of the hand with a quick rotary motion and using the left arm as a screen that made it extremely difficult to determine in advance which ball was which. 'Alf'

Valentine was an orthodox left-armer with an unusual power of spin.

Their match figures, on a wicket plumb throughout tell an astonishing story:

	Overs	Maidens	Runs	Wickets
Ramadhin	115	70	152	11
Valentine	116	75	127	7

So far as I recall by the end of the match the strolling bands were already singing the calypso that became famous, about 'Those little pals of mine, Ramadhin and Valentine.'

The West Indians had arrived with a vengeance – and at Lord's, too.

1950

GENTLEMEN v PLAYERS
Played at Lord's, 26, 27, 28 July, 1950.
Result: Match drawn.

Gentlemen: First innings
R.T. Simpson c and b Bedser	10
J.G. Dewes c Washbrook b Tattersall	94
G.H.G. Doggart b Wright	75
D.B. Carr b Tattersall	0
D.J. Insole c Evans b Wright	4
N.W.D. Yardley run out	5
T.E. Bailey c Parkhouse b Bedser	5
F.R. Brown b Tattersall	122
J.J. Warr b Wright	2
D.V. Brennan b Hollies	0
C.J. Knott not out	1
Extras (b 5, lb 2)	7
Total	325

Bowling: Bedser 23-2-77-2, Shackleton 18-3-51-0, Tattersall 16.4-6-38-3, Hollies 23-8-49-1, Wright 25-4-103-3.

Players: First innings
H. Gimblett lbw b Brown	23
C. Washbrook c Insole b Bailey	0
W.G.A. Parkhouse b Brown	29
D.J. Kenyon lbw b Brown	5
H.E. Dollery c Brennan b Doggart	123
T.G. Evans b Bailey	19
D. Shackleton c Simpson b Knott	25
A.V. Bedser c Dewes b Knott	59
R. Tattersall lbw b Doggart	12
D.V.P. Wright not out	6
W.E. Hollies not out	1
Extras (b 2, lb 4)	6
Total (9 wickets declared)	308

Bowling: Bailey 25-6-65-2, Warr 21-5-66-0, Yardley 10-1-23-0, Brown 28-3-63-3, Knott 21-2-63-2, Carr 2-0-11-0, Doggart 4-1-11-2.

Gentlemen: Second innings
R.T. Simpson lbw b Hollies	69
J.G. Dewes b Tattersall	48
G.H.G. Doggart lbw b Wright	36
D.B. Carr c Bedser b Wright	17
D.J. Insole not out	38
F.R. Brown not out	22
N.W.D. Yardley	
T.E. Bailey	
J.J. Warr ⎫ did not bat	
D.V. Brennan	
C.J. Knott	
Extras (b 1, lb 3, nb 1)	5
Total (4 wickets declared)	235

Bowling: Bedser 12-0-41-0, Shackleton 13-0-60-0, Tattersall 10-0-35-1, Hollies 12-1-43-1, Wright 9-0-51-2.

Players: Second innings
H. Gimblett c Knott b Bailey	14
C. Washbrook c and b Brown	43
W.G.A. Parkhouse c Brown b Knott	81
D.J. Kenyon c Brennan b Bailey	54
H.E. Dollery c Yardley b Knott	20
T.G. Evans st Brennan b Knott	9
D. Shackleton c Insole b Knott	2
A.V. Bedser b Bailey	10
R. Tattersall st Brennan b Knott	0
D.V.P. Wright not out	2
W.E. Hollies not out	0
Extras (b 2, lb 5)	7
Total (9 wickets)	242

Bowling: Bailey 14-2-59-3, Warr 8-1-38-0, Yardley 4-0-13-0, Brown 10-0-59-1, Knott 11-0-66-5.

ABOVE RIGHT F.R. Brown, England captain at the age of forty

F. R. BROWN HITS 122 OUT OF 131 IN 1¾ HOURS

Cambridge Men Rescue The Gentlemen
From E. W. SWANTON

Daily Telegraph, 27 July, 1950

GENTLEMEN v PLAYERS was always a specially important match when an when an MCC side was due to be picked for an overseas tour. In late July 1950 the spotlight was even brighter than usual because the leadership of the tour to Australia was due to be announced forthwith. It had recently become known that F.G. Mann and N.W.D. Yardley, both experienced as Test captains, had had to decline for business reasons. The names canvassed included Tom Dollery, the popular captain of Warwickshire, D.J. Insole, and G.H.G. Doggart, Cambridge University captains in 1949 and 1950 and

F.R. Brown, an all-rounder of the ripe 1930s vintage now leading Northamptonshire with spirit, but in his fortieth year.

The choice of Brown looks to have been more obvious retrospectively than it did at the time. As it happened he seized the occasion to play a magnificent forcing innings against the cream of the professional bowling and he proved a great success in Australia both as captain and cricketer. Brown's innings set the character for a gloriously exciting match which ended with the Players' last wicket pair together needing 11 runs for victory.

AMES HITS 100th CENTURY
Gives Kent Victory

Star, 11 August, 1950

1950

ON THE LAST day of the 1950 Canterbury Week Leslie Ames won a match for Kent and in the process reached his 100th hundred. Only eleven batsmen in history had previously done so, and only eight more have since reached this truly prestigious goal. None of them has been a wicket-keeper, as Ames was through the greatest part of his career, though not at the end.

I happened to be on the air as he approached and finally reached the hundred. One sees Les clearly in the mind's eye chasing nimbly down the pitch, hitting the spinners on the half-volley or on the full, always balanced, never in a rush. There seemed little reason why he should not continue for several years more, but after leading a Commonwealth team to India and Ceylon that winter he broke down with the recurrence of a back injury in Kent's opening match of 1951 and could not play again.

KENT v MIDDLESEX
Played at Canterbury, 9, 10, 11 August, 1950.
Result: Kent won by four wickets.

Middlesex: First innings

J.D. Robertson st Evans b Wright	40
J.G. Dewes c Evans b Wright	60
W.J. Edrich b Ridgeway	6
H.P. Sharp b Dovey	62
S.M. Brown b Wright	19
L.H. Compton b Wright	7
F.J. Titmus c Evans b Ridgeway	9
J.M. Sims c Fagg b Ridgeway	13
J.J. Warr b Wright	4
J.A. Young b Dovey	14
A.E. Moss not out	7
Extras (b 4, lb 4)	8
Total	249

Bowling: Ridgeway 31-9-86-3, Mallett 20-5-58-0, Dovey 19.5-4-36-2, Wright 30-8-61-5.

Kent: First innings

A.E. Fagg run out	88
D.G. Clark c L. Compton b Warr	6
L.E.G. Ames c L. Compton b Warr	4
P. Hearn st L. Compton b Sims	17
H.A. Pawson not out	103
T.G. Evans c Sims b Warr	6
A. Woollett c Young b Warr	10
A.W.H. Mallett not out	15
R.R. Dovey	
D.V.P. Wright } did not bat	
F. Ridgeway	
Extras (lb 4, w 1)	5
Total (6 wickets declared)	254

Bowling: Warr 26-8-67-4, Moss 21-4-76-0, Sims 16-2-53-1, Young 14-8-15-0, Titmus 11-2-38-0.

Middlesex: Second innings

J.D. Robertson b Dovey	54
J.G. Dewes c Pawson b Dovey	32
W.J. Edrich not out	77
H.P. Sharp c Clark b Wright	21
S.M. Brown not out	51
L.H. Compton	
F.J. Titmus	
J.M. Sims	
J.J. Warr } did not bat	
J.A. Young	
A.E. Moss	
Extras (b 6)	6
Total (3 wickets declared)	241

Bowling: Ridgeway 22-8-59-0, Mallett 27-8-65-0, Dovey 20-4-64-2, Wright 11-2-47-1.

Kent: Second innings

A.E. Fagg c L. Compton b Warr	0
D.G. Clark run out	3
L.E.G. Ames c Moss b Young	131
P. Hearn b Young	30
H.A. Pawson b Warr	57
A. Woollett not out	0
A.W.H. Mallett b Warr	9
R.R. Dovey not out	5
T.G. Evans	
D.V.P. Wright } did not bat	
F. Ridgeway	
Extras (b 4)	4
Total (6 wickets)	239

Bowling: Warr 11-1-57-3, Moss 5-2-18-0, Sims 14-1-53-0, Young 19-3-90-2, Titmus 0.5-0-4-0, Edrich 1-0-13-0.

LEFT L.E.G. Ames: the only wicket-keeper to reach a hundred hundreds

1951

AUSTRALIA v ENGLAND

Played at Melbourne,
23, 24 (no play), 26, 27, 28 February, 1951.
Result: England won by eight wickets.

Australia: First innings

J.W. Burke c Tattersall b Bedser	11
A.R. Morris lbw b Brown	50
A.L. Hassett* c Hutton b Brown	92
R.N. Harvey c Evans b Brown	1
K.R. Miller c and b Brown	7
G.B. Hole b Bedser	18
I.W. Johnson lbw b Bedser	1
R.R. Lindwall c Compton b Bedser	21
D. Tallon† c Hutton b Bedser	1
W.A. Johnston not out	12
J.B. Iverson c Washbrook b Brown	0
Extras (b 2, lb 1)	3
Total	217

Fall of Wickets: 1/23, 2/111, 3/115, 4/123, 5/156, 6/166, 7/184, 8/187, 9/216, 10/217.
Bowling: Bedser 22-5-46-5, Bailey 9-1-29-0, Brown 18-4-49-5, Wright 9-1-50-0, Tattersall 11-3-40-0.

England: First innings

L. Hutton b Hole	79
C. Washbrook c Tallon b Miller	27
R.T. Simpson not out	156
D.C.S. Compton c Miller b Lindwall	11
D.S. Sheppard c Tallon b Miller	1
F.R. Brown* b Lindwall	6
T.G. Evans† b Miller	1
A.V. Bedser b Lindwall	11
T.E. Bailey c Johnson b Iverson	5
D.V.P. Wright lbw b Iverson	3
R. Tattersall b Miller	10
Extras (b 9, lb 1)	10
Total	320

Fall of Wickets: 1/40, 2/171, 3/204, 4/205, 5/212, 6/213, 7/228, 8/236, 9/246, 10/320.
Bowling: Lindwall 21-1-77-3, Miller 21.7-5-76-4, Johnston 12-1-55-0, Iverson 20-4-52-2, Johnson 11-1-40-0, Hole 5-0-10-1.

Australia: Second innings

J.W. Burke c Hutton b Bedser	1
A.R. Morris lbw b Bedser	4
A.L. Hassett* b Wright	48
R.N. Harvey lbw b Wright	52
K.R. Miller c and b Brown	0
G.B. Hole b Bailey	63
I.W. Johnson c Brown b Wright	0
R.R. Lindwall b Bedser	14
D. Tallon† not out	2
W.A. Johnston b Bedser	1
J.B. Iverson c Compton b Bedser	0
Extras (b 2, lb 8, w 1, nb 1)	12
Total	197

Fall of Wickets: 1/5, 2/6, 3/87, 4/89, 5/142, 6/142, 7/192, 8/196, 9/197, 10/197.
Bowling: Bedser 20.3-4-59-5, Bailey 15-3-32-1, Brown 9-1-32-1, Wright 15-2-56-3, Tattersall 5-2-6-0.

England: Second innings

L. Hutton not out	60
C. Washbrook c Lindwall b Johnston	7
R.T. Simpson run out	15
D.C.S. Compton not out	11
Extras (lb 2)	2
Total (2 wickets)	95

D.S. Sheppard, F.R. Brown*, T.G. Evans†, A.V. Bedser, T.E. Bailey, D.V.P. Wright and R. Tattersall did not bat.

Fall of Wickets: 1/32, 2/62.
Bowling: Lindwall 2-0-12-0, Miller 2-0-5-0, Johnston 11-3-36-1, Iverson 12-2-32-0, Johnson 1-0-1-0, Hole 1-0-3-0, Hassett 0.6-0-4-0.

RIGHT Victory at last: Hassett applauds

AT MELBOURNE in the Fifth Test of the MCC tour of 1950-51 England at last tasted the fruits of a post-war victory over Australia. They did so by eight wickets after losing the toss on a pitch that remained plumb throughout, and in so doing gained tangible redress for the ill-luck that they endured in the earlier Tests.

Yet this win, though comfortable in the end, would probably have eluded them but for an improbable stand of 74 for the last wicket which stretched the first innings lead from 29 to 103. This was Reg Simpson's finest hour. After Hutton and he had made 131 together for the second wicket England's batting folded against Miller and Lindwall so that after Hutton left seven further wickets fell for 75 runs. Simpson was 92 when joined by the number 11, Roy Tattersall (career average 9.35!). Simpson thereupon cut loose with a stream of fine strokes, taking out his bat for 156. Tattersall contributed a staunch defence and 10 runs. (On being

ENGLAND WIN LAST TEST BY EIGHT WICKETS

Bedser, Hutton and Simpson the Heroes

From E. W. SWANTON
MELBOURNE, Wednesday.

AT last! England's victory by eight wickets in the fifth Test here this evening has altered the whole aspect of the tour as it will be remembered by the players taking part and by those both at home and in Australia who have been following the fortunes of the series.

Daily Telegraph, 1 March, 1951

drafted out from Manchester to join the team in January he found that his feet swelled and his boots grew too tight. I am proud to reveal that for this Test he borrowed mine!)

By adding five wickets to his five in the first innings Alec Bedser kept Australia on a tight rein, as he had done throughout the series. The English out-cricket in Australia's second innings was admirable, as indeed it had been constantly during the series. Bedser with 30 wickets and Hutton, who averaged 88 where only two other men exceeded 20, were both at their peak on this tour. So also, as all-rounder and captain, was Freddie Brown.

102

CAMBRIDGE WERE strong favourites to win the University Match of 1951, but in an intensely and keenly-contested game they were beaten by 21 runs with seventeen minutes to spare.

Michael Melford had joined the *Daily Telegraph* in 1950 as understudy to me for the cricket and rugger, and so remained until he transferred to the *Sunday Telegraph* on its foundation in 1961. As I was covering a Test at Old Trafford he reported this match, and as an Oxford man will have hailed the result with quiet satisfaction – only slightly tempered by the fact that his fellow-Carthusians, Peter May (whose biography he wrote many years later) and Oliver Popplewell were on the losing side. It was a strange fact that May, by general consent the best of all English post-war batsmen, in his three years in the Cambridge XI failed to reach 40 against Oxford.

The University Match, though no longer a notable social occasion, still at this time enjoyed considerable prestige and public support. The two sides at Lord's in 1951 contained six current or budding Test cricketers.

EXCITING WIN FOR OXFORD

DIVECHA BOWLS OUT CAMBRIDGE

By MICHAEL MELFORD

The sustained tension and excitement of the last afternoon of the University match of 1951 is not likely to be forgotten by anyone present at Lord's yesterday. At the end of it, Oxford had won by 21 runs, with only 17 minutes remaining for play.

Since one o'clock Cambridge had fought desperately on an awkward, turning wicket against some magnificent bowling by Divecha, who took seven for 62, for the 219 they required to win. But with 45 minutes left they still needed 63 from their last two wickets.

A stout-hearted ninth wicket stand by Hayward and Marlar added 41 in 25 minutes and brought Cambridge within sight of victory. But Divecha, who had been bowling his off-breaks almost unchanged since lunch, had Hayward caught at the wicket in his 44th over and gained for Oxford a victory that on all known form had seemed next to impossible.

If ever a game of cricket was won by fielding, this was it. Oxford were, and looked, a mediocre batting side. They certainly bowled to the limit of their ability, but it was the power to back their bowling with some of the best fielding of recent years that won the day.

BOOBBYER'S FINE INNINGS

There had been only a little rain in the night and while Oxford batted in the morning the wicket was placid enough. In 80 minutes, however, the last four wickets could make only 49.

Mitchell batted capably for half an hour until Boobbyer's innings of 80 ended after he had batted for 10 minutes under five hours.

It was not pretty to watch, for Boobbyer's main assets are a wonderful eye and endless patience; but the value of the performance is obvious.

Cambridge had 4½ hours in which to make their runs. They were away to an excellent start, but when May came in at 44 the ball had begun to come through at odd heights.

Soon Sheppard met an almost unplayable ball from Divecha which stood up and, from his glove, flew high into the leg trap. Cockett and Stevenson soon followed the same way, and with the score 75 for four, May was left with an oppressive responsibility on a deteriorating wicket.

Daily Telegraph, 11 July, 1951

OXFORD v CAMBRIDGE
Played at Lord's, 7, 9, 10 July, 1951.
Result: Oxford won by 21 runs.

Oxford: First innings

M.B. Hofmeyr* lbw b Warr	40
B. Boobbyer c May b Marlar	17
P.J. Whitcombe c Subba Row b Marlar	10
D.B. Carr c Popplewell b Marlar	34
P.D.S. Blake c Subba Row b Marlar	24
C.E. Winn c Warr b Stevenson	6
D.J. Lewis c Hayward b Warr	19
R.V. Divecha b Warr	0
W.M. Mitchell c May b Warr	9
A.D. Jose b Marlar	1
J.N. Bartlett not out	4
Extras (b 11, lb 2, w 1)	14
Total	178

Bowling: Warr 21-13-31-4, Wait 14-2-26-0, Hayward 9-1-28-0, Marlar 26-11-41-5, Subba Row 14-5-31-0, Stevenson 5-2-7-1.

Cambridge: First innings

D.S. Sheppard c Whitcombe b Divecha	23
K.P.A. Mathews lbw b Mitchell	25
W.I.D. Hayward lbw b Jose	9
P.B.H. May c sub b Divecha	30
J.A. Cockett b Jose	0
R. Subba Row not out	37
M.H. Stevenson c Jose b Mitchell	0
O.B. Popplewell run out	10
J.J. Warr* lbw b Jose	5
R.G. Marlar b Jose	0
O.J. Wait run out	2
Extras (b 22, lb 5)	27
Total	168

Bowling: Jose 16.4-4-46-4, Divecha 23-10-36-2, Mitchell 17-5-45-2, Carr 3-2-2-0, Bartlett 11-7-12-0.

Oxford: Second innings

M.B. Hofmeyr* run out	19
B. Boobbyer c and b Subba Row	80
P.J. Whitcombe c Subba Row b Wait	5
D.B. Carr c Subba Row b Marlar	50
P.D.S. Blake c Cockett b Subba Row	1
C.E. Winn st Popplewell b Subba Row	0
D.J. Lewis c Popplewell b Subba Row	0
R.V. Divecha c Sheppard b Warr	14
W.M. Mitchell not out	17
A.D. Jose b Marlar b Subba Row	0
J.N. Bartlett c Popplewell b Warr	0
Extras (b 14, lb 2, w 5, nb 1)	22
Total	208

Bowling: Warr 29-9-45-2, Wait 19-5-32-1, Hayward 12-3-16-0, Marlar 26-8-64-1, Subba Row 9.1-2-21-5, Stevenson 6-3-8-0.

Cambridge: Second innings

D.S. Sheppard c Boobbyer b Divecha	42
K.P.A. Mathews lbw b Divecha	15
W.I.D. Hayward c Whitcombe b Divecha	35
P.B.H. May c Whitcombe b Bartlett	33
J.A. Cockett c Carr b Divecha	0
R. Subba Row b Bartlett	4
M.H. Stevenson c Carr b Divecha	7
O.B. Popplewell b Divecha	1
J.J. Warr* b Divecha	28
R.G. Marlar c Whitcombe b Bartlett	17
O.J. Wait not out	0
Extras (b 8, lb 6, w 1)	15
Total	197

Bowling: Jose 5-0-17-0, Divecha 43.2-19-62-7, Mitchell 16-5-42-0, Carr 6-0-14-0, Bartlett 34-16-47-3.

LEFT R.V. Divecha in action against Cambridge at Lord's

1952

Heartbreak for 'Mankad the marvel'

By PETER LAKER

THIS second Test at Lord's—a good thing for England today—will always be remembered by India's gallant little warrior, Vinoo Mankad, as the "heartbreak Test."

The "Haslingden marvel" gave more than can be expected of any man during a marathon innings of 184 in four hours twenty-five minutes, the highest individual score by any Indian in a Test—and the finest exhibition of fighting cricket ever seen at Lord's.

When he finally left with the total at 270, his third wicket stand with Vijay Hazare (49) had yielded 211 in three hours thirty-five minutes

And India, 32 runs behind, were still in a position to cheat their opponents of victory No. 2. Then . . . well, you just couldn't call it Test cricket!

Then the side's strange temperament took over and the remaining batsmen panicked, playing wild strokes that would have shamed a schoolboy

The score tumbled sensationally to 323 for eight, and although Gopinath Ramchand clouted 42 in a hectic record ninth wicket Test partnership of 54 with Shinde, it was too late. Freddie Trueman stepped in and polished off the innings for 378, and England required 77.

The world has surely never produced a cricketer to surpass the astonishing all-round ability and guts of this thirty-five-year-old player Mankad.

Then it happened Jim Laker unexpectedly pushed an off-spinner past Mankad's aggressive bat

Daily Mirror, 24 June, 1952

The Queen congratulates Mankad the Test 'wizard'

India's cricket "wizard," Vinoo Mankad, was congratulated by the Queen after his magnificent "back to the wall" innings of 184 for India in the Test Match against England at Lord's yesterday. The Queen arrived at Lord's after lunch and watched play from the pavilion

Daily Mirror, 24 June, 1952

RIGHT Vinoo Mankad: hero on the losing side

THE INDIANS of 1952, like their teams to England hitherto and for many years afterwards, were no match for their opponents on English pitches, formidable though they were on their own. In Vinoo Mankad they had an all-rounder of world class and it was the height of misfortune that he was contracted to Haslingden and could play only in this and the subsequent two Tests. His performance in the Second Test at Lord's in terms of sheer stamina had seldom been approached. He scored 72 and 184, going in first despite bowling 73 overs of slow left-arm spin in England's first innings for a return of 5 for 196. In the second he bowled another 24.

Note that Len Hutton, the first professional to lead England at home, was considered very much on trial in this, his second Test as captain. The *Daily Mirror* gives the news of his appointment for the remaining two Tests. Peter Laker, who had played a little for Sussex, was in 1952 at the start of a long career as the paper's cricket-writer. Hence perhaps a predilection for superlatives.

ENGLAND v INDIA

Played at Lord's,
19, 20, 21, 23, 24 June, 1952.
Result: England won by eight wickets.

India: First innings

M.H. Mankad c Watkins b Trueman	72
Pankaj Roy c and Bedser	35
P.R. Umrigar b Trueman	5
V.S. Hazare* not out	69
V.L. Manjrekar lbw b Bedser	5
D.G. Phadkar b Watkins	8
H.R. Adhikari lbw b Watkins	0
G.S. Ramchand b Trueman	18
M.K. Mantri† b Trueman	1
S.G. Shinde st Evans, b Watkins	5
Ghulam Ahmed b Jenkins	0
Extras (b 7, nb 10)	17
Total	235

Fall of Wickets: 1/106, 2/116, 3/118, 4/126, 5/135, 6/139, 8/167, 8/180, 9/221, 10/235.
Bowling: Bedser 33-8-62-2, Trueman 25-3-72-4, Jenkins 7.3-1-26-1, Laker 12-5-21-0, Watkins 17-7-37-3.

England: First innings

L. Hutton* c Mantri b Hazare	150
R.T. Simpson b Mankad	53
P.B.H. May c Mantri b Mankad	74
D.C.S. Compton lbw b Hazare	6
T.W. Graveney c Mantri b Ghulam Ahmed	73
A.J. Watkins b Mankad	0
T.G. Evans† c and b Ghulam Ahmed	104
R.O. Jenkins st Mantri b Mankad	21
J.C. Laker not out	23
A.V. Bedser c Ramchand b Mankad	3
F.S. Trueman b Ghulam Ahmed	17
Extras (b 8, lb 5)	13
Total	537

Fall of Wickets: 1/106, 2/264, 3/272, 4/292, 5/292, 6/451, 7/468, 8/506, 9/514, 10/537.
Bowling: Phadkar 27-8-44-0, Ramchand 29-8-67-0, Hazare 24-4-196-5, Mankad 73-24-196-5, Ghulam Ahmed 43.4-12-106-3, Shinde 6-0-43-0, Umrigar 4-0-15-0.

India: Second innings

M.H. Mankad b Laker	184
Pankaj Roy b Bedser	0
P.R. Umrigar (7) b Trueman	14
V.S. Hazare* c Laker b Bedser	49
V.L. Manjrekar b Laker	1
D.G. Phadkar b Laker	16
H.R. Adhikari (3) b Trueman	16
G.S. Ramchand (9) b Trueman	42
M.K. Mantri† (8) c Compton b Laker	5
S.G. Shinde c Hutton b Trueman	14
Ghulam Ahmed not out	1
Extras (b 29, lb 3, nb 4)	36
Total	378

Fall of Wickets: 1/7, 2/59, 3/270, 4/272, 5/289, 6/312, 7/314, 8/323, 9/377, 10/378.
Bowling: Bedser 36-13-60-2, Trueman 27-4-110-4, Jenkins 10-1-40-0, Laker 39-15-102-4, Watkins 8-0-20-0, Compton 2-0-10-0.

England: Second innings

L. Hutton* not out	39
R.T. Simpson run out	2
P.B.H. May c Roy b Ghulam Ahmed	26
D.C.S. Compton not out	4
T.W. Graveney	
A.J. Watkins	
T.G. Evans†	
R.O. Jenkins	did not bat
J.C. Laker	
A.V. Bedser	
F.S. Trueman	
Extras (b 4, lb 4)	8
Total (2 wickets)	79

Fall of Wickets: 1/8, 2/71.
Bowling: Ramchand 1-0-5-0, Hazare 1-1-0-0, Mankad 24-12-35-0, Ghulam Ahmed 23.2-9-31-1.

HUTTON AGAIN

Len Hutton has accepted the England captaincy for remaining two matches against India

Lock is no-balled for throwing

By JOHN ROBERTSON

CONTROVERSY raged at the Oval yesterday when Fred Price, the former Middlesex wicketkeeper, thrice no-balled Tony Lock, the England and Surrey bowler, for throwing against the Indians.

It is almost unheard-of for a class slow left-hand bowler to be so treated and Price's action raises big problems for the M.C.C. and England.

Lock played in the last Test at Manchester, taking a number of Indian wickets, and no exception was then taken to his action.

In view of the Australian tour next season and our crying need for another Verity it must be settled once and for all whether Lock's action is fair or not.

He has played a big part in taking Surrey to the head of the championship and obviously his whole future may be at stake.

Our umpires are a vigilant, independent race and only last month Paddy Corrall, the former Leicester wicketkeeper, five times no-balled Cuan McCarthy, the South African fast bowler.

From time immemorial fast bowlers' actions have been queried but a slow, left-hander —I ask you!

Sections of the crowd showed their disapproval by yelling "no ball" continuously as Lock finished his over. After the innings there were some boos, apparently aimed at Price, and cries of "well bowled Lock."

Price, who refused to comment, was square-leg umpire.

Sunday Graphic, 27 July, 1952

THE FIRST of five matches during his career wherein Tony Lock was no-balled for throwing was that between Surrey and the Indians at The Oval at the end of July 1951. When earlier that summer Cuan McCarthy, the South African Test bowler in residence at Cambridge, had been called for throwing playing for the University at Worcester, it was the first case in England for forty-four years. For all practical purposes throwing had been eliminated from the game, largely by the combined efforts of Lord Harris and Sydney Pardon (editor of *Wisden*) at the turn of the century.

The case of Lock was specially significant because he had been capped by England for the first time only the previous week. It also boded ill that the umpire in question, Fred Price, the old Middlesex wicket-keeper, was roundly booed both by the crowd and the Surrey members. In calling Lock, Price had given expression to the thoughts of many that his faster ball at least was suspect. Would the selectors now name him for the next Test? John Robertson of the *Sunday Graphic* states here, reasonably enough, that the legitimacy or otherwise of his action should be settled once and for all. In fact they did choose him and their successors continued to do so for the next six years, albeit he was subsequently no-balled both in a Test and in a colony match during the MCC's West Indian tour of 1953-54.

Lock's bowling at times was an open reproach to all concerned, not excluding us cricket-writers, the only defence perhaps being that in the case of a slowish bowler no physical threat was involved and that, this being so, there was an understandable reluctance to put a livelihood in jeopardy. As is well-known, Lock remodelled his action on his own volition, after having seen in New Zealand an amateur film showing him bowling in Tests in England the previous summer; he was said to be horrified by what he saw.

The universal crack-down on illegal actions, in Australia as well as England, was not due for a long while yet. It was only effected following a debate on the matter at the ICC annual meeting at Lord's in July 1960.

RIGHT Tony Lock: from this position a throw could follow. His faster ball was particularly suspect

1953

THE *MANCHESTER GUARDIAN* headlines of 8 June 1953 tell a melancholy story which the report by H.M. (Harold Mather) explains plainly enough. It might however be added that the Somerset authorities must have been ludicrously optimistic if they had supposed that a pitch relaid in October would be fit for first-class cricket, whatever the intervening weather, and Coronation festivities or not, by the following May. 'Bertie' Buse was indeed hardly used.

Lancashire obviously ran away with the match when Marner and Wharton decided to take the long handle and made 70 together in twenty-five minutes. Nor could a captain wish for a better bowler in such circumstances than Roy Tattersall with his admirably controlled slow-medium off-breaks. This, by the way, was the first appearance for Somerset of another off-spinner, Brian Langford, the future captain and chairman of the county cricket committee, who, aged seventeen, in the following two matches in the Bath Festival took an astonishing 25 wickets.

Matches completed in a day have always been very rare occurrences – fewer than thirty cases in the last hundred years. Yet this was the fourth time Somerset had so suffered at Lancashire's expense.

SOMERSET v LANCASHIRE
Played at Bath, 8 June, 1953.
Result: Lancashire won by an innings and 24 runs.

Somerset: First innings 55 (Tattersall 7-25).

Lancashire: First innings 158 (P. Marner 44; Buse 6-41).

Somerset: Second innings 79 (J. Redman 27*; Tattersall 6-44, Statham 4-13).

RIGHT R. Tattersall: thirteen wickets in the match for Lancashire who defeated Somerset in a day. He was a very skilful – and underrated – bowler who should have played more than his 16 Tests

REMARKABLE DAY'S PLAY AT BATH
Cruel Blow to Buse's Benefit Match

FROM OUR SPECIAL CORRESPONDENT

BATH, SATURDAY.

At the end of one of the most remarkable days' cricket in recent years Lancashire not only had beaten Somerset by an innings and 24 runs here to-day, but had done so when some 55 minutes still remained for play.

Exponents of brighter cricket certainly could not have wished for more excitement than they had in this match, but even they could not want it produced by false conditions, as it was to-day. H. T. F. Buse, whose benefit match this was, lives here and is greatly respected in this city, possibly even a little more than he is elsewhere in the county. But it was more than regrettable that he chose a game on this ground for such an occasion. The club ground undoubtedly is not without its beauty, but the wicket is far from being up to county match standards. Though it was relaid in October the cold winds and other unhelpful weather retarded the normal process of knitting together. This in itself was a headache for the groundsman, but added to his troubles were the facts that the turf was unsuitable from the start and that because of Coronation festivities on the ground he was unable to give it the strict attention it required. The result was that when it was mowed on Wednesday only a negligible amount of grass was removed. Even before the start of play to-day the wicket itself was lacking in grass generally. and what there was looked more like dried moss. To-day's proceedings were. therefore. a natural outcome, for even bowlers could not predict what any ball would do.

An Ironic Fact

Criticism of batsmanship in such conditions would be futile and unjust. The bowlers made the most of their chances. Indeed, it was somewhat ironic that Buse should bowl so well as to take six for 41 and thus contribute to his own misfortune. It was, however, necessary only for any bowler to pitch an approximate length and immediately the unfortunate batsman had to decide what stroke to attempt to make or even whether to make one at all. Not surprisingly many wrong decisions were made, but in spite of the bowlers' efforts, and particularly those of Tattersall who never once lost his length, one's sympathy was with the strikers. The effects can perhaps best be seen from the details of Somerset's first innings. Not one man was bowled and apart from Buse and Deshon those who were caught fell almost the first time they chanced their arm.

Somerset are not strong at the best of times and to-day were without Hall. It must, therefore. have been cruel in the extreme that their opponents on such a wicket should be Lancashire, with one of the strongest, most varied attacks in the championship. Washbrook's opinion of the pitch was immediately shown, for he opened his attack with Statham and Tattersall. The former was not successful, but ninety minutes later the home side was out for 55. Tattersall having taken seven for 25 and not having had to work hard to do so. Lancashire did start somewhat better. but the dismissal of Ikin began a collapse and with five men out

Manchester Guardian, 8 June, 1953

for 46 they were not certain to gain the lead. But then came the most controlled and yet the boldest batting of the day.

Marner and Wharton were quiet only for a few balls, but then they began an onslaught. Fifteen runs were scored off an over by Lawrence, Marner hit the last four balls of the next over by Buse for six, two, four, six, and the pair later hit Redman for eighteen in an over. This may suggest wild hitting; in fact, it was not, and indeed it was refreshing to see the young Marner watch the ball so carefully and get so well over and behind it that when Wharton was bowled by Redman one thought their stand of seventy had lasted even fewer than 26 minutes. In the end Lancashire gained a lead of 103 and two hours twenty minutes still were left for play when Gimblett and Lawrence came out a second time.

Last Vain Effort

By this time the pitch was in an even worse condition, for the ball removed grass and earth each time it pitched. and soon Somerset were seven for four, three of the wickets this time having fallen to Statham. Buse and Stephenson, who hit Tattersall for a four and six off successive balls, then added nineteen, but nine wickets were down for 44 at 5 15 p.m., 65 minutes from the close of play. Fine batting by Redman and dour defiance by Langford then held up Lancashire for twenty minutes and added 35 runs, but the end was obvious. Tattersall this time took six for 44, and thus had thirteen wickets in one day for only 69 runs, easily the best bag of his career.

This was the first of three matches of the Bath cricket festival and at a meeting afterwards the home officials were considering taking the matches against Kent and Leicestershire to other grounds. If they do not a repetition of to-day's happenings is far from impossible. H. M.

THE FAMOUS partnership between W. Watson and T.E. Bailey which, against all the odds, saved their side from defeat in the Lord's Test of 1953 achieved the almost unprecedented distinction of providing the page one lead in the *Manchester Guardian*. Note that the story was written by Neville Cardus, no less. After the war he did not again write cricket for the paper on a regular basis but – such was the anticipation – was drafted in to report the 1953 series. It is a colourful, dramatic piece, reflecting the day's cricket in characteristically Cardusian language. My old nose tells me, though, that the opening paragraph for some reason was written in the office. Perhaps Neville had omitted to record the plain fact of the result. 'Terrific' is not his word for it! But 'Panic gibbered on the ground...' That's the ticket!

It is good to be reminded of that nostalgic summer. Lindsay Hassett's Australians wanted to see the Coronation, so their game with Nottinghamshire was amiably reduced to two days. The royal aura was still abroad when it came to the Lord's Test which is by its nature something of a Command Performance anyway. This was the exciting climax to what had been from the first a gripping Test Match. On the last morning Watson and Bailey came together with the score 74 for 4 and all but five hours of play yawning ahead against an attack consisting of Lindwall, Miller, Johnston, Davidson, Benaud and Ring. The occasion was hand-made for Trevor Bailey who, as the *Daily Telegraph* correspondent observed, 'expresses his true nature in a long, defensive vigil. Never has the dead bat stroke, both forward and back, been played hour after hour with more evident relish'.

Willie Watson, by contrast, was a left-hander with a good range of stroke

1953

and a fondness for deploying it. He batted now as the occasion called for, and for four hours and a bit the gallant partnership survived. Watson and Bailey were out in quick succession shortly before six o'clock. The latter, wrote Cardus 'drove mistakenly, and as he realised he was out threw his head back, put a hand to his brow, the living image of remorse and self-distrust'.

For a few overs now Australia were in with a chance, but Brown saw attack as the best defence, and by the time he stepped off the Test arena for the last time the day had been honourably, if narrowly saved.

MANCHESTER GUARDIAN

No. 33,286 ✠✠✠ WEDNESDAY JULY 1 1953 Price 3d

MIRACLE OF FAITH AT LORD'S

The Astonishing Watson and Bailey

LEFT NO TIME TO LOSE

Australia: 346 and 368. England: 372 and 282 for 7.
Match Drawn.

BY NEVILLE CARDUS

LORD'S, TUESDAY.

In a terrific closing period this evening there was still a chance for Australia to win. As six o'clock approached a heroic match-saving stand by Watson and Bailey was broken. Soon after this mishap to England Bailey got out. Now, with less than half an hour to pass, Australia strove to capture four wickets. England 246 for six.

Panic gibbered on the ground when Evans was nearly stumped off Benaud. Brown sent the temperature to fever point by massive hell-for-leather drives, powerful and ponderous and brave. Evans stood his ground impertinently, aggressively. So all the alarums died away in the evening's lovely mellowing sunshine.

It had been an afternoon of intense strain. We could suffer no further tug on the nerves when Brown was out after 25 minutes past six, except to feel he should have survived, because plainly he wanted to stay in the fight to the last.

The result, I think, did justice to both teams; neither quite deserved to win, and Watson's and Bailey's stand was not made of the stuff of which lost causes are compounded. It was a stand of noble martyrdom, and at the end it was the martyrs who each had been crowned with a laurel wreath.

who made the proper or fashionable genuflexion. And he nearly had Watson caught at the wicket when Watson was 74 at twenty-five minutes past three; but fortunately Watson missed his aim on the off-side.

Hassett Grows Impatient

At twenty minutes to four Lindwall went out of action; the only question which tormented me now was what he would be able to recapture of his true fire after tea. But Watson and Bailey, in spite of recurrent vicissitudes, seldom suggested a fatal error; and Australia's reserve bowling was palpably dependent on good luck and a batsman's miscalculation. Ten minutes before tea Lindwall was called back; clearly Hassett was getting troubled and unusually impatient.

A curious fact about Watson's batting was that he played the good balls with more certainty than he played the

OLD TRAFFORD NEXT

Len Hutton will again captain England in the third Test match which begins at Old Trafford a week to-morrow. The England team will be picked on Sunday.

amorphous spin and slower stuff of the day. At tea Watson and Bailey remained obdurate and not out: England 183 for four.

It would be a poor compliment to Watson and Bailey to say that they batted better than the Australians

ENGLAND v AUSTRALIA

Played at Lord's,
25, 26, 27, 29, 30 June, 1953.
Result: Match drawn.

Australia: First innings 346 (A.L. Hassett 104, A.K. Davidson 76, R.N. Harvey 59; Bedser 5-105, Wardle 4-77).

England: First innings 372 (L. Hutton 145, T.W. Graveney 78, D.C.S. Compton 57; Lindwall 5-66).

Australia: Second innings 368 (K.R. Miller 109, A.R. Morris 89, R.R. Lindwall 50; Brown 4-82).

England: Second innings

L. Hutton* c Hole b Lindwall	5
D. Kenyon c Hassett b Lindwall	2
T.W. Graveney c Langley b Johnston	2
D.C.S. Compton lbw b Johnston	33
W. Watson c Hole b Lindwall	109
T.E. Bailey c Benaud b Ring	71
F.R. Brown c Hole b Benaud	28
T.G. Evans† not out	11
J.H. Wardle not out	0
A.V. Bedser } did not bat	
J.B. Statham	
Extras (b 7, lb 6, w 2, nb 6)	21
Total (7 wickets)	282

Fall of Wickets: 1/6, 2/10, 3/12, 4/73, 5/236, 6/246, 7/282.
Bowling: Lindwall 19-3-26-2, Miller 17-8-17-0, Johnston 29-10-70-2, Ring 29-5-84-2, Benaud 17-6-51-1, Davidson 14-5-13-0, Hole 1-1-0-0.

LEFT Bailey hits out! While this may be an untypical picture of a batsman better known for stonewalling, 'The Boil' could attack when the occasion demanded

107

1953

PETER WILSON says

WE SAW A MIGHTY VICTORY !

BY the beard of W. G. Grace, we've done it !

After nineteen years of frustration, war, humiliation and near misses, we've got those old Ashes back where they belong — in England, where we have taught the best part of the world how to play cricket . . . and what it means.

At 2.53, with a sweep to leg, Denis Compton signed Australia's death warrant, and we had won by eight wickets

The "old enemy" was so completely nung, drawn and quartered that I almost expected groundsman Lock to pin a notice on the Oval gates saying that having been executed according to the due processes of the law, the victim was legally pronounced dead.

Critics could say that the rate of scoring was slow So it was—little over a run every two minutes. But the crowd of round about 30,000 would have stayed there if England had been scoring only a little over a run every two hours.

Men Who Counted

It wasn't just Bill Edrich gnawing his way to victory, or celtish Peter May thumping the skin off the ball, or Denis Compton determined to be in at the death

It was the rain and shine, near victory and even closer defeat of the whole five Tests—a distillation of the heart-breaks and heart-failures of Nottingham, Lord's, Manchester and Leeds.

It was the dourness of Trevor Bailey and Willie Watson, the indomitability of that willing horse Alec Bedser, the batsmanship of Hutton and the galvanic acrobatics of Godfrey Evans.

As the runs mounted and the gap narrowed, we all thought of the men who had sculpted this final monumental victory. Some of them were in the pavilion—Fred Trueman, for one, who had proved himself something very much more than a pigeon-toed, bandy-legged pit-boy, as one Australian had so contemptuously described him.

Lordly Lock and laudable Laker were there. And there were others who hadn't quite made the final Test, but who had done their bit to ensure that **THIS WAS THE MATCH THAT COUNTED.**

Daily Mirror, 20 August, 1953

OF ALL MODERN Tests the one beyond all other that gripped public interest and provoked patriotic fervour was the last Oval Test of 1953 wherein the Ashes surrendered in 1934 were at last recaptured. Here is the recording of it in the purple prose of the *Daily Mirror*.

Peter Wilson (the lucky man to witness the victory for the *Mirror*) was son of F.B. Wilson, a triple Cambridge blue and cricket captain early in the century who was an all-round games-writer. Peter was father of Julian Wilson, the racing commentator.

ENGLAND v AUSTRALIA
Played at The Oval,
15, 17, 18, 19 August, 1953.
Result: England won by eight wickets.

Australia: First innings

A.L. Hassett* c Evans b Bedser	53
A.R. Morris lbw b Bedser	16
K.R. Miller lbw b Bailey	1
R.N. Harvey c Hutton b Trueman	36
G.B. Hole c Evans b Trueman	37
J.H. de Courcy c Evans b Trueman	5
R.G. Archer c and b Bedser	10
A.K. Davidson c Edrich b Laker	22
R.R. Lindwall c Evans b Trueman	62
G.R.A. Langley† c Edrich b Lock	18
W.A. Johnston not out	9
Extras (b 4, nb 2)	6
Total	275

Fall of Wickets: 1/38, 2/41, 3/107, 4/107, 5/118, 6/160, 7/160, 8/207, 9/245, 10/275.
Bowling: Bedser 29-3-88-3, Trueman 24.3-3-86-4, Bailey 14-3-42-1, Lock 9-2-19-1, Laker 5-0-34-1.

England: First innings

L. Hutton* b Johnston	82
W.J. Edrich lbw b Lindwall	21
P.B.H. May c Archer b Johnston	39
D.C.S. Compton c Langley b Lindwall	16
T.W. Graveney c Miller b Lindwall	4
T.E. Bailey b Archer	64
T.G. Evans† run out	28
J.C. Laker c Langley b Miller	1
G.A.R. Lock c Davidson b Lindwall	4
F.S. Trueman b Johnston	10
A.V. Bedser not out	22
Extras (b 9, lb 5, w 1)	15
Total	306

Fall of Wickets: 1/37, 2/137, 3/154, 4/167, 5/170, 6/210, 7/225, 8/237, 9/262, 10/306.
Bowling: Lindwall 32-7-70-4, Miller 34-12-65-1, Johnston 45-16-94-3, Davidson 10-1-26-0, Archer 10.3-2-25-1, Hole 11-6-11-0.

Australia: Second innings

A.L. Hassett* lbw b Laker	10
A.R. Morris lbw b Lock	26
K.R. Miller (5) c Trueman b Laker	0
R.N. Harvey b Lock	1
G.B. Hole (3) lbw b Laker	17
J.H. de Courcy run out	4
R.G. Archer c Edrich b Lock	49
A.K. Davidson b Lock	21
R.R. Lindwall c Compton b Laker	12
G.R.A. Langley† c Trueman b Lock	2
W.A. Johnston not out	6
Extras (b 11, lb 3)	14
Total	162

Fall of Wickets: 1/23, 2/59, 3/60, 4/61, 5/61, 6/85, 7/135, 8/140, 9/144, 10/162.
Bowling: Bedser 11-2-24-0, Trueman 2-1-4-0, Lock 21-9-45-5, Laker 16.5-2-75-4.

England: Second innings

L. Hutton* run out	17
W.J. Edrich not out	55
P.B.H. May c Davidson b Miller	37
D.C.S. Compton not out	22
T.W. Graveney	
T.E. Bailey	
T.G. Evans†	
J.C. Laker	did not bat
G.A.R. Lock	
F.S. Trueman	
A.V. Bedser	
Extras (lb 1)	1
Total (2 wickets)	132

Fall of Wickets: 1/24, 2/88.
Bowling: Lindwall 21-5-46-0, Miller 11-3-24-0, Johnston 29-14-52-0, Archer 1-1-0-0, Hassett 1-0-4-0, Morris 0.5-0-5-0.

OPPOSITE Compton on the attack as the England victory approaches.

LEFT Hutton, Hassett and the two teams acknowledge the cheers from The Oval balcony

1954

Four police guard umpire's house

RIOT SQUAD WILL STAND BY AT TEST

From ALEX BANNISTER

GEORGETOWN, Sunday.

POLICE strength will be doubled and the steel-helmeted riot squad will stand by at the Bourda Cricket Ground tomorrow when the third Test between the West Indies and England is resumed.

Mr. Charles Palmer, player-manager of the touring M.C.C. team, made this request this morning. It was immediately granted.

He told the British Guiana Cricket Board of Control officials : " While I am not an alarmist, I am concerned with the safety of the 15 England players under my charge."

Trembling

It was decided, in view of the delicacy of the situation, against asking the Argyll and Sutherland Highlanders, stationed here, to patrol the ground.

Daily Mail, 1 March, 1954

WEST INDIES v ENGLAND
Played at Georgetown,
24, 25, 26, 27 February, 1, 2 March, 1954.
Result: England won by nine wickets.

England: First innings 435 (L. Hutton 169, D.C.S. Compton 64; Ramadhin 6-113).

West Indies: First innings 251 (E. de C. Weekes 94, C.A. McWatt 54; Statham 4-64).

West Indies: Second innings 256 (J.K. Holt 64, J.B. Stollmeyer 44; Wardle 3-24).

England: Second innings 75 for 1.

RIGHT The Saturday evening scene at Georgetown as the bottles fly and the riot stops play

THE THIRD TEST of the MCC West Indies tour of 1953-54 at Georgetown, British Guiana (as it then was) contained the first case of crowd mis-behaviour stopping play since the earliest days of international cricket in Australia. When the West Indian, Clifford McWatt, was comfortably run out in attempting the run that would have brought up a 100 partnership between him and J.K. Holt the spectators behind the square-leg umpire began throwing bottles in the direction of umpire Menzies who had given the decision.

As mounted police made a show of strength in the area of the trouble the chairman of the British Guiana Board suggested to Len Hutton, the England captain, that he should take his men off the field. Hutton declined the offer, preferring to press home his side's pronounced advantage. This undoubtedly saved further misbehaviour – and earned England the ninth West Indian wicket before close of play soon afterwards.

The incident happened after the early editions of the London Sunday papers had gone to press, but the *Daily Mail* and other nationals made it front page news on the Monday. Before the match was continued C.H. Palmer, the MCC player-manager, asked for and obtained additional police protection, as Alex Bannister reports. There was no further disorder and England went on to win the match easily. By a second easy victory in the Fifth Test they had the satisfaction of halving the series after two initial defeats.

The Governor of what was still a colony, decided against the use of the battalion of Argyll and Sutherland Highlanders which were stationed in Georgetown. It was, as I remember, something of a comfort that British troops were at hand, but although the authorities attributed the affair to political elements, and an air of tension overhung the country, there was no hostility towards the English party. Rum and betting – there would have been sidestakes on the hundred partnership – were other factors in the outbreak. The least enviable person was the little umpire, whose house was provided with a police guard. On each of the following two MCC tours to the West Indies matches were interrupted by the crowds; at Port-of-Spain, 1959-60 and at Kingston in 1967-68.

LANCASHIRE v YORKSHIRE

Played at Manchester, 31 July, 2, 3 August 1954.
Result: Yorkshire won by an innings and 38 runs.
Yorkshire: First innings 248 (J.V. Wilson 130*).

Lancashire: First innings

W. Place c Lowson b Wardle	2
A. Wharton c Booth b Wardle	41
A. Wilson c Wilson b Wardle	7
G.A. Edrich c Lowson b Wardle	5
K. Grieves c Trueman b Wardle	4
J.T. Ikin c Wilson b Appleyard	0
S. Smith c Wilson b Wardle	0
C.S. Smith c Lowson b Wardle	4
M.J. Hilton c Illingworth b Wardle	2
J.B. Statham c Appleyard b Wardle	6
R. Tattersall not out	0
Extras (b 2)	2
Total	73

Fall of Wickets: 1/14, 2/30, 3/48, 4/60, 5/61, 6/61, 7/65, 8/66, 9/73.
Bowling: Trueman 10-2-19-0, Appleyard 16-7-27-1, Wardle 21.2-12-25-9.

Lancashire: Second innings

W. Place c Wilson b Wardle	6
A. Wharton c Booth b Appleyard	16
A. Wilson b Appleyard	6
G.A. Edrich c Yardley b Appleyard	17
K. Grieves c Trueman b Appleyard	4
J.T. Ikin c Booth b Appleyard	0
S. Smith c Wilson b Appleyard	21
C.S. Smith c Close b Wardle	27
M.J. Hilton b Appleyard	11
J.B. Statham c Yardley b Wardle	10
R. Tattersall not out	0
Extras (b 14, lb 5)	19
Total	137

Fall of Wickets: 1/26, 2/26, 3/34, 4/34, 5/59, 6/106, 7/106, 8/122, 9/135.
Bowling: Trueman 5-3-5-0, Appleyard 23-8-33-7, Wardle 33.2-11-60-3, Close 6-0-20-0.

ONLY IN the ninth post-war summer did Yorkshire for the first time lower Lancashire's colours. The victory – by an innings and 38 runs in the end was foreshadowed on the Bank Holiday Monday when J.H. Wardle accomplished the bowling feat of the season.

Two factors helped in the selection of this story. No survey of post-war cricket should omit commendable mention of Johnny Wardle's gifts as a cricketer. He took 1,846 wickets between 1946 and 1958, 102 of them for England. If he had not the quiet philosophy of most of the great slow left-armers he could be as deadly as any.

The front page *Yorkshire Post* story also gives a brief illustration of the spare, balanced, evocative prose of the *Yorkshire Post*'s long-serving (1934-76) cricket-writer, J.M. Kilburn, surely a model to all of his craft.

One is reminded of the pull that the Roses Matches used to exert on both sides of the Pennines. Despite a wet night and morning 7,000 waited until tea-time to see the cricket. In the Whitsuntide match between the ancient rivals at Headingley in 1954, 20,000 waited through intermittent showers and saw not a ball bowled.

BELOW The canny Johnny Wardle

1954

Wardle makes the Red Rose wilt

All out 73, Lancashire follow on

By J. M. KILBURN

TWO and a half hours was the permitted span for cricket at Old Trafford yesterday, and, in that time, Yorkshire contrived a position of overwhelming advantage over Lancashire. From their weekend's 30 for 2, Lancashire collapsed to 73 all out, and following on, scored 17 for no wicket, thus leaving themselves in need of another 158 runs to avoid an innings defeat.

The attenuated day brought triumph to Wardle, who bowled unchanged through the remainder of the Lancashire first innings, and bowled again immediately the second innings began. His first innings figures were:—

Overs.	maidens.	runs.	wickets.
21.2	12	25	9

a performance to be remembered all his days and losing no sweetness in this particular setting.

Complete domination

An achievement of some distinction could scarcely have been avoided in the circumstances for once the pitch had begun to dry, the conditions were ideally suited to the slow left-hander, but Wardle's domination was so complete that there need be no disparagement of the analysis, no reservation of acclaim. The bowling and the result were magnificent.

The wet night and early morning threatened no Bank Holiday cricket at all, but Old Trafford's astonishing powers of recovery from flooding and the experienced ministrations of the groundsmen enabled a start to be made at quarter past four, and even at that late hour there were 7,000 eager spectators.

Best of Wardle's career

J. H. Wardle's bowling performance yesterday was not only the best of his career, but was outstanding in this season's first-class cricket. He had once previously taken nine wickets in an innings; nine for 48 against Sussex at Hull two months ago. His best performance before then was eight for 26 against Middlesex in 1950. He has been particularly hard on Middlesex, taking seven for 66 in 1947 and seven for 49 against them in 1952.

He took two wickets when Lancashire batted on Saturday and seven, at a cost of 17 runs, yesterday.

Wardle so far this season has taken 111 wickets, 98 of them for Yorkshire.

Yorkshire Post, 3 August, 1954

1955

THIS ALTOGETHER extraordinary New Year Test Match at Melbourne had an ending beyond the realms of fiction. The fifth morning started with Australia at 73 for 2, needing 165 more to win. It seemed anyone's match. Yet in an hour's play and 12 eight-ball overs the remaining eight wickets had fallen for 36 runs to Tyson and Statham, leaving the former with the exceptional analysis of 7 for 27. Relative speeds can never be more than matters of opinion, so I will only add that I have never seen faster bowling anywhere by anyone, than that of Frank Tyson in the second innings of this match and in the Sydney Test preceding it.

The first of Colin Cowdrey's 22 Test hundreds, made immediately after his twenty-second birthday, was perhaps at least as great an innings as any of them: made out of a total of 192 all out and out of 160 while he was at the wicket. Youthful mastery in the bud! When the second day ended with Australia 188 for 8 there was nothing in it, but after a week-end of dry scorching heat brought in by the dreaded Melbourne 'Northerly' wind the teams on the Monday morning were staggered to discover that the pitch was definitely damp. The *Age* led the paper with the allegation – accepted gradually on all sides as having been true – that the

BELOW Tyson bowling at the time when many regarded him as the fastest ever. His action put excessive strain on his frame however and after 1955 he never really fulfilled his early promise

pitch had been watered by the curator to prevent it breaking up. As it happened England benefited in their second innings with the best batting conditions of the match, wherein Peter May scored a hundred of a quality comparable with Cowdrey's.

There was only one scar on England's peformance in this match, and that was a drop in the over-rate at which a crowd of 60-odd thousand showed loud disapproval. In a five-hour day on the Saturday England bowled 54 overs – which corresponds to just over 14 six-ball overs an hour. It was the first time I had noticed slowing-down used as what was evidently a tactical ploy. Within a few years it had become commonplace with resort to subtle techniques, and now, of course, we have minimum rates (16 overs per hour for home Tests) as prescribed regulations.

This Test victory, followed by a third successively at Adelaide, left the Ashes with Len Hutton's side, deservedly indeed. It is, though, an interesting speculation what the Australian Board would have done if the watering had worked to their side's advantage and England had been beaten. Whatever had been decided, what a palaver!

MAGNIFICENT TYSON HERO OF TEST TRIUMPH

Australia Routed by Pace Attack

From E. W. SWANTON
MELBOURNE, Wednesday.

THE history of cricket is a story of surprises, but in the chronicle of Test matches the suddenness and utter completeness of Australia's collapse to-day, which gave England victory by 128 runs, will rank as a startling curiosity many years ahead.

The last eight Australian wickets went down, six of them to the formidable Tyson, for 36 runs and that is a thing, I suppose, no one has seen before when the result was at stake since Syd Gregory's team floundered on an Oval gluepot in 1912.

Rhodes and Hirst, of course, bowled out Australia for 36 at Birmingham in 1902. There was also the fantastic epilogue to the Old Trafford Test on Hassett's tour, when Australia on the last evening made 35 for eight, the game then being a certain draw with Australia ahead when their innings started. In any case, all these strange things happened in England on wet wickets.

Tyson and Statham have shown themselves once more, as they did at Sydney, altogether too good for Australia's batsmen when there has been anything in the wicket to help tilt the balance.

TYSON'S ANALYSIS
Best Ever for Fast Bowler

Tyson's has been the more dramatic part. His analysis in this second innings has never been bettered by a fast bowler in a match between England and Australia. But they have worked essentially in harness as a pair, and each has generally bowled better when his counterpart was at the other end. Tyson has taken 19 wickets in the two matches, Statham 12—31 out of the total of 40.

Daily Telegraph, 6 January, 1955

AUSTRALIA v ENGLAND
Played at Melbourne,
31 December, 1, 3, 4, 5 January, 1955.
Result: England won by 128 runs.

England: First innings

L. Hutton* c Hole b Miller		12
W.J. Edrich c Lindwall b Miller		4
P.B.H. May c Benaud b Lindwall		0
M.C. Cowdrey b Johnson		102
D.C.S. Compton c Harvey b Miller		4
T.E. Bailey c Maddocks b Johnston		30
T.G. Evans† lbw b Archer		20
J.H. Wardle b Archer		0
F.H. Tyson b Archer		6
J.B. Statham b Archer		3
R. Appleyard not out		1
Extras (b 9)		9
Total		191

Fall of Wickets: 1/14, 2/21, 3/29, 4/41, 5/115, 6/169, 7/181, 8/181, 9/190, 10/191.
Bowling: Lindwall 13-0-59-1, Miller 11-8-14-3, Archer 13.6-4-33-4, Benaud 7-0-30-0, Johnston 12-6-26-1, Johnson 11-3-20-1.

Australia: First innings

L.E. Favell lbw b Statham		25
A.R. Morris lbw b Tyson		3
K.R. Miller c Evans b Statham		7
R.N. Harvey b Appleyard		31
G.B. Hole b Tyson		11
R. Benaud c sub (J.V. Wilson) b Appleyard		15
R.G. Archer b Wardle		23
L.V. Maddocks† c Evans b Statham		47
R.R. Lindwall b Statham		13
I.W. Johnson* not out		33
W.A. Johnston b Statham		11
Extras (b 7, lb 3, nb 2)		12
Total		231

Fall of Wickets: 1/15, 2/38, 3/43, 4/65, 5/92, 6/115, 7/134, 8/151, 9/205, 10/231.
Bowling: Tyson 21-2-68-2, Statham 16.3-0-60-5, Bailey 9-1-33-0, Appleyard 11-3-38-2, Wardle 6-0-20-1.

England: Second innings

L. Hutton* lbw b Archer		42
W.J. Edrich b Johnston		13
P.B.H. May b Johnston		91
M.C. Cowdrey c Benaud		7
D.C.S. Compton c Maddocks b Archer		23
T.E. Bailey not out		24
T.G. Evans† c Maddocks b Miller		22
J.H. Wardle b Johnson		38
F.H. Tyson c Harvey b Johnston		6
J.B. Statham c Favell b Johnston		0
R. Appleyard b Johnston		6
Extras (b 2, lb 4, w 1)		7
Total		279

Fall of Wickets: 1/40, 2/96, 3/128, 4/173, 5/185, 6/211, 7/257, 8/273, 9/273, 10/279.
Bowling: Lindwall 18-3-52-0, Miller 18-6-35-1, Archer 24-7-50-2, Benaud 8-2-25-1, Johnston 24.5-2-85-5, Johnson 8-2-25-1.

Australia: Second innings

L.E. Favell b Appleyard		30
A.R. Morris c Cowdrey b Tyson		4
K.R. Miller (5) c Edrich b Tyson		6
R.N. Harvey c Evans b Tyson		11
G.B. Hole (6) c Evans b Statham		5
R. Benaud (3) b Tyson		22
R.G. Archer b Statham		15
L.V. Maddocks† b Tyson		0
R.R. Lindwall lbw b Tyson		0
I.W. Johnson* not out		4
W.A. Johnston c Evans b Tyson		0
Extras (b 1, lb 13)		14
Total		111

Fall of Wickets: 1/23, 2/57, 3/77, 4/86, 5/87, 6/97, 7/98, 8/98, 9/110, 10/111.
Bowling: Tyson 12.3-1-27-7, Statham 11-1-38-2, Bailey 3-0-14-0, Appleyard 4-1-17-1, Wardle 1-0-1-0.

LEFT A delighted Hutton returns to England with the Ashes. Against Australia he averaged over 50 and in 23 Tests as England captain never lost a rubber

113

1955

THE PARTNERSHIP of 347 for the seventh wicket between D.St.E. Atkinson and C. Depeiza for the West Indies against Australia at Bridgetown in May 1955 was remarkable both in itself and for the circumstances surrounding it.

The Test was the Fourth in the first-ever visit of the Australians to the Caribbean. They were already two up in the series, and when Depeiza, the wicket-keeper, joined his captain the West Indian reply to Australia's mammoth score of 668 stood at 147 for 6. But now the seventh wicket persisted on the perfect Kensington pitch for more than a day, Atkinson producing a full array of strokes while his partner based his game on an elongated forward push which earned him his nickname 'The leaning tower Depeiza'! They were not parted until they had beaten the world record for the seventh wicket, and established what is still a West Indian Test record for any wicket. (*The Times* headline over a somewhat undistinguished report is one run adrift.)

Behind the scenes the story was an unhappy one. Jeffrey Stollmeyer had been nominated as the West Indian captain and Denis Atkinson as his vice-captain before the series began. Both were white. Stollmeyer was the senior West Indian cricketer in age and was rich in experience of captaincy, but when injury prevented his leading the team in the First, Fourth and Fifth Tests there was violent press comment and public demonstration in favour of one of the three Ws. These were sensitive times politically with the territories emerging from colonial status towards independence.

Such factors aside however, it had become difficult, to say the least, in view of the high repute as cricketers

RECORD STAND BY W. INDIES

SEVENTH PAIR BAT ALL DAY

348 ADDED SO FAR

FROM OUR SPECIAL CORRESPONDENT

BRIDGETOWN, BARBADOS,

The Times, 19 May, 1955

and sportsmen of Frank Worrell, Clyde Walcott and Everton Weekes, to justify the attitude of the West Indian Board, who maintained their choice was governed not by racial considerations but by what they saw as the necessity for an amateur rather than a professional captain. Six more Test series in five years were to be contested by the West Indies before Worrell was appointed captain, with brilliant results, for the tour to Australia of 1960-61.

As for Denis Atkinson he answered the situation in the only way he could, by putting his heart and soul into the job and by doing his best to carry the very weak West Indian bowling. He took 13 wickets in the series at 35 runs each. No one else had more than six, while Valentine and Ramadhin, the scourges of English batsmen, were taking 10 between them for 72 runs apiece.

LEFT Denis Atkinson: a captain's innings of 219. Interestingly this was his only century in 22 Test matches

WEST INDIES v AUSTRALIA

Played at Bridgetown,
14, 16, 17, 18, 19, 20 May, 1955.
Result: Match drawn.

Australia: First innings

C.C. McDonald run out	46
L.E. Favell c Weekes b Atkinson	72
R.N. Harvey c Smith b Worrell	74
W.J. Watson c Depeiza b Dewdney	30
K.R. Miller c Depeiza b Dewdney	137
R. Benaud c Walcott b Dewdney	1
R.G. Archer b Worrell	98
R.R. Lindwall c Valentine b Atkinson	118
I.W. Johnson* b Dewdney	23
G.R.A. Langley† b Sobers	53
J.C. Hill not out	8
Extras (b 1, lb 2, w 4, nb 1)	8
Total	668

Fall of Wickets: 1/108, 2/126, 3/226, 4/226, 5/233, 6/439, 7/483, 8/562, 9/623, 10/668.
Bowling: Worrell 40-7-120-2, Dewdney 33-5-125-4, Walcott 26-10-57-0, Valentine 31-9-87-0, Ramadhin 24-3-84-0, Atkinson 48-14-108-2, Smith 22-8-49-0, Sobers 11.5-6-30-1.

West Indies: First innings

J.K. Holt b Lindwall	22
G. St A. Sobers c Hill b Johnson	43
C.L. Walcott c Langley b Benaud	15
E. de C. Weekes c Langley b Miller	44
F.M.M. Worrell run out	16
O.G. Smith c Langley b Miller	2
D. St E. Atkinson* c Archer b Johnson	219
C.C. Depeiza† b Benaud	122
S. Ramadhin c and b Benaud	10
D.T. Dewdney b Johnson	0
A.L. Valentine not out	2
Extras (b 5, lb 4, w 2, nb 4)	15
Total	510

Fall of Wickets: 1/52, 2/69, 3/105, 4/142, 5/143, 6/147, 7/494, 8/504, 9/504, 10/510.
Bowling: Lindwall 25-3-96-1, Miller 22-2-113-2, Archer 15-4-44-0, Johnson 35-13-77-3, Hill 24-9-71-0, Benaud 31.1-6-73-3, Harvey 4-0-16-0, Watson 1-0-5-0.

Australia: Second innings

C.C. McDonald b Smith	17
L.E. Favell run out	53
R.N. Harvey c Valentine b Smith	27
W.J. Watson b Atkinson	0
K.R. Miller lbw b Atkinson	10
R. Benaud b Sobers	5
R.G. Archer lbw b Atkinson	28
R.R. Lindwall (9) b Atkinson	10
I.W. Johnson* (8) c Holt b Smith	57
G.R.A. Langley† not out	28
J.C. Hill c Weekes b Atkinson	1
Extras (b 9, lb 4)	13
Total	249

Fall of Wickets: 1/71, 2/72, 3/73, 4/87, 5/107, 6/119, 7/151, 8/177, 9/241, 10/249.
Bowling: Worrell 7-0-25-0, Dewdney 10-4-23-0, Valentine 6-1-16-0, Ramadhin 2-0-10-0, Atkinson 36.2-16-56-5, Smith 34-12-71-3, Sobers 14-3-35-1.

West Indies: Second innings

J.K. Holt lbw b Hill	49
G. St A. Sobers lbw b Archer	11
C.L. Walcott b Benaud	83
E. de C. Weekes run out	6
F.M.M. Worrell c Archer b Miller	34
O.G. Smith b Lindwall	11
D. St E. Atkinson† not out	20
C.C. Depeiza† not out	11
S. Ramadhin ⎫	
D.T. Dewdney ⎬ did not bat	
A.L. Valentine ⎭	
Extras (b 6, lb 2, w 1)	9
Total (6 wickets)	234

Fall of Wickets: 1/38, 2/67, 3/81, 4/154, 5/193, 6/207.
Bowling: Lindwall 8-1-39-1, Miller 21-3-66-1, Archer 7-1-11-1, Johnson 14-4-30-0, Hill 11-2-44-0, Benaud 11-3-35-1.

FOUNDATION OF VICTORY?

The Genius of Washbrook

TEST WEATHER : Cloudy ; bright periods by afternoon ; wind E. moderate.

By Denys Rowbotham

Manchester Guardian, 13 July, 1956

ENGLAND v AUSTRALIA

Played at Leeds,
12, 13, 14 (no play), 16, 17 July, 1956.
Result: England won by an innings and 42 runs.

England: First innings

P.E. Richardson c Maddocks b Archer	5
M.C. Cowdrey c Maddocks b Archer	0
A.S.M. Oakman b Archer	4
P.B.H. May* c Lindwall b Johnson	101
C. Washbrook lbw b Benaud	98
G.A.R. Lock c Miller b Benaud	21
D.J. Insole c Mackay b Benaud	5
T.E. Bailey not out	33
T.G. Evans† b Lindwall	40
J.C. Laker b Lindwall	5
F.S. Trueman c and b Lindwall	0
Extras (b 4, lb 9)	13
Total	325

Fall of Wickets: 1/2, 2/8, 3/17, 4/204, 5/226, 6/243, 7/248, 8/301, 9/321, 10/325.
Bowling: Lindwall 33.4-11-67-3, Archer 50-24-68-3, Mackay 13-3-29-0, Benaud 42-9-89-3, Johnson 29-8-59-1.

Australia: First innings

C.C. McDonald c Evans b Trueman	2
J.W. Burke lbw b Lock	41
R.N. Harvey c Trueman b Lock	11
P.J.P. Burge lbw b Laker	2
K.D. Mackay c Bailey b Laker	2
K.R. Miller b Laker	41
R.G. Archer b Laker	4
R. Benaud c Oakman b Laker	30
L.V. Maddocks† c Trueman b Lock	0
I.W. Johnson* c Richardson b Lock	0
R.R. Lindwall not out	0
Extras (b 4, lb 6)	10
Total	143

Fall of Wickets: 1/2, 2/40, 3/59, 4/59, 5/63, 6/69, 7/142, 8/143, 9/143, 10/143.
Bowling: Trueman 8-2-19-1, Bailey 7-2-15-0, Laker 29-10-58-5, Lock 27.1-11-41-4.

Australia: Second innings

C.C. McDonald b Trueman	6
J.W. Burke b Laker	16
R.N. Harvey c and b Lock	69
P.J.P. Burge (5) lbw b Laker	5
K.D. Mackay (8) b Laker	2
K.R. Miller (4) c Trueman b Laker	26
R.G. Archer (9) c Washbrook b Lock	1
R. Benaud (6) b Laker	1
L.V. Maddocks† (10) lbw b Lock	0
I.W. Johnson* (7) c Oakman b Laker	3
R.R. Lindwall not out	0
Extras (b 7, lb 4)	11
Total	140

Fall of Wickets: 1/10, 2/45, 3/108, 4/120, 5/128, 6/136, 7/138, 8/140, 9/140, 10/140.
Bowling: Trueman 11-3-21-1, Bailey 7-2-13-0, Laker 41.3-21-55-6, Lock 40-23-40-3.

THE RETURN TO Test cricket of Cyril Washbrook for the Third Test against Australia at Headingley in 1956 is generally recalled as a triumph of selection. He was forty-one and, though captain of Lancashire, had not played in a Test for five years. He was also one of the four selectors along with L.E.G. Ames and W. Wooller under the chairmanship of G.O. Allen, the captain P.B.H. May being coopted on appointment.

The idea, much criticized before the event, was to stiffen the middle batting. Washbrook's comment when the team was announced was 'one does not decline to play for England – one will do one's best but it will not be easy'. When he joined May at the end of an hour on the first morning the score was 17 for 3. Scarcely an 'easy' situation! Washbrook stayed all day while 184 were being added, of which his share was an undefeated 90. May was out for 101 a few minutes before the close with the board showing 204 for 4. The captain, who had needed persuasion to fall in with the decision, said on his return: 'Thank goodness I listened.'

The sub-editor who used the word 'genius' in the *Manchester Guardian's* page one heading over-stated the case and failed to reflect the tenor of Denys Rowbotham's report, which spoke of his judgement and self-mastery. Washbrook had not the genius of a Compton or a Hutton but he 'brought to England's batting what his selectors hoped and asked of him – solidity, stability and endurance'.

With 'Foundation of Victory?' however the sub was on surer ground. As soon as Laker and Lock began to turn the ball on the dry pitch already beginning to dust it was clear that England's score of 325 was ample for the winning of the match. The early deterioration of the wicket reflected no credit whatever on the Yorkshire authorities. At close of play Australia were 81 for 6, five wickets having fallen to the spinners. More would no doubt have been made of the state of the pitch had not rain set in that night and washed out Saturday's play. After the week-end, and as soon as the sun got to work, Australia were hopelessly trapped. Laker and Lock spun their side to victory, but the foundation had been laid by Washbrook and his captain.

ABOVE Washbrook going out at Headingley to continue his memorable – and invaluable – innings of 98

1956

IT WAS NOT easy to find a fresh angle to what is, statistically at least, the most celebrated feat in cricket history. The *Yorkshire Post* however seized the occasion to remind its readers that J.C. Laker was a Yorkshireman, that he hailed from Shipley and was educated at the Salts High School, Saltaire. Hence the 'Congratulations to an Old Salt'! As a teenager in the early years of the war, Jim Laker played for Saltaire in the Bradford League. It was the accident of being posted to the War Office at the end of his service and being billeted at Catford in South London, that led to his being recruited to the Surrey staff.

Laker was a modest, laconic fellow, as suggested in the accompanying photograph. But for the formal applause of David Sheppard, left, and Brian Statham, right, he strolls in, sweater over shoulder, as though he might be returning from a net rather than taking nineteen wickets in a Test Match.

His success was the result of off-spin bowling of immaculate length in widely contrasting conditions. In Australia's first innings on a pitch which was dry and dusty and accordingly helpful, without being so difficult as the Australians made it seem, he enjoyed a spell, after tea on the second day that baffled belief. In the space of half an hour the score declined from 64 for 2 to 84 all out, Laker 9 for 36. The collapse was compounded of the Australians' dread of high-class off-spin (a type little practised in their own country) and of a particular inferiority complex against Laker who had taken all 10 against

them for Surrey early in the tour and 11 in the Headingley Test preceding this one.

As the weather closed in on Manchester, allowing a few overs only on the Saturday and a bare hour on the Monday it became a question whether the sudden collapse of Australian morale would escape its due reward. It nearly did, for on the last day on a dead wicket on which the ball turned slowly Australia batted with traditional tenacity and England's victory came with only an hour to spare. Laker's analysis this time was – 51.2 – 21 – 53 – 10. Not the least phenomenal thing about the game was that Lock who generally shared the wickets fairly evenly with Laker when the ball was turning (he took 155 wickets during the season as compared with Laker's 132) on this occasion had 1 for 106.

BELOW Jim Laker's final victim: Maddocks is lbw for 2

Many will be wondering how it was that England, batting first, managed to put up such a big score. Well, they had much the better of the pitch and batted extremely well on it. Just as importantly, Australia's slow bowling amounted only to Johnson, a flighter rather than a spinner, and Benaud whose wrist-spin, apart from one momentous occasion five years hence, was seldom a threat on English pitches.

ENGLAND v AUSTRALIA
Played at Manchester,
26, 27, 28, 30, 31 July, 1956.
Result: England won by an innings and 170 runs.

England: First innings
P.E. Richardson c Maddocks b Benaud	104
M.C. Cowdrey c Maddocks b Lindwall	80
Rev D.S. Sheppard b Archer	113
P.B.H. May* c Archer b Benaud	43
T.E. Bailey b Johnson	20
C. Washbrook lbw b Johnson	6
A.S.M. Oakman c Archer b Johnson	10
T.G. Evans† st Maddocks b Johnson	47
J.C. Laker run out	3
G.A.R. Lock not out	25
J.B. Statham c Maddocks b Lindwall	0
Extras (b 2, lb 5, w 1)	8
Total	459

Fall of Wickets: 1/174, 2/195, 3/288, 4/321, 5/327, 6/339, 7/401, 8/417, 9/458, 10/459.
Bowling: Lindwall 21.3-6-63-2, Miller 21-6-41-0, Archer 22-6-73-1, Johnson 47-10-151-4, Benaud 47-17-123-2.

Australia: First innings
C.C. McDonald c Lock b Laker	32
J.W. Burke c Cowdrey b Lock	22
R.N. Harvey b Laker	0
I.D. Craig lbw b Laker	8
K.R. Miller c Oakman b Laker	6
K.D. Mackay c Oakman b Laker	0
R.G. Archer st Evans b Laker	6
R. Benaud c Statham b Laker	0
R.R. Lindwall not out	6
L.V. Maddocks† b Laker	4
I.W. Johnson* b Laker	0
Extras	0
Total	84

Fall of Wickets: 1/48, 2/48, 3/62, 4/62, 5/62, 6/73, 7/73, 8/78, 9/84, 10/84.
Bowling: Statham 6-3-6-0, Bailey 4-3-4-0, Laker 16.4-4-37-9, Lock 14-3-37-1.

Australia: Second innings
C.C. McDonald c Oakman b Laker	89
J.W. Burke c Lock b Laker	33
R.N. Harvey c Cowdrey b Laker	0
I.D. Craig lbw b Laker	38
K.R. Miller (6) b Laker	0
K.D. Mackay (5) c Oakman b Laker	0
R.G. Archer c Oakman b Laker	0
R. Benaud b Laker	18
R.R. Lindwall c Lock b Laker	8
L.V. Maddocks† (11) lbw b Laker	2
I.W. Johnson* (10) not out	1
Extras (b 12, lb 4)	16
Total	205

Fall of Wickets: 1/28, 2/55, 3/114, 4/124, 5/130, 6/130, 7/181, 8/198, 9/203, 10/205.
Bowling: Statham 16-10-15-0, Bailey 20-8-31-0, Laker 51.2-23-53-10, Lock 55-30-69-0, Oakman 8-3-21-0.

RIGHT Laker leaves the field – applauded by Sheppard and Statham, but seemingly unmoved by his historic feat. It was a curious twist of fate that his great spinning partner had only one victim in the match

19 WICKETS FOR 90 RUNS
Jim Laker's feat is unique in Tests
Shipley congratulations for an 'Old Salt'
By our sports editor

IT is not often that an individual cricketer becomes as important as the game, but yesterday at Old Trafford, Manchester, where England beat Australia by an innings and 170 runs, Jim Laker, of Shipley and Surrey, whose style was moulded at Salts High School and Headingley nets, became the current toast of cricket.

Yorkshire Post, 1 August, 1956

117

1957

THE LONG and skilful rearguard action executed by Peter May and Colin Cowdrey which rescued their side in the First Test of 1957 against the West Indies at Edgbaston evoked a fairly hysterical response by press and public of which the *Daily Sketch*'s treatment is a fair sample. The 411 runs they put on for the fourth wicket was, and remains, a Test record of its kind. When the long partnership began early on the fourth morning England in their second innings with three men out were 275 runs in arrears. They had been undermined by 'Sonny' Ramadhin whose 7 for 49 in 31 overs on the first day was a grisly reminder of the psychological advantage which he had established over England's batsmen seven years before and had never lost.

Unable to spot for certain which way the ball would turn, May and Cowdrey thrust forward the left leg, bat and pad together to every ball from Ramadhin that pitched outside the off-stump. Umpires in those days were even more reluctant than now to give an lbw decision to an off-break if the leg is well forward. Appeal after appeal was turned down by C.S. Elliott and E. Davies, and Ramadhin grew more and more deflated, as May and Cowdrey, with the utmost concentration and no shortage of scoring strokes, batted on and on. May might even have won the match against a frustrated enemy if he had declared a little earlier. As it was, he took out his bat for 285, the highest score ever by an England captain, and the decline in West Indian morale lasted through the series.

In keeping Ramadhin on for 98 overs, the largest number ever bowled in an innings, John Goddard, his captain, laid himself open to strong criticism. Ramadhin was never quite the same bowler afterwards.

ABOVE Peter May showing stern concentration during his record-breaking innings. The wicketkeeper is R.B. Kanhai

ENGLAND v WEST INDIES
Played at Birmingham,
30, 31 May, 1, 3, 4 June, 1957.
Result: Match drawn.

England: First innings

P.E. Richardson c Walcott b Ramadhin	47
D.B. Close c Kanhai b Gilchrist	15
D.J. Insole b Ramadhin	20
P.B.H. May* c Weekes b Ramadhin	30
M.C. Cowdrey c Gilchrist b Ramadhin	4
T.E. Bailey b Ramadhin	1
G.A.R. Lock b Ramadhin	0
T.G. Evans† b Gilchrist	14
J.C. Laker b Ramadhin	7
F.S. Trueman not out	29
J.B. Statham b Atkinson	13
Extras (b 3, lb 3)	6
Total	186

Fall of Wickets: 1/32, 2/61, 3/104, 4/115, 5/116, 6/118, 7/121, 8/130, 9/150, 10/186.
Bowling: Worrell 9-1-27-0, Gilchrist 27-4-74-2, Ramadhin 31-16-49-7, Atkinson 12.4-3-30-1.

West Indies: First innings

B.H. Pairaudeau b Trueman	1
R.B. Kanhai† lbw b Statham	42
C.L. Walcott c Evans b Laker	90
E. de C. Weekes b Trueman	9
G. St A. Sobers c Bailey b Statham	53
O.G. Smith lbw b Laker	161
F.M.M. Worrell b Statham	81
J.D.C. Goddard* c Lock b Laker	24
D. St E. Atkinson c Statham b Laker	1
S. Ramadhin not out	5
R. Gilchrist run out	0
Extras (b 1, lb 6)	7
Total	474

Fall of Wickets: 1/4, 2/83, 3/120, 4/183, 5/197, 6/387, 7/466, 8/469, 9/474, 10/474.
Bowling: Statham 39-4-114-3, Trueman 30-4-99-2, Bailey 34-11-80-0, Laker 54-17-119-4, Lock 34.4-15-55-0.

England: Second innings

P.E. Richardson c sub (N.S. Asgarali) b Ramadhin	34
D.B. Close c Weekes b Gilchrist	42
D.J. Insole b Ramadhin	0
P.B.H. May* not out	285
M.C. Cowdrey c sub (N.S. Asgarali) b Smith	154
T.G. Evans† not out	29
T.E. Bailey	
G.A.R. Lock	
J.C. Laker ⎫ did not bat	
F.S. Trueman	
J.B. Statham	
Extras (b 23, lb 16)	39
Total (4 wickets declared)	583

Fall of Wickets: 1/63, 2/65, 3/113, 4/524.
Bowling: Gilchrist 26-2-67-1, Ramadhin 98-35-179-2, Atkinson 72-29-137-0, Sobers 30-4-77-0, Smith 26-4-72-1, Goddard 6-2-12-0.

West Indies: Second innings

B.H. Pairaudeau b Trueman	7
R.B. Kanhai† c Close b Trueman	1
C.L. Walcott (6) c Lock b Laker	1
E. de C. Weekes c Trueman b Lock	33
G. St A. Sobers (3) c Cowdrey b Lock	14
O.G. Smith (7) lbw b Laker	5
F.M.M. Worrell (5) c May b Lock	0
J.D.C. Goddard* not out	0
D. St E. Atkinson not out	4
S. Ramadhin ⎫ did not bat	
R. Gilchrist	
Extras (b 7)	7
Total (7 wickets)	72

Fall of Wickets: 1/1, 2/9, 3/25, 4/27, 5/43, 6/66, 7/68.
Bowling: Statham 2-0-6-0, Trueman 5-3-7-2, Laker 24-20-13-2, Lock 27-19-31-2, Close 2-1-8-0.

118

Thanks, Compton for such a fairy tale end—143

By FRANK ROSTRON

DENIS COMPTON, sunniest cricketer of his generation, went out in a fairy-story blaze of sunshine and glory yesterday with a century—his 122nd—in his last match as a Middlesex professional at Lord's.

Daily Express, 29 August, 1957

1957

DENIS COMPTON had a wonderful knack of rising to the occasion anywhere, but especially at Lord's. He made a hundred the first time he stepped on to the ground, 114 as a 14-year-old, for the London Elementary Schoolboys. He made 143 in three hours thirty-five years later on his last professional appearance for Middlesex.

He made 47 of his 123 hundreds at Lord's, three in Tests, five in the annual Bank Holiday match with Sussex, including – inevitably – 182 in his Benefit. He would probably have got another in brother Leslie's Benefit if he had not run out three of his partners including the beneficiary! As it was, he had to take out his bat for 72.

Denis made 38,942 runs, at an average of 51.85 – and there would have been several thousand more but for the knee injuries which plagued his latter years. He took 622 wickets, at 32.27, and when he happened to be looking – as John Warr might have observed – he caught 415 catches.

MIDDLESEX v WORCESTERSHIRE
Played at Lord's, 28, 29, 30 August, 1957.
Result: Worcestershire won by two wickets.

Middlesex: First innings
J.D. Robertson c Kenyon b Coldwell	104
R.A. Gale c Broadbent b Flavell	17
A.C. Walton c Booth b Coldwell	37
D.C.S. Compton b Flavell	143
W.J. Edrich b Flavell	9
J.T. Murray st Booth b Chesterton	27
F.J. Titmus not out	8
D. Bennett, J.J. Warr, R.J. Hurst, A.E. Moss — did not bat	
Extras (b 1, lb 4)	5
Total (6 wickets declared)	350

Fall of Wickets: 1/24, 2/76, 3/301, 4/305, 5/330, 6/350.
Bowling: Flavell 18-0-83-3,' Coldwell 28-4-121-2, Chesterton 27.4-5-91-1, Horton 20-5-50-0.

Worcestershire: First innings 354 for 9 declared (D.W. Richardson 113, R.G. Broadbent 56; Hurst 4-70).

Middlesex: Second innings 203 for 7 declared (D.C.S. Compton 48, A.C. Walton 42).

Worcestershire: Second innings 200 for 8 (R.G. Broadbent 42).

LEFT Denis Compton: goodbye to a 'Golden Boy'

1958

THE TROUBLES surrounding J.H. Wardle in August 1958 damaged both the image of cricket in general and the prospects of the forthcoming MCC tour of Australia in particular. A few days after he was chosen by the MCC selectors Yorkshire announced that they were not renewing his contract for 1959. That in itself, though not making an ideal situation, would not have affected his Australian invitation.

However cheque-book journalism then brought matters to a bitter and tragic climax. Although Wardle was pictured stroking his chin behind a typewriter, the *Daily Mail* articles fiercely critical of the Yorkshire Committee, the captain, J.R. Burnet, and members of the team, were certainly ghosted. Of these the MCC Committee were bound to take cognizance, and a fortnight later, after hearing his side of the dispute, they withdrew his invitation. Ronald Aird, the MCC secretary told him, according to Alex Bannister, 'I'm sorry, Johnny, you're out.' To this the victim's reaction was, 'It is my own fault and I asked for it.'

No one was more disappointed than Peter May, due to lead MCC in Australia, under whose captaincy Wardle had had the record haul of 90 wickets (chiefly with left-arm wrist-spin), in South Africa two winters before. Since no substitute was chosen May's team which surrendered the Ashes so emphatically was seriously weakened and unbalanced as a result.

Having travelled with him on three overseas tours I must say I never saw or heard of his stepping out of line either on the field or off. With Yorkshire it was plainly different, though Wardle was far from being the only culprit. As J.M. Kilburn, the historian of Yorkshire cricket, put it succinctly:

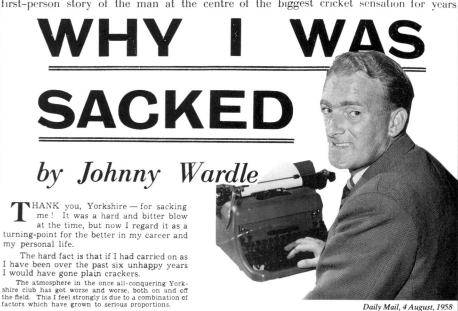

WHY I WAS SACKED

by Johnny Wardle

THANK you, Yorkshire — for sacking me! It was a hard and bitter blow at the time, but now I regard it as a turning-point for the better in my career and my personal life.

The hard fact is that if I had carried on as I have been over the past six unhappy years I would have gone plain crackers.

The atmosphere in the once all-conquering Yorkshire club has got worse and worse, both on and off the field. This I feel strongly is due to a combination of factors which have grown to serious proportions.

Daily Mail, 4 August, 1958

Daily Mail MORNING SPECIAL

NO. 19,387 FOR QUEEN AND COMMONWEALTH WEDNESDAY, AUGUST 20 1958 PRICE 2½D.

'Welfare of cricket must override all else'

M.C.C. SACKS WARDLE

Greece rejects Cyprus plan

Comment

WEDNESDAY AUG. 20 1958

NEXT ON THE LIST?

COMMITTEE SAYS

Grave disservice

JOHNNY SAYS

I asked for it

By ALEX BANNISTER

JOHNNY WARDLE, star spin bowler, was sacked by the M.C.C. yesterday from the England team which tours Australia this winter. They considered his case at Lord's. They heard his side of his row with Yorkshire.

DAVID (I hit him / I hit him / I hit him again)

AND THE BULLOCK

By JACK CROSSLEY

FLOODS SWEEP HOLIDAY TOWNS

THE WORST-HIT AREA IS SHADED

GIRL DEAD — MAN SHOT

Yorkshire teams in the 1950s contained much individual playing talent but lacked a thread to bind together some ill-assorted temperaments. Dressing-room disaffection inevitably became reflected in attitudes and performances on the field. The common interest was too frequently obscured by the personal concern.

Wardle was not a silent witness in an uncomfortable atmosphere.

Yorkshire, however, could point to the fact that whereas they finished 11th with Wardle included in 1958 they won the Championship in the two following years and indeed their placings over the next decade were: 1, 1, 2, 1, 1, 5, 4, 1, 1, and 1.

HANIF MOHAMMAD'S diminutive figure belies the fact that he achieved two ultimate batting records, the highest and the longest individual innings in history.

For most people it was fitting that the most prolific batsman in history, Sir Donald Bradman, should hold the record for the highest individual score in first-class cricket; at least that was from 1929, when he made 452 for New South Wales against Queensland, until 12 January 1959, when Hanif was

1959

run out attempting his 500th run while playing for Karachi against Bahawalpur in the Quaid-e-Azam Trophy, Pakistan's major domestic competition. Elation and exhaustion must have been coloured with disappointment that the magical figure of 500 had so narrowly eluded him – obviously Bahawalpur were giving no quarter.

One season earlier, in 1957-58, in the first Test Match between West Indies and Pakistan at Bridgetown, Hanif batted for sixteen hours and ten minutes to score 337 when Pakistan followed on 473 behind. At the time it was the second highest individual Test score after Hutton's 364, but not for long. Two Tests later West Indies' rising star Gary Sobers, not content with his first Test hundred, went on to score 365 not out.

The key to Hanif's ability to play innings of such endurance was a combination of strict discipline and concentration, easy economy in his attacking strokes and an unshakeable defence guaranteed to frustrate the most determined of bowlers.

The fact that Hanif's 499 was achieved in Pakistan's domestic competition accounts for why it only afforded one short paragraph in *The Times*. Most English papers failed to record it at all. No doubt, however, he got full adulation from his own country's press.

BAHAWALPUR v KARACHI
Played at Karachi, 8, 9, 11, 12 January, 1959.
Result: Karachi won by an innings and 479 runs.

Bahawalpur: First innings 185 (M. Ramzan 64; Ikram Elahi 4-68).

Karachi: First innings 772 for 7 declared (Hanif Mohammad 499, Wallis Mathais 103).

Bahawalpur: Second innings 108.

LEFT Hanif at Bridgetown in 1958: 337 runs in a gruelling 16 hours 10 minutes. Later in the series Sobers scored his 365 not out

1960

THE NO-BALLING of Geoffrey Griffin, a 20-year-old opening bowler from Natal, in the Lord's Test of 1960 scarred the memory of the game as well as convincing the South African authorities at long last that to continue to expose him to the umpires' scrutiny was unfair and unkind both to the English umpires and to the young man himself.

No overseas bowler had ever before been called in England. Yet before the Second Test no fewer than six umpires had no-balled Griffin. D.J. McGlew, the captain and the tour manager, Dudley Nourse, notwithstanding this decided, presumably, on a show-down at headquarters where Sid Buller, the leading umpire, was standing with Frank Lee. McGlew avoided putting on Griffin at the end at which Buller would judge him at square-leg. Lee however no-balled him eleven times. At the end of the second day Griffin had M.J.K. Smith caught behind for 99 off the last ball of one over, and with

CHUCKER'S HAT-TRICK

By BRIAN CHAPMAN

WORDS, except the 600-odd I intend to set down right now, fail me. The second day of the second Test at Lord's yesterday erupted into a volcanic crescendo of excitement.

Daily Mirror, 25 June, 1960

England throwing the bat in the knowledge of a weekend declaration, he picked up Walker and Trueman from the first two balls of his next. Although this is the only Test hat-trick ever done at Lord's, in the circumstances it passed relatively unnoticed.

A final bizarre note. An exhibition match followed England's victory early on the fourth day, and in this Buller took his only opportunity of no-balling Griffin. The President of the South African Board, G.W.A. Chubb, thereupon announced that Griffin would not bowl again on the tour. He was a likeable young man, but it was a nice point, to my mind, whether Meckiff or he was the more obvious chucker.

ENGLAND v SOUTH AFRICA
Played at Lord's, 23, 24, 25, 27 June, 1960.
Result: England won by an innings and 73 runs.

England: First innings

M.C. Cowdrey* c Maclean b Griffin	4
R. Subba Row lbw b Adcock	90
E.R. Dexter c MacLean b Adcock	56
K.F. Barrington lbw b Goddard	24
M.J.K. Smith c Waite b Griffin	99
J.M. Parks† c Fellows-Smith b Adcock	3
P.M. Walker b Griffin	52
R. Illingworth not out	0
F.S. Trueman b Griffin	0
J.B. Statham not out	2
A.E. Moss did not bat	
Extras (b 6, lb 14, w 1, nb 11)	32
Total (8 wickets declared)	362

Fall of Wickets: 1/7, 2/103, 3/165, 4/220, 5/227, 6/347, 7/360, 8/360.
Bowling: Adcock 36-11-70-3, Griffin 30-7-87-4, Goddard 31-6-96-1, Tayfield 27-9-64-0, Fellows-Smith 5-0-13-0.

South Africa: First innings

D.J. McGlew* lbw b Statham	15
T.L. Goddard b Statham	19
S. O'Linn c Walker b Moss	18
R.A. McLean c Cowdrey b Statham	15
J.H.B. Waite† c Parks b Statham	3
P.R. Carlstein c Cowdrey b Moss	12
C. Wesley c Parks b Statham	11
J.P. Fellows-Smith c Parks b Moss	29
H.J. Tayfield c Smith b Moss	12
G.M. Griffin b Statham	5
N.A.T. Adcock not out	8
Extras (lb 4, nb 1)	5
Total	152

Fall of Wickets: 1/33, 2/48, 3/56, 4/69, 5/78, 6/88, 7/112, 8/132, 9/138, 10/152.
Bowling: Statham 20-5-63-6, Trueman 13-2-49-0, Moss 10.3-0-35-4.

South Africa: Second innings

D.J. McGlew* b Statham	17
T.L. Goddard c Parks b Statham	24
S. O'Linn lbw b Trueman	8
R.A. McLean c Parks b Trueman	13
J.H.B. Waite† lbw b Statham	0
P.R. Carlstein c Parks b Moss	6
C. Wesley b Dexter	35
J.P. Fellows-Smith not out	27
H.J. Tayfield b Dexter	4
G.M. Griffin b Statham	0
N.A.T. Adcock b Statham	2
Extras (nb 1)	1
Total	137

Fall of Wickets: 1/26, 2/49, 3/49, 4/50, 5/63, 6/72, 7/126, 8/132, 9/133, 10/137.
Bowling: Statham 21-6-34-5, Trueman 17-5-44-2, Moss 14-1-41-1, Illingworth 1-1-0-0, Dexter 4-0-17-2.

LEFT Griffin is reduced to bowling under-arm having been no-balled for throwing

THE ANNUAL ICC meeting at Lord's in July 1960 was the key event in the controversy over illegal bowling actions which had particularly threatened relations between England and Australia. The outcome was not immediately apparent as may be judged from my initial reaction in the *Daily Telegraph* to the press release while two days later I was speculating whether the 1961 visit of the Australians should be postponed. The no-balling of Griffin only a few weeks before had left among all present a deep scar not easy perhaps to appreciate so many years later.

While the ICC and the separate countries had been agonizing over a comprehensive definition of a throw the authorities had been acquiring positive evidence in the shape of photographs – film as well as stills – and the opinions of umpires and players.

The crucial meeting was an unofficial one between Sir Donald Bradman and W.J. Dowling (chairman of the Australian Board) on the one hand and Gubby Allen and Sir Hubert Ashton on the other. Both parties concluded that suspect bowlers simply must not be chosen for county or state sides, and Bradman and Allen, chairman of the respective selection committees, were men with the prestige and personality to bring this about. The Australian situation, with chuckers in almost every

1960

state, was the more acute. Yet they promptly disappeared, apart from Ian Meckiff – whose bowling had undermined England on the ill-fated tour of 1958-59 – and he was not chosen to come to England in 1961.

Note that although Imperial had long been an anachronism the I of the ICC title was not amended to International for several years yet.

THROWING GETS ANOTHER NEW DEFINITION

◆

No Move to Exclude Bowlers With Doubtful Actions

By E. W. SWANTON

Daily Telegraph, 16 July, 1960

AUSTRALIA TOUR MIGHT BE BETTER POSTPONED

◆

Meckiff's Selection Could Cause Major Fracas

By E. W. SWANTON

Daily Telegraph, 18 July, 1960

BELOW The ICC group (BACK ROW) R. Aird (Secretary MCC), HH The Maharaja Gaekwar of Baroda (India), R.E. Foster Bowley (South Africa), A.H.H. Gilligan (New Zealand), A. Drayton (West Indies), Sir Donald Bradman (Australia), G.O. Allen (MCC). (SEATED) HE Lieut-General Mohammed Yousef (Pakistan), M.A. Chidambaram (India), J. St F. Dare (West Indies), W.J. Dowling (Australia), H.S. Altham (President MCC), G.W.A. Chubb (South Africa), Sir Hubert Ashton (President-designate MCC), Sir Arthur Sims (New Zealand)

1960

"THE GREATEST TEST MATCH OF ALL TIME"

The Times, 15 December, 1960

SIR DONALD BRADMAN is the last man in cricket to make extravagant, ill-considered judgements, and at the end of this First Test of the Australia-West Indies series of 1960-61 he declared it to be 'the greatest'. Yet the result surely was a singularly happy fluke.

What enthused the Don and everyone else present at Brisbane was the skill and spirit of the struggle, the dramatic shifts and turns, the brave response to challenges by two exceptional captains and the high degree of sportsmanship shown from first to last. Fine deeds were done by great cricketers: Sobers, Davidson, Hall and the captains themselves, Benaud and Worrell. *The Times* correspondent thought that the expectation of victory never oscillated more frequently between two sides.

When what was sure to the last eight-ball over began Australia needed six runs to win with three wickets left. A leg-bye came off Hall's first ball, Benaud was caught behind (for 52) off the second. No run came off the third; a sneaked single off the fourth, another off the fifth as Hall dropped a skier. Three runs to get, three balls to go. Meckiff swung the sixth towards the mid-wicket boundary where Hunte took the ball on the bounce and ran out

Grout by a foot as, going like men possessed, they went through for a third run. With the scores level:

> In came Kline, looking pale and drawn. He took guard and not a bird moved. He lashed out like a man in a nightmare fighting off phantoms: the ball flew to midwicket, there was a flurry of desperate fieldsmen, Solomon flung at the wicket and to an incredulous shout of joy and anguish, scattered the stumps. The umpire's finger shot up and Meckiff was out. It was a tie.

This report and others conveyed the frenzied scene lucidly enough – which is as well as it seems the excitement was apparently too much for the broadcast since no coherent recording of that last over exists.

The series maintained a high note throughout. The Test record attendance for one day of 90,800 watched the second day of the fifth and final game at Melbourne, after which match (Australia having won the rubber 2-1), half a million people lined the Melbourne streets to give Worrell and his men a tumultuous farewell.

AUSTRALIA v WEST INDIES

Played at Brisbane, 9, 10, 12, 13, 14 December, 1960. Result: Match tied.

West Indies: First innings

C.C. Hunte c Benaud b Davidson		24
C.W. Smith c Grout b Davidson		7
R.B. Kanhai c Grout b Davidson		15
G. St A. Sobers c Kline b Meckiff		132
F.M.M. Worrell* c Grout b Davidson		65
J.S. Solomon hit wkt b Simpson		65
P.D. Lashley c Grout b Kline		19
F.C.M. Alexander† c Davidson b Kline		60
S. Ramadhin c Harvey b Davidson		12
W.W. Hall st Grout b Kline		50
A.L. Valentine not out		0
Extras (lb 3, w 1)		4
Total		453

Fall of Wickets: 1/23, 2/42, 3/65, 4/239, 5/243, 6/283, 7/347, 8/366, 9/452, 10/453.
Bowling: Davidson 30-2-135-5, Meckiff 18-0-129-1, Mackay 3-0-15-0, Benaud 24-3-93-0, Simpson 8-0-25-1, Kline 17.6-6-52-3.

Australia: First innings

C.C. McDonald c Hunte b Sobers		57
R.B. Simpson b Ramadhin		92
R.N. Harvey b Valentine		15
N.C. O'Neill c Valentine b Hall		181
L.E. Favell run out		45
K.D. Mackay b Sobers		35
A.K. Davidson c Alexander b Hall		44
R. Benaud* lbw b Hall		10
A.T.W. Grout† lbw b Hall		4
I. Meckiff run out		4
L.F. Kline not out		3
Extras (b 2, lb 8, w 1, nb 4)		15
Total		505

Fall of Wickets: 1/84, 2/138, 3/194, 4/278, 5/381, 6/469, 7/484, 8/489, 9/496, 10/505.
Bowling: Hall 29.3-1-140-4, Worrell 30-0-93-0, Sobers 32-0-115-2, Valentine 24-6-82-1, Ramadhin 15-1-60-1.

West Indies: Second innings

C.C. Hunte c Simpson b Mackay		39
C.W. Smith c O'Neill b Davidson		6
R.B. Kanhai c Grout b Davidson		54
G. St A. Sobers b Davidson		14
F.M.M. Worrell* c Grout b Davidson		65
J.S. Solomon lbw b Simpson		47
P.D. Lashley b Davidson		0
F.C.M. Alexander† b Benaud		5
S. Ramadhin c Harvey b Simpson		6
W.W. Hall b Davidson		18
A.L. Valentine not out		7
Extras (b 14, lb 7, w 2)		23
Total		284

Fall of Wickets: 1/13, 2/88, 3/114, 4/127, 5/210, 6/210, 7/241, 8/250, 9/253, 10/284.
Bowling: Davidson 24.6-4-87-6, Meckiff 4-1-19-0, Mackay 21-7-52-1, Benaud 31-6-69-1, Simpson 7-2-18-2, Kline 4-0-14-0, O'Neill 1-0-2-0.

Australia: Second innings

C.C. McDonald b Worrell		16
R.B. Simpson c sub (L.R. Gibbs) b Hall		0
R.N. Harvey c Sobers b Hall		5
N.C. O'Neill c Alexander b Hall		26
L.E. Favell c Solomon b Hall		7
K.D. Mackay b Ramadhin		28
A.K. Davidson run out		80
R. Benaud* c Alexander b Hall		52
A.T.W. Grout† run out		2
I. Meckiff run out		2
L.F. Kline not out		0
Extras (b 2, lb 9, nb 3)		14
Total		232

Fall of Wickets: 1/1, 2/7, 3/49, 4/49, 5/57, 6/92, 7/226, 8/228, 9/232, 10/232.
Bowling: Hall 17.7-3-65-5, Worrell 16-3-41-1, Sobers 8-0-30-0, Valentine 10-4-27-0, Ramadhin 17-3-57-1.

OPPOSITE The most memorable action photograph in Test history: Solomon's throw breaks the stumps and the match is tied

LEFT The West Indians' motorcade through Melbourne as the city says farewell

1961

PROMISE – AND REALITY! The Old Trafford Test of 1961 was a magnificent match with, for England, a tantalizing – almost a heart-searching – climax. When it started, the series stood level at one win apiece. Australia were defending the Ashes won resoundingly under Richie Benaud in 1958-59.

The game went England's way from the start, with Australia, chiefly in the ever-combative, angular form of Bill Lawry, fighting every inch of the way. Crawford White was overstating it when on the last morning he opined that with four wickets to get and Australia leading by 154, 'England are poised for victory'.

It did almost seem so, though, not many minutes after the start of play on that fifth day when Australia's number 11, Graham McKenzie joined Alan Davidson at 334 for 9. David Allen's off-breaks had taken 3 for 0 in 15 balls. The difference then was a mere 157. There followed the historic stand of 98 for the last wicket, with Davidson hitting brilliantly and McKenzie supporting him admirably.

So in the end England needed to make 256 in three hours 50 minutes on a dry pitch taking spin. So many to get in the fourth innings was a tough proposition, even if time had not been a factor. As it was the required rate was 66 runs an hour. The start was brisk, then came Ted Dexter at his most commanding. In 84 minutes he made 76 and twenty minutes before tea he and the patient Subba Row were together with the board showing 150 for 1. It was at this point that Benaud played his last despairing card, switching the line of his attack to the right-handed Dexter by bowling his leg-breaks round the wicket into the foot marks. First Dexter was caught behind, and then May bowled round his legs for a duck. A few

Poised for victory in photo-finish

By CRAWFORD WHITE

THIS magnificent fourth Test promises to produce today one of the most exciting finishes since Australia and the West Indies tied with 737 each last December.

Australia start this morning 154 runs on with only four wickets in hand. So England are poised for victory.

Daily Mail, 1 August, 1961

England ripped apart in 20 deadly mins

Daily Mail, 2 August, 1961

feverish moments of Close and not only he but also Subba Row were gone. All four to Benaud – England at tea 163 for 5. The batting following Peter May's departure was not only fragile but rudderless. So it continued, the margin finally being 54 runs and twenty minutes.

Thus the Ashes remained with Australia and they continued to hold them – thanks to those momentous twenty minutes – through the next four series, three of them halved, the other won by one match: 1962-63, 1964, 1965-66, and 1968, until the last Test of the 1970-71 series in Australia.

Australia: First innings 190 (W.M. Lawry 74, B.C. Booth 46; Statham 5-53, Dexter 3-16).
England: First innings 367 (P.B.H. May 95, K.F. Barrington 78, G. Pullar 63, Simpson 4-23).
Australia: Second innings 432 (W.M. Lawry 102, A.K. Davidson 77*, N.C. O'Neill 67, R.B. Simpson 51; Allen 4-58).

England: Second innings

G. Pullar c O'Neill b Davidson	26
R. Subba Row b Benaud	49
E.R. Dexter c Grout b Benaud	76
P.B.H. May* b Benaud	0
D.B. Close c O'Neill b Benaud	8
K.F. Barrington lbw b Mackay	5
J.T. Murray† c Simpson b Benaud	4
D.A. Allen c Simpson b Benaud	10
F.S. Trueman c Benaud b Simpson	8
J.B. Statham b Davidson	8
J.A. Flavell not out	0
Extras (b 5, w 2)	7
Total	201

Fall of Wickets: 1/40, 2/150, 3/150, 4/158, 5/163, 6/171, 7/171, 8/189, 9/193, 10/201.
Bowling: Davidson 14.4-1-50-2, McKenzie 4-1-20-0, Mackay 13-7-33-1, Benaud 32-11-70-6, Simpson 8-4-21-1.

RIGHT The beginning of the end for England: Dexter is caught behind for 76 off Benaud

HAMPSHIRE'S FLAG ON SUMMIT AT LAST

CHAMPIONS AFTER 66 YEARS

The long, hard climb is over. The chains at last are broken. At Bournemouth yesterday, soon after four o'clock, Hampshire won the county championship after 66 years of trying and in the 98th year of their history. They beat Derbyshire by 140 runs, on the same ground and at much the same time of day as Glamorgan won their only title in 1948.

As the sun broke through the haze, there followed all the joys of victory. The winning team were serenaded and appeared on the balcony with their glasses in their hands. Ingleby-Mackenzie, in a short and cheerful speech, called himself "the luckiest captain of all time" to be so fortunate in his players. One sensed the spirit of unity and humour and comradeship which has turned a good side into a championship one. Mr. Altham, the president of the club, spoke of the captain's adventurous example, which has brought its reward and to which the team has reacted so well.

The Times, 2 September, 1961

HAMPSHIRE'S FIRST Championship was a highly popular event everywhere for they were an attractive side which under Colin Ingleby-Mackenzie's direction played enterprising cricket. Three men behind the scenes had much to do with their success: Desmond Eagar, the preceding captain and at this point half-way through his 32 years as secretary; Arthur Holt, the admirable coach, under whose care most of the staff had graduated; and Harry Altham, who inspired Hampshire cricket and cricketers off the field as successfully as Ingleby-Mackenzie on it.

As a Hampshire man John Woodcock – *The Times* Cricket Correspondent – must have found this the most enjoyable to write of all his many thousand reports. In his last paragraphs he really let sentiment have its head.

Then, of course, there is the captain. His has been a triumph not of tactics, nor of theory, nor even of leadership, but of personality. Ingleby-Mackenzie has a zest for cricket which he can communicate to others. He has, too, an old world charm which in this day and age it is a joy to meet. And around him he has a friendly, keen, and modest side—the heirs of Hambledon. More cosmopolitan they may be, but now supreme, in all England, like William Beldam and Richard Nyren, John Small and Thomas Brett on Broad-Halfpenny Down so long ago.

Hampshire 1961: (BACK ROW) M.D. Burden, H. Horton, D.A. Livingstone, A. Wassell, M. Heath, D.W. White, P.J. Sainsbury, D.O. Baldry, N. Drake (scorer) (SEATED) J.R. Gray, D. Shackleton, A.C.D. Ingleby-Mackenzie (captain), R.E. Marshall

1962

RAIN TO RESCUE OF THE GENTLEMEN

PLAYERS WELL AHEAD OF CLOCK

The Times, 21 July, 1962

THE GENTLEMEN played first against the Players at Lord's (the Dorset Square ground) in 1806. It was thus the oldest first-class fixture and for most of its long history this was the prime classic of the summer.

When the 137th Lord's Gentlemen and Players took place as usual in July 1962 no one knew it would be the last because the decision to abolish the distinction between amateurs and professionals had yet to be taken. However, as it turned out, the game as usual was keenly fought and provided much admirable cricket, with honours even on the run of play – for although the Players had only 29 runs to get in thirty-five minutes when rain brought down the final curtain Dexter had declared his side's second innings with five wickets standing.

Dexter had just emerged, somewhat luckily, as the selectors' choice for the captaincy of MCC in Australia in the coming winter following a long and lively debate as to the respective merits also of Colin Cowdrey and David Sheppard, both of whom were also Test captains. In the event Cowdrey, after having been named to lead the Gentlemen, fell out of the running at the crucial moment, removed to hospital with an internal complaint which kept him off the field for three weeks, while Sheppard, who had arranged for sabbatical leave from his wardenship of an east end mission, in the event of his being chosen for the tour, still had to prove current form. This he did to everyone's satisfaction in this match.

Of the 137 matches between Gentlemen and Players at Lord's the Players won 68, the Gentlemen 41, and 28 were drawn. Most of the best English batsmen scored hundreds in these matches. It is a fitting coincidence that whereas of the Gentlemen's 44 hundreds Dr

W.G. Grace, the undisputed champion, contributed seven, while of the Players 46, J.B. Hobbs, greatest of professional batsmen, likewise scored seven.

For younger readers one might repeat the old tag that this was a game where all the Players were gentlemen and all the Gentlemen players. The maintenance to the end of the ancient title was generally accepted as being out of respect for tradition and without any possible other implication. Limited elements of the press, however, inevitably used it as a cheap dig at 'the diehard reactionaries at Lord's'.

ABOVE Dexter is applauded to the wicket by the fielding Players. His captaincy of MCC for the tour to Australia has just been announced

GENTLEMEN v PLAYERS
Played at Lord's, 18, 19, 20 July, 1962.
Result: Match drawn.

Gentlemen: First innings
Rev D.S. Sheppard c and b Titmus	112
E.J. Craig b Trueman	4
E.R. Dexter* c Trueman b Shackleton	55
M.J.K. Smith run out	44
R.M. Prideaux b Trueman	14
A.R. Lewis lbw b Shackleton	2
R.W. Barber run out	0
D.E. Pithey run out	30
T.E. Bailey c Walker b Shackleton	5
A.C. Smith† c Sharpe b Shackleton	33
O.S. Wheatley not out	14
Extras (b 4, lb 6)	10
Total	323

Fall of Wickets: 1/12, 2/109, 3/204, 4/221, 5/227, 6/229, 7/239, 8/226, 9/275.
Bowling: Trueman 13-6-59-2, Shackleton 38-9-101-4, Walker 28-4-64-0, Titmus 20-6-46-1, Gifford 14-4-43-0.

Players: First innings
M.J. Stewart c A. Smith b Bailey	0
J.H. Edrich b Bailey	19
P.H. Parfitt c Sheppard b Dexter	9
T.W. Graveney c Craig b Wheatley	21
P.J. Sharpe c and b Barber	39
P.M. Walker b Bailey	15
F.J. Titmus c Dexter b Bailey	70
F.S. Trueman* c Wheatley b Barber	63
K.V. Andrew† c A. Smith b Bailey	17
N. Gifford c A. Smith b Bailey	2
D. Shackleton not out	1
Extras (b 4)	4
Total	260

Fall of Wickets: 1/0, 2/15, 3/41, 4/56, 5/86, 6/104, 7/194, 8/255, 9/257.
Bowling: Bailey 30.3-10-58-6, Wheatley 19-6-37-1, Dexter 18-2-49-1, Barber 21-7-90-2, Pithey 8-2-22-0.

Gentlemen: Second innings
Rev D.S. Sheppard b Titmus	34
E.J. Craig c Titmus b Trueman	0
E.R. Dexter* run out	1
M.J.K. Smith not out	15
R.M. Prideaux b Shackleton	109
A.R. Lewis c Andrew b Titmus	10
R.W. Barber not out	3
D.E. Pithey	
T.E. Bailey	did not bat
A.C. Smith†	
O.S. Wheatley	
Total (5 wickets declared)	172

Fall of Wickets: 1/0, 2/73, 3/95, 4/115, 5/166.
Bowling: Shackleton 19-8-38-1, Trueman 10-6-8-1, Titmus 24-5-69-2, Walker 9-2-21-0, Gifford 7-0-36-0.

Players: Second innings
M.J. Stewart c A. Smith b Wheatley	3
J.H. Edrich not out	77
P.H. Parfitt c Dexter b Barber	63
T.W. Graveney c A. Smith b Bailey	41
P.J. Sharpe not out	12
P.M. Walker	
F.J. Titmus	
F.S. Trueman*	did not bat
K.V. Andrew†	
N. Gifford	
D. Shackleton	
Extras (b 1, lb 10)	11
Total (3 wickets)	207

Fall of Wickets: 1/3, 2/121, 3/177.
Bowling: Bailey 13-1-45-1, Wheatley 12-1-46-1, Pithey 4-0-27-0, Dexter 7-0-35-0, Barber 7-0-43-1.

Lord's calls time, Gents, please

By FRANK ROSTRON

THERE will be no more "Call me mister" in England's cricket, no more "fancy caps" as the paid players mockingly call the unpaid gentlemen.

For they're all the same cricketing flesh and blood now, under the flannels.

From February 1 next there will be no amateurs. There will also be no professionals. There will only be "Players."

So with this abolish-the-amateur decision of the M.C.C. advisory committee after an historic seven-hour meeting at Lord's yesterday, the last link with cricket's squire and peasant tradition is shattered.

Daily Express, 27 November, 1962

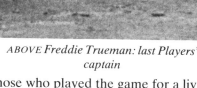

1962

THE ABOLITION of the distinction between amateurs and professionals was brought about when the MCC Committee in November 1962 accepted a recommendation of the Advisory County Cricket Committee to that effect reached by a majority of ten votes to seven. Although economic pressures would eventually have driven amateurs out of the regular county game the decision was a surprise, coming when it did, both because the counties' preference was a narrow one which MCC were not obliged to accept without wider consultation among cricketers and also because a representative committee which they had set up only four years before to examine the matter in depth had come down strongly against any change in the system.

Here are the immediate results of the abolition. In 1962 fifty amateurs had played in county cricket, twelve of them as captains. The other five counties were led already by professionals. In 1963 the counties were led by eight who had been amateurs while four counties replaced their amateur captains with men who had always been pros. About one third of the fifty 1962 amateurs were not seen in county cricket again.

My reaction in the *Daily Telegraph* was one of lament for the passing of the *independent* element. I maintained that the game was generally at its best when there was a balance between

ABOVE Freddie Trueman: last Players' captain

those who played the game for a living and those who did not. I foresaw difficulties in finding future leaders. Looking back, I believe there to be a connection between the departure of the amateur spirit and the ultra-defensive mood of much of the county cricket of the middle and late 1960s which in turn led to the 40-over Sunday League and the recruiting of overseas stars.

This however was a minority view – at any rate in the press. Frank Rostron, for instance, on the front page of the *Daily Express* was clearly rejoicing that 'the last link with cricket's squire and peasant tradition is shattered'.

1963

The most fantastic over Lord's has ever seen

By IAN WOOLDRIDGE

STOP pounding, pulse, while I tell the story of cricket's greatest last over. It began at Lord's last night at 5.55. It ended just after six.

LEFT Moment of drama: Cowdrey comes out to bat with a broken arm in plaster. Twenty-one years later Paul Terry was to emulate Cowdrey's brave feat for England against the 1984 West Indians

THE 1963 TEST against the West Indies at Lord's will remain longer in my memory than almost every other Test of the modern age. It was evenly and aggressively contested throughout and spiced with great individual performances, the climax sustained until the last over began with all four endings to a cricket match possible. Wes Hall, who had kept up his speed astonishingly in an unbroken spell (apart from tea) of three hours, twenty minutes, was the bowler, eight wickets were down and eight runs were needed. Off the first three balls, David Allen and Derek Shackleton scored a single apiece. Off the fourth Shackleton was run out. Enter to the non-striker's end Colin Cowdrey, broken left arm in plaster. Allen kept his head. How could he contrive six runs without the risk of exposing Cowdrey to the last ball?

In the view of the best judges who saw it Dexter's 70 in 80 minutes against

130

In those few minutes blue-bloods cavorted like children on the Pavilion balconies, newspapermen stood and roared.

So ended the second Test between England and West Indies. In a draw.

After 29 hours and 55 minutes England needed eight runs to win when the last over began.

Wesley Hall, the world's fastest bowler, was turning at the end of his 22-yard run. Derek Shackleton, greying 38-year-old veteran from Hampshire, had to face him.

He was last but one man in. For England's last hope, Colin Cowdrey, was still in the dressing-room with his fractured left arm in plaster.

BALL ONE: Hall unleashed it like a bullet. At 90 m.p.h. it swung viciously away. Shackleton lashed out and missed.

Sprinting

BALL TWO: It was just as fast, but straighter. Shackleton dropped his bat on it and ran. Hall flung himself down the wicket to try to run out David Allen, racing from the other end. Hall stumbled. England seven to win.

BALL THREE: Allen turned it away down the leg side for a single. Six to win.

BALL FOUR: Shackleton lashed out, missed and stumbled. He looked up to find Allen racing at him. He ran. But Murray, West Indies 19-year-old wicketkeeper, coolly tossed the ball to captain Frank Worrell.

Worrell could not trust himself to throw. He had a two-yard start on Shackleton and ran like an Olympic sprinter to the other end. He won the race. Shackleton was run out.

England, six to win, two balls to go. And in came Colin Cowdrey. For 30 minutes he had been practising batting one-handed in the dressing-room for this moment.

Flying

Cowdrey, said many, was showing fool's courage to bat at all. It will already probably be 12 weeks before he can return to cricket. Another blow could finish his career. But mercifully it was Allen facing the bowling.

BALL FIVE: Allen pushed it back.

BALL SIX: Hall, in utter silence, tossed it from hand to hand and looked imploringly at the sky. He began to run, gold crucifix flying out behind him.

England could win with a six. West Indies could win with a wicket.

It was probably the fastest ball of Hall's life. It seared straight for Allen's middle stump. But Allen leant forward like a master and met it with a bold British bat.

Cricket's great last over was done.

Daily Mail, 26 June, 1963

the extreme pace of Hall and Griffith was one of the finest innings ever played. Barrington, Butcher and Kanhai batted admirably; Trueman rarely, if ever, bowled better; Close on the last day played his highest and best innings for England, impervious as ever to physical hurt.

Blows were given and received, yet the game was chivalrously fought. Although by far the most exciting, the match was the only draw in the series. England went on to win the Third Test comfortably, but Frank Worrell's side – having won the First Test – won the last two to take the series 3-1.

ENGLAND v WEST INDIES
Played at Lord's,
20, 21, 22, 24, 25 June, 1963.
Result: Match drawn.

West Indies: First innings

C.C. Hunte c Close b Trueman	44
E.D.A. St J. McMorris lbw b Trueman	16
G. St A. Sobers c Cowdrey b Allen	42
R.B. Kanhai c Edrich b Trueman	73
B.F. Butcher c Barrington b Trueman	14
J.S. Solomon c Murray b Shackleton	56
F.M.M. Worrell* b Trueman	0
D.L. Murray† c Cowdrey b Shackleton	20
W.W. Hall not out	25
C.C. Griffith c Cowdrey b Shackleton	0
L.R. Gibbs c Stewart b Shackleton	0
Extras (b 10, lb 1)	11
Total	301

Fall of Wickets: 1/51, 2/64, 3/127, 4/145, 5/219, 6/219, 7/263, 8/297, 9/297, 10/301.
Bowling: Trueman 44-16-100-6, Shackleton 50.2-22-93-3, Dexter 20-6-41-0, Close 9-3-21-0, Allen 10-3-35-1.

England: First innings

M.J. Stewart c Kanhai b Griffith	2
J.H. Edrich c Murray b Griffith	0
E.R. Dexter* lbw b Sobers	70
K.F. Barrington c Sobers b Worrell	80
M.C. Cowdrey b Gibbs	4
D.B. Close c Murray b Griffith	9
J.M. Parks† b Worrell	35
F.J. Titmus not out	52
F.S. Trueman b Hall	10
D.A. Allen lbw b Griffith	2
D. Shackleton b Griffith	8
Extras (b 8, lb 8, nb 9)	25
Total	297

Fall of Wickets: 1/2, 2/20, 3/102, 4/115, 5/151, 6/206, 7/235, 8/271, 9/274, 10/297.
Bowling: Hall 18-2-65-1, Griffith 26-6-91-5, Sobers 18-4-45-1, Gibbs 27-9-59-1, Worrell 13-6-12-2.

West Indies: Second innings

C.C. Hunte c Cowdrey b Shackleton	7
E.D.A. St J. McMorris c Cowdrey b Trueman	8
G. St A. Sobers (5) c Parks b Trueman	8
R.B. Kanhai (3) c Cowdrey b Shackleton	21
B.F. Butcher (4) lbw b Shackleton	133
J.S. Solomon c Stewart b Allen	5
F.M.M. Worrell* c Stewart b Trueman	33
D.L. Murray† c Parks b Trueman	2
W.W. Hall c Parks b Trueman	2
C.C. Griffith b Shackleton	1
L.R. Gibbs not out	1
Extras (b 5, lb 2, nb 1)	8
Total	229

Fall of Wickets: 1/15, 2/15, 3/64, 4/84, 5/104, 6/214, 7/224, 8/226, 9/228, 10/229.
Bowling: Trueman 26-9-52-5, Shackleton 34-14-72-4, Allen 21-7-50-1, Titmus 17-3-47-0.

England: Second innings

M.J. Stewart c Solomon b Hall	17
J.H. Edrich c Murray b Hall	8
E.R. Dexter* b Gibbs	2
K.F. Barrington c Murray b Griffith	60
M.C. Cowdrey not out	19
D.B. Close c Murray b Griffith	70
J.M. Parks† lbw b Griffith	17
F.J. Titmus c McMorris b Hall	11
F.S. Trueman c Murray b Hall	0
D.A. Allen not out	4
D. Shackleton run out	4
Extras (b 5, lb 8, nb 3)	16
Total (9 wickets)	228

Fall of Wickets: 1/15, 2/27, 3/31, 4/130, 5/158, 6/203, 7/203, 8/219, 9/228.
Bowling: Hall 40-9-93-4, Griffith 30-7-59-3, Sobers 4-1-4-0, Gibbs 17-7-56-1.

ABOVE LEFT The end of the match: players and umpires rush off as excited spectators surge on to the field. Fortunately Cowdrey was spared facing a ball; so ended one of the most exciting Tests ever

1963

Wembley touch as Sussex win Cup

from JOHN ARLOTT

LORD'S, September 7

THIS STIRRING match was a happy triumph, by 14 runs, for Sussex and, equally, for the promoters of the county cricket knock-out competition. The final was played as a hard, tactical, team operation. Worcestershire, their flawless out-cricket shrewdly directed, might have won in the first half but for the handsome front-foot batting of Parks.

No Worcester batsman could quite match him on a pitch where, so long as the bowlers bowled straight on a full length, a packed front-of-the-wicket field would contain almost any batsman. Worcestershire's consolation was the Man of the Match award to Gifford.

Runs, wickets, time . . . runs, wickets, time: 128 for six . . . 132 for seven: 37 to get . . . three wickets and nine overs left!

If the promoters had stage-managed the affair they could not have kept the crowd in a more savage state of suspense.

When Snow took the wickets of Gifford and Flavell with consecutive balls it seemed that Sussex had achieved the final break-through. But Booth, intelligently adventurous, with Carter his game henchman, chased the game to within two overs and 15 runs of a win for his side before they embarked on one close run too many.

Then "Sussex-by-the-Sea" broke out from the front of the Tavern.

Perhaps it was not, strictly speaking, first-class cricket. But as entertainment it is with us for the foreseeable future.

Let us be grateful for it.

Observer, 8 September, 1963

THE FIRST OF the one-day finals at Lord's, won by Sussex on the first Saturday of September 1963, was that for The Knock-Out Competition, *not* for the Gillette Cup. It may read oddly today but several of the counties (and notably Yorkshire) were very luke-warm in 1963 about both sponsorship and the limited-over game generally. Hence Gillette's initial patronage was extremely low-key. They believed in the idea and gave it time to sell itself. They provided indeed an ideal pattern for future commercial involvement, and the game is indebted for their example which in England, though not Australia, has been followed by their rivals and successors.

The Gillette Cup became known generally as such in 1964, and was that year again won by Sussex: these were very much Dexter days. In addition to leading Sussex to victory he was writing a column each week for the *Observer*. Today Dexter is better known as a television commentator.

SUSSEX v WORCESTERSHIRE
The Knock-out Competition final
Played at Lord's, 7 September, 1963.
Result: Sussex won by 14 runs.

Sussex
R.J. Langridge b Gifford	34
A.S.M. Oakman c Slade b Gifford	19
K.G. Suttle b Gifford	9
E.R. Dexter* c Broadbent b Horton	3
J.H. Parks† b Slade	57
L.J. Lenham c Booth b Gifford	7
G.C. Cooper lbw b Slade	0
N.I. Thomson lbw b Flavell	1
A. Buss c Booth b Carter	3
J.A. Snow b Flavell	10
D.L. Bates not out	3
Extras (b 9, lb 10, nb 3)	22
Total	168

Fall of Wickets: 1/62, 2/67, 3/76, 4/98, 5/118, 6/123, 7/134, 8/142, 9/157.
Bowling: Flavell 14.2-3-31-2, Carter 12-1-39-1, Slade 11-2-23-2, Gifford 15-4-33-4, Horton 8-1-20-1.

Worcestershire
D. Kenyon* lbw b Buss	1
M.J. Horton c and b Buss	26
R.G.A. Headley c Snow b Bates	25
T.W. Graveney c Dexter b Oakman	29
D.W. Richardson c Parks b Thomson	3
R.G. Broadbent c Bates b Snow	13
R. Booth† not out	33
D.N.F. Slade b Buss	3
N. Gifford b Snow	0
J.A. Flavell b Snow	0
R.G. Carter run out	2
Extras (b 8, lb 9, nb 2)	19
Total	154

Fall of Wickets: 1/7, 2/38, 3/80, 4/91, 5/103, 6/128, 7/132, 8/133, 9/133.
Bowling: Thomson 13.2-4-35-1, Buss 15-2-39-3, Oakman 13-4-17-1, Suttle 5-2-11-0, Bates 9-2-20-1, Snow 8-0-13-3.

RIGHT Jim Parks driving handsomely through the covers during his top-scoring 57. The advent of one-day cricket was ideal for his belligerent strokeplay

JUST WHEN the palaver about throwing seemed to have been resolved the Australian selectors surprised everyone by naming Meckiff after a gap of three seasons to play in another Test Match. As John Woodcock observes here how he came to be chosen was a mystery seeing that the selectors were still, as for many years, Sir Donald Bradman, J.S. Ryder and Dudley Seddon. Had the 84-year-old patriarch, Jack Ryder, arguing the case for his fellow-Victorian, won over one of the other two? The Don is not the man to break confidentiality, but it is safe to say that it was Seddon who allowed himself to be persuaded.

Reuter's short report from Brisbane makes clear that as usual in these cases it is the umpire who comes in for the crowd's abuse while the offender becomes a hero.

1963

ABOVE *Ian Meckiff: no-balled for throwing*

AUSTRALIA IN DILEMMA OVER MECKIFF

From Our Cricket Correspondent

It was with both sympathy and relief that I heard the news from Brisbane on Saturday morning that I. Meckiff had been called for throwing in the first Test match against South Africa: sympathy, obviously, for Meckiff and the umpire, C. Egar, in their embarrassing ordeal, and a deep sense of relief that we shall not be burdened next summer with a full scale throwing controversy.

How Meckiff came to be chosen for Brisbane is, itself, a mystery. On his own admission his action is the same now as it was in 1958-59 when he headed the Australian bowling averages against England. It is unchanged since last winter, when, although the most successful bowler in Australia, he was not chosen for the Test matches. He was, it is true, called twice for throwing in the Sheffield Shield, but there seemed to exist a tacit acceptance of his action.

Even if people in their heart of hearts regarded him as a thrower there was a natural reluctance on the part of the umpires to finish his career. It may help in filling in the background to know that Meckiff is one of Australia's most popular players. At Melbourne, his home ground he is a hero. Everyone likes him, friend and foe, and he is delightfully keen. I make this point because there seem these days to be so many players who are *blasé* to a degree in their attitude to the game.

Meckiff's action has all the symptoms of a throw: the front foot splayed in the delivery stride, the body wide open, the sudden disconcerting speed off a leisurely run. On seeing him, first people have been inclined to let forth a rather hollow laugh. When, during the West Indian visit to Australia in 1960-61, he made a resolute effort to straighten his arm, he lost all his sting. In 1958, when I saw him take so many vital English wickets, and again last winter, when playing for Victoria, he was, I thought, a worse offender than the South African Griffin, the centre of the rumpus at the Lord's Test in 1960.

INVIDIOUS POSITION

How, then, was Meckiff chosen for Brisbane? Why this unexpected and inconsistent decision to put him to the test? Why the *volte-face*? Was it the desire to end, once and for all, an ambiguous situation? Was it anxiety at the prospect of coming to England next summer with a weak opening attack? Was it a misguided attempt to be fair to Meckiff? Was it that Sir Donald Bradman found, as he had not found before, that J. S. Ryder and D. Seddon, his fellow selectors, agreed to outvote him? Whatever the reason, Australia's two leading umpires were placed in a wholly invidious position. No doubt they discussed it beforehand and decided that "the time had come".

As the result of Egar's censure it is hardly possible for the Victorian selectors to choose Meckiff for their next match against Queensland, and they have in fact deferred the announcement of their team. As a result of it, too, the umpires on the English list will have rested more easily over the weekend. So, no doubt, will the officials at Lord's, who could scarce conceal their anxiety when he was chosen. So, also, will the English journalists. It is a hateful thing having to say of such a enthusiast as Meckiff that you think he infringes the law. So, finally, will English batsmen, for Meckiff in this country could have been devilishly effective.

MAN OF DECISION

It must have been like a dawn execution at Brisbane: one from the days of the guillotine, with the crowd cheering and booing. It was finished in the first over. Benaud, a man of decision, has said he will not bowl Meckiff again in the match. By the demonstrations that followed Meckiff must have been made to feel a martyr and Egar an ogre. In a cold, premeditated way, the Australian selectors had brought the whole matter to a head, and vindicated, in the process, those Englishmen who, whenever they have watched Meckiff turn his arm, have let their thoughts be known.

Had Meckiff not been called at Brisbane, today's meeting of the Advisory County Cricket Committee at Lord's would no doubt have been disturbed by speculation of what might happen in England next summer. As it is, the counties will be able to concentrate their thoughts upon the canker of seam bowling. There are numerous proposals and possibilities to be considered. One would restrict the bowler in the length of his run-up; another would prevent him from polishing the ball; a third would affect the preparation of pitches. They are all aimed at reviving the dying art of slow bowling, and of making cricket a more attractive and diverse game to watch.

TENSE SILENCE

BRISBANE, Dec. 8.—There was loud applause as Benaud handed the ball to Meckiff to bowl, then a tense silence as Meckiff marked out his run-up and came up to bowl. The first ball went wide of Goddard's off stump. Egar called his second and third balls and Benaud went over from slip to speak to Meckiff. There followed an apparently legitimate ball, then another no-ball, three good balls, and then a fourth no-ball.

The crowd jeered and hooted as Egar shouted "no ball" each time. There was more booing when Meckiff was replaced. Benaud was barracked for the remainder of the afternoon, and at close of play an embarrassed Meckiff was carried shoulder-high from the pitch by a section of the crowd who had swarmed on to the field. After chairing Meckiff the same group of spectators returned to the pitch and booed Egar as he left the pitch.

The Times, 7 December, 1963

<table>
<tr><td>

1964

</td><td>

WORCESTER CHAMPIONS
FOR FIRST TIME

Daily Telegraph, 26 August, 1964

</td></tr>
</table>

Triumph for Kenyon's leadership

IT is a great thing in the cricket world when a county win their first championship, as Worcestershire did yesterday.

They are the champions of 1964, with their Warwickshire neighbours irrevocably runners-up.

Only five now of the 17 first-class counties, Essex, Leicestershire, Northants, Somerset and Sussex, have never been champions, but more remarkable than this is the fact that until Worcestershire's very popular success, only two new ones, Glamorgan in 1948, and Hampshire in 1961, have added their names to the illustrious list since before the first war.

Daily Telegraph, 26 August, 1964

25 AUGUST 1964 was a gala day for Worcestershire who beat their southern neighbours Gloucestershire at Worcester while those of Warwickshire to the east had their title hopes eliminated by a narrow defeat at the hands of Hampshire. So it was Worcestershire's Championship, their first, and therefore an occasion significant for English cricket. For though the disparity between the strong and the weak had been growing less for quite a while Glamorgan in 1948 and Hampshire in 1961 were the only other counties to have won their first Championships since the Second World War.

The final table told the story of the shift in power. Who would have thought it possible that the first three would be Worcestershire, Warwickshire and Nottinghamshire, with the traditional leaders, Surrey, Yorkshire, Middlesex and Kent following in that order? To show it was no fluke Worcestershire won again in 1965.

Kenyon led a well-balanced side in a cool, philosophical way. Still a fine player at forty he made his 70th hundred in the Gloucestershire match that settled the Championship. Tom Graveney was the great batsman of the side, and there was plenty of bowling with Jack Flavell, Len Coldwell and young Norman Gifford, England bowlers all, in the van.

Worcestershire's winning team. (STANDING) W. Faithful (scorer), D.N.F. Slade, R.G.A. Headley, R.G.M. Carter, L.J. Coldwell, N. Gifford, C.D. Fearnley, W.B. Powell (masseur); (SEATED) R. Booth, J.A. Flavell, D. Kenyon, T.W. Graveney, M.J. Horton, D.W. Richardson

ON THE LAST morning of the First Test at Kingston, Jamaica between the West Indies and Australia in February, 1965, with the state of the match favouring the home side but the issue undecided, an article by Richie Benaud was published in the *Jamaica Gleaner*, under the heading 'Charlie Griffith is a chucker'. The piece was syndicated throughout the West Indies and India and appeared, of course, in the newspaper of which Benaud was cricket correspondent, the *Sydney Sun*.

The sensational effect of this allegation can no doubt be imagined. For it came from the recently retired captain of Australia, who had been the opposite number to Frank Worrell in the Australia v West Indies series of 1960-61 which is universally recognized as the best ever played. The spirit in which this series had been fought, coupled with the excitement of the matches themselves, made for a 'special relationship' as between Australia and the West Indies under these two admirable captains, and this allegation by one of them dealt the relationship an all but mortal blow.

There had been talk among cricketers and in the press about Charlie Griffith's action for several years. He had been once called in Barbados playing against the Indians, and he was to be no-balled once more against Lancashire on the West Indies tour to England of 1966. The ball that was suspect was the one bowled open-chested from the edge of the crease. I know that the West Indies authorities were nervous on this matter, not least Worrell, who had retired and was now managing the side. There was clear evidence as to this in the fact that although Sobers, Worrell's successor as captain, never fielded anywhere except round the bat, for every over bowled by Griffith prior to the allegation he had stood at mid-off, watching the bowler's feet and no doubt reminding him, if necessary, to keep close to the stumps.

Sitting in the press-box with Benaud I knew what was in his mind and even presumed, as a friend, to suggest that after the match he might seek a meeting with Worrell and the West Indies Board and produce evidence. Richie, however, was not to be deflected. At Brisbane in 1963 he had been Australia's captain when, in the First Test of the series against South Africa, Ian Meckiff had been no-balled out of Test cricket. After that dramatic experience he told me, 'If I could prove that my own brother threw I would expose him'. It was Meckiff's no-balling that determined Benaud to disclose the truth as he saw it, come what may.

BELOW C.C. Griffith: a fearsome fast bowler who became involved in the 'chucking' crisis

WEST INDIES v AUSTRALIA
Played at Kingston, 3, 4, 5, 6, 8 March, 1965.
Result: West Indies won by 179 runs.

West Indies: First innings 239 (A.W. White 57*, C.C. Hunte 41; Mayne 4-43).

Australia: First innings 217 (N.J.N. Hawke 45*, N.C. O'Neill 40; Hall 5-60).

West Indies: Second innings 373 (C.C. Hunte 81, J.S. Solomon 76, B.F. Butcher 71; Mayne 4-56, Philpott 4-109).

Australia: Second innings 216 (B.C. Booth 56; Hall 4-45).

BENAUD ACCUSES GRIFFITH OF THROWING

AUSTRALIA'S former captain, Richie Benaud, has raised a hornet's nest about his ears here by denouncing Charles Griffith's action in an article on the front page of the *Daily Gleaner*, cables E. W. Swanton

Daily Telegraph, 9 March, 1965

1965

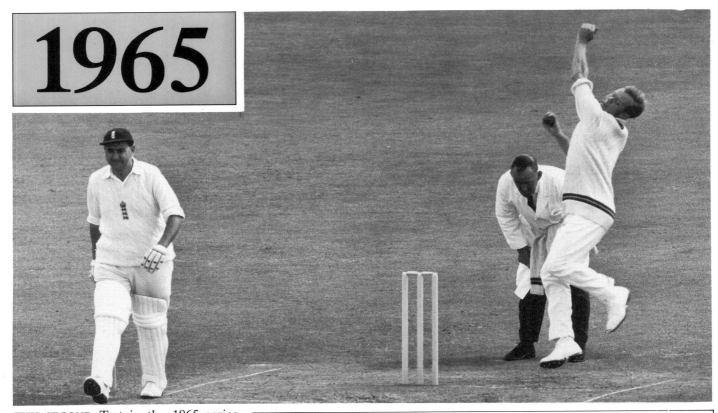

THIS SECOND Test in the 1965 series of three developed into a fraternal triumph without parallel in Test cricket for the two Pollocks, Graeme and Peter. Looking back over twenty-odd years my assessment of the 21-year-old Graeme does not seem in any way exaggerated. I can imagine either of two other left-handers playing such an innings as his 125, Frank Woolley and Gary Sobers: no one else. I rated Peter Pollock, the senior by three years, as in 1964 'the best fast bowler in the world outside the West Indies'. He took here five wickets in each innings, Graeme intervening with 59 towards South Africa's second innings 289 which left England to get 319 to win.

This was England's first defeat in 15 Tests under the captaincy of M.J.K. Smith. They missed Dexter in this series, injured in a car accident, while Cartwright, who had taken 6 for 94 in the first innings, was unable to bowl in the second because of a fractured thumb. There was, however, no dis-credit in losing the short series to this South African side in what turned out to be their last tour to England.

Second Test—First Day

POLLOCK'S GLORIOUS 125 SAVES SOUTH AFRICA

◆

TWO ENGLAND WICKETS LOST FOR 16 RUNS

South Africa were all out for 269 and England have scored 16 runs for the loss of two wickets.

By E. W. SWANTON

TRENT BRIDGE, Thursday.

AN innings was played here today by Graeme Pollock which in point of style and power, of ease and beauty of execution, is fit to rank with anything in the annals of the game.

Pollock came in when after 50 anxious minutes South Africa's score stood at 16 for two. Between this point and lunch he batted easily and without inhibition or restraint while two more wickets fell, and his companions struggled in every sort of difficulty against some very good swing bowling by Cartwright. *Daily Telegraph, 6 August, 1965*

ENGLAND v SOUTH AFRICA
Played at Nottingham,
5, 6, 7, 9 August, 1965.
Result: South Africa won by 94 runs.

South Africa: First innings

E.J. Barlow	c Cowdrey b Cartwright	19
H.R. Lance	lbw b Cartwright	7
D.T. Lindsay†	c Parks b Cartwright	0
R.G. Pollock	c Cowdrey b Cartwright	125
K.C. Bland	st Parks b Titmus	1
A. Bacher	b Snow	12
P.L. van der Merwe*	run out	38
R. Dumbrill	c Parfitt b Cartwright	30
J.T. Botten	c Parks b Larter	10
P.M. Pollock	c Larter b Cartwright	15
A.H. McKinnon	not out	8
Extras (lb 4)		4
Total		269

Fall of Wickets: 1/16, 2/16, 3/42, 4/43, 5/80, 6/178, 7/221, 8/242, 9/252, 10/269.
Bowling: Larter 17-6-25-1, Snow 22-6-63-1, Cartwright 31.3-9-94-6, Titmus 22-8-44-1, Barber 9-3-39-0.

England: First innings

G. Boycott	c Lance b P.M. Pollock	0
R.W. Barber	c Bacher b Dumbrill	41
K.F. Barrington	b P.M. Pollock	1
F.J. Titmus	c R.G. Pollock b McKinnon	20
M.C. Cowdrey	c Lindsay b Botten	105
P.H. Parfitt	c Dumbrill b P.M. Pollock	18
M.J.K. Smith*	b P.M. Pollock	32
J.M. Parks†	c and b Botten	6
J.A. Snow	run out	3
J.D.F. Larter	b P.M. Pollock	2
T.W. Cartwright	not out	1
Extras (b 1, lb 3, w 1, nb 6)		11
Total		240

Fall of Wickets: 1/0, 2/8, 3/63, 4/67, 5/133, 6/225, 7/229, 8/236, 9/238, 10/240.
Bowling: P.M. Pollock 23.5-8-53-5, Botten 23-5-60-2, McKinnon 28-11-54-1, Dumbrill 18-3-60-1, R.G. Pollock 1-0-2-0.

South Africa: Second innings

E.J. Barlow (4)	b Titmus	76
H.R. Lance	c Barber b Snow	0
D.T. Lindsay† (1)	c Cowdrey b Larter	9
R.G. Pollock (5)	c Titmus b Larter	59
K.C. Bland (6)	b Snow	10
A. Bacher (3)	lbw b Larter	67
P.L. van der Merwe*	c Parfitt b Larter	4
R. Dumbrill	b Larter	13
J.T. Botten	b Larter	18
P.M. Pollock	not out	12
A.H. McKinnon	b Titmus	9
Extras (b 4, lb 5, nb 3)		12
Total		289

Fall of Wickets: 1/2, 2/35, 3/134, 4/193, 5/228, 6/232, 7/243, 8/265, 9/269, 10/289.
Bowling: Larter 29-7-68-5, Snow 33-6-83-3, Titmus 19.4-5-46-2, Barber 3-0-20-0, Boycott 26-10-60-0.

England: Second innings

G. Boycott	b McKinnon	16
R.W. Barber	c Lindsay b P.M. Pollock	1
K.F. Barrington (5)	c Lindsay b P.M. Pollock	1
F.J. Titmus (3)	c Lindsay b McKinnon	4
M.C. Cowdrey (6)	st Lindsay b McKinnon	20
P.H. Parfitt (7)	b P.M. Pollock	86
M.J.K. Smith* (8)	lbw b R.G. Pollock	24
J.M. Parks† (9)	not out	44
J.A. Snow (4)	b Botten	0
J.D.F. Larter (11)	c van der Merwe b P.M. Pollock	10
T.W. Cartwright (10)	lbw b P.M. Pollock	0
Extras (lb 5, w 2, nb 11)		18
Total		224

Fall of Wickets: 1/1, 2/10, 3/10, 4/13, 5/41, 6/59, 7/114, 8/207, 9/207, 10/224.
Bowling: P.M. Pollock 24-15-34-5, Botten 19-5-58-1, McKinnon 27-12-50-3, Dumbrill 16-4-40-0, R.G. Pollock 5-2-4-1, Barlow 7-1-20-0.

Second Test—Fourth Day

ENGLAND WELL BEATEN BY SOUTH AFRICA

◆

TRIUMPHANT MATCH FOR POLLOCK BROTHERS

South Africa beat England by 94 runs in the second Test

By E. W. SWANTON

TRENT BRIDGE, Monday.

SOUTH AFRICA fully deserved their first victory over England in 12 Test matches, and one can imagine the celebrations tonight in Port Elizabeth, the home place of the remarkable brothers Pollock. Their joint contribution makes a page without parallel in cricket history.

Daily Telegraph, 10 August, 1965

FAR LEFT Peter Pollock – South Africa's foremost fast bowler – in action. ABOVE LEFT The two brothers – Peter (LEFT) and Graeme (RIGHT), who overpowered England with their bowling and batting

137

1966

HAWKE PUTS AUSTRALIA BACK IN FIGHT

◆

NOTHING CAN DIM GLORY OF BARBER'S 185

Daily Telegraph, 8 January, 1966

THE INNINGS of Bob Barber on the first day of the Sydney Test of 1966 is one that sticks in an old critic's memory when the detail of most of the 270 Tests he covered is blurred beyond definition. Boycott and Barber went in on a sunny day with just enough breeze to temper the heat, and after a few overs Barber began to show his complete left-handed armoury, with a penchant for the cover-drive, beautifully timed and executed. With Boycott the subordinate partner, the pair put on 234, a number only twice exceeded by England's first wicket against Australia. Accompanied by John Edrich, Barber completed a chanceless innings of 185 out of 303 in just under five hours, his 19 fours finding the boundary at all points of the compass.

Neil Hawke, in a brilliant spell with the second new ball that brought him four wickets, salvaged a share of the honours of the day. Edrich and the England tail however saw to it that the innings of Barber's life was the cornerstone of what was only the third innings victory by England in Australia since 1901.

The figures of Barber's career, respectable though they are, do nothing to fortify one's opinion that as forcing batsman (once he left his native Lancashire for Warwickshire), wrist-spin bowler, and top-class fielder anywhere he had more natural all-round talent than any post-war English cricketer, Botham excepted.

I recall a happy personal touch. His innings was watched by his father, who had flown in from England that very morning.

AUSTRALIA v ENGLAND
Played at Sydney,
7, 8, 10, 11 January, 1966.
Result: England won by an innings and 93 runs.

England: First innings

G. Boycott c and b Philpott	84
R.W. Barber b Hawke	185
J.H. Edrich c and b Philpott	103
K.F. Barrington c McKenzie b Hawke	1
M.C. Cowdrey c Grout b Hawke	0
M.J.K. Smith* c Grout b Hawke	6
D.J. Brown c Grout b Hawke	1
J.M. Parks† c Grout b Hawke	13
F.J. Titmus c Grout b Walters	14
D.A. Allen not out	50
I.J. Jones b Hawke	16
Extras (b 3, lb 8, w 2, nb 2)	15
Total	488

Fall of Wickets: 1/234, 2/303, 3/309, 4/309, 5/317, 6/328, 7/358, 8/395, 9/433, 10/488.
Bowling: McKenzie 25-2-113-0, Hawke 33.7-6-105-7, Walters 10-1-38-1, Philpott 28-3-86-2, Sincock 20-1-98-0, Cowper 6-1-33-0.

Australia: First innings

W.M. Lawry c Parks b Jones	0
G. Thomas c Titmus b Brown	51
R.M. Cowper st Parks b Allen	60
P.J.P. Burge c Parks b Brown	6
B.C. Booth* c Cowdrey b Jones	8
D.J. Sincock c Parks b Brown	29
K.D. Walters st Parks b Allen	23
N.J.N. Hawke c Barber b Brown	0
A.T.W. Grout† b Brown	0
G.D. McKenzie c Cowdrey b Barber	24
P.I. Philpott not out	5
Extras (b 7, lb 8)	15
Total	221

Fall of Wickets: 1/0, 2/81, 3/91, 4/105, 5/155, 6/174, 7/174, 8/174, 9/203, 10/221.
Bowling: Jones 20-6-51-2, Brown 17-1-63-5, Boycott 3-1-8-0, Titmus 23-8-40-0, Barber 2.1-1-2-1, Allen 19-5-42-2.

Australia: Second innings

W.M. Lawry c Cowdrey b Brown	33
G. Thomas c Cowdrey b Titmus	25
R.M. Cowper c Boycott b Titmus	0
P.J.P. Burge run out	1
B.C. Booth* b Allen	27
D.J. Sincock (7) c Smith b Allen	27
K.D. Walters (6) not out	35
N.J.N. Hawke (9) c Smith b Titmus	2
A.T.W. Grout† (10) c Smith b Allen	3
G.D. McKenzie (11) c Barber b Titmus	12
P.I. Philpott (8) lbw b Allen	5
Extras (b 3, lb 1)	4
Total	174

Fall of Wickets: 1/46, 2/50, 3/51, 4/86, 5/86, 6/119, 7/131, 8/135, 9/140, 10/174.
Bowling: Jones 7-0-35-0, Brown 11-2-32-1, Titmus 17.3-4-40-4, Barber 5-0-16-0, Allen 20-8-47-4.

LEFT Bob Barber, whose 185 was the innings of his life. On the 1965-66 tour to Australia he made over 1,000 runs at an average of 50

CLARK'S TEAM OPT FOR TWO COMPETITIONS

---◆---

CHANGE WOULD MEAN ONLY 20 FEWER PLAYING DAYS

By E. W. SWANTON

AFTER much heart-searching and almost an agony of self-analysis, English first-class cricket approaches the crux. I feel that the impending decision is the most momentous of its kind during my time as a critic.

Daily Telegraph, 20 December, 1966

Readers of these columns will need no reminding of where my sympathies lie. I go for one-day cricket in the '60s as a supplement to the traditional version, and my belief is that, as with the Gillette Cup, the public would give a new competition a fair chance.

Ideally I would prefer it given some time at the weekend, and myself, I see many advantages in the Yorkshire League principle whereby in a limited-over system a straight win, obtained by bowling the opposition out, is specially rewarded. Both these developments could eventually come—if the new shape is accepted.

Daily Telegraph, 20 December, 1966

BY THE mid-1960s all concerned with first-class cricket in England were greatly concerned by the drastic drop in attendance at matches and the serious financial position of all those counties which did not greatly profit from football pools and other forms of revenue from supporters' clubs. Accordingly the counties asked the MCC to set up a Committee under D.G. Clark, chairman of Kent, to examine the future of County Cricket in the widest terms and come up with a practical plan to revive flagging interest and make the game viable once more. They had to face the fact that whereas nearly 2 million watched Championship cricket in the post-war boom period around 1950 that figure had sunk by 1966 to just over 500,000.

The Committee of twelve, distinguished in all walks of cricket life, went through a mass of evidence. They denounced the negative approach to the game of most county sides, and thought sub-standard pitches led to sub-standard cricket. They thought that players were jaded by too much cricket. These views were all but unanimous.

They accordingly recommended a reduction of Championship matches to sixteen or twenty of three days each, played on Saturdays, Sundays and Mondays, with a separate 65-over one-day mid-week competition of 16 matches under the unrestricted Laws of Cricket (e.g. no limit on overs bowled by individuals) and given first-class status. The Gillette Cup should remain as it was. They also provided an analysis of current ills and difficulties most of which are still relevant today.

BELOW David Clark, whose committee looked closely at the depressed state of English cricket during the 1960s

My comment at the time favoured the main proposal, as will be seen. Was it accepted by the counties? Was it... hell! They voted against 16–4. As usual throughout history a Committee had got through a mountain of work for little immediate result. However by loosening qualification rules for overseas players the Clark Report led indirectly to the much shorter-length John Player Sunday League begun in 1969.

1967

JOHN WOODCOCK'S report of the final stages of the Warwickshire–Yorkshire match in mid-August 1967, along with one in similar vein by Michael Melford in the *Daily Telegraph*, had a crucial effect on Brian Close's career and on the shape and character of the current England team. As the incumbent Test captain with five victories in six successive Tests behind him Brian Close was assured of taking MCC to the West Indies in the winter before the allegations of time-wasting to a degree that deprived his opponents of victory questioned his suitability for the job.

After hearing the evidence (culminating in Yorkshire dawdling to the extent of bowling only two overs in the last eleven minutes) the counties' Executive Committee (comprising six former county captains) found Yorkshire guilty of unfair play against the spirit of the game. They held the Yorkshire captain entirely responsible and severely censured him. Close left the meeting at Lord's to lead England to another victory (over Pakistan) at The Oval. But when the MCC Committee a week later chose their team for the West Indies they gave the leadership to Colin Cowdrey.

Twenty years on the same thought recurs. It was a cast-iron case. If Close had expressed sincere regret and promised there would be no repetition those fellow cricketers sitting in judgement must have added a rider to that effect, and this in turn could only have helped to mollify the MCC Committee. He might well have been forgiven. As it was he made it no secret that in similar circumstances he would act in the same way again. That obduracy cooked his goose.

RIGHT Close receives notice during the Oval Test of his censure for time-wasting

Yorkshire fall from grace
Two dishonourable points
From JOHN WOODCOCK, Cricket Correspondent

BIRMINGHAM. — *Warwickshire (6pts.) drew with Yorkshire (2pts.)*

By resorting to some of the more questionable tricks of the trade and with the help of the rain, Yorkshire acquired two dishonourable points. When time was called Warwickshire were nine runs short of victory with five wickets standing.

Without exception, Yorkshire's performance was, of its kind, the least attractive I have seen on a cricket field, and the blame lies, squarely, at the door of England's captain and Yorkshire's. From the moment Warwickshire came out for their second innings, needing 142 to win in 102 minutes, Yorkshire employed all the known methods of wasting time. There was only one factor in their defence. The rain, coming and going, made the ball wet and meant that it frequently needed drying.

The Times, 19 August, 1967

After the match Close left for Northampton to help choose the England side for the next Test. I wished it had been Mike Smith instead. A man capable of condoning and conducting such an operation as Yorkshire's last evening would seem a peculiar choice to take an M.C.C. side to the West Indies on an expedition that demands from its leader a strong sense of sportsmanship and responsibility. Smith had a good match—with the bat, in the field and in the spirit in which he played it.

The Times, 19 August, 1967

WARWICKSHIRE v YORKSHIRE
Played at Birmingham, 16, 17, 18 August, 1967. Result: Match drawn.

Yorkshire: First innings 238 (J.H. Hampshire 102, G. Boycott 57).

Warwickshire: First innings 242 (D.L. Amiss 53, K. Ibadulla 52; Nicholson 6-50).

Yorkshire: Second innings 145 (Cartwright 4-26, Cook 4-66).

Warwickshire: Second innings 133 for 5 (D.L. Amiss 46; Hutton 3-48).

NOT MANY sportsmen have rated a leading two-column obituary in *The Times*. But S.F. Barnes is generally thought of as the best bowler ever seen. It is intriguing to speculate on the anonymous author. The style could have been that of H.S. Altham. It might have been R.B. Vincent, a former *Times* cricket correspondent. Whoever it was he contents himself with calling him one of England's greatest, a judgement beyond dispute.

For many years, even in his very old age, Sydney Barnes used to come to the Tests at Lord's and Edgbaston, where it was a privilege to watch in his company. One at once noticed his hands as he smoked his pipe; strong, supple, long-fingered. (He had the most symmetrical flowing hand-writing to the end.)

After a model, rigid run-up these hands at the instant of delivery imparted both varieties of break and swing at a pace varying from slow-medium to distinctly brisk. Add to the armoury a mastery of length and natural life off the pitch, and it is not difficult to imagine the problems he posed to the best batsmen.

He was however reputed to be difficult to handle, and after a few years with Lancashire at the turn of the century preferred to play his county cricket with Staffordshire, for whom he performed with no diminution of skill until he was over sixty. Plum Warner always said he had no trouble with him, and it was with Warner's second MCC side to Australia in 1911-12 that he and F.R. Foster made perhaps the most lethal partnership of any: S.F.B. 34

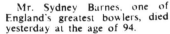

wickets at 22.88 each, F.R.F. 32 at 21.62. On the South African mat two years later, when nearing 41, Barnes in only four Tests took 49 wickets (the most ever in a Test series) at 10.93 runs each. Such was the faith in his powers he was sounded out about making yet another trip to Australia in 1920-21, when he was forty-seven – but he was too wise to sign on for that.

LEFT Sydney Barnes in old age, with Wilfred Rhodes

OBITUARY

MR SYDNEY BARNES

A great England bowler

Mr. Sydney Barnes, one of England's greatest bowlers, died yesterday at the age of 94.

Sydney Francis Barnes turned to splendid advantage his physical advantages. Right-arm fast-medium, he made full use of his height—he stood fully six feet—and possessed a most deceptive flight, exceptional accuracy of length and command of both swerve and break. Though he generally brought the ball in from leg he could turn it either way, and could bowl for long spells without loss of effectiveness.

Up till the First World War, and for some time afterwards, two international bowlers were widely accepted as supreme: Spofforth and Barnes. Debates on which was the deadlier remained inconclusive, if only for chronological causes. Sydney Barnes, born on April 19, 1873, some 20 years after Spofforth, was the slower to prove his genius. As an amateur for Warwickshire in 1894 and 1895, he was unimpressive and revealed scarcely more promise as a Lancashire professional in 1899.

He might never have developed as he did but for the perception of A. C. MacLaren, who reimported him from League cricket into the Lancashire side for the last match of 1901, and invited him to Australia—provoking the inevitable outcry.

A raw recruit can seldom have confuted criticism more completely: five for 66 against South Australia, 12 for 99 against Victoria, and—in the first Test match—five for 65 (after a useful little 26 not out), paving the way for England's only victory.

34 wickets to Barnes and 32 to Foster.

Foster bowled left-handed, round the wicket, in the classic manner. Barnes was a " lively medium who could make the ball do something either way ", wrote Moyes.

The Times, 27 December, 1967

IT WOULD need a riot or some disaster of a major kind for a national newspaper's cricket correspondent to lead the front page. This was the only time in thirty years that I did so, and a deeply saddening affair it was. Jamaica was going through a difficult time politically, and the disorder was considered in retrospect to have been fomented by elements demonstrating against authority generally. There was antipathy against neither players nor umpires, for though the bottle-throwing followed the dismissal of Basil Butcher, finely caught by Jim Parks behind the wicket, he had walked straight away without waiting for Douglas Sang Hue's decision.

The subsequent post-mortem blamed the police for a mis-judgement which at this range of time seems laughable, though scarcely so then. They fired their tear-gas towards the troubled area but into the prevailing wind which carried it across the field into the pavilion and even as far as the parliament building, causing the Jamaican cabinet to suspend its sitting.

The Daily

No. 35084.   LONDON, TUESDAY, FEBRUARY 13, 1968.   and

RIOT STOPS PLAY IN TEST

Police use tear gas in fight with crowd

COWDREY STRUCK BY BOTTLE

```
2006: SPORT -- SCORES 10 KINGSTON
WEST INDIES 204 FOR FIVE -- RIOT HALTED PLAY.
```

By E. W. SWANTON

KINGSTON, Jamaica, Monday.

My report was written with eyes and nose affected by tear-gas since although the little Sabina Park press-box had been fitted with an air-conditioner – a unique experience for all of us – the door could not be held against spectators escaping from the fumes!

Since the newly-laid pitch was doing strange things the result was an all but certain win for England when the fourth afternoon's play was suspended.

When after a delay of seventy minutes it re-started England could not recapture their lost impetus and Sobers and his young cousin, David Holford, lasted out the day. The genius of Sobers, defying both the malevolence of the pitch and the efforts of a varied attack, monopolized the fifth day which took place in a strangely flat atmosphere. The riot had taken the heart out of the match.

Sobers, taking out his bat for 113,

ultimately set England 159 to win at a run a minute, and promptly had the wickets of Boycott and Cowdrey in his first over. With England 19 for 4 at the close Sobers opted to take, on the sixth day, the seventy minutes lost (which by arrangement either captain could ask for). As the score-card shows, those seventy minutes did not pass without much English anxiety and in the end they only just held on to a draw having looked certain victors until upset by the riot.

WEST INDIES v ENGLAND
Played at Kingston,
8, 9, 10, 12, 13, 14 February, 1968.
Result: Match drawn.

England: First innings 376 (M.C. Cowdrey 101, J.H. Edrich 96; Hall 4-63).

West Indies: First innings 143 (Snow 7-49).

West Indies: Second innings
G.S. Camacho b D'Oliveira	25
D.L. Murray† lbw b Brown	14
R.B. Kanhai c Edrich b Jones	36
S.M. Nurse b Snow	73
C.H. Lloyd b Brown	7
G. St A. Sobers* not out	113
B.F. Butcher c Parks b D'Oliveira	25
D.A.J. Holford lbw b Titmus	35
C.C. Griffith lbw b Jones	14
W.W. Hall c Parks b Jones	0
L.R. Gibbs not out	1
Extras (b 33, lb 10, nb 5)	48
Total (9 wickets declared)	391

Fall of Wickets: 1/102, 2/122, 3/164, 4/174, 5/204, 6/314, 7/351, 8/388, 9/388.
Bowling: Brown 33-9-65-2, Snow 27-4-91-1, Jones 30-4-90-3, D'Oliveira 32-12-51-2, Titmus 7-2-32-1, Barrington 6-1-14-0.

England: Second innings
G. Boycott b Sobers	0
J.H. Edrich b Hall	6
M.C. Cowdrey* lbw b Sobers	0
K.F. Barrington lbw b Griffith	13
T.W. Graveney c Griffith b Gibbs	21
J.M. Parks† lbw b Gibbs	3
B.L. D'Oliveira not out	13
F.J. Titmus c Camacho b Gibbs	4
D.J. Brown b Sobers	0
J.A. Snow / I.J. Jones } did not bat	
Extras (b 8)	8
Total (8 wickets)	68

Fall of Wickets: 1/0, 2/0, 3/19, 4/19, 5/38, 6/51, 7/61, 8/68.
Bowling: Hall 3-2-3-1, Griffith 5-2-13-1, Sobers 16.5-7-33-3, Gibbs 14-11-11-3.

LEFT Riot police bearing batons and shields in their attempt to restore order after the riot at Kingston

143

1968

THIS FOURTH TEST of the 1967-68 MCC tour to the West Indies at Port-of-Spain was noteworthy in several respects. First, it is the second and last among all the 1,000-odd Tests played to be won against a declaration, and certainly the only one to be lost by a side that has declared twice. Second, as the only Test of the series that was finished it gave the Wisden Trophy to England. The Trophy, first presented a quarter of a century ago, had been competed for in 11 series between England and the West Indies and this is one of only two of them won by England, as against eight such successes by the West Indies.

Not least it was the decisive point of a series that was contested hard but with exemplary sportsmanship by Sobers and Cowdrey and their respective sides. One should associate in this regard the managership of Leslie Ames, an old friend of the West Indies

who had toured there in 1929-30 and, incidentally, scored two hundreds in this first Test rubber on their home territory: he and Cowdrey complemented one another admirably.

There was both moral justice and irony in the result in that England had made nearly all the running in the first three Tests. But for a missed catch by Boycott at the critical moment they must have won the highly exciting First at Port-of-Spain. But for the riot they were highly probable winners of the Second at Kingston. They had all the better of the Third at Bridgetown. The irony lay that in this Fourth match it was the West Indians who had called the tune from the start. England never looked like winning until the last moment.

Though the unique prestige surrounding his name stood him in good stead Sobers was inevitably criticized throughout the Caribbean for his declaration. The generosity of his decision lay in his having made it in the knowledge that Griffith had broken down early in England's first innings. Without Griffith the bowling was slender. As I wrote after the match Sobers had slightly misread his hand.

ENGLAND TRIUMPH WITH MINUTES TO SPARE

◆

COWDREY & BOYCOTT LEAD 78-AN-HOUR DASH

By E. W. SWANTON

PORT OF SPAIN, Trinidad, Tuesday.

ENGLAND won a victory this evening that had been beyond all human prediction, until Sobers made what, on the face of it, was the most "sporting" of all sporting declarations, by seven wickets.

They made 215 in two hours 42 mins, getting the final run off the fourth ball of what would have been the penultimate over after a last hour and a half of cricket that maintained a crescendo of excitement from first to last.

Daily Telegraph, 20 March, 1968

WEST INDIES v ENGLAND
Played at Port-of Spain,
14, 15, 16, 18, 19 March, 1968.
Result: England won by seven wickets.

West Indies: First innings

G.S. Camacho c Knott b Brown	87
M.C. Carew c Lock b Brown	36
S.M. Nurse c Edrich b Barrington	136
R.B. Kanhai c Barrington b Lock	153
C.H. Lloyd b Jones	43
G. St A. Sobers* c Jones b Brown	48
B.F. Butcher not out	7
W.V. Rodriguez b Jones	0
D.L. Murray† not out	5
C.C. Griffith } did not bat	
L.R. Gibbs	
Extras (lb 6, nb 5)	11
Total (7 wickets declared)	526

Fall of Wickets: 1/119, 2/142, 3/415, 4/421, 5/506, 6/513, 7/514.
Bowling: Brown 27-2-107-3, Snow 20-3-68-0, Jones 29-1-108-2, D'Oliveira 15-2-62-0, Lock 32-3-129-1, Barrington 10-2-41-1.

England: First innings

J.H. Edrich c Lloyd b Carew	32
G. Boycott c Nurse b Rodriguez	62
M.C. Cowdrey* c Murray b Butcher	148
K.F. Barrington lbw b Gibbs	48
T.W. Graveney c Murray b Rodriguez	8
B.L. D'Oliveira b Rodriguez	0
A.P.E. Knott† not out	69
J.A. Snow b Butcher	0
D.J. Brown c Murray b Butcher	0
G.A.R. Lock lbw b Butcher	3
I.J. Jones b Butcher	1
Extras (b 13, lb 11, w 2, nb 7)	33
Total	404

Fall of Wickets: 1/86, 2/112, 3/245, 4/260, 5/260, 6/373, 7/377, 8/377, 9/381, 10/404.
Bowling: Sobers 36-8-87-0, Griffith 3-1-7-0, Gibbs 57-24-68-1, Rodriguez 35-4-145-3, Carew 25-18-23-1, Butcher 13.4-2-34-5, Lloyd 4-2-7-0, Nurse 2-2-0-0.

West Indies: Second innings

G.S. Camacho c Graveney b Snow	31
M.C. Carew not out	40
S.M. Nurse run out	9
R.B. Kanhai not out	2
C.H. Lloyd	
G. St A. Sobers*	
B.F. Butcher	
W.V. Rodriguez } did not bat	
D.L. Murray†	
C.C. Griffith	
L.R. Gibbs	
Extras (b 1, lb 7, nb 2)	10
Total (2 wickets declared)	92

Fall of Wickets: 1/66, 2/88.
Bowling: Brown 10-2-33-0, Snow 9-0-29-1, Jones 11-2-20-0.

England: Second innings

J.H. Edrich b Rodriguez	29
G. Boycott not out	80
M.C. Cowdrey* c Sobers b Gibbs	71
T.W. Graveney b Gibbs	2
B.L. D'Oliveira not out	12
K.F. Barrington	
A.P.E. Knott†	
J.A. Snow	
D.J. Brown } did not bat	
G.A.R. Lock	
I.J. Jones	
Extras (b 11, lb 6, nb 4)	21
Total (3 wickets)	215

Fall of Wickets: 1/55, 2/173, 3/182.
Bowling: Sobers 14-0-48-0, Gibbs 16.4-1-76-2, Rodriguez 10-1-34-1, Carew 7-2-19-0, Butcher 5-1-17-0.

RIGHT Colin Cowdrey and Gary Sobers with the Wisden Trophy which they contested in the most sporting manner in 1967-68. It was the last Test series in which England beat West Indies

1968

THE PROTRACTED and bitter upset known as the 'D'Oliveira Affair' erupted on 28 August 1968 when his name was not included in the MCC team chosen shortly to tour South Africa. There were known to be doubts whether D'Oliveira, designated a 'Cape Coloured' by his native country, would be acceptable to the South African Government on account of its rigid apartheid policy.

The very day the selectors met to finalize the touring team England had squared the rubber against Australia at The Oval with a highly exciting victory to which D'Oliviera had contributed a superb innings of 158, besides taking a vital wicket. Whereas several places in the party for South Africa were in doubt it seemed that D'Oliveira's crucial contribution when all attention was focused upon him must have secured his place. The selectors answered criticism of his omission by asserting that it was a decision reached

This sad illusion that cricket is only a game

ALAN ROSS argues that the case of Basil D'Oliveira cannot be discussed in a political vacuum and that the MCC was unwise to attempt to do so.

IN TRYING to be 'non-political' the MCC selectors have in fact made a sad political blunder. Their decision to leave out Basil D'Oliveira from the side to tour South Africa makes no sense at all in cricketing terms, and the reasons given to defend it can hardly be taken seriously.

In wider terms—and cricket, like any human activity, can never be considered in a political vacuum, as though it were played and watched by a species of robots —a golden opportunity has been missed. In a flexible situation the wrong gamble was taken.

The arguable case against D'Oliveira is that he had a disappointing tour in quite different conditions as a bowler in the West Indies and a comparatively lean county season here; also that at 33, he is getting on in years. The case for D'Oliveira is that his temperament makes him as effective a Test batsman as we have in England—his record in this respect is unrivalled; that as a bowler he was brought up on South African wickets, which have recently become exactly suited to his style: and that his presence as the only all-rounder would materially improve the balance of the side. To my mind these are, in relation to his current form, incontrovertible factors, especially when one considers others who have been preferred to him.

The side as chosen is a dull, unimaginative one, and its cautious, unimaginative aspect is one of the two reasons that has cost D'Oliveira his place. What he innocently stands for—as a symbol of hope and achievement in a repressive society—is the other.

A year or two ago, in commenting on a monstrous statement by a South African Cabinet Minister on the subject of race and sport, the MCC dragged its feet like an arthritic grandmother. In the end, under pressure of public opinion, it was announced that no compromises would be acceptable in the choice of players to tour South Africa or in the treatment they received when they got there. Well and good. Even so, it was plain that D'Oliveira's potential presence would create all kinds of anomalies and possible embarrassments, as well as a general sharpening of political tension. Those who put a quiet life and the maintenance of the *status quo* before all else—and the MCC has all the instincts of outer suburbia when it comes to avoiding 'trouble'—hoped it would never happen.

Their wishes have been granted. Yet despite the assurances given, it is impossible to allow that non-cricketing considerations of any kind played no part in the long-drawn-out discussions of last Tuesday night. It was obvious that if reasons could be produced for omitting D'Oliveira, then most of those concerned would heave a sigh of relief and sleep that much more soundly. There are reasons for omitting anyone and in this instance, predictably, they were found.

It was in precisely this situation that a committee more politically sensitive, more courageous and generous in its appreciation of human values, would have acted in the opposite fashion. D'Oliveira last week, as both batsman and bowler, was crucial in winning an historic Test match. The conditions for the greater part of it were similar to those that may be found in South Africa. It is inconceivable in the light of this that he could not find a place among the 16 players chosen for the tour, had all else been equal.

All else, of course, was not equal. On the Test match grounds of Johannesburg and Cape Town, of Durban and Port Elizabeth, the races are strictly segregated, the more obviously coloured ones shut off behind barbed wire. In hotels, buses, trains, lavatories and restaurants, it is whites only; in the sports arenas it is always white against white, black against black. The Olympic ideal finds no favour in South Africa, as their athletes have latterly and painfully discovered.

It is a naive illusion that the profoundly political attitudes that dominate South African thinking about sport have in reality nothing to do with the case—sport seeming to exist in a kind of blissful vacuum of its own—and it is this illusion that the MCC seems to share. It may or may not be subconscious, but the fact remains that whenever discussion takes place on this subject, in committee or elsewhere, the assumption is that to accept the establishment's view is admirably non-political, whereas to argue the alternative is dragging politics into sport.

South Africa's racial system is as ruthless to its opponents and as offensive in its principles as much that was done by the Nazis, and is still being done, in the name of Communism, by the Soviet Union.

The rejection of D'Oliveira, *whatever* the ostensible reasons, will now come as a soothing breeze to the sweating but complacent apostles and fellow-travellers of *apartheid*—it was received with cheers in Afrikaner circles—and as an unexpected blow in the face to those of D'Oliveira's colour. Any sophisticated committee with a healthy sense of priorities—with so little in it and the issues so delicately balanced—would have made absolutely sure that, if humanly possible, this should not happen.

If this is bringing politics into sport, then it is a negligible and entirely proper price to pay. Coloured enclaves in South Africa will be that much more dejected in the New Year, and those who have left countries of persecution or neglect to make their homes and take their chances with us, can scarcely be blamed if they feel a lot is still stacked against them. Unless I believed that D'Oliveira was not even worth considering for the South African tour, I should feel the same. There are issues in the world in which even a wooden rifle is better than no rifle at all. D'Oliveira, unpolitical, inscrutable and unassuming as he is, might have been, especially in terms of the white population, more use than either.

Observer, 1 September, 1968

on purely cricketing grounds. That was the position when Alan Ross wrote his perceptive comment in the *Observer* of the following Sunday.

From this point the sad saga developed like a Greek tragedy. In mid-September Tom Cartwright, an all-rounder who was a much better bowler than batsman, dropped out of the touring team through injury. Thereupon the selectors, who had stated in reply to press questioning when the team was announced that D'Oliveira was considered chiefly as a batsman rather than an all-rounder, named him as Cartwright's replacement. The South African Prime Minister, John Vorster, promptly said that the revised team was not that of MCC but of anti-apartheid groups and as such would not be welcome. That was that. MCC cancelled the visit for reasons 'beyond the control of the South African Cricket Association'.

The final act of the drama was a Special General Meeting of MCC demanded according to rule by members, headed by the Rev D.S. Sheppard, now Bishop of Liverpool, who put three motions expressing no confidence in the Committee. A hardhitting debate at Church House, Westminster ended in the substantial defeat of 'the rebels' when the postal votes of members were announced. Voting from the floor gave the Committee a much narrower majority.

Considering how active MCC had been from the beginning of the century in fostering the game almost wherever English was spoken it was ironic that their direct responsibility for official English tours abroad should end in such a way.

Triple defeat for MCC critics

By DAVID GRAY

The critics of the MCC committee's handling of the matter of Basil d'Oliveira and the selection of the team to tour South Africa failed last night. Of the 10,000 members of the club, 4,357 voted, by post and in person, in support of the committee and 1,570 backed the Rev. David Sheppard and his group.

Two other motions were also defeated : the one urging that no further tours of South Africa should be undertaken until evidence could be given of actual progress towards nonracial cricket there was lost by 4,664 votes to 1,214 and the other which asked for proposals to be submitted by the South African Cricket Association to MCC on the question of non-racial cricket, went down by 4,508 votes to 1,352.

Guardian, 6 December, 1968

ENGLAND v AUSTRALIA
Played at The Oval,
22, 23, 24, 26, 27 August, 1968.
Result: England won by 226 runs.

England: First innings 494 (J.H. Edrich 164, B.L. D'Oliveira 158, T.W. Graveney 63).

Australia: First innings 324 (W.M. Lawry 135, I.R. Redpath 67).

England: Second innings 181 (Connolly 4-65).

Australia: Second innings 125 (R.J. Inverarity 56; Underwood 7-50).

LEFT D'Oliveira on his way to 158 against Australia at The Oval

1968

6·6·6 6·6·6

Sobers hits six sixes in one over

WEST Indian Gary Sobers set a world record when he hit six sixes in an over for Nottinghamshire off Malcolm Nash, the Glamorgan bowler, at Swansea, yesterday.

The Sunday Times, 1 September, 1968

ABOVE Gary Sobers in big hitting mood

THE FIRST point to note about Gary Sobers's record-breaking sixes at Swansea is that they were hit not late in a match with the result perhaps foregone but after tea on the first afternoon when Glamorgan and Nottinghamshire were keenly contesting third place in the Championship. As will be seen Gary timed his feat nicely to catch the early editions of *The Sunday Times* which rightly informed its readers that this was a world record. (It has since been equalled – it cannot be bettered! – by the Indian Test cricketer R.J. Shastri for Bombay v Baroda in 1984-85.)

What one wanted to know was the nature and direction of the strokes against the hapless young left-arm medium-pacer, Malcolm Nash – an admirable cricketer, by the way, who has never been allowed to forget his involuntary contribution to history. I had the information from O.S. Wheatley, who was enjoying the performance from the field of play.

Sobers was batting with his back to Mumbles Bay on the curiously shaped (and capacious) St Helen's ground, Swansea. The first six over long-on cleared the wall and smacked against a pub in Gorse Lane. The second went to mid-wicket, and apparently connected with another pub a little down the road. The third landed among the spectators at long-off, the fourth similarly at mid-wicket. The fifth was the one that Roger Davis at long-off caught before falling over the boundary line, and the last and biggest again flew over mid wicket, down a side street towards the Town Hall, and was not recovered until next day.

It is this ball, I suppose, which now has a home in the Trent Bridge Museum.

148

1969

FOR LANCASHIRE, who had been languishing at the wrong end of the County Championship for most of the 1960s, the advent of the John Player League was like manna from heaven. Greatly strengthened by the arrival of Clive Lloyd they carried off the title in the initial year, 1969, and in 1970 went one better, not only repeating this victory but winning also the first of three successive Gillette Cup finals. They owed much to the shrewd leadership of Jack Bond.

By reputation Warwickshire were at least as strong a side as Lancashire, and up to a point they were very much in contention here. They took longer, however to acclimatize themselves to the abbreviated version of cricket. This must be the last *Daily Sketch* heading – for this once well-esteemed picture paper folded the following year.

LEFT Jack Bond: captain of Lancashire during their heyday of success in limited-over cricket, which began with winning the first John Player League

Lancashire are Sunday Kings

By REX BRIAN

LANCASHIRE, for so long the poor County cousins to Yorkshire, are sitting on top of the cricket world this weekend as first champions of the Player's Sunday League. They took the title yesterday by beating Warwick at Nuneaton while chief challengers Hants lost to Essex.

Daily Sketch, 25 August, 1969

1969

THE *SUN* HEADLINES tell the story eloquently enough of Glamorgan's 1969 Championship. The youngest county (admitted in 1921) had won a worthy if surprising victory in 1948 under Wilfred Wooller. This second win was more dramatic and more notable in that they were the first side to go through the summer unbeaten since Lancashire back in 1930. Amid mounting Welsh enthusiasm Glamorgan won their last three home matches to bring the title home, the penultimate against Essex by one run.

They won led by a boy from the valleys in Tony Lewis, and although Majid was one of the star batsmen most of the side were born and bred Welsh-

SALUTE TO TONY LEWIS AND GLAMORGAN

'A LOT OF HARD WORK..A LOT OF HAPPINESS'

By CLIVE TAYLOR

Sun, 6 September, 1969

men. It was an additional bonus that the senior of them, the well-loved Don Shepherd in this deciding match against Worcestershire took his 2,000th wicket.

There were 6,000 at Sophia Gardens, that day, to hail the conquerors and to sing 'Land of My Fathers' with the huyl that only those familiar with Cardiff Arms Park on the great days can truly know. Clive Taylor was one of the most popular and most talented members of the press box. He was the chief cricket writer for the *Sun* from the birth of the paper in 1965 until his sudden death in 1977 aged only fifty.

By 3.8 p m. Glamorgan had won the county championship. By 3.10 pm. the crowd were singing: 'Land Of My Fathers' outside the pavilion. The delay is explained by the fact that they are more conservative in Cardiff than in other parts of Wales.

The defeat of Worcestershire, that had been predicted for three days, came with the dismissal of Brian Brain peering down the leg side and caught on the off.

Worcestershire's 147-run defeat was entirely expected and ruthlessly achieved by Don Shepherd and Tony Cordle bowling on a worn-out wicket. Between them they took nine wickets to bring to Wales for the first time since 1948 a title that took even them by surprise.

DECISIVE MATCH

"All we set out to do was finish in the first six," said captain Tony Lewis. "Even that is putting it optimistically. We just wanted to be in the top half of the table. We did not think about winning it until we had beaten Gloucestershire for the first time.

Sun, 6 September, 1969

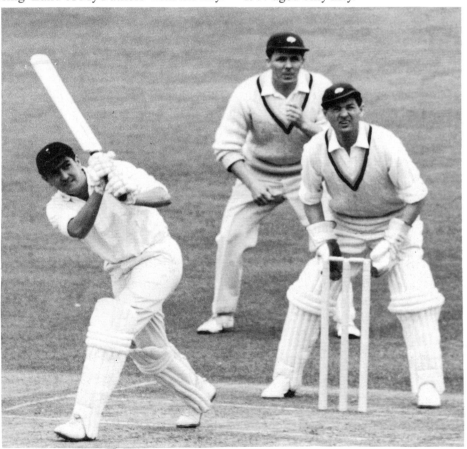

RIGHT Tony Lewis, 'a boy from the valleys', shows the forceful style which helped his county win the Championship in 1969. It was a popular and well-deserved win

150

GOVERNMENT DEMANDS STOP TOUR

Umpire Callaghan 'carries the can'

By PETER THORNTON

THE CRICKET Council will hold an emergency meeting at Lord's today to decide on their answer to the Government's demand to call off the Springbok's tour.

Daily Telegraph, 22 May, 1970

THROUGHOUT THE early months of 1970 newspaper readers were regaled with a running serial on the forthcoming tour of the South Africans due to start (on a basis already restricted) at the end of May. While the touring Springbok Rugby team were being subjected to continual harrassment, and matches interrupted despite the presence of police forces numbered in thousands, the Cricket Council in England and the Cricket Association in South Africa continued to say that the cricket tour would proceed come hell or high water. Barbed wire on top of the walls of Test grounds was erected and watch kept on pitches to protect them against damage caused at night by anti-apartheid activists. Artificial pitches were laid. It was estimated that security arrangements at Edgbaston for two matches, would cost £250,000.

The Prime Minister, Harold Wilson, said on television that he thought the decision to allow the tour to go ahead was 'a big mistake', and that he hoped people would feel free to demonstrate if they wished. A fortnight before the South Africans were due there was a full-scale House of Commons debate. With an election pending neither the Conservative nor the Labour party were anxious to commit themselves unequivocally to abandonment. Most followed the line of the Home Secretary, James Callaghan, who urged the Cricket Council to call the tour off. So did the Sports Council, the Race Relations Board, the Royal Commonwealth Society, the Archbishop of Canterbury, the Chief Rabbi, *et al.*

1970

Many who instinctively reacted against such attempts at coercion came, however, to feel, as I did myself, that the tour had simply become impracticable. Cricket, spread over several days, is a much easier game to disrupt than football. Our grounds would become scenes of violence, and the atmosphere completely removed from the spirit of sport. No one would enjoy the tour, least of all surely the South African team. It would become not so much a cricket series as an ideological battle-ground.

The climax came when, with the visitors' arrival only a few days away, Maurice Allom and S.C. Griffith, chairman and secretary respectively of the Cricket Council, were called to the Home Office where Mr Callaghan formally requested that the tour be cancelled 'on the grounds of broad public policy'. The Council, regarding this as a Government directive, complied without a vote being taken. As the barbed wire and barricades came down the prevailing feeling was of relief that a protracted ordeal had been averted.

I was left to reflect personally on what might have been if the SACA had adopted the policy I had first advocated more than a year earlier of bringing a multi-racial tour party sufficient to make two teams playing in England simultaneously. There were coloured cricketers good enough to earn a place in the first thirty. An appropriate fixture programme could have been set up, and such a party could have come over without any infringement of South African law.

LEFT The Rev David Sheppard, (now Bishop of Liverpool), a leading advocate of stopping the tour, addressing an anti-apartheid rally in Trafalgar Square

1970

FOLLOWING THE abandonment of the tour by the South Africans the TCCB hurriedly substituted on the corresponding dates a series of five unofficial Tests against a powerful Rest of the World team made up of five of the leading South Africans, five West Indians playing in county cricket, two Pakistanis, an Indian and an Australian also thus engaged. Sobers, still at the height of his powers, was captain of what was arguably the strongest side ever to play in England. It was completely equipped, and it played throughout, with the utmost zeal and dedication. The team's managers, F.R. Brown and Leslie Ames, testified to an exemplary team spirit – a practical refutation, if you like, of the obnoxious doctrine of apartheid.

The TCCB organized the series for three reasons. They needed it as an examination-ground for the coming winter tour of Australia. The counties needed the profits. And the game itself needed to put on a summer spectacle rather than leave the television, radio and press a clear field for the football World Cup. The firm of Guinness provided the sponsorship. Retrospectively the status of the five games has been queried, and individual performances therein are not now included in official records. The fact remains that in 1970 they were announced, sponsored, and reported on as Tests, they were so named in the 1971 *Wisden*, and a statement after the 1971 ICC annual meeting was made that the Conference 'confirmed the Cricket Council's stated view that the Rest of the World Series of 1970 were unofficial Test Matches'.

The First Test unfortunately coincided with the General Election, and resulted in a wholesale English defeat from which interest in the series took time to recover. However England gained a well-earned and conclusive victory in the Second Test, as shown here. Although they lost the last three the Rest of the World had to make 223 to win the Fourth by two wickets and 285 to win the Fifth by four.

From the averages shown here can be judged the opposition England were up against.

REST OF THE WORLD v ENGLAND
Played at Nottingham, 2, 3, 4, 6, 7 July, 1970.
Result: England won by eight wickets.

Rest of the World: First innings 276 (C.H. Lloyd 114*, B.A. Richards 64; D'Oliveira 4-43, Greig 4-59).

England: First innings 279 (R. Illingworth 97; Barlow 5-66).

Rest of the World: Second innings 286 (E.J. Barlow 142).

England: Second innings 284 for 2 (B.W. Luckhurst 113*, K.W.R. Fletcher 69*, M.C. Cowdrey 64).

BELOW The closing scenes of the Oval Test

REST OF THE WORLD
Batting

	Tests	Inns.	Not Outs	Runs	Highest Inns.	Average
G.S. Sobers	5	9	1	588	183	73.50
C.H. Lloyd	5	9	1	400	114*	50.00
M.J. Procter	5	9	3	292	62	48.66
D.L. Murray	3	4	0	172	95	43.00
E.J. Barlow	5	9	0	353	142	39.22
B.A. Richards	5	8	1	257	64	36.71
Intikhab Alam	5	8	1	240	61	34.28
R.B. Kanhai	5	9	0	284	100	31.55
R.G. Pollock	5	8	0	250	114	31.25
Mushtaq Mohammed	2	4	0	29	14	7.25
G.D. McKenzie	3	4	2	10	6	5.00
L.R. Gibbs	4	5	3	7	3	3.50
F.M. Engineer	2	3	0	3	2	1.00

Also batted: P.M. Pollock, 23*   *Signifies not out.*

Bowling

	Overs	Maidens	Runs	Wickets	Average
E.J. Barlow	152	33	396	20	19.80
C.H. Lloyd	53	13	120	6	20.00
G.S. Sobers	272.4	106	452	21	21.52
M.J. Procter	211.1	82	359	15	23.93
G.D. McKenzie	122.2	31	283	9	31.44
Intikhab Alam	283.5	99	637	14	45.50
L.R. Gibbs	167	53	307	3	102.33

Also Bowled: P.M. Pollock 33-6-110-2, R.B. Kanhai 1-0-4-0, R.G. Pollock 0.2-0-5-0, Mushtaq Mohammad 55-18-135-1.

England's greatest victory, says 'Illy'

Daily Express, 8 July, 1970

THERE IS NO county side surely that enjoys more widespread support within its borders than Kent, despite which their XIs of the 1950s and early 1960s were quite unable to match standards which hitherto had been taken for granted. Over the span of half a century in only two summers did they finish in the lower half of the Championship table. Great was the delight then when in 1967 they won the Gillette Cup. 1970 was the club's centenary year and on 1 July Cowdrey's promising young side stood plumb last in the table.

From this point all went wonderfully well, and the strong advantage gained on the first two days of the last match against Surrey at The Oval put them, humanly speaking, out of range of Lancashire who by then were their only challengers. The dressing-room balcony could now be safely festooned with hops! It was the more to their credit that Kent consistently contributed either three or four men to the five-match series between England and the Rest of the World and in their absence the reserves rose to the occasion and put in many decisive – and at times match-winning – performances. This was the start of the most successful decade in Kent's long and distinguished history.

1970

COWDREY CENTURY SETS SEAL ON KENT'S TRIUMPH

Kent have scored 256 for six in 84 overs in reply to Surrey's first innings of 151 for nine declared.

By E. W. SWANTON at The Oval

COLIN COWDREY has made no secret of nourishing over his career two ambitions; to lead M C C in Australia, and to bring the county championship back to Kent.

Deprived of the more likely honour, he is now reaping the second, and nothing could have been more appropriate than that he should crown the day with a distinguished and completely characteristic hundred.

Daily Telegraph, 11 September, 1970

BELOW Colin Cowdrey, who led Kent to the Championship, batting at Canterbury in 1970. Walking in from cover is his old colleague – and adversary – Tom Graveney

1971

THE ASHES which had been in Australia's keeping for twelve years returned to England on 17 February 1971 by virtue of their victory at Sydney by 62 runs in what was termed the Seventh Test. This however concealed the fact that only six were contested, the Third being abandoned without a ball bowled and an extra one brought into the programme.

Ray Illingworth's side had been the stronger in bowling throughout the series though only able to drive their advantage home to victory in the Fourth Test (also at Sydney). For this crucial game on a suspect pitch – exceptional rain had interfered with the preparation – the Australian selectors made history by dropping their captain, Bill Lawry, most obdurate of left-handers, in favour of Ian Chappell.

England were without Boycott, their best batsman, through injury, while Snow, their leading bowler, after two overs in Australia's second innings put himself out of action by breaking his hand on the boundary pickets.

A game of many fluctuations was marred by a serious show of dissent by England after Snow had been warned for intimidation. Illingworth joined Snow in angry conversation with umpire Rowan, and when he saw Snow tangling with a spectator, one on either side of the fence, and several cans of beer being thrown, the captain without reference to the umpires led his team off the field. They only returned after being warned that otherwise they might lose the match by default. This incident took some of the gilt off the gingerbread, and was no doubt the chief reason for the warning against ill-discipline and dissent issued by the Cricket Council on the team's return home.

This aspect apart, Illingworth's contribution to the series both as captain and all-rounder had much to do with the result.

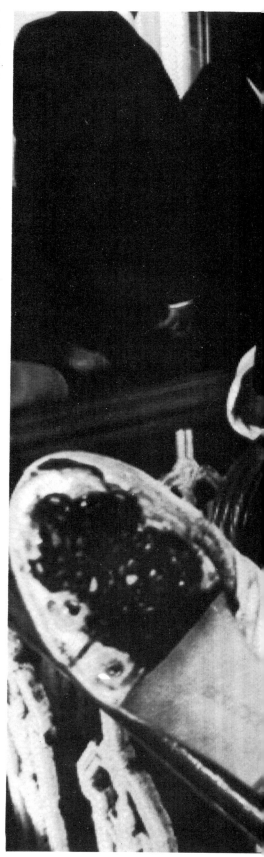

ILLINGWORTH LEADS STRICKEN ENGLAND SIDE TO ASHES TRIUMPH

England took Australia's last five second innings wickets for 37 runs yesterday to win the seventh Test by 62 runs. They thus won the series 2-0 and regained the Ashes.

By E. W. SWANTON in Sydney

THE Ashes, after 12 long years in Australia's keeping, were recaptured with the minimum of excitement in Sydney yesterday after an hour and a half's cricket with more than a day of the seventh Test to spare.

Daily Telegraph, 18 February, 1971

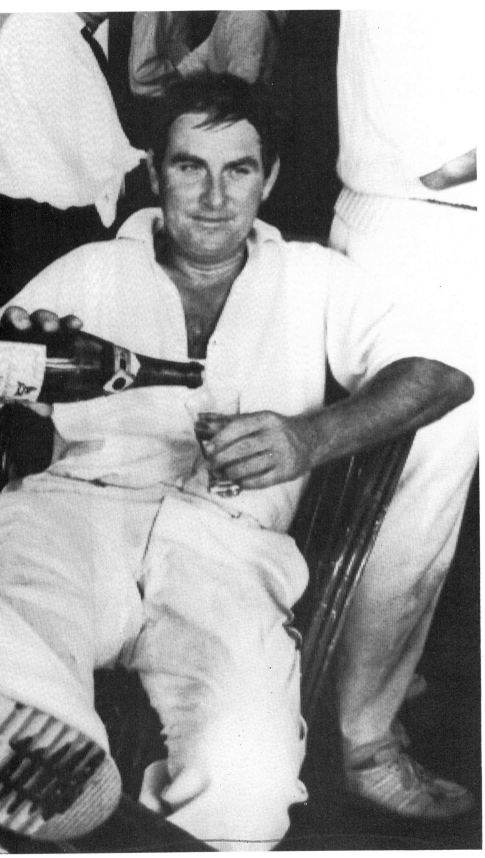

AUSTRALIA v ENGLAND

Played at Sydney,
12, 13, 14, 16, 17 February, 1971.
Result: England won by 62 runs.

England: First innings

J.H. Edrich c G.S. Chappell b Dell	30
B.W. Luckhurst c Redpath b Walters	0
K.W.R. Fletcher c Stackpole b O'Keeffe	33
J.H. Hampshire c Marsh b Lillee	10
B.L. D'Oliveira b Dell	1
R. Illingworth* b Jenner	42
A.P.E. Knott† c Stackpole b O'Keeffe	27
J.A. Snow b Jenner	7
P. Lever c Jenner b O'Keeffe	4
D.L. Underwood not out	8
R.G.D. Willis b Jenner	11
Extras (b 4, lb 4, w 1, nb 2)	11
Total	184

Fall of Wickets: 1/5, 2/60, 3/68, 4/69, 5/98, 6/145, 7/156, 8/165, 9/165, 10/184.
Bowling: Lillee 13-5-32-1, Dell 16-8-32-2, Walters 4-0-10-1, G.S. Chappell 3-0-9-0, Jenner 16-3-42-3, O'Keeffe 24-8-48-3.

Australia: First innings

K.H. Eastwood c Knott b Lever	5
K.R. Stackpole b Snow	6
R.W. Marsh† c Willis b Lever	4
I.M. Chappell* b Willis	25
I.R. Redpath c and b Underwood	59
K.D. Walters st Knott b Underwood	42
G.S. Chappell b Willis	65
K.J. O'Keeffe c Knott b Illingworth	3
T.J. Jenner b Lever	30
D.K. Lillee c Knott b Willis	6
A.R. Dell not out	3
Extras (lb 5, w 1, nb 10)	16
Total	264

Fall of Wickets: 1/11, 2/13, 3/32, 4/66, 5/147, 6/162, 7/178, 8/235, 9/239, 10/264.
Bowling: Snow 18-2-68-1, Lever 14.6-3-43-3, D'Oliveira 12-2-24-0, Willis 12-1-58-3, Underwood 16-3-39-2, Illingworth 11-3-16-1.

England: Second innings

J.H. Edrich c I.M. Chappell b O'Keeffe	57
B.W. Luckhurst c Lillee b O'Keeffe	59
K.W.R. Fletcher c Stackpole b Eastwood	20
J.H. Hampshire c I.M. Chappell b O'Keeffe	24
B.L. D'Oliveira c I.M. Chappell b Lillee	47
R. Illingworth* lbw b Lillee	29
A.P.E. Knott† b Dell	15
J.A. Snow c Stackpole b Dell	20
P. Lever c Redpath b Jenner	17
D.L. Underwood c Marsh b Dell	0
R.G.D. Willis not out	2
Extras (b 3, lb 3, nb 6)	12
Total	302

Fall of Wickets: 1/94, 2/130, 3/158, 4/165, 5/234, 6/251, 7/276, 8/298, 9/299, 10/302.
Bowling: Lillee 14-0-43-2, Dell 26.7-3-65-3, Walters 5-0-18-0, Jenner 21-5-39-1, O'Keeffe 26-8-96-3, Eastwood 5-0-21-1, Stackpole 3-1-8-0.

Australia: Second innings

K.H. Eastwood b Snow	0
K.R. Stackpole b Illingworth	67
R.W. Marsh† (7) b Underwood	16
I.M. Chappell* (3) c Knott b Lever	6
I.R. Redpath (4) c Hampshire b Illingworth	14
K.D. Walters (5) c D'Oliveira b Willis	1
G.S. Chappell (6) st Knott b Illingworth	30
K.J. O'Keeffe c sub (K. Shuttleworth) b D'Oliveira	12
T.J. Jenner c Fletcher b Underwood	4
D.K. Lillee c Hampshire b D'Oliveira	0
A.R. Dell not out	3
Extras (b 2, nb 5)	7
Total	160

Fall of Wickets: 1/0, 2/22, 3/71, 4/82, 5/96, 6/131, 7/142, 8/154, 9/154, 10/160.
Bowling: Snow 2-1-7-1, Lever 12-2-23-1, D'Oliveira 5-1-15-2, Willis 9-1-32-1, Underwood 13.6-5--28-2, Illingworth 20-7-39-3, Fletcher 1-0-9-0.

*LEFT The fruits of victory for England's
captain, Ray Illingworth, after a hard-fought
– and at times contentious – series which
England won 2-0*

1971

THE FIRST negro life peer, who became Sir Learie Constantine and finally Baron Constantine of Maraval in Trinidad and Tobago and of Nelson in the County Palatine of Lancaster, was by any computation a man of singular qualities and achievements. He was first and foremost a cricketer of unparalleled exuberance and panache, possessed of an eye so keen, reflexes so responsive and limbs so flexible that as a fielder anywhere he was, as they say, out of this world. His fast bowling and his hitting were spectacular to a degree, and if anyone was made to be a crowd-puller in league cricket it was he. In Nelson, his adopted home, he was the uncrowned king, and when the war came he was an ideal man to fuse community effort for the common cause.

Like Sir Frank Worrell he educated himself in the law while pursuing the career of a professional cricketer, and was called to the bar at the ripe age of fifty-four. Returning home to take a prominent part in government, he came back to London on independence as the first High Commissioner for Trinidad. To one who knows the little patch of Maraval on the outskirts of Port-of-Spain from which he `sprang, 'Conny's' story is a legend indeed.

Learie Constantine: cricketer (BELOW), lawyer (RIGHT), and peer (ABOVE)

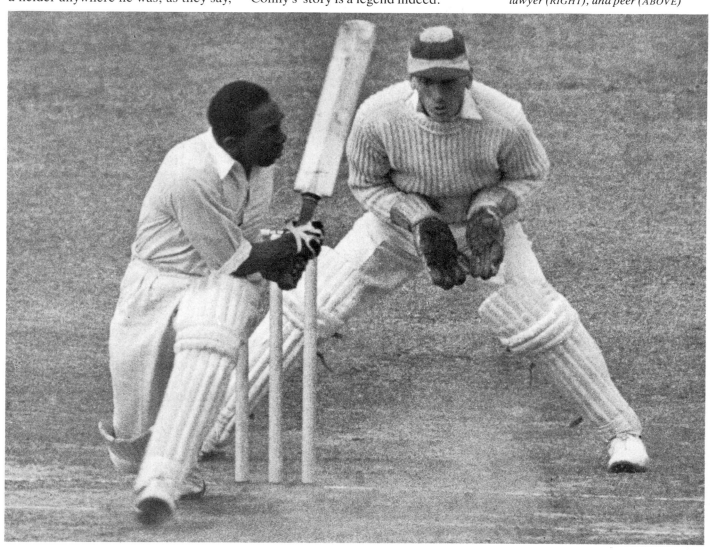

156

Lord Constantine, first Negro life peer, dies

By E. W. SWANTON

LORD CONSTANTINE, who has died, aged 69, built a life of noted public service in several fields on the original base of his fame as a cricketer.

Daily Telegraph, 2 July, 1971

1971

9 O'CLOCK SHADOWS!

Fans go wild as Hughes settles Cup thriller in grand manner

LANCASHIRE, the Gillette Cup-holders, are through to the final again after the longest-ever cricket cup-tie in history.

At seven minutes to nine at Old Trafford last night, and in the most appalling light, they finally won a ten-hour duel with Gloucestershire as skipper Jack Bond pushed the fifth ball of the fifty-seventh over for the single that clinched victory by three wickets.

Daily Mirror, 29 July, 1971

ABOVE The players run for the pavilion among the invading spectators as the game ends in twilight. Five years later David Hughes hit 26 in an over in the Gillette final off Bishen Bedi

THE GILLETTE CUP semi-final between Lancashire and Gloucestershire which because of earlier rain was prolonged until almost nine o'clock was won in semi-darkness by the youngest Lancashire player, David Hughes. Batting with his captain, Jack Bond, he said when 27 runs were needed off the last six overs, 'If I can see 'em I can hit 'em,' and promptly did so to the tune of 24 in an over from John Mortimore.

This was the heyday of Lancashire's one-day successes. The match was watched by 23,500, and it was all but ten o'clock before they had all dispersed. Lancashire went on to beat Kent in the final and to retain the Gillette Cup – having won it the year before. The following year – in 1972 – they established a record of three consecutive wins in the competition which has yet to be equalled. Sixteen years later only Jack Simmons and David Hughes are still playing for their county.

LANCASHIRE v GLOUCESTERSHIRE
The Gillette Cup (semi-final)
Played at Manchester, 28 July, 1971.
Result: Lancashire won by three wickets.

Gloucestershire

R.B. Nicholls b Simmons	53
D.M. Green run out	21
R.D.V. Knight c Simmons b Hughes	31
M.J. Procter c Engineer b Lever	65
M. Bissex not out	29
A.S. Brown* c Engineer b Sullivan	6
H. Jarman not out	0
J.B. Mortimore	
B.J. Meyer† } did not bat	
J. Davey	
Extras (b 2, lb 14, w 1, nb 1)	18
Total (6 wickets)	229

Fall of Wickets: 1/57, 2/87, 3/113, 4/150, 5/201, 6/210.
Bowling: Lever 12-3-40-1, Shuttleworth 12-3-33-0, Wood 12-3-39-0, Hughes 11-0-68-1, Simmons 12-3-25-2, Sullivan 1-0-6-1.

Lancashire

D. Lloyd lbw b Brown	31
B. Wood run out	50
H. Pilling b Brown	21
C.H. Lloyd b Mortimore	34
J. Sullivan b Davey	10
F.M. Engineer† hit wkt b Mortimore	2
J.D. Bond* not out	16
J. Simmons b Mortimore	25
D.P. Hughes not out	26
P. Lever	
K. Shuttleworth } did not bat	
Extras (b 1, lb 13, nb 1)	15
Total (7 wickets, 56.5 overs)	230

Fall of Wickets: 1/61, 2/105, 3/136, 4/156, 5/160, 6/163, 7/203.
Bowling: Procter 10.5-3-38-0, Davey 11-1-22-1, Knight 12-2-42-0, Mortimore 11-0-81-3, Brown 12-0-32-2.

AS JOHN WOODCOCK remarked in his report India's first Test win on English soil, at The Oval in August 1971, had taken 39 years to achieve. It came after an absorbing struggle dominated by the spin bowlers of each side: Bedi, Chandra and Venkat for India, Illingworth, the captain, and Underwood for England. The performance which proved decisive was that of Chandra, the wrist-spinner with the polio-afflicted right shoulder whose googly, bowled at a full slow-medium pace, was his most dangerous ball. Between lunch and tea in England's second innings he took 6 for 38 to give his side the prospect of a victory which seemed beyond imagining after England had scored 355 on the first day.

India under Ajit Wadekar were a sporting and attractive side, and the fact that their successes were based on spin made them the more popular. Only Kapil Dev among Indian bowlers exceeds the 266 Test wickets of the slow left-arm Bedi, an artist if ever there was one. Chandra had 242 in Tests, Prasanna (present, but not needed in this series) 189 and his fellow off-spinner Venkat 156.

Within a few years India won series against England (two), the West Indies and New Zealand and lost a close one only to Australia.

India at Kennington Oval were clearly encouraged by the vocal support of their expatriate countrymen: so much so that Ray Illingworth remarked ruefully that India seemed to be the home side rather than his.

ENGLAND v INDIA

Played at The Oval,
19, 20 (no play), 21, 23, 24 August, 1971.
Result: India won by four wickets.

England: First innings

B.W. Luckhurst c Gavaskar b Solkar	1
J.A. Jameson run out	82
J.H. Edrich c Engineer b Bedi	41
K.W.R. Fletcher c Gavaskar b Bedi	1
B.L. D'Oliveira c Mankad b Chandrasekhar	2
A.P.E. Knott† c and b Solkar	90
R. Illingworth* b Chandrasekhar	11
R.A. Hutton b Venkataraghavan	81
J.A. Snow c Engineer b Solkar	3
D.L. Underwood c Wadekar b Venkataraghavan	22
J.S.E. Price not out	1
Extras (b 4, lb 15, w 1)	20
Total	355

Fall of Wickets: 1/5, 2/111, 3/135, 4/139, 5/143, 6/175, 7/278, 8/284, 9/352, 10/355.
Bowling: Abid Ali 12-2-47-0, Solkar 15-4-28-3, Gavaskar 1-0-1-0, Bedi 36-5-120-2, Chandrasekhar 24-6-76-2, Venkataraghavan 20.4-3-63-2.

India: First innings

S.M. Gavaskar b Snow	6
A.V. Mankad b Price	10
A.L. Wadekar* c Hutton b Illingworth	48
D.N. Sardesai b Illingworth	54
G.R. Viswanath b Illingworth	0
E.D. Solkar c Fletcher b D'Oliveira	44
F.M. Engineer† c Illingworth b Snow	59
S. Abid Ali b Illingworth	26
S. Venkataraghavan lbw b Underwood	24
B.S. Bedi c D'Oliveira b Illingworth	2
B.S. Chandrasekhar not out	0
Extras (b 6, lb 4, nb 1)	11
Total	284

Fall of Wickets: 1/17, 2/21, 3/114, 4/118, 5/125, 6/222, 7/230, 8/278, 9/284, 10/284.
Bowling: Snow 24-5-68-2, Price 15-2-51-1, Hutton 12-2-30-0, D'Oliveira 7-5-5-1, Illingworth 34.3-12-70-5, Underwood 25-6-49-1.

England: Second innings

B.W. Luckhurst c Venkataraghavan b Chandrasekhar	33
J.A. Jameson run out	16
J.H. Edrich b Chandrasekhar	0
K.W.R. Fletcher c Solkar b Chandrasekhar	0
B.L. D'Oliveira c sub (K. Jayantilal) b Venkataraghavan	17
A.P.E. Knott† c Solkar b Venkataraghavan	1
R. Illingworth* c and b Chandrasekhar	4
R.A. Hutton not out	13
J.A. Snow c and b Chandrasekhar	0
D.L. Underwood c Mankad b Bedi	11
J.S.E. Price lbw b Chandrasekhar	3
Extras (lb 3)	3
Total	101

Fall of Wickets: 1/23, 2/24, 3/24, 4/49, 5/54, 6/65, 7/72, 8/72, 9/96, 10/101.
Bowling: Abid Ali 3-1-5-0, Solkar 3-1-10-0, Bedi 1-0-1-1, Chandrasekhar 18.1-3-38-6, Venkataraghavan 20-4-44-2.

India: Second innings

S.M. Gavaskar lbw b Snow	0
A.V. Mankad c Hutton b Underwood	11
A.L. Wadekar* run out	45
D.N. Sardesai c Knott b Underwood	40
G.R. Viswanath c Knott b Luckhurst	33
E.D. Solkar c and b Underwood	1
F.M. Engineer† not out	28
S. Abid Ali not out	4
S. Venkataraghavan	
B.S. Bedi } did not bat	
B.S. Chandrasekhar	
Extras (b 6, lb 5, nb 1)	12
Total (6 wickets)	174

Fall of Wickets: 1/2, 2/37, 3/76, 4/124, 5/134, 6/170.
Bowling: Snow 11-7-14-1, Price 5-0-10-1, D'Oliveira 9-3-17-0, Illingworth 36-15-40-0, Underwood 38-14-72-3, Luckhurst 2-0-9-1.

BELOW India taste Victory at last: The Oval 1971

India's three exciting hours to fame
The Times, 25 August, 1971

What Massie d

Jack Fingleton looks back in joy at the man who beat England by going round and around

---

ENGLAND v AUSTRALIA
Played at Lord's, 22, 23, 24, 26 June, 1972.
Result: Australia won by eight wickets.

England: First innings

G. Boycott b Massie	11
J.H. Edrich lbw b Lillee	10
B.W. Luckhurst b Lillee	1
M.J.K. Smith b Massie	34
B.L. D'Oliveira lbw b Massie	32
A.W. Greig c Marsh b Massie	54
A.P.E. Knott† c Colley b Massie	43
R. Illingworth* lbw b Massie	30
J.A. Snow b Massie	37
N. Gifford c Marsh b Massie	3
J.S.E. Price not out	4
Extras (lb 6, w 1, nb 6)	13
Total	272

Fall of Wickets: 1/22, 2/23, 3/28, 4/84, 5/97, 6/193, 7/200, 8/260, 9/265, 10/272.
Bowling: Lillee 28-3-90-2, Massie 32.5-7-84-8, Colley 16-2-42-0, G.S. Chappell 6-1-18-0, Gleeson 9-1-25-0.

Australia: First innings

K.R. Stackpole c Gifford b Price	5
B.C. Francis b Snow	0
I.M. Chappell* c Smith b Massie	56
G.S. Chappell b D'Oliveira	131
K.D. Walters c Illingworth b Snow	1
R. Edwards c Smith b Illingworth	28
J.W. Gleeson c Knott b Greig	1
R.W. Marsh† c Greig b Snow	50
D.J. Colley c Greig b Price	25
R.A.L. Massie c Knott b Snow	0
D.K. Lillee not out	2
Extras (lb 7, nb 2)	9
Total	308

Fall of Wickets: 1/1, 2/7, 3/82, 4/84, 5/190, 6/212, 7/250, 8/290, 9/290, 10/308.
Bowling: Snow 32-13-57-5, Price 26.1-5-87-2, Greig 29-6-74-1, D'Oliveira 17-5-48-1, Gifford 11-4-20-0, Illingworth 7-2-13-1.

England: Second innings

G. Boycott b Lillee	6
J.H. Edrich c Marsh b Massie	6
B.W. Luckhurst c Marsh b Lillee	4
M.J.K. Smith c Edwards b Massie	30
B.L. D'Oliveira c G.S. Chappell b Massie	3
A.W. Greig c I.M. Chappell b Massie	3
A.P.E. Knott† c G.S. Chappell b Massie	12
R. Illingworth* c Stackpole b Massie	12
J.A. Snow c Marsh b Massie	0
N. Gifford not out	16
J.S.E. Price c G.S. Chappell b Massie	19
Extras (w 1, nb 4)	5
Total	116

Fall of Wickets: 1/12, 2/16, 3/18, 4/25, 5/31, 6/52, 7/74, 8/74, 9/81, 10/116.
Bowling: Lillee 21-6-50-2, Massie 27.2-9-53-8, Colley 7-1-8-0.

Australia: Second innings

K.R. Stackpole not out	57
B.C. Francis c Knott b Price	9
I.M. Chappell c Luckhurst b D'Oliveira	6
G.S. Chappell not out	7
K.D. Walters	
J.W. Gleeson	
R.W. Marsh†	
D.J. Colley	did not bat
R.A.L. Massie	
D.K. Lillee	
Extras (lb 2)	2
Total (2 wickets)	81

Fall of Wickets: 1/20, 2/51.
Bowling: Snow 8-2-15-0, Price 7-0-28-1, Greig 3-0-17-0, D'Oliveira 8-3-14-1, Luckhurst 0.5-0-5-0.

A LOOK BACK at Lord's is pertinent for a number of reasons, none more so than the phenomenal success of Bob Massie and his tactics of bowling round the wicket.

Massie caught the English batsmen napping. One understands that "around" tactics are seldom employed in English cricket—it could well become a vogue now—although McKenzie and Hawke, two preceding Australian bowlers, often varied their tactics by bowling round the stumps. Never, however, as much as Massie did at Lord's.

An Australian won't be expected to dissect too closely an experiment that succeeded so handsomely. Its main problems are for the English selectors, and it will be interesting to see the results of their probing when they announce their batting side for Nottingham. The only crumb for thought one is prepared to offer is that there was one particular English batsman in the past decade who was eminently equipped by his technique to handle these round-the-stumps tactics. If that sounds mysterious, it is only nationalistically so.

This is not to suggest that Massie's strategy will succeed again in the immediate Tests ahead. The English, sound thinkers on technique, might well come up with the answer for Nottingham. Nor is this to be interpreted as crowing over a Test success that has been a long time in coming. The cock that crows the loudest is in greatest danger of losing its head. What delights me is that Australian cricket, after such a run of defeat, can now stand with pride on equal ground.

It is wise to acknowledge the important part Lillee played in Massie's success. One complements the other. It is apparent that several Englishmen don't appreciate Lillee's speed. It makes them jumpy. The older Australian batsmen demurred most against Lol Larwood's tactics in Australia in the early thirties. Most of the younger men did their best to make the most of an awkward job, and it could be that some of England's present batsmen are a little late in their careers to adjust against Lillee's speed and Massie's tactics.

The Sunday Times, 2 July, 1972

d to England

Robin Marlar insists that Massie is no wonder bowler despite those 16 wickets at Lord's

IT WILL come as no surprise to regular readers that there was no singing or dancing, no cascading champagne, no fizzing funsters in the Marlar household after the Australians had won at Lord's. Monday was no *jour de fête* there, but a day whose Tati-ness was spelt with a difference. It was a magnificent victory for the Australians, all the sweeter for being played out in front of the largest crowd likely to see them, a crowd enthralled by Greg Chappell, Bob Massie and Dennis Lillee, now heroes of cricketing history.

Lord's knows its game, and liked what it saw. There was much chat about opening up the series, a result good for the game and all that sort of stuff. Those who utter such views deserve respect, though not necessarily agreement. I am not impressed by the argument that the "gates" at Nottingham, Leeds and the Oval will be bigger because the series is now level. We like these days to see a winning side, and will buy tickets in advance to see one in action.

The Sunday Times, 2 July, 1972

OF ALL FLASHES in the pan the performance of Robert Arnold Lockyear Massie in the Lord's Test of 1972 was surely the flashiest. He took 16 wickets for 137 in what was his first Test, a number only ever exceeded in a Test by Laker and Barnes, and England were routed. Yet Massie played through ten seasons, on and off, for Western Australia, and took in all only 179 first-class wickets. He was only chosen for five further Tests, wherein he did nothing exceptional.

What helped to make it all seem the more unreal was that he bowled right-arm fast-medium round the wicket – a mode of attack not recommended in any text-book. All that can be added is that his late swing both ways bamboozled everyone. *The Sunday Times* printed a double-sided post-mortem showing a jubilant Jack Fingleton. Robin Marlar correctly diagnosed it as a seven-day wonder.

FAR LEFT Massie in action at Lord's

BELOW Boycott is comprehensively bowled

1972

LEICESTERSHIRE won their first title in 1972, the inaugural year of the Benson and Hedges Cup, and there was a distinct piquancy in their doing so since they were led by Ray Illingworth and the team they beat in the final were Yorkshire. The situation would not have been lost on Sir Leonard Hutton, who in Leicestershire's semi-final against Warwickshire had named Illingworth, his fellow-Yorkshireman and colleague, winner of the Gold Award for the best personal performance. Ironically enough the Award in the Final at Lord's went to another expatriate Yorkshireman, Chris Balderstone.

Illingworth in a close association with the Leicestershire Secretary, F.M. Turner, had begun to make a strong mark on Leicestershire's fortunes soon

BENSON AND HEDGES TROPHY FINAL
Gently to the slaughter

Observer, 23 July, 1972

after his leaving Yorkshire to take on the captaincy in 1969.

For most of the match runs were strangely hard to come by on a fast pitch, Yorkshire being pinned down by the strong Leicestershire attack of McKenzie, Higgs, Spencer, Davison and Illingworth. Yorkshire's 136 was too slender a total to defend once Balderstone and Haywood finally decided it was safe to put their bats to the ball.

The *Daily Telegraph*'s hoary old reactionary reported that 'illustrious old cricketers were asking one another in puzzled tones why the art of batsmanship nowadays seemed so complicated and difficult, and seemed unconvinced by the ironical answer: "Oh, it's the tension"!'

BELOW Graham McKenzie, Leicestershire's Australian opening bowler, bowls Richard Lumb for seven

LEICESTERSHIRE v YORKSHIRE
The Benson and Hedges Cup Final
Played at Lord's, 22 July, 1972.
Result: Leicestershire won by five wickets.

Yorkshire
P.J. Sharpe* c Tolchard b Higgs	14
R.G. Lumb b McKenzie	7
B. Leadbeater run out	32
J.H. Hampshire lbw b McKenzie	14
R.A. Hutton c Spencer b Steele	8
J.D. Woodford c Spencer b Illingworth	1
C. Johnson b Higgs	20
C.M. Old lbw b Illingworth	6
D.L. Bairstow† c Tolchard b McKenzie	13
H.P. Cooper not out	7
A.G. Nicholson not out	4
Extras (lb 9, nb 1)	10
Total (9 wickets, 55 overs)	136

Fall of Wickets: 1/17, 2/21, 3/60, 4/65, 5/77, 6/83, 7/113, 8/122, 9/124.
Bowling: McKenzie 11-2-22-3, Higgs 11-1-33-2, Spencer 7-2-11-0, Davison 11-2-22-0, Illingworth 10-3-21-2, Steele 5-1-17-1.

Leicesterhsire
B. Dudleston c Bairstow b Nicholson	6
M.E. Norman c Sharpe b Woodford	38
R.W. Tolchard† c Bairstow b Cooper	3
B.F. Davison b Cooper	17
J.C. Balderstone not out	41
R. Illingworth* c Bairstow b Hutton	5
P.R. Haywood not out	21
J.F. Steele ⎫	
G.D. McKenzie ⎬ did not bat	
C.T. Spencer ⎪	
K. Higgs ⎭	
Extras (b 2, lb 2, w 4, nb 1)	9
Total (5 wickets, 46.5 overs)	140

Fall of Wickets: 1/16, 2/24, 3/58, 4/84, 5/97.
Bowling: Old 9.5-1-35-0, Nicholson 9-2-17-1, Hutton 11-1-24-1, Cooper 9-0-27-2, Woodford 8-1-28-1.

GLENN TURNER Of New Zealand in 1973 became the seventh and last batsman to start an English season by scoring a thousand runs before the end of May. Moreover so long as the pattern of fixtures maintains its present shape he well may remain the last of a hallowed line which starts with W.G. Grace and continues with the names of Hayward, Hallows, Hammond, Bradman (twice) and W.J. Edrich.

Turner reached the target on the last day of the month and only after a considerable struggle against the Northamptonshire bowling on what the *Evening Standard* described as 'a difficult wicket'. He was a fine batsman, very sound and straight in method, whom one-day cricket for Worcestershire transformed from a somewhat sticky player to one who could bat with attractive freedom.

He belonged to a more seasoned and successful generation of New Zealand batsmen than preceding ones, and though the first Test win over England

BELOW LEFT Glenn Turner, reaches his record and BELOW RIGHT being congratulated by Sharp, Northamptonshire's wicket-keeper

1973

was still five years away New Zealand gave them plenty to think about on their short tour that summer. In the Lord's Test England, after squeaking home by 38 runs at Trent Bridge, were only saved by a mammoth innings of 178 by Keith Fletcher.

New Zealander Turner bats into cricket history
BANG! AND THAT'S THE MAGIC 1000

Evening Standard, 31 May, 1973

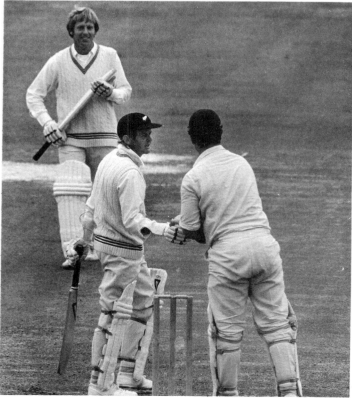

1973

THE LORD'S Test Match of 1973, between England and West Indies, was the one occasion when the spectre of terrorism reared its ugly head at cricket's headquarters. It must have been with ghastly trepidation that the then secretary of MCC, S.C. Griffith, shortly after lunch on the Saturday, announced over the loud-speaker system that the capacity crowd of 28,000 should leave the ground – knowing that there was no possibility that they could do so quickly. In the event the bomb threat, which had been telephoned via the *Sunday Mirror* newspaper, was a hoax, but coming as it did in the middle of a concerted IRA terrorist campaign in London, it had to be taken seriously. Certainly events showed how pitifully vulnerable crowded sports arenas could be to such attacks.

For eighty-five minutes Lord's presented the extraordinary spectacle of empty stands and thousands of spectators milling about on the ground – 'Dickie' Bird fiercely guarding the wicket all the while. When play was resumed it rapidly became clear that the lost time was in no way going to effect England's sorry slide to the second worst margin of defeat in their Test history. Having scored 652 for 8 West Indies proceeded to bowl England out twice and win by the devastating margin of an innings and 226 runs.

'Alert' to meet I.R.A. terror

Bank blast: Test match halted

Sunday Telegraph, 26 August, 1973

ENGLAND v WEST INDIES
Played at Lord's, 23, 24, 25, 27 August, 1973.
Result: West Indies won by an innings and 226 runs.

West Indies: 652 for 8 declared (R.B. Kanhai 157, G. St A. Sobers 150*, B.D. Julien 121; Willis 4-118).

England: First innings 233 (K.W.R. Fletcher 68, A.W. Greig 44; Boyce 4-50, Holder 4-56).

England: Second innings 193 (K.W.R. Fletcher 86*; Boyce 4-49, Gibbs 3-26).

BELOW Police approach a single, recalcitrant figure in an otherwise empty stand and RIGHT umpire Bird guards the wicket during the delay and enforced pitch invasion by the crowd

164

Crowd at Lord's told to leave

By MICHAEL MELFORD

A CROWD of 28,000, including thousands of West Indians, was ordered to evacuate Lord's yesterday afternoon after a telephoned bomb threat. The third day's play in the final Test was suspended in an incident without precedent.

Sunday Telegraph, 26 August, 1973

1974

Amiss rescues the lost Test

Daily Mail, 22 February, 1974

DENNIS AMISS, the quiet man of Warwickshire who was once a temperamental flop, yesterday completed one of the epic innings of cricket to deny the West Indies a victory in the second Test which we all thought was there for the taking.

The genial 30-year-old Amiss — a professional since he left school at Birmingham —led England's great escape with a masterly unbeaten 262 of unbelievable concentration.

He batted throughout the 9½-hour innings knowing that one slip, one lapse of concentration, would cost England defeat.

DENNIS AMISS enjoyed a golden period as opening batsman for England in 1973 and 1974. In 20 successive Tests he scored over 2,000 runs with an average of 71. In eighteen months he made 8 Test hundreds. The MCC tour of the West Indies in the middle of this sequence saw him at his peak and the finest of his innings in that rubber was surely the monumental 262 not out with which he saved the Kingston, Jamaica Test.

A great second innings stand of 209 between Amiss and Boycott had failed to avail England in the First Test at Port-of-Spain, and when they went in again at Kingston on the fourth afternoon with a deficit of 230 and ten long hours stretching ahead the odds seemed long on their going two down in the series with three to play. At the close Amiss came in not out 123, after four hours, but with five wickets down all the other specialist batsmen were gone.

On the last day, in the scorching bowl of Sabina Park, Dennis with a staunch succession of partners, Underwood, Knott, Old and Pocock, defied fatigue and all the wiles of a varied attack, standing firm until, when Pocock left, a maxium of 75 minutes' batting time remained and England were in credit to the tune of 163.

Only now could he feel that his job was done. With the West Indian effort slackening off Willis kept him company to the end. After nine and a half hours at the crease Amiss came in tired but smiling. He had hit 40 fours and a six and had given just one chance, a very sharp one to Gary Sobers of all people, standing three yards from the bat at short leg first thing on the last morning.

WEST INDIES v ENGLAND

Played at Kingston,
16, 17, 19, 20, 21 February, 1974.
Result: Match drawn.

England: First innings

G. Boycott c Kanhai b Sobers	68
D.L. Amiss c Kanhai b Barrett	27
J.A. Jameson st Murray b Gibbs	23
F.C. Hayes c Boyce b Sobers	10
M.H. Denness* c Fredericks b Boyce	67
A.W. Greig c Fredericks b Barrett	45
A.P.E. Knott† c Murray b Barrett	39
C.M. Old c Murray b Julien	2
D.L. Underwood c Fredericks b Sobers	24
P.I. Pocock c Gibbs b Julien	23
R.G.D. Willis not out	6
Extras (lb 7, nb 12)	19
Total	353

Fall of Wickets: 1/68, 2/104, 3/133, 4/134, 5/224, 6/278, 7/286, 8/322, 9/333, 10/353.
Bowling: Boyce 19-2-52-1, Julien 18-3-40-2, Sobers 33-11-65-3, Barrett 39-16-86-3, Gibbs 40-16-78-1, Fredericks 4-0-11-0, Lloyd 4-2-2-0.

West Indies: First innings

R.C. Fredericks b Old	94
L.G. Rowe lbw b Willis	120
A.I. Kallicharran c Denness b Old	93
C.H. Lloyd* b Jameson	49
R.B. Kanhai c Willis b Greig	39
G. St A. Sobers c Willis b Greig	57
B.D. Julien c Denness b Greig	66
K.D. Boyce c Greig b Willis	8
D.L. Murray† not out	6
A.G. Barrett lbw b Willis	0
L.R. Gibbs not out	6
Extras (b 16, lb 18, nb 11)	45
Total (9 wickets declared)	583

Fall of Wickets: 1/206, 2/226, 3/338, 4/401, 5/439, 6/551, 7/563, 8/567, 9/574.
Bowling: Willis 24-5-97-3, Old 23-6-72-2, Pocock 57-14-152-0, Underwood 36-12-98-0, Greig 49-14-102-3, Jameson 7-2-17-1.

England: Second innings

G. Boycott c Murray b Boyce	5
D.L. Amiss not out	262
J.A. Jameson c Rowe b Barrett	38
F.C. Hayes run out	0
M.H. Denness* c Rowe b Barrett	28
A.W. Greig b Gibbs	14
A.P.E. Knott† (8) run out	6
C.M. Old (9) b Barrett	19
D.L. Underwood (7) c Murray b Sobers	12
P.I. Pocock c sub (V.A. Holder) b Boyce	4
R.G.D. Willis not out	3
Extras (b 10, lb 11, w 1, nb 19)	41
Total (9 wickets)	432

Fall of Wickets: 1/32, 2/102, 3/107, 4/176, 5/217, 6/258, 7/271, 8/343, 9/392.
Bowling: Boyce 21-4-70-2, Julien 13-3-36-0, Sobers 34-13-73-1, Barrett 54-24-87-3, Gibbs 44-15-82-1, Fredericks 6-1-17-0, Lloyd 3-1-5-0, Kanhai 3-1-8-0, Rowe 2-1-1-0, Kallicharran 3-0-12-0.

LEFT A watchful Dennis Amiss, who made one of the outstanding match-saving innings in Test Cricket during a marvellous run of personal form in 1973-74

All out for 42! India collapse in Test fiasco

Evening Standard, 24 June, 1974

1974

APART FROM the gross disparity in the scores India's visit to Lord's in 1974 was significant in that Mike Denness was able to reverse the result of the two immediately preceding rubbers wherein Ray Illingworth at home and Tony Lewis in India had lost by the odd match. This game also saw the first of four Test hundreds made inside a twelvemonth by England's captain.

The largest score ever made by England at Lord's meant that India would have a long rearguard to fight. They made England work hard on the Saturday, but on the Monday, with two full days to go and a leeway still to make up of 325, they made a bad start after which the utter hopelessness of the situation took over. All credit nevertheless to two masters in their day of swing and seam, Geoff Arnold and Chris Old. The innings was all over in seventy-seven minutes. This was the lowest Test score at Lord's, and the third lowest in England, worsened (if that is the word) only by South Africa's 30 in 1924 and Australia's 36 in 1902, both at Edgbaston.

Evening newspaper reports tend naturally to end in mid-air: this time the experienced and well-travelled John Thicknesse was able to take the story to its conclusion.

ENGLAND v INDIA
Played at Lord's,
20, 21, 22, 24 June, 1974.
Result: England won by an innings and 285 runs.

England: First innings 629 (D.L. Amiss 188, M.H. Denness 118, A.W. Greig 106, J.H. Edrich 96; Bedi 6-226).

India: First innings 302 (F.M. Engineer 86, G.R. Viswanath 52; Old 4-67).

India: Second innings	
S.M. Gavaskar lbw b Arnold	5
F.M. Engineer† lbw b Arnold	0
A.L. Wadekar* b Old	3
G.R. Viswanath c Knott b Arnold	5
B.P. Patel c Knott b Arnold	1
E.D. Solkar not out	18
S. Abid Ali c Knott b Old	3
Madan Lal c Hendrick b Old	2
E.A.S. Prasanna b Old	5
B.S. Bedi b Old	0
B.S. Chandrasekhar absent hurt	–
Total	42

Fall of Wickets: 1/2, 2/5, 3/12, 4/14, 5/25, 6/28, 7/30, 8/42, 9/42.
Bowling: Arnold 8-1-19-4, Old 8-3-21-5, Hendrick 1-0-2-0.

LEFT Geoff Arnold and Chris Old, architects of India's defeat with respectively 4-19 and 5-21 in India's second innings

1974

RECORDS OF the magnitude of the partnership between John Jameson and Rohan Kanhai for Warwickshire against Gloucestershire in July 1974 need for their achievement the most favourable circumstances possible. These were abundantly in evidence, notably a beautifully plumb pitch and an attack, not very dangerous at full strength, from which the two best bowlers, Mike Procter and Tony Brown, though present as batsmen, were unfit to turn their arms over. Championship regulations at that time limited the first innings of each side to 100 overs, and it was within that span, and occupying five hours and twelve minutes, that the 465 runs were scored.

Wisden describes the assault as 'brutal and ruthless', and to be sure Gloucestershire, after getting a wicket with the second ball of the match, were unlucky in running up against these two in such punishing form. Jameson in his prime batted like the best type of forcing amateur of other days, a powerful fellow who gave the ball a rare thump with the full face of the bat. As to Kanhai, there was scarcely a finer stroke-maker in the game.

It was a story of superlatives right up the street of the *News of the World*, coming to hand late on Saturday afternoon, just right for the early editions. The reporter records the various milestones that were passed, culminating in the 435 by the Indians, Nimbalkar and Bhandarkar which was the best ever for the second wicket hitherto.

WARWICKSHIRE v GLOUCESTERSHIRE
Played at Birmingham, 27, 29 July, 1974.
Result: Warwickshire won by an innings and 61 runs.

Warwickshire: 465 (J.A. Jameson 240*, R.B. Kanhai 213*).

Gloucestershire: First innings 243 (J.C. Foat 52; Hemmings 6-87).

Gloucestershire: Second innings 161 (M.J. Procter 46; Blenkiron 4-18, Willis 4-31).

RIGHT Jameson and Kanhai before the record-breaking scoreboard

OWZAT!— 465 NOT OUT

'SALUTE Warwickshire world-beaters John Jameson and Rohan Kanhai, county cricket's No. 1 entertainers.

Edgbaston, used to batting spectaculars from this wonder pair, had never seen anything like it as the two cavaliers cracked an unbeaten 465 for the second wicket in just 100 overs against suffering Gloucestershire.

Chances

Jameson, rejected by England because he is too adventurous and prone to giving chances, finished on a career-best 240 (a six and 34 fours).

Kanhai, sacked as West Indies Test skipper, ended with 213 (a six and 30 fours). And they took only five hours to beat the previous world record for the second wicket . . . the 455 by Indian batsmen Bhandarkar and Nimbalkar in Poona in 1948-49.

News of the World, 28 July, 1974

ENGLAND WIN LAST BATTLE – DESPITE DEFIANT CHAPPELL

By E. W. SWANTON in Melbourne

England bowled out Australia for 373 to win the match by an innings and four runs. Australia took the rubber 4-1 with one match drawn.

Daily Telegraph, 14 February, 1975

A PERSONAL TOUCH! I wrote my first cricket reports as a member of the *Evening Standard* staff in 1928. This from Melbourne forty-seven years later was my last. By a happy chance I had an England victory, not – alas! – for the rubber since Australia, largely by dint of the efforts of the most consistently fast pair I ever saw in harness together, Lillee and Thomson, had won four Tests out of the first five.

Since Australia started the last day at 274 for 3 needing only 103 runs to make England bat again, the result was anything but foregone. At lunch it was 367 for 6 with Greg Chappell needing four for his hundred and Max Walker, that likeable, obdurate fellow, with him. It was far from being sewn up yet.

The finale I saw in the happiest circumstances from the luncheon room of the Melbourne Cricket Club Committee whose President, Sir Albert Chadwick, had been kind enough to propose my health. Hardly had he done so when Tony Greig caught and bowled Walker and Peter Lever 'found a break-back of rare quality to bowl Chappell immediately after he had reached his hundred'. That was that. England actually just won by an innings – something that had happened only once before in the 42 Tests I had seen in Australia. Before long I was writing the last paragraph in a peaceful press box:

My last sight of Melbourne Cricket Ground was an impromptu little gathering on the outfield in front of the banner reading 'MCC Fans Thank Colin – six Tours'. The central figure, wearing a large straw sun-hat, was signing endless autographs, posing for photographs and exchanging friendly talk with young and old in the way that has made him as popular a cricketer as has ever visited Australia.'

What a pleasant way to take one's bow!

1975

AUSTRALIA v ENGLAND
Played at Melbourne,
8, 9, 10, 12, 13 February, 1975.
Result: England won by an innings and four runs.

Australia: First innings
I.R. Redpath c Greig b Lever	1
R.B. McCosker c Greig b Lever	0
I.M. Chappell* c Knott b Old	65
G.S. Chappell c Denness b Lever	1
R. Edwards c Amiss b Lever	0
K.D. Walters c Edrich b Old	12
R.W. Marsh† b Old	29
M.H.N. Walker not out	20
D.K. Lillee c Knott b Lever	12
A.A. Mallett b Lever	7
G. Dymock c Knott b Greig	0
Extras (b 2, lb 1, nb 2)	5
Total	152

Fall of Wickets: 1/0, 2/5, 3/19, 4/23, 5/50, 6/104, 7/115, 8/141, 9/149, 10/152.
Bowling: Arnold 6-2-24-0, Lever 11-2-38-6, Old 11-0-50-3, Greig 8.7-1-35-1.

England: First innings
D.L. Amiss lbw b Lillee	0
M.C. Cowdrey c Marsh b Walker	7
J.H. Edrich c I.M. Chappell b Walker	70
M.H. Denness* c and b Walker	188
K.W.R. Fletcher c Redpath b Walker	146
A.W. Greig c sub (T.J. Jenner) b Walker	89
A.P.E. Knott† c Marsh b Walker	5
C.M. Old b Dymock	0
D.L. Underwood b Walker	11
G.G. Arnold c Marsh b Walker	0
P. Lever not out	6
Extras (b 4, lb 2, nb 1)	7
Total	529

Fall of Wickets: 1/4, 2/18, 3/167, 4/359, 5/507, 6/507, 7/508, 8/514, 9/514, 10/529.
Bowling: Lillee 6-2-17-1, Walker 42.2-7-143-8, Dymock 39-6-130-1, Walters 23-3-86-0, Mallett 29-8-96-0, I.M. Chappell 12-1-50-0.

Australia: Second innings
I.R. Redpath c Amiss b Greig	83
R.B. McCosker c Cowdrey b Arnold	76
I.M. Chappell* c Knott b Greig	50
G.S. Chappell b Lever	102
R. Edwards c Knott b Arnold	18
K.D. Walters b Arnold	3
R.W. Marsh† c Denness b Lever	1
M.H.N. Walker c and b Greig	17
D.K. Lillee (11) not out	0
A.A. Mallett (9) c Edrich b Greig	0
G. Dymock (10) c Knott b Lever	0
Extras (b 9, lb 5, w 4, nb 5)	23
Total	373

Fall of Wickets: 1/111, 2/215, 3/248, 4/289, 5/297, 6/306, 7/367, 8/373, 9/373, 10/373.
Bowling: Arnold 23-6-83-3, Lever 16-1-65-3, Old 18-1-75-0, Greig 31.7-7-88-4, Underwood 18-5-39-0.

'Ashes to ashes, dust to dust — if Thomson don't get ya, Lillee must . . .'

Sunday Telegraph, Sydney

LEFT Australia's view of the tour: Paul Rigby's cartoon from the Sunday Telegraph, Sydney, which does not, however, account for England's face-saving victory in the last Test after four consecutive defeats. On the succeeding New Zealand leg of the tour the England batsmen continued their run of good form

Eclipso! It's the best thing since the Ashes

THE FIRST Prudential World Cup – an enterprise towards which the authorities looked forward with some apprehension, if only from the weather angle – went off like a dream. For the fifteen days of the tournament, there was never a cloud in the sky, albeit only a week before its commencement cricket had been halted by snow.

Robin Marlar, not a critic given to half measure, bestowed on all concerned unqualified praise. After noting the West Indians' utter determination to win and paying due tribute to Clive Lloyd for his magnificent 102 in only 24 overs he went on:

> IN AN optimist's world, great events evoke great deeds. As Clive Lloyd and his West Indian team have come ever closer to the glittering prize of the first Prudential World Cup, their captain's heart and mind have been slowly but totally captured by the ambition to win it. Nothing, neither pressure nor their own volatility, nothing in fact was to deter them.
>
> As for Lloyd, his batting, so full of pyrotechnics, is hardly a faithful reflection of an essentially calm personality. But on this, the most important occasion of his cricketing life, Lloyd staged a midsummer Guy Fawkes celebration to take the Man of the Match award, making 102 in the 24 overs he was at the wicket, the second 50 off 32 balls, thus helping the West Indies to reach the unconquerable height of 291 for 8 off their 60 overs.
>
> After giving the West Indies first innings, the Australians had to bat through late afternoon into evening and even later than that. They bravely kept in contact and contention with Ian Chappell leading, but in the end, as Lloyd predicted, the West Indies were able to defend their total, notably by the positive virtue of running out three of the top four Australians.
>
> And so, in all the glory of a Lords' full to the corners, the West Indians beat out their rhythms and rang their bells. Thus ended the best innovation in the history of cricket since that notice in The Times which gave birth to the Ashes. Thanks to effective and imaginative administration, hardly a carp has been heard, while by their cricket the players, especially those of West Indies, the winners, Australia and Pakistan have invested two of the happiest and finest June weeks with a substantial dollop of international goodwill.
>
> This Cup has certainly worked wonders. Quite apart from extending the game's audience from theatre to cinema proportions it has struck a rich seam of gold. There will be a surplus from the pool of expenses and television fees and the gate, some £190,000 from not far short of 200,000 spectators, will be sheer profit for cricket all over the world. *The Sunday Times, 22 June, 1975*

ABOVE Clive Lloyd raises the World Cup after his century LEFT

AUSTRALIA v WEST INDIES
The Prudential World Cup Final
Played at Lord's, 21 June, 1975.
Result: West Indies won by 17 runs.

West Indies

R.C. Fredericks hit wkt b Lillee	7
C.G. Greenidge c Marsh b Thomson	13
A.I. Kallicharran c Marsh b Gilmour	12
R.B. Kanhai b Gilmour	55
C.H. Lloyd* c Marsh b Gilmour	102
I.V.A. Richards b Gilmour	5
B.D. Julien not out	26
D.L. Murray† c and b Gilmour	14
V.A. Holder not out	6
A.M.E. Roberts did not bat	
Extras (lb 5, nb 11)	17
Total (8 wickets, 60 overs)	291

Fall of Wickets: 1/12, 2/27, 3/50, 4/199, 5/206, 6/209, 7/261, 8/285.
Bowling: Lillee 12-1-55-1, Gilmour 12-2-48-5, Thomson 12-1-44-2, Walker 12-1-71-0, G.S. Chappell 7-0-33-0, Walters 5-0-23-0.

Australia

A. Turner run out	40
R.B. McCosker c Kallicharran b Boyce	7
I.M. Chappell* run out	62
G.S. Chappell run out	15
K.D. Walters b Lloyd	35
R.W. Marsh† b Boyce	11
R. Edwards c Fredericks b Boyce	28
G.J. Gilmour c Kanhai b Boyce	14
M.H.N. Walker run out	7
J.R. Thomson run out	21
D.K. Lillee not out	16
Extras (b 2, lb 9, nb 7)	18
Total (58.4 overs)	274

Fall of Wickets: 1/25, 2/81, 3/115, 4/162, 5/170, 6/195, 7/221, 8/231, 9/233.
Bowling: Julien 12-0-58-0, Roberts 11-1-45-0, Boyce 12-0-50-4, Holder 11.4-1-65-0, Lloyd 12-1-38-1.

1975

THE UNIVERSAL enjoyment of the 1975 season, with glorious weather throughout, the hugely successful first Prudential World Cup and a series between England and Australia, was rudely and violently interrupted when, during the early hours of the final day of the Third Test at Headingley, vandals sabotaged the wicket forcing the match to be abandoned. Those responsible were supporters of George Davis, a mini-cab driver from east London who, in March 1975, had been imprisoned for twenty years for his part in an armed robbery.

From then his supporters protested his innocence by a series of demonstrations aimed at bringing the case into the public eye.

The major attraction of the visiting Australian team were the two fast bowlers, Lillee and Thomson who, the previous winter, had largely destroyed the English team in Australia. After victory by Australia in the First Test and a draw in the second the four-match series was poised at Headingley with only one further Test to play at The Oval. At the end of the fourth day at Headingley England had every chance of victory, with Australia 220 for 3, 224 runs behind. The abandonment of the match as a draw ensured that Australia retained the Ashes.

Events however subsequently proved the question-mark in the *Guardian* front-page headline to be unfounded. The saboteurs were indeed prosecuted, in January 1976. Peter Chappell, a close friend of Davis was jailed for eighteen months. Three others who admitted damaging the walls and pitch at Headingley received suspended sentences.

ENGLAND v AUSTRALIA

Played at Leeds,
14, 15, 16, 18, 19 August, 1975.
Result: Match drawn.

England: First innings 288 (D.S. Steele 73, J.H. Edrich 62, A.W. Greig 51; Gilmour 6-85).

Australia: First innings 135 (Edmonds 5-28, Underwood 3-22).

England: Second innings 291 (D.S. Steele 92, A.W. Greig 49).

Australia: Second innings 220 for 3 (R.B. McCosker 95*, I.M. Chappell 65).

BELOW Slogans daubed on the walls of Headingley spell out the dismal message and RIGHT members of the Press look on as police experts inspect the vandalized wicket

Test saboteurs may escape prosecution

The Guardian, 20 August, 1975

1976

Unflinching to disaster

Robin Marlar sees England savaged

The Sunday Times, 11 July, 1976

THE MANCHESTER Test of 1976 between England and West Indies brought overwhelming victory to the latter but at serious cost to their reputation. Another reputation also suffered, that of the Lancashire authorities who provided a cracked, uneven pitch on which the fast bowling even when of a fair length was intrinsically dangerous.

When England went in a second time on the Saturday evening, having been bowled out in their first innings for 71, there were a little over thirteen hours of the match to go and the margin between the sides was 551. Before close of play John Edrich and Brian Close were then subjected to a physical battering from which they were lucky to escape with nothing worse than bruises. There could have been broken bones or worse, so short and fast did Holding, Roberts and Daniel bowl, without reproof from their captain, Clive Lloyd and inhibited by only one umpire's warning for intimidation, uttered by Bill Alley the Australian, to Holding.

Lloyd's comment, as quoted by *Wisden* was: 'Our fellows got carried away. They knew they had only eighty minutes that night to make an impression, and they went flat out sacrificing accuracy for speed. They knew afterwards they had bowled badly'. The excuse palpably begged the question. The bowling was accurate enough in its intended shortness as well as extremely fast. Even on a plumb pitch it would have been a serious menace. Lloyd's excuse was inadequate in a more basic respect because by implication it ignored cricket's traditional axiom that a captain should be responsible for the conduct of his team. Lloyd could not

have been unaware out there in the field of the sickly odour of intimidation. All that could have been pleaded in his defence was that he was following the fashion of Ian Chappell, of Australia, and, before him, of Ray Illingworth in the Ashes series of 1970-71, which assumes that the conduct of the game is to be left wholly and entirely in the hands of the umpires.

I write thus now of a happening of eleven years ago because the evil of intimidation is still a serious scar on the game which neither captains are willing to curb nor cricket authority to tackle by reform of the law.

The first two games of the series

having been drawn, the West Indies went on to win the Fourth Test at Headingley by 55 runs after a fine match and the Fifth at The Oval very easily. The West Indies made 687 for 8 in the first innings, their highest score ever against England.

ENGLAND v WEST INDIES
Played at Manchester,
8, 9, 10, 12, 13 July, 1976.

West Indies: 211 (C.G. Greenidge 134; Selvey 4-41, Underwood 3-55).

England: First innings 71 (Holding 5-17, Roberts 3-32).

West Indies: Second innings 411 for 5 declared (I.V.A Richards 135, C.G. Greenidge 101, R.C. Fredericks 50).

England: Second innings 126 (Roberts 6-37).

Ordeal by fire for veterans John Edrich LEFT and Brian Close BELOW

1976

England women dispel flippancy and the Australian challenge

By Alan Gibson

WOMEN AT LORD'S! In August of 1976, the Jubilee Year of the Women's Cricket Association they came, they saw, and they conquered the hearts of those who had turned up to see history made. It was a perfect summer's day, and the opposition, fittingly enough, was provided by the Australian touring team. Moreover, to make the celebration complete, England easily won the 60-over-a-side match under the captaincy of the leading figure in the feminine game, Rachel Heyhoe (now Heyhoe Flint).

In opening the gates of Lord's to women cricketers MCC were recognizing both the game's ancient beginnings and its well-conducted modern state. The first reference is to a match between 'eleven maids of Bramley and eleven maids of Hambledon', at Gosden Common near Guildford, Surrey as recorded in the *Reading Mercury* of July 1745. Women seem to have played as a regular thing, if in limited numbers, throughout the nineteenth century prior to the forming in 1887 of the fashionable White Heather Club, whose players included the wife of a future Prime Minister, Stanley Baldwin. Following the formation of the WCA in 1926 overseas tours were organized and territorial Associations sprouted, and in 1958 came the International Women's Cricket Council. This body has now fourteen countries affiliated, four of them West Indian. The game has not taken off to the same degree as, for instance, lawn tennis or athletics, but support is maintained at a healthy level.

Alan Gibson in his *Times* report thought that the 'girls', as he termed them, batted better than they bowled. The fact is that they scarcely have the physical strength either to bowl very fast or to give the ball sufficient of a tweak to produce sharp turn. On the other hand they play well and gracefully the strokes that call for touch and timing. I write as one who not only saw this game at Lord's but was also among the mourners at The Oval in 1937 when in the match which climaxed the first Australian tour to England poor Miss Betty Snowball was run out for 99 – there was scarcely a dry eye on the ground!

As to 1976 at Lord's the atmosphere was refreshingly, delightfully sporting – I almost said gentlemanly.

ENGLAND v AUSTRALIA
60 overs
Played at Lord's, 4 August, 1976.
Result: England won by eight wickets.

Australia: 161, 59.4 overs (S. Tredrea 54).

England: 162 for 2, 56.2 overs (C. Watmough 50*, E. Bakewell 50).

BELOW Australia's Jannette Lumsden is run out

LORD'S : *England women beat Australia by eight wickets.*

The notices were still there on the pavilion doors: "The attention of all members of MCC, and Middlesex, their guests and visitors, is drawn to the conditions contained in regulation 3 (v) of the regulations of MCC which require them to wear a necktie and jacket whilst in the pavilion."

Regulation 3 (v) has never taken such a battering as it did yesterday. The doorkeepers turned their eyes away as the skirts whisked up to the dressing rooms. For this, as you will already know—it is not Rachael Flint's fault if you do not—was the first time the women had taken over Lord's. The editor of *The Cricketer* told me he had raced to the ground to be sure of seeing the first ball bowled. Not many others had. Only a few hundred were there at the start, and when Australia lost a wicket to the second ball, the noise was rather less than it will be if the same thing happens in the men's match next year. But, as a sunny afternoon drew on, more and more people came along until there was a larger crowd than Middlesex often get.

The Times, 5 August, 1976

176

Mushtaq men cut it fine

Sunday Telegraph, 5 September, 1976

NORTHAMPTONSHIRE, the first-class county with the lowest population among the 17, for whom existence, let alone prosperity on the field was precarious for so many years, at last won something in 1976. Their victory in the Gillette Cup under the leadership of Mushtaq Mohammad, fourth of the five famous Pakistani brothers, was gained with an understandably cosmopolitan side – for there is a limited source of supply in the schools and clubs within the county. They were also runners-up in the Championship in 1976, a side in fact very much to be reckoned with. Four years later came a second success at Lord's in the final of the Benson and Hedges Cup, this time captained by P.J. Watts of Bedfordshire, almost a local boy.

It was a tight contest rather than a brilliant one as reported by Tony Lewis. Lancashire had on their side the confidence that came from having won four Gillettes in the last six years, but after many a palpitating moment Northamptonshire's nerve just held.

LANCASHIRE v NORTHAMPTONSHIRE
The Gillette cup final
Played at Lord's, 4 September, 1976.
Result: Northamptonshire won by four wickets.

Lancashire: 195 for 7, 60 overs (D. Lloyd 48, J. Abrahams 46; Bedi 3-52).

Northamptonshire: 199 for 6, 58.1 overs (P. Willey 65, R.T. Virgin 53; Lee 2-29).

NORTHAMPTONSHIRE carried off the Gillette Cup, the first major success in the history of the club. Lancashire's 195-7 after Mushtaq had put them in, never appeared adequate, yet balancing Lancashire's vast experience in these competitions against the jitters of the novice, left the result wide open.

Twenty-five thousand spectators paying a record £82,500 earned the suspense if not the brilliance. Indeed, it was a dark and sinister start for Lancashire who had won the Cup four out of the last six times.

Sunday Telegraph, 5 September, 1976

BELOW Northamptonshire in a jubilant mood after their victory. Peter Willey (CENTRE) was a deserving Man of the Match

1977

A FICTION-WRITER would have been pressed to write a script better illustrative of the things that make cricket what it is than the actual happenings of the Centenary Test at Melbourne in March 1977. The ebb and sway of fortunes, the quality of several individual performances, the brilliance of the fielding, and the closeness of the final stages all combined to do a unique occasion full justice.

For Australia Dennis Lillee impressed his greatness on the scene and spared the spectators sight of the indiscipline which so sadly marred his reputation. His was the sustained performance of the match – in 48 overs he took 11 wickets for 165 – supported as it was by an unbeaten hundred from his old crony and state colleague Rodney Marsh.

All the England bowlers came out well from the match, while of the batsmen Derek Randall, helped in the biggest stand of the match by Dennis Amiss, stole the show – and very nearly the match. In the end Australia's margin of victory, 45 runs, was exactly that of the first of all Test matches, on the same ground just a hundred years earlier.

The Melbourne Cricket Club and the Victorian Cricket Association combined to bring to reality the vision of the old Test cricketer of the 1930s, Hans Ebeling. The reunion of former England and Australian cricketers was on a grand scale. J.S. Ryder, eighty-seven and P.G.H. Fender, eighty-four, were the senior players of their respective countries, and of the 244 invitees only twenty-six were prevented by infirmity from attending.

In several ways this Centenary Test marked a peak in Anglo-Australian relations not touched before nor since attained.

Randall's our pride and joy !

Pat Gibson: Melbourne

THEY are all going home now . . . the Queen back to the Royal Yacht, Bradman to Adelaide, Larwood to Sydney and Voce to Nottingham.

But none will ever forget the Centenary Test which began with a batting shambles which must have made the old ones shudder and finished in a death or glory struggle which made them wish they were young again.

Daily Express, 18 March, 1977

AUSTRALIA v ENGLAND
Played at Melbourne,
12, 13, 14, 16, 17 March, 1977.
Result: Australia won by 45 runs.

Australia: First innings

I.C. Davis lbw b Lever	5
R.B. McCosker b Willis	4
G.J. Cosier c Fletcher b Lever	10
G.S. Chappell* b Underwood	40
D.W. Hookes c Greig b Old	17
K.D. Walters c Greig b Willis	4
R.W. Marsh† c Knott b Old	28
G.J. Gilmour c Greig b Old	4
K.J. O'Keeffe c Brearley b Underwood	0
D.K. Lillee not out	10
M.H.N. Walker b Underwood	2
Extras (b 4, lb 2, nb 8)	14
Total	138

Fall of Wickets: 1/11, 2/13, 3/23, 4/45, 5/51, 6/102, 7/114, 8/117, 9/136, 10/138.
Bowling: Lever 12-1-36-2, Willis 8-0-33-2, Old 12-4-39-3, Underwood 11.6-2-16-3.

England: First innings

R.A. Woolmer c Chappell b Lillee	9
J.M. Brearley c Hookes b Lillee	12
D.L. Underwood c Chappell b Walker	7
D.W. Randall c Marsh b Lillee	4
D.L. Amiss c O'Keeffe b Walker	4
K.W.R. Fletcher c Marsh b Walker	4
A.W. Greig* b Walker	18
A.P.E. Knott† lbw b Lillee	15
C.M. Old c Marsh b Lillee	3
J.K. Lever c Marsh b Lillee	11
R.G.D. Willis not out	1
Extras (b 2, lb 2, w 1, nb 2)	7
Total	95

Fall of Wickets: 1/19, 2/30, 3/34, 4/40, 5/40, 6/61, 7/65, 8/78, 9/86, 10/95.
Bowling: Lillee 13.3-2-26-6, Walker 15-3-54-4, O'Keeffe 1-0-4-0, Gilmour 5-3-4-0.

Australia: Second innings

I.C. Davis c Knott b Greig	68
R.B. McCosker (10) c Greig b Old	25
G.J. Cosier (4) c Knott b Lever	4
G.S. Chappell* (3) b Old	2
D.W. Hookes (6) c Fletcher b Underwood	56
K.D. Walters (5) c Knott b Greig	66
R.W. Marsh† not out	110
G.J. Gilmour b Lever	16
K.J. O'Keeffe (2) c Willis b Old	14
D.K. Lillee (9) c Amiss b Old	25
M.H.N. Walker not out	8
Extras (lb 10, nb 15)	25
Total (9 wickets declared)	419

Fall of Wickets: 1/33, 2/40, 3/53, 4/132, 5/187, 6/244, 7/277, 8/353, 9/407.
Bowling: Lever 21-1-95-2, Willis 22-0-91-0, Old 27.6-2-104-4, Underwood 12-2-38-1, Greig 14-3-66-2.

England: Second innings

R.A. Woolmer lbw b Walker	12
J.M. Brearley lbw b Lillee	43
D.L. Underwood (7) b Lillee	7
D.W. Randall (3) c Cosier b O'Keeffe	174
D.L. Amiss (4) b Chappell	64
K.W.R. Fletcher (5) c Marsh b Lillee	1
A.W. Greig* (6) c Cosier b O'Keeffe	41
A.P.E. Knott† (7) lbw b Lillee	42
C.M. Old (8) c Chappell b Lillee	2
J.K. Lever (9) lbw b O'Keeffe	4
R.G.D. Willis not out	5
Extras (b 8, lb 4, w 3, nb 7)	22
Total	417

Fall of Wickets: 1/28, 2/113, 3/279, 4/290, 5/346, 6/369, 7/380, 8/385, 9/410, 10/417.
Bowling: Lillee 34.4-7-139-5, Walker 22-4-83-1, O'Keeffe 33-6-108-3, Gilmour 4-0-29-0, Chappell 16-7-29-1, Walters 3-2-7-0.

TOP RIGHT Randall hooks Lillee
BOTTOM RIGHT O'Keeffe caught by Brearley

1977

THE FACT THAT thirty-five of the world's leading cricketers had signed highly lucrative contracts to play cricket for three years in the Australian summer for the newspaper and television tycoon Kerry Packer burst upon an astonished public on 9 May 1977. It emerged at the same time that Tony Greig who had led England in the Centenary Test at Melbourne only two months earlier was simultaneously acting as a clandestine recruiting agent for the rebel organization, and the Cricket Council lost no time in stripping him of the captaincy.

After the euphoria of the Centenary Test, which had shown cricket and cricketers in the best possible light, for those to whom the traditions of cricket were dear the blow was hard to bear. The *Sunday Telegraph*, at its first opportunity to comment on the news which had leaked six days earlier, printed four articles on the subject.

Tony Lewis went into the financial temptation which had been too much for the man who had been sitting on top of the cricket world immediately following his successes in India where he, Lewis, had led an MCC side including Greig four years earlier. Tim Rice contributed a disillusioned, contemptuous piece wherein he asked whether 'if our handsome ex-captain is prepared to hawk his talents in any market-place, would he like a role in *Jesus Christ Superstar*?' Alan Lee revealed that the secret was not meant to break when it did and gave the reactions to the news of the cricket authorityies. Colin Cowdrey, lamenting Greig's fall from grace, discussed possible contenders for the England captaincy in the forthcoming series against Australia and named three, Mike Brearley, John Edrich and Geoffrey Boycott, the first of whom landed the job.

The great god, TV...

By TIM RICE

IT hasn't been the greatest of weeks for cricket what with the rain and this Kerry Packer business.

Rain hasn't ever dampened my enthusiasm for the game but Kerry and his accomplices might well succeed almost overnight where the elements have failed, in my case, for 25 years. Already I don't care who wins this series.

No selector has ever managed to induce such an outbreak of indifference in this cricket lover before. No individual performance in the Packer matches, even if they are deemed to be first class, could really impress me.

Even if Tony Greig scored 364 before lunch it could not rank with Len Hutton's most famous innings. Should Derek Underwood take 19 for 90 in one match I shall remain unmoved. Should he take 20 for 90, I shall still consider Jim Laker's finest hour a vastly more memorable performance, not least because I know it would have happened whether the TV cameras had been there or not.

Obviously there is no reason whatsoever for any great team performance to take place in Kerry's circus. I like to feel that cricketers at the highest level are selected for their cricketing skills and for their value to their side, not because they are good "TV. material."

Is Derek Randall pleased with Packer's assessment of his talents? His superb innings in the Centenary Test is not to be compared with, say, Compton's 184 at Nottingham in 1948, but with the Eurovision song contest. (At least Randall's innings might have beaten the French song).

Is Greig so short of a few bob that he has to go to these clandestine lengths to make a buck? I could tell he felt slightly shifty about the whole affair when he began talking like Nixon.

"Test match situation" ... "at this moment in time" ... "my motivation", were some of the phrases propping up his meaningful dialogue at Hove. If our handsome ex-captain is prepared to hawk his talents in any market place would he like a role in *Jesus Christ Superstar*? I am sure he is a member of Equity and I may well be able to fix it if he would let me know which part would best suit him.

If all this simply meant that Test cricketers would at last get paid a fair wage for playing in Test matches, then one could treat this whole hoohah as a temporary crisis, but I have a feeling that it won't simply mean that, which is sad because the financial lot of cricketers could, and would, have been improved anyway without threatening the whole structure of international cricket.

There will be other changes, too. Cads will begin to suggest that Greig is not really British anyway. Some things of course not even Kerry Packer can alter. I still cannot understand what Geoff Boycott's statements mean.

I suppose one must remain optimistic however. Cricket after all is greater than Packer, Greig and all the Aussies put together. The game has survived other major assaults over the years. But I, if I were the producer of It's A Knockout, I'd be worried.

180

For Greig, a case of paradise lost

THE BIG TOP MONEY SPINNER

Sunday Telegraph, 9 May, 1977

The 1977 Test series, won easily by England against an Australian side all but four of whom were revealed as Packer signatories, proceeded against a noisy background of meetings, threats and counter-threats. The most crucial decision was that unanimously made in July by the Test-playing countries of the International Cricket Conference which barred from Test cricket any player who 'has made himself available to play in a match previously disapproved by the Conference.' This ban was contested successfully in the English courts by Packer on behalf of the players as an undue restraint of trade. The case lasted seven weeks, and involved the ICC and the TCCB in punitive costs.

For the Australian winters Packer's 'World Series Cricket' of one-day matches, with most of the best West Indians and Australians as well as a sprinkling from the other countries involved, was promoted while simultaneously official Test and first-class programmes continued. The Packer circus even toured the West Indies, the matches provoking several serious disorders.

Suddenly in May 1979 – just two years after the original news broke – the Australian Cricket Board announced they had come to an accommodation with Packer's PBL which was to be responsible *for the next ten years* for the marketing and promotion of cricket in Australia. The other countries had no option but to accept a *fait accompli*, however little they liked the vulgarizing of the game which it was sure to involve. Senior critics such as Jack

ABOVE The razzmatazz of World Series Cricket: the drinks buggy arrives, with female attendants

FAR LEFT Kerry Packer and Tony Greig outside the Law Courts in London

Fingleton and Bill O'Reilly warned of the consequences to be expected, but the deed was done. The war was over, at great cost which is still being added up eight years later now the glorification of one-day cricket at the expense of first-class and Test cricket has led to a disastrous fall in Australian playing standards. As this is being written Packer has sold his television and kindred interests to the America's Cup winner Alan Bond, with what likely effect on cricket, only time will show. One can merely record an instinctive first feeling of relief.

Over the whole affair of the Packer involvement one question has been unanswered from 1979 until now. Cricket's ruling bodies naturally render to their constituent member clubs and associations an account of their stewardship. What revenues have they gathered through what channels, gate money, sponsorship and so on; what were the out-goings; how will the profit be distributed? The Australian Cricket Board have never divulged under what financial arrangements they and their promoters have worked or how profitable the deal has been to either party. If the other interested countries have been curious, who can blame them?

1977

Boycott obliges the Yorkshire faithful

Guardian, 12 August, 1977

OF MODERN English batsmen it was perhaps more probable that Geoffrey Boycott would reach the coveted milestone of 100 first-class hundreds than any other, such was the relentless appetite for runs that he revealed throughout his career. When John Arlott commented in his *Guardian* report, 'His mind was set so firmly on that objective that no one, not even the Australian team, could bar his way', he put his finger on the pulse of Boycott's at times seemingly infallible consistency; the harnessing of his considerable batting talent to a deeply entrenched mental attitude. Such single-mindedness, rarely – if ever – matched by another Test cricketer, has been the root of the contrasting facets of Boycott's remarkable, but controversial career.

The circumstances of his achievement at Headingley in July 1977 are very revealing. Only a fortnight previ-

ously he had returned to Test cricket after a self-imposed exile of three years and 30 Tests. At the time of Boycott's departure the Editor of *Wisden* commented drily; 'Indeed, Boycott by his deeds and words has all England wondering whether he will ever be a force again in Test cricket'. At the time Boycott had scored 4,839 Test runs, including 13 hundreds; by the end of his career he had progressed to the then record total of 8,114, including 22 hundreds.

On his return in the Third Test against Australia at Trent Bridge in 1977 Boycott had scored 107 and 80 and batted on all five days of the match – something that would have afforded him as much pleasure as his scores. That was his 98th hundred. A week later his 99th was knocked off against Warwickshire and the stage was set, in front of his own Yorkshire crowd, for what was probably the zenith of his extraordinary career – certainly of his

popularity. As he became not only the eighteenth man to score 100 hundreds, but the first to do so in a Test Match, his acclaim for once extended far beyond those devoted supporters in the county whose fierce loyalties and prejudices have always been his meat and drink.

ENGLAND v AUSTRALIA

Played at Leeds, 11, 12, 13, 15 August, 1977.
Result: England won by an innings and 85 runs.

England: First innings

J.M. Brearley* c Marsh b Thomson	0
G. Boycott c Chappell b Pascoe	191
R.A. Woolmer c Chappell b Thomson	37
D.W. Randall lbw b Pascoe	20
A.W. Greig b Thomson	43
G.R.J. Roope c Walters b Thomson	34
A.P.E. Knott† lbw b Bright	57
I.T. Botham b Bright	0
D.L. Underwood c Bright b Pascoe	6
M. Hendrick c Robinson b Pascoe	4
R.G.D. Willis not out	5
Extras (b 5, lb 9, w 3, nb 22)	39
Total	436

Fall of Wickets: 1/0, 2/82, 3/105, 4/201, 5/275, 6/398, 7/398, 8/412, 9/422, 10/436.
Bowling: Thomson 34-7-113-4, Walker 48-21-97-0, Pascoe 34.4-10-91-4, Walters 3-1-5-0, Bright 26-9-66-2, Chappell 10-2-25-0.

Australia: First innings

R.B. McCosker run out	27
I.C. Davis lbw b Hendrick	0
G.S. Chappell* c Brearley b Hendrick	4
D.W. Hookes lbw b Botham	24
K.D. Walters c Hendrick b Botham	4
R.D. Robinson c Greig b Hendrick	20
R.W. Marsh† c Knott b Botham	2
R.J. Bright not out	9
M.H.N. Walker c Knott b Botham	7
J.R. Thomson b Botham	0
L.S. Pascoe b Hendrick	0
Extras (lb 3, b 1, nb 2)	6
Total	103

Fall of Wickets: 1/8, 2/26, 3/52, 4/57, 5/66, 6/77, 7/87, 8/100, 9/100, 10/103.
Bowling: Willis 5-0-35-0, Hendrick 15.3-2-41-4, Botham 11-3-21-5.

Australia: Second innings

R.B. McCosker c Knott b Greig	12
I.C. Davis c Knott b Greig	19
G.S. Chappell* c Greig b Willis	36
D.W. Hookes lbw b Hendrick	21
K.D. Walters lbw b Woolmer	15
R.D. Robinson b Hendrick	20
R.W. Marsh† c Randall b Hendrick	63
R.J. Bright c Greig b Hendrick	5
M.H.N. Walker b Willis	30
J.R. Thomson b Willis	0
L.S. Pascoe not out	0
Extras (b 1, lb 4, w 4, nb 18)	27
Total	248

Fall of Wickets: 1/31, 2/35, 3/63, 4/97, 5/130, 6/167, 7/179, 8/244, 9/245, 10/248.
Bowling: Willis 14-7-32-3, Hendrick 22.5-6-54-4, Botham 17-3-47-0, Greig 20-7-64-2, Woolmer 8-4-8-1, Underwood 8-3-16-0.

LEFT Boycott returns, the hero of his devoted supporters

Frank Woolley, one of cricket's greats

IT IS DOUBTFUL whether any cricketer has ever evoked such a degree of hero-worship over so many years as did the great left-handed all-rounder Frank Woolley in the county of Kent. Nor perhaps, until this TV-watching age, has any given so much pleasure to so many for so long. He stepped into the side, a tall, slim youth, early in 1906, the year of Kent's first Championship, aged just nineteen. Three years later he played in the first of 52 successive Tests for England, for many years a record sequence. When at the age of fifty-one he felt the moment for retirement had come he was batting in the same free, uninhibited way as ever, and showing little sign of mortal decay. Indeed in that last year, 1938, he returned the compliment of leading the Players at Lord's by giving, for many on both sides young enough to be his sons, a copy-book illustration of the way to play fast bowling.

Genius is not to be measured by the yardstick of figures. Yet the basic facts are clear enough. Only Sir Jack Hobbs narrowly bettered his aggregate of 58,969 runs, including 145 hundreds. Only 26 bowlers in history have taken more than his 2,068 wickets. No one has approached his tally of 1,017 catches (chiefly at slip). If his Test batting record is less impressive it needs remembering that until half-way through it he was played as an all-rounder, batting no higher than number six or seven: also that home Tests were of three days only. In 1912 he took 10 for 54 against Australia at The Oval. In those days he was rated just about the best slow left-arm bowler in the country.

Frank lived to 91, and until his last two years, when in the grip of cancer, came over annually from their home in Nova Scotia to Canterbury Week with his second wife, previously Mrs Martha Morse, a remarkable American lady

with whose literary aid he wrote the memoirs of his early life. After ten years of widowerhood he had married again in 1971.

A moving illustration of the admiration and affection in which he was held in Kent was the size of the congregation at his Memorial Service in Canterbury Cathedral. Although it was forty years since he had played his last innings 600 people filled the quire.

ABOVE Frank Woolley, who never lost his devotion to cricket, watches the 12-year-old Nawab of Pataudi bowling at Alf Gover's cricket school

Charm is a difficult virtue to dissect. The late R. C. Robertson-Glasgow began his Print of Frank Woolley, in that delightful series of his, by saying that " he was easy to watch, difficult to bowl to, and impossible to write about."

True pendulum

The key to his play, as with all the very greatest, was an extraordinary refinement of timing and that again seemed to derive from the severe simplicity and correctness of his method.

Here was this extremely tall slim figure, swinging his bat in the fullest and truest pendulum through the line of the ball. There were no kinks or ornamentations—no one surely was ever so free from mannerism...

what endeared him to the ringside, and at the same time made him so devastating an opponent, was his whole approach to batsmanship.

Aloof antagonist

The modest, self-effacing companion of the dressing-room quickly became an utterly disdainful, aloof antagonist at the wicket.

He seemed superbly indifferent to who was bowling, or how they were bowling.

He sometimes got out, I believe, because he had refused to recognise a particular trap set for him. He certainly paid the penalty, now and then, for taking to himself a bowler whom a comrade did not relish, seeking to knock him off.

The thing he never seemed to comtemplate, let alone to fear, was getting out himself. He was the antithesis of the calculating, bread-and-butter run collector. He played the ball on its merits, and he played for his side.

In the nineties he batted precisely as he would bat after the century was reached.

He was a Kentish cricketer of the county's golden age.

" We were never allowed to play for averages in the Kent side," he wrote in Wisden on his retirement, and went on to say that it was never the policy that the pitch must be occupied all day after winning the toss. Such was his early environment, the influence of which so firmly shaped his attitude throughout his cricket life.

Daily Telegraph, 20 October, 1978

1979

CHAMPAGNE ESSEX

IN 1979, 103 years after their foundation, Essex first caught the habit of winning – and in the eight summers starting with that one they've gone from strength to strength, with four Championships, one NatWest Trophy, one Benson and Hedges Cup and three John Player titles, nine in all.

They first tasted success in 1979 by winning the Benson and Hedges Cup, after a great final against Surrey in which they made what was the highest score at Lord's in 55 overs of 290 for 6. But the Championship was *the* thing and the ease of the victory was such as to recall Surrey in the 1950s, by 77 points and with more than a fortnight of the season left. Essex actually won 13 matches, six more than Worcestershire, the runners-up.

Essex were a well-seasoned lot without an overseas Test player, though the South African Ken McEwan would have been one, no doubt, in happier times. About half their staff were born or bred within the county. Keith Fletcher, in his sixth year of leadership, had already been acclaimed as a remarkably shrewd captain, under whom his side enjoyed playing. There was no more dangerous opening bowler in the country – and certainly no more dedicated cricketer – than John Lever.

The *Sun*'s adjoining column is a reminder of the then rising hopes in the west, with Botham's already fruitful Test career only two years old, Garner just coming up to his prime and Richards almost at the pinnacle. Somerset, too, were on the threshold of success – soon to be realized.

RIGHT Graham Gooch in action for Essex in 1979. Although his appearances were limited by Test calls his contribution to the county's success was decisive

Champs at last but only 650 see it

By IAN JARRETT

ESSEX last night uncorked the champagne that has been on ice for nearly three months.

The runaway £8,000 Schweppes championship leaders — on top since the end of May—swept to their first-ever title success at Northampton.

But no one of the country's most unglamorous grounds, a crowd of only 650—less than 100 of them Essex supporters watched the final flourish of the new champions.

It was something of a Tartan triumph for Keith Fletcher's terrors. Brian Hardie, with an unbeaten 103, and fellow Scot Mike Denness, with 51, set Essex on the way to their 11th victory of the season.

Their opening partnership of 113 powered Essex towards their target of 229, a task they achieved with seven wickets and nine overs to spare.

Sun, 22 August, 1979

Somerset's jackpot trio

By STEVE WHITING

SOMERSET skipper Brian Rose is backing his Three Musketeers to swing today's facinating Gillette Cup smi-final duel with Middlesex at Lord's.

Rose pinpoints the current cut and thrust of Test men Ian Botham, Viv Richards and Joel Garner as three good reasons why Somerset are just about to put the record-book straight.

184

Champagne fizz by cider men

Observer, 9 September, 1979

A SUMMER admirably satisfactory in almost all respects came to a fitting close when Somerset – the only county now without a trophy to their name picked up two on successive days. They had fallen at the last hurdle in 1978, both in the Gillette and the John Player League. Now they won both, the Lord's match conclusively, and well justifying by virtue of Vivian Richards' innings and some destructive overs by Garner, a second champagne heading. The *Observer*'s youthful correspondent, Scyld Berry, reminded his readers that the first of the legendary Somerset heroes, Sammy Woods, used to breakfast off lobsters and champagne. So he did and he refreshed himself and his companions on Sunday walks from bottles of beer shrewdly hidden in unlikely places. For Somerset in 1979, though, there were no Sunday walks, only regular calls to duty in the John Player League; Brian Rose's team accordingly left St John's Wood for Trent Bridge where next day they summoned up the energy to complete a notable double.

SOMERSET v NORTHAMPTONSHIRE
The Gillette Cup Final
Played at Lord's, 8 September, 1979.
Result: Somerset won by 45 runs.

Somerset

B.C. Rose* b Watts	41
P.W. Denning c Sharp b Sarfraz	19
I.V.A. Richards b Griffiths	117
P.M. Roebuck b Willey	14
I.T. Botham b T.M. Lamb	27
V.J. Marks b Griffiths	9
G.I. Burgess c Sharp b Watts	1
D. Breakwell b T.M. Lamb	5
J. Garner not out	24
D.J.S. Taylor† not out	1
K.F. Jennings did not bat	
Extras (b 5, lb 3, nb 3)	11
Total (8 wickets, 60 overs)	269

Fall of Wickets: 1/34, 2/95, 3/145, 4/185, 5/213, 6/214, 7/219, 8/268.
Bowling: Sarfraz 12-3-51-1; Griffiths 12-1-58-2; Watts 12-2-34-2; T.M. Lamb 12-0-70-2; Willey 12-2-45-1.

Northamptonshire

G. Cook run out	44
W. Larkins lbw b Garner	0
R.G. Williams hit wkt b Garner	8
A.J. Lamb st Taylor b Richards	78
P. Willey c Taylor b Garner	5
T.J. Yardley c Richards b Burgess	20
G. Sharp† b Garner	22
Sarfraz Nawaz not out	16
T.M. Lamb b Garner	4
B.J. Griffiths b Garner	0
P.J. Watts* absent hurt	–
Extras (b 6, lb 9, w 5, nb 7)	27
Total (56.3 overs)	224

Fall of Wickets: 1/3, 2/13, 3/126, 4/138, 5/170, 6/182, 7/218, 8/224, 9/224.
Bowling: Garner 10.3-3-29-6, Botham 10-3-27-0, Jennings 12-1-29-0, Burgess 9-1-37-1, Marks 4-0-22-0, Richards 9-0-44-1, Breakwell 2-0-9-0.

RIGHT Richards batting during his chanceless 117 – one of the outstanding innings of Gillette Cup Finals

1980

ENGLAND v AUSTRALIA

Played at Lord's,
28, 29, 30 August, 1, 2 September, 1980.
Result: Match drawn.

Australia: First innings

G.M. Wood st Bairstow b Emburey	112
B.M. Laird c Bairstow b Old	24
G.S. Chappell* c Gatting b Old	47
K.J. Hughes c Athey b Old	117
G.N. Yallop lbw b Hendrick	2
A.R. Border not out	56
R.W. Marsh† not out	16
R.J. Bright	
D.K. Lillee	did not bat
A.A. Mallett	
L.S. Pascoe	
Extras (b 1, lb 8, nb 2)	11
Total (5 wickets declared)	385

Fall of Wickets: 1/64, 2/150, 3/260, 4/267, 5/320.
Bowling: Old 35-9-91-3, Hendrick 30-6-67-1, Botham 22-2-89-0, Emburey 38-9-104-1, Gooch 8-3-16-0, Willey 1-0-7-0.

England: First innings

G.A. Gooch c Bright b Lillee	8
G. Boycott c Marsh b Lillee	62
C.W.J. Athey b Lillee	9
D.I. Gower b Lillee	45
M.W. Gatting lbw b Pascoe	12
I.T. Botham* c Wood b Pascoe	0
P. Willey lbw b Pascoe	5
D.L. Bairstow† lbw b Pascoe	6
J.E. Emburey lbw b Pascoe	3
C.M. Old not out	24
M. Hendrick c Border b Mallett	5
Extras (b 6, lb 8, nb 12)	26
Total	205

Fall of Wickets: 1/10, 2/41, 3/137, 4/151, 5/158, 6/163, 7/164, 8/173, 9/200, 10/205.
Bowling: Lillee 15-4-43-4, Pascoe 18-5-59-5, Chappell 2-0-2-0, Bright 21-6-50-0, Mallett 7.2-3-25-1.

Australia: Second innings

G.M. Wood lbw b Old	8
B.M. Laird c Bairstow b Old	6
G.S. Chappell* b Old	59
K.J. Hughes lbw b Botham	84
A.R. Border not out	21
G.N. Yallop	
R.W. Marsh†	
R.J. Bright	did not bat
D.K. Lillee	
A.A. Mallett	
L.S. Pascoe	
Extras (b 1, lb 8, nb 2)	11
Total (4 wickets declared)	189

Fall of Wickets: 1/15, 2/28, 3/139, 4/189.
Bowling: Old 20-6-47-3, Hendrick 15-4-53-0, Botham 9.2-1-43-1, Emburey 9-2-35-0.

England: Second innings

G.A. Gooch lbw b Lillee	16
G. Boycott not out	128
C.W.J. Athey c Laird b Pascoe	1
D.I. Gower b Mallett	35
M.W. Gatting not out	51
I.T. Botham*	
P. Willey	
D.L. Bairstow†	did not bat
J.E. Emburey	
C.M. Old	
M. Hendrick	
Extras (b 3, lb 2, nb 8)	13
Total (3 wickets)	244

Fall of Wickets: 1/19, 2/43, 3/124.
Bowling: Lillee 19-5-53-1, Pascoe 17-1-73-1, Bright 25-9-44-0, Mallett 21-2-61-1.

ABOVE The gloomy scene at Lord's on the Saturday of the Centenary Test

THE CENTENARY TEST at Lord's in August 1980, marking as it did the first Test in England – which, incidentally, was played at The Oval – was secondary in all respects to its forerunner at Melbourne. The chief adverse factor was the weather which held up play for fifty minutes on the first day, and allowed only one and a quarter hours on the second. On the third day early morning rain had affected old pitches on the Tavern end of the square, the umpires, after several inspections, not judging the conditions fit until a quarter to four. They became the arbiters in the matter once Greg Chappell and Ian Botham, the respective captains, disagreed. The former, whose side were batting and in the stronger position, was keen to play, Botham not so.

Keen frustration was felt all round with the sun shining and a helpful breeze blowing. It became known that the groundstaff considered the field fit for play after lunch, and on all the

evidence the umpires, H.D. Bird and D.J. Constant, seem to have been too pernickety by half. Allowing all this, it was deplorable that a few members addressed words to the umpires during their progress on to the ground down the steps from the pavilion door, and two of them jostled umpire Constant. For this lapse of conduct MCC were obliged to issue a public apology.

Australia made all the running throughout, Kim Hughes, with innings of 117 and 84, batting brilliantly. He made the stroke of the match when he drove Old on to the top tier of the pavilion. On the last day Chappell with his second declaration left England to make 370 in 350 minutes. When England's score at three o'clock stood at 112 for 2 with play due to go on until seven the general feeling was that a challenge for victory would have fitted

The Test that lost its head

By PETER SMITH

ENGLAND'S senior Test umpires, David Constant and Dickie Bird, were close to being replaced at Lord's on Saturday following the manhandling they received from a group of MCC members.

Both men were in such a state of shock in the dressing room after the abuse and jostling they received that they needed attention from the Australian team doctor.

Bird, who is 47, was so upset at his treatment by members and by the pressure from MCC officials to get play started that he was in tears.

Constant, 39, had to be treated for shock after being attacked on the Long Room steps.

Unprecedented

At one time things looked bad enough for fellow umpires John Langridge and Lloyd Budd to be asked to stand by.

Australian captain Greg Chappell sent in his team doctor after seeing the unprecedented attacks on the umpires both inside and outside the Lord's pavilion.

Daily Mail, 1 September, 1980

RIGHT: Kim Hughes showing sparkling style during his century

the spirit of the occasion. However Boycott ground on at his own slow pace up to and beyond his sixth hundred against Australia. England moved unhurriedly 'amid more boos than cheers' according to *Wisden* to a score of 244 for 3 at the close.

Thanks to the sponsorship of Cornhill the social side of the occasion, with over 200 famous old cricketers present, was scarcely less glamorous than its Melbourne predecessor.

1981

THE THIRD TEST between West Indies and England at Bridgetown in March, 1981 was overshadowed by the death during it of Ken Barrington, the team's assistant-manager and coach. It cannot be suggested that the tragedy was likely to have affected the result because the West Indians were well on top when, on the second night of the match, Ken suffered his fatal heart attack. Nevertheless the loss was a demoralizing blow to a side which had already suffered a severe and unexpected setback quite separate from cricket.

Much more probably there was something of cause and effect in the cancellation of the Second Test in Guyana because of political interference and the sudden collapse of a man deeply sensitive to the well-being of the team. For the current players had a special place in their affections for Barrington just as he had for them in his. The action of the Guyana Government in withdrawing, three days before the Test was due to start, the visitor's permit of Robin Jackman (who had been sent out from England as a replacement) because of his South African connections led to the cancellation of the match by the Cricket Council on the grounds that an

BELOW Ken Barrington breakfasting with journalist Frank Keating in Georgetown, Guyana shortly before his tragic death

Test team stunned by tragedy

Barrington dies of heart attack

From PETER SMITH in Barbados

THE cricket world was yesterday mourning the death of Ken Barrington, one of the game's greatest post - war players.

He suffered a heart attack in Bridgetown, Barbados, where he was on tour as assistant manager of the England team.

His wife Ann was with him when he collapsed in his hotel room after returning from dinner with friends.

Daily Mail, 16 March, 1981

unacceptable restriction had been imposed on the selection of the team. The tense situation resulting and the hurried rearrangements before the team flew out of Georgetown inevitably put a severe strain on the tour management. Barrington had had a heart-attack in Australia twelve years before. Now in the comparative anticlimax of a peaceful Barbados and with his wife, Ann, just arrived to join him came the mortal blow.

This indeed was an ill-starred tour as was the later one of David Gower's side to India, though the latter at least had a

happy ending. The authorities were discovering that Botham's virtues as a cricketer did not extend to a gift for leadership which moreover took almost all the flair and effectiveness from his own play.

There were however redeeming features, not so much in this Test as the following two at Antigua and Kingston, Jamaica both of which were saved by staunch rearguard actions wherein Gooch, Boycott, Willey and Gower all defied the fast attack of Holding, Croft, Garner and Roberts to make hundreds. Gower subdued all his natural impulses

in the Fifth Test by taking out his bat after seven and three quarter hours for 154.

England then, having lost the First Test at Port-of-Spain by an innings, succumbed in the series, 2-0. It was the bowling which failed, for once, rather than the batting as the West Indies Test scores make clear: 426 for 9 declared, 265 and 379 for 7 declared, 468 for 9 declared and 442.

BELOW The England team remember in silence a universal friend and unstinting servant of the game

1981

Botham's a miracle!

THE amazing Ian Botham had the mourners dancing in the aisles at Headingley last night with the greatest comeback since Lazarus.

Daily Express, 21 July, 1981

ENGLAND v AUSTRALIA

Played at Leeds, 16, 17, 18, 20, 21 July, 1981.
Result: England won by 18 runs.

Australia: First innings

J. Dyson b Dilley	102
G.M. Wood lbw b Botham	34
T.M. Chappell c Taylor b Willey	27
K.J. Hughes* c and b Botham	89
R.J. Bright b Dilley	7
G.N. Yallop c Taylor b Botham	58
A.R. Border lbw b Botham	8
R.W. Marsh† b Botham	28
G.F. Lawson c Taylor b Botham	13
D.K. Lillee not out	3
T.M. Alderman not out	0
Extras (b 4, lb 13, w 2, nb 12)	32
Total (9 wickets declared)	401

Fall of Wickets: 1/55, 2/149, 3/196, 4/220, 5/332, 6/354, 7/357, 8/396, 9/401.
Bowling: Willis 30-8-72-0, Old 43-14-91-0, Dilley 27-4-78-2, Botham 39.2-11-95-6, Willey 13-2-31-1, Boycott 3-2-2-0.

England: First innings

G.A. Gooch lbw b Alderman	2
G. Boycott b Lawson	12
J.M. Brearley* c Marsh b Alderman	10
D.I. Gower c Marsh b Lawson	24
M.W. Gatting lbw b Lillee	15
P. Willey b Lawson	8
I.T. Botham c Marsh b Lillee	50
R.W. Taylor† c Marsh b Lillee	5
G.R. Dilley c and b Lillee	13
C.M. Old c Border b Alderman	0
R.G.D. Willis not out	1
Extras (b 6, lb 11, w 6, nb 11)	34
Total	174

Fall of Wickets: 1/12, 2/40, 3/42, 4/84, 5/87, 6/112, 7/148, 8/166, 9/167, 10/174.
Bowling: Lillee 18.5-7-49-4, Alderman 19-4-59-3, Lawson 13-3-32-3.

England: Second innings

G.A. Gooch c Alderman b Lillee	0
G. Boycott lbw b Alderman	46
J.M. Brearley* c Alderman b Lillee	14
D.I. Gower c Border b Alderman	9
M.W. Gatting lbw b Alderman	1
P. Willey c Dyson b Lilley	33
I.T. Botham not out	149
R.W. Taylor† c Bright b Alderman	1
G.R. Dilley b Alderman	56
C.M. Old b Lawson	29
R.G.D. Willis c Border b Alderman	2
Extras (b 5, lb 3, w 3, nb 5)	16
Total	356

Fall of Wickets: 1/0, 2/18, 3/37, 4/41, 5/105, 6/133, 7/135, 8/252, 9/319, 10/356.
Bowling: Lillee 25-6-94-3, Alderman 35.3-6-135-6, Lawson 23-4-96-1, Bright 4-0-15-0.

Australia: Second innings

J. Dyson c Taylor b Willis	34
G.M. Wood c Taylor b Botham	10
T.M. Chappell c Taylor b Willis	8
K.J. Hughes* c Botham b Willis	0
R.J. Bright (8) b Willis	19
G.N. Yallop (5) c Gatting b Willis	0
A.R. Border (6) b Old	0
R.W. Marsh† (7) c Dilley b Willis	4
G.F. Lawson c Taylor b Willis	1
D.K. Lillee c Gatting b Willis	17
T.M. Alderman not out	0
Extras (lb 3, w 1, nb 14)	18
Total	111

Fall of Wickets: 1/13, 2/56, 3/58, 4/58, 5/65, 6/68, 7/74, 8/75, 9/110, 10/111.
Bowling: Willis 15.1-3-43-8, Old 9-1-21-1, Dilley 2-0-11-0, Botham 7-3-14-1, Willey 3-1-4-0.

190

Willis sets Ashes ablaze

Daily Express, 22 July, 1981

THE ASHES series of 1981 makes one of the more sensational stories in cricket history. After the Second Test at Lord's England under Ian Botham in their last 12 Tests had won none, drawn eight and lost four. The captain's contribution in these 12 matches had been a batting average of 13.80 and 35 wickets at 32 runs each. At Lord's he had made a pair, and afterwards resigned as captain, pre-empting the selectors who would surely have relieved him of the burden.

With Mike Brearley restored as leader for the Third Test at Headingley, England, one down in the series, looked so sure to lose again that at their direst moment the bookmakers offered 500 to one against them. On the Saturday morning England, having followed on 227 behind, had lost Gooch in the second innings without a run on the board.

On the Monday, on a pitch rated unsatisfactory by both sides, they had declined against Lillee and Alderman, to 135 for 8, still 92 behind. When Dilley joined Botham in mid-afternoon the mood at first was simply that they might as well die fighting. Now, as they say, read on.

'Botham's a miracle', sang the *Daily Express* and Pat Gibson, stretching the analogy somewhat as between Botham and Lazarus, thought it the moment to bring out one of the biblical allusions so beloved of the late Lord Beaverbrook. Botham embarked on a furious assault; nor was Dilley (who has always had an orthodox left-handed method) all that far behind. In eighty minutes they added 117, of which Dilley's share when Alderman bowled him was 56. First Old and then Willis helped

Botham in stands of 77 and 37 respectively before early on the fifth morning Botham took out his bat for an unbeaten 149.

Even so Australia needed only 130, which, despite an untrustworthy pitch, seemed to be well within their capacity: the more so by the time Brearley switched Willis's end with the score 56 for 1. Those who saw Willis's bowling that day whether in the flesh or on the television screen will never forget it. If ever a man summoned undreamt of powers for a supreme effort it was he. The catches close and behind the wicket from hurried stabs as one man after another was undone by a combination of sheer pace and unpredictable lift and movement told their

ABOVE Willis's penultimate wicket: Lawson is caught by Taylor for 1
FAR LEFT Botham hooks another boundary

own story. One was reminded of Frank Tyson's devastating 7 for 27 to win the Melbourne Test of 1954-55.

As most readers will know England after this providential escape went on to retain the Ashes with a narrow victory at Edgbaston and by a larger margin at Old Trafford. In this latter match Botham's 118 according to *Wisden* 'for its ferocious yet effortless power and dazzling cleanness of stroke can surely never have been bettered in a Test match even by the legendary Jessop'. So be it. But it was the 'miracle' of Headingley that started it all.

Sussex clinch their first Sunday title

The Times, 30 August, 1982

SUSSEX IN the 1980s under John Barclay were a good and popular side who in his first year of leadership, 1981, came nearer even than their predecessors had done in the 1930s to winning the Championship that has narrowly eluded them throughout their history. The margin was a mere two points and the issue was not determined until the penultimate day of the season. In 1982 they slipped back but made their mark not only by winning the John Player Special League but by doing so with the best record of any County in its history. To have won 14 out of 16 matches and lost only one (to Worcestershire narrowly at Horsham) was a particularly striking record

considering what a succession of quick sprints the competition demands. Such overseas stars as Imran Khan, Mendis and Le Roux were specially suited to 40-over cricket, but there was not a weak spot. The crucial match at Hove watched by a full house of 7,000 or more was that at the end of August against Middlesex, the runners-up. Victory by 23 runs clinched the title which they ultimately won by 12 points.

A new provision whereby four fielders and the wicket-keeper must be stationed within fielding circles thirty yards from the stumps was tried with success this summer. Barclay resigned during the 1986 season because of a hand injury that badly affected his bowling. It was therefore Ian Gould, the wicket-keeper, who, succeeding him, led Sussex to another win in the final of the NatWest Trophy.

SUSSEX v MIDDLESEX

Played at Hove, 29 August, 1982.
Result: Sussex won by 23 runs.

Sussex

G.D. Mendis run out	100
I.J. Gould† c Radley b Slack	58
C.M. Wells b Slack	2
P.W.G. Parker b Cowans	17
G.S. le Roux c Cook b Cowans	23
C.P. Phillipson c Downton b Cowans	8
I.A. Greig c Slack b Cowans	2
J.R.T. Barclay* not out	0
A.P. Wells ⎤	
A.C.S. Pigott ⎬ did not bat	
C.E. Waller ⎦	
Extras (b 2, lb 13, w 1, nb 2)	18
Totl (7 wickets, 40 overs)	228

Fall of Wickets: 1/134, 2/150, 3/194, 4/205, 5/224, 6/226, 7/228.
Bowling: Daniel 8-0-56-0, Cowans 8-0-44-4, Slack 8-0-43-2, Emburey 8-1-20-0, Hughes 8-0-47-0.

Middlesex

W.N. Slack lbw b Barclay	31
J.M. Brearley* lbw b le Roux	8
R.O. Butcher b Greig	59
P.R. Downton† b Pigott	40
R.G.P. Ellis b Greig	6
C.T. Radley c and b le Roux	18
C.R. Cook c Gould b le Roux	3
J.E. Emburey run out	2
W.W. Daniel b Pigott	6
N.G. Cowans not out	14
S.P. Hughes run out	2
Extras (b 2, lb 11, w 2, nb 1)	16
Total (39.1 overs)	205

Fall of Wickets: 1/22, 2/80, 3/142, 4/158, 5/160, 6/179, 7/182, 8/185, 9/197.
Bowling: Wells 6-0-23-0, le Roux 7.1-0-27-3, Greig 7-0-44-2, Barclay 8-0-36-1, Waller 3-0-16-0, Pigott 8-0-43-2.

RIGHT John Barclay, Sussex's captain, proudly displays the trophy after his team have beaten Middlesex

Cricket: Cairns man of the match, New Zealand men of the century

The underdogs break their chains

The Times, 2 August, 1983

1983

ABOVE Coney, having just played the shot which brought New Zealand their first Test victory in England, salutes the triumph

15 AUGUST 1983 was a gala day indeed for New Zealand whose team led by G.P. Howarth beat England for the first time in a Test in England. They had come close to victory more than once, and in 1977-78 they had won for the first time in New Zealand, under the leadership of M.G. Burgess. Now they could come over here with confidence, as they forthwith showed by winning the three-Test rubber of 1986 hands down.

When New Zealand were first introduced to the Test arena they showed all the courage that their sporting and other history led England to expect. Of the first 18 Tests between them England won only three. But their cricket was wholly amateur, and the bowling was never strong enough to bowl England out twice. Gradually over the last twenty years or so they have largely

overcome the handicaps of a small field of choice and restricted income to the point when no country can take them lightly. In the last few years they have won series against all the Test-playing countries.

At Headingley New Zealand's victory was clear-cut and extraordinary only in that Richard Hadlee, their champion bowler, by the strangest of chances failed to take a wicket. He nevertheless had a big say in the result with an important innings of 75. The chief figure was Lance Cairns, who used the customary swinging conditions at Yorkshire's headquarters to return match figures of 10 for 144.

ENGLAND v NEW ZEALAND

Played at Leeds, 28, 29, 30 July, 1 August, 1983.
Result: New Zealand won by five wickets.

England: First innings

G. Fowler c Smith b Chatfield	9
C.J. Tavaré c Smith b Coney	69
D.I. Gower c Coney b Cairns	9
A.J. Lamb c M.D. Crowe b Cairns	58
I.T. Botham c Howarth b Cairns	38
D.W. Randall c Coney b Cairns	4
P.H. Edmonds c Smith b Cairns	8
G.R. Dilley b Cairns	0
R.W. Taylor† not out	10
R.G.D. Willis* c J.J. Crowe b Coney	9
N.G. Cowans c Bracewell b Cairns	0
Extras (b 4, lb 7)	11
Total	225

Fall of Wickets: 1/18, 2/35, 3/135, 4/175, 5/185, 6/205, 7/205, 8/209, 9/225, 10/225.
Bowling: Hadlee 21-9-44-0, Chatfield 22-8-67-1, Cairns 33.2-14-74-7, Coney 12-3-21-2, Bracewell 1-0-8-0.

New Zealand: First innings

J.G. Wright c Willis b Cowans	93
B.A. Edgar b Willis	84
G.P. Howarth* run out	13
M.D. Crowe lbw b Cowans	37
J.J. Crowe run out	0
J.V. Coney c Gower b Willis	19
R.J. Hadlee b Cowans	75
J.G. Bracewell c Dilley b Edmonds	16
I.D.S. Smith† c Tavaré b Willis	2
B.L. Cairns not out	24
E.J. Chatfield lbw b Willis	0
Extras (b 1, lb 4, w 1, nb 8)	14
Total	377

Fall of Wickets: 1/52, 2/168, 3/169, 4/169, 5/218, 6/304, 7/348, 8/351, 9/377, 10/377.
Bowling: Willis 23.3-6-57-4, Dilley 17-4-36-0, Botham 26-9-81-0, Cowans 28-8-88-3, Edmonds 45-14-101-1.

England: Second innings

G. Fowler c Smith b Chatfield	19
C.J. Tavaré b Chatfield	23
D.I. Gower not out	112
A.J. Lamb c Coney b Cairns	28
I.T. Botham c Howarth b Coney	4
D.W. Randall c Smith b Chatfield	16
P.H. Edmonds c Smith b Chatfield	0
G.R. Dilley c Smith b Chatfield	15
R.W. Taylor† b Cairns	9
R.G.D. Willis* c Coney b Cairns	4
N.G. Cowans c M.D. Crowe b Cairns	10
Extras (b 8, lb 3, w 1)	12
Total	252

Fall of Wickets: 1/39, 2/44, 3/116, 4/126, 5/142, 6/142, 7/190, 8/217, 9/221, 10/252.
Bowling: Hadlee 26-9-45-0, Chatfield 29-5-95-5, Cairns 24-2-70-3, Coney 8-1-30-2.

New Zealand: Second innings

J.G. Wright c Randall b Willis	26
B.A. Edgar c Edmonds b Willis	2
G.P. Howarth* c Randall b Willis	20
M.D. Crowe c Lamb b Willis	1
J.J. Crowe b Willis	13
J.V. Coney not out	10
R.J. Hadlee not out	6
J.G. Bracewell	
I.D.S. Smith† did not bat	
B.L. Cairns	
E.J. Chatfield	
Extras (b 8, lb 7, nb 10)	25
Total (5 wickets)	103

Fall of Wickets: 1/11, 2/42, 3/60, 4/61, 5/83.
Bowling: Willis 14.5-3-35-5, Dilley 8-2-16-0, Botham 0.1-0-4-0, Cowans 5-0-23-0.

193

1983

INDIA'S VICTORY over West Indies in the final of the 1983 Prudential World Cup was without doubt the greatest upset in all three of these highly successful and popular competitions. Their achievement is here proclaimed by the *Sunday Mirror* in characteristically strident tabloid style – revealing a tendency for the headline to be catchy rather than informative.

It was, indeed, a remarkable effort, considering that at one stage of the competition there was no certainty that India would qualify even for the semifinals, and that they ended their qualifying matches second to the West Indies. At the time Clive Lloyd's team were not only twice winners of the cup, but virtually invincible in both one- and five-day cricket. Despite this, however, India had shown their mettle by beating the West Indies in the first match of the competition.

When the final came it was universally expected that the cup-holders would cruise to the total of 183 reached by India. They had, after all, scored 228, 252, 218, 282, 276, 172 for 0 and 188 for 2 in their progress to the final. And yet, in less than three hours they had been bowled out in 52 overs for 140. Their downfall was brought about more by India's highly disciplined and innovative all-round team than by any outstanding individual effort.

As for the previous two competitions – in 1975 and 1979 – the popularity of the Prudential World Cup was borne out by the capacity attendance of nearly 25,000 for the final, although it is interesting that whereas the overall attendance for the whole competition only went up a small amount between 1975 and 1979 – from nearly 118,000 to nearly 133,000 – for the 1983 competition it leapt up to 232,000.

COWBOY
Dev's devils are

S and INDIANS!

the new one-day wonders

Sunday Mirror, 26 June, 1983

INDIA v WEST INDIES
The Prudential World Cup Final
Played at Lord's, 25 June, 1983.
Result: India won by 43 runs.

India

S.M. Gavaskar c Dujon b Roberts	2
K. Srikkanth lbw b Marshall	38
M. Amarnath b Holding	26
Yashpal Sharma c sub b Gomes	11
S.M. Patil c Gomes b Garner	27
Kapil Dev* c Holding b Gomes	15
K.B.J. Azad c Garner b Roberts	0
R.M.H. Binny c Garner b Roberts	2
Madan Lal b Marshall	17
S.M.H. Kirmani† b Holding	14
B.S. Sandhu not out	11
Extras (b 5, lb 5, w 9, nb 1)	20
Total (54.4 overs)	183

Fall of Wickets: 1/2, 2/59, 3/90, 4/92, 5/110, 6/111, 7/130, 8/153, 9/161.
Bowling: Roberts 10-3-32-3, Garner 12-4-24-1, Marshall 11-1-24-2, Holding 9.4-2-26-2, Gomes 11-1-49-2, Richards 1-0-8-0.

West Indies

C.G. Greenidge b Sandhu	1
D.L. Haynes c Binny b Madan Lal	13
I.V.A. Richards c Kapil Dev b Madan Lal	33
C.H. Lloyd* c Kapil Dev b Binny	8
H.A. Gomes c Gavaskar b Madan Lal	5
S.F.A. Bacchus c Kirmani b Sandhu	8
P.J. Dujon† b Amarnath	25
M.D. Marshall c Gavaskar b Amarnath	18
A.M.E. Roberts lbw b Kapil Dev	4
J. Garner not out	5
M.A. Holding lbw b Amarnath	6
Extras (lb 4, w 10)	14
Total (52 overs)	140

Fall of Wickets: 1/5, 2/50, 3/57, 4/66, 5/66, 6/76, 7/119, 8/124, 9/126.
Bowling: Kapil Dev 11-4-21-1, Sandhu 9-1-32-2, Madan Lal 12-2-31-3, Binny 10-1-23-1, Amarnath 7-0-12-3, Azad 3-0-7-0.

FAR LEFT Ladbroke's may not have agreed with his odds but optimism paid off for Patel's bookies, even if 'Super Dev' did let him down!

LEFT To undisguised joy Amarnath bowls Dujon and breaks his threatening partnership with Marshall: India's momentous victory is not far away

IN TERMS of results 1984 was a sorry year for English Test cricket. All three Test series completed were lost – including the home one against West Indies by a spectacular 5-0 margin – and England did not actually win a Test until the eleventh hour, in India at the end of December.

It was the combined tour at the beginning of the year, to New Zealand and Pakistan – with a short stop-over for two goodwill matches in Fiji en route – which was particularly unhappy. In New Zealand one decisive win by the home country gave them their first ever series victory against England. Only a few days after leaving Auckland the jaded and discontented England team were faced with quite a different problem in the First Test against Pakistan at Karachi – the inspired leg-spin bowling of Abdul Qadir. His revival of what had become a virtually obsolete craft brought him 8 for 133 in the match and bewitched the already limp visitors into losing England's first Test Match ever on Pakistan soil. Two draws in the ensuing matches enabled Pakistan to follow New Zealand's example and claim their first series win against England.

Most depressing was the fact that it was not only the standard of cricket which appeared to be at fault; after New Zealand's victory Willis accused his team of the worst bowling he had known in 80 Tests and at Karachi both teams were guilty of plumbing the depths of batting ineptitude. A number of newspaper reports, which included accusations of drug-taking in New Zealand, soured relations between members of the press and the players and greatly contributed to the general malaise of the tour party. The reports also appear to have set something of a precedent for sensational and investi-

England in a trance as wily Qadir spins his web of mystery

ENGLAND'S batsmen read Abdul Qadir's leg breaks, googlies, top-spinners and flippers about as well as they read Urdu.

And that is just about the whole story of how they became the first England side to lose a Test match in Pakistan here yesterday.

Daily Express, 7 March, 1984

ABOVE Pakistan's wizard, Qadir, traps Gower lbw in the First Test at Karachi

gative journalism, with no interest in the cricket. This aspect became far worse during the England tour of the West Indies in 1986 and was evident again in Australia in 1986-87.

PAKISTAN v ENGLAND
Played at Karachi, 2, 3, 4, 6 March, 1984.
Result: Pakistan won by 3 wickets.

England: First innings 182 (D.I. Gower 58; Qadir 5-74, Sarfraz 4-42).

Pakistan: First innings 277 (Salim Malik 74, Mohsin Khan 40; Cook 6-65).

England: Second innings 159 (D.I. Gower 57; Tausif 3-37, Qadir 3-59).

Pakistan: Second innings 66 for 7 (Cook 5-18).

196

Great, good, nasty, brutish and short

Sunday Times, 19 August, 1984

ABOVE The picture says it all. Gower takes evasive action during the Oval Test

IN HIS ASSESSMENT of the 1984 West Indians who beat England on their own pitches by five Tests to none Robin Marlar gave due credit to Clive Lloyd and his team. They were well led and:

> won so convincingly because their fast bowlers were penetrative and controlled, and because they batted in depth with reliability. No England side of recent memory could have lived with them. Lloyd's leadership has matured: 'old man Hubert' is as justifiably popular as 'Old Man River!

The Sunday Times cricket correspondent followed with special bouquets – for the deadly triple-forked attack of Marshall, Garner and Holding, for Greenidge and Gomes, who averaged 80 apiece, and Dujon who created a fan club. Having dissected England's problems and weaknesses he asked how many West Indians realized that their batsmen against their own attack 'would be made to look as puny as England's'. He then returned to the methods adopted by the West Indian fast bowlers and delivered his judgement:

> However, it is my conviction that the current West Indian method, developed to perfection by Clive Lloyd, is deeply offensive to the essence of cricket, which is the defence of the stumps by a batsman, rather than the defence of his own body.

ENGLAND v WEST INDIES
Played at The Oval,
9, 10, 11, 13, 14 August, 1984.
Result: West Indies won by 172 runs.

West Indies: First innings

C.G. Greenidge	lbw b Botham	22
D.L. Haynes	b Allott	10
H.A. Gomes	c Botham b Ellison	18
I.V.A. Richards	c Allott b Botham	8
P.J.L. Dujon†	c Tavaré b Botham	3
C.H. Lloyd*	not out	60
M.D. Marshall	c Gower b Ellison	0
E.A.E. Baptiste	c Fowler b Allott	32
R.A. Harper	b Botham	18
M.A. Holding	lbw b Botham	0
J. Garner	c Downton b Allott	6
Extras	(b 1, lb 4, w 7, nb 1)	13
Total		190

Fall of Wickets: 1/19, 2/45, 3/64, 4/64, 5/67, 6/70, 7/124, 8/154, 9/154, 10/190.
Bowling: Agnew 12-3-46-0, Allott 17-7-25-3, Botham 23-8-72-5, Ellison 18-3-34-2.

England: First innings

G. Fowler	c Richards b Baptiste	31
B.C. Broad	b Garner	4
P.I. Pocock	c Greenidge b Marshall	0
C.J. Tavaré	c Dujon b Holding	16
D.I. Gower*	c Dujon b Holding	12
A.J. Lamb	lbw b Marshall	12
I.T. Botham	c Dujon b Marshall	14
P.R. Downton†	c Lloyd b Garner	16
R.M. Ellison	not out	20
P.J.W. Allott	b Marshall	16
J.P. Agnew	b Marshall	5
Extras	(b 2, lb 4, nb 10)	16
Total		162

Fall of Wickets: 1/10, 2/22, 3/45, 4/64, 5/83, 6/84, 7/116, 8/133, 9/156, 10/162.
Bowling: Garner 18-6-37-2, Marshall 17.5-5-35-5, Holding 13-2-55-2, Baptiste 12-4-19-1, Harper 1-1-0-0.

West Indies: Second innings

C.G. Greenidge	c Botham b Agnew	34
D.L. Haynes	b Botham	125
H.A. Gomes	c Tavaré b Ellison	1
I.V.A. Richards	lbw b Agnew	5
P.J.L. Dujon† (6)	c Lamb b Ellison	49
C.H. Lloyd* (5)	c Downton b Ellison	36
M.D. Marshall (8)	c Lamb b Botham	12
E.A.E. Baptiste (7)	c Downton b Allott	5
R.A. Harper	c Downton b Allott	17
M.A. Holding	lbw b Botham	30
J. Garner	not out	10
Extras	(lb 12)	12
Total		346

Fall of Wickets: 1/51, 2/52, 3/69, 4/132, 5/214, 6/237, 8/293, 9/329, 10/346.
Bowling: Agnew 14-1-51-2, Allott 26-1-96-2, Botham 22.3-2-103-3, Ellison 26-7-60-3, Pocock 8-3-24-0.

England: Second innings

G. Fowler	c Richards b Marshall	7
B.C. Broad	c Greenidge b Holding	39
P.I. Pocock (10)	c and b Holding	0
C.J. Tavaré (3)	c Richards b Garner	49
D.I. Gower* (4)	lbw b Holding	7
A.J. Lamb (5)	c Haynes b Holding	1
I.T. Botham (6)	c Marshall b Garner	54
P.R. Downton† (7)	lbw b Garner	10
R.M. Ellison (8)	c Holding b Garner	13
P.J.W. Allott (9)	c Lloyd b Holding	4
J.P. Agnew	not out	2
Extras	(lb 2, w 1, nb 13)	16
Total		202

Fall of Wickets: 1/15, 2/75, 3/88, 4/90, 5/135, 6/181, 7/186, 8/200, 9/200, 10/202.
Bowling: Garner 18.4-3-51-4, Marshall 22-5-71-1, Holding 13-2-43-5, Baptiste 8-3-11-0, Harper 8-5-10-0.

1984

Enter Sid and Company with a grand flourish

Guardian, 24 August, 1984

THE LIGHT-HEARTED note in the *Guardian* headline echoes what was most people's initial reaction to this, Sri Lanka's first Test Match in England; a bit of respite for England after their mauling by the West Indies and a friendly welcome to the babies of Test cricket. In the event nothing the West Indian Goliath threw at England compared with the shock brought about by the Sri Lankan David. A team which, during the preceding weeks, had been largely overshadowed during its round of the counties, gave an inspired performance. Their spirit, if naive, was filled with a refreshing sense of enjoyment noticeably lacking in their opponents, who, to ensure a draw humiliatingly in Sri Lanka's favour,

played some of the dullest cricket seen at Lord's for many years – and were deservedly castigated for it by the crowd.

What a dream come true for 'Sid' – Sidath Wettimuny, whose 190 in the first innings was the highest score by any batsman on his first appearance in a Test in England. Few people minded that it was also the longest innings played at Lord's. It was a great occasion too for the Sri Lankan captain, Duleep Mendis, who raced to a hundred in the first innings and was only six runs short in the second of equalling George Headley's unique record of a hundred in both innings of a Lord's Test.

To date Sri Lanka have not given a performance of comparable merit in

any subsequent Test matches, although they achieved the milestone of their first Test victory in 1985, against India. Lord's 1984 will certainly pass into the folklore of the island's cricket.

ENGLAND v SRI LANKA
Played at Lord's, 23, 24, 25, 27, 28 August, 1984.
Result: Match drawn.

Sri Lanka: First innings

S. Wettimuny c Downton b Allott	190
S.A.R. Silva† lbw b Botham	8
R.S. Madugalle b Ellison	5
R.L. Dias c Lamb b Pocock	32
A. Ranatunga b Agnew	84
L.R.D. Mendis* c Fowler b Pocock	111
P.A. De Silva c Downton b Agnew	16
A.L.F. De Mel not out	20
J.R. Ratnayake not out	5
D.S. De Silva V.B. John } did not bat	
Extras (b 2, lb 8, w 2, nb 8)	20
Total (7 wickets declared)	491

Fall of Wickets: 1/17, 2/43, 3/144, 4/292, 5/442, 6/456, 7/464.
Bowling: Agnew 32-3-123-2, Botham 29-6-114-1, Ellison 28-6-70-1, Pocock 41-17-75-2, Allott 36-7-89-1.

England: First innings

G. Fowler c Madugalle b John	25
B.C. Broad c Silva b De Mel	86
C.J. Tavaré c Ranatunga b D.S. De Silva	14
D.I. Gower* c Silva b De Mel	55
A.J. Lamb c Dias b John	107
I.T. Botham c sub (D.M. Vonhagt) b John	6
R.M. Ellison c Ratnayeke b D.S. De Silva	41
P.R. Downton† c Dias b De Mel	10
P.J.W. Allott b De Mel	0
P.I. Pocock c Silva b John	2
J.P. Agnew not out	1
Extras (b 5, lb 7, w 5, nb 6)	23
Total	370

Fall of Wickets: 1/49, 2/105, 3/190, 4/210, 5/218, 6/305, 7/354, 8/354, 9/369, 10/370.
Bowling: De Mel 37-10-110-4, John 39.1-12-98-4, Ratnayeke 22-5-50-0, D.S. De Silva 45-16-85-2, Madugalle 3-0-4-0, Ranatunga 1-1-0-0.

Sri Lanka: Second innings

S. Wettimuny c Gower b Botham	13
S.A.R. Silva† not out	102
R.S. Madugalle b Botham	3
R.L. Dias lbw b Botham	38
A. Ranatunga lbw b Botham	0
L.R.D. Mendis* (7) c Fowler b Botham	94
P.A. De Silva (6) c Downton b Pocock	3
A.L.F. De Mel c Ellison b Botham	14
J.R. Ratnayeke not out	7
D.S. De Silva V.B. John } did not bat	
Extras (b 5, lb 4, nb 11)	20
Total (7 wickets declared)	294

Fall of Wickets: 1/19, 2/27, 3/111, 4/115, 5/118, 6/256, 7/276.
Bowling: Agnew 11-3-54-0, Botham 27-6-90-6, Ellison 7-0-36-0, Pocock 29-10-78-1, Allott 1-0-2-0, Lamb 1-0-6-0, Tavaré 3-3-0-0, Fowler 1-0-8-0.

LEFT Wettimuny, perhaps not used to such high-level exertions, receives treatment for cramp from the England fielders during his innings of 190

Hadlee in a class of his own

By PAT GIBSON

STAND aside Ian Botham . . . and Imran Khan and Kapil Dev . . . and anyone else who lays claims to the title.

For now there can be no doubt that Richard Hadlee, the 33-year-old New Zealander who plays county cricket for Notts, is the greatest all-rounder in the game today.

Daily Express, 28 August, 1984

1984

ACHIEVEMENT OF 'the double' was, in the past, the hallmark of an above average all-rounder; difficult, but always realistic. Wilfred Rhodes and George Hirst were admittedly slight exceptions, doing it sixteen and fourteen times respectively, but Trevor Bailey and Fred Titmus both did it eight times – along with 'W.G.' and Woolley. In the lowest bracket, forty-eight players – including overseas visitors – achieved it once. That was until 1969, when the number of County Championship matches was much reduced to make way for more one-day cricket and it seemed that the last of Titmus's efforts, in 1967, had lowered the curtain on this particular record.

It required a player with both the exceptional talent and gritty determination of Richard Hadlee to re-open the books. Having reached his 100 wickets in 658 overs the 1000th run came in his 21st innings – with three matches to spare. He ended the season with 1,179 runs and 117 wickets. As Pat Gibson of the *Daily Express* hints, there had been for some time constant discussion as to the best all-rounder among the quartet of contemporaries; Ian Botham, Kapil Dev, Imran Khan – and Hadlee. His 'double' is something none of the others have approached.

Ever since his first Test for New Zealand in 1972-73 Hadlee's efforts have been decisive in his country's steadily rising fortunes. Similarly, when he joined Nottinghamshire in 1978, his all-round contribution boosted the county's performances no end, never more so than in 1984 when his 'double' helped them to within an ace of winning the County Championship.

BELOW Richard Hadlee: great all-rounder

1985

England set to end tour drought after six years

The Times, 19 January, 1985

TEST SERIES follow one another nowadays as though on a conveyor belt, so that the star players must sometimes feel, to vary the simile slightly, as though they were on an everlasting escalator. Thus England's 2-1 victory in India in the winter of 1984-85 may seem long, long ago. It is however well worth memorizing in the light of subsequent misfortunes that England under David Gower accomplished the hitherto unprecedented feat of winning a rubber in India after the home side had drawn first blood.

On their arrival they ran into the assassination of Mrs Gandhi and had to be shielded from the political unrest by an unscheduled diversion to Sri Lanka. Then on the eve of the First Test at Bombay came the murder of the British Deputy High Commissioner, Mr Percy Norris, their host of the previous evening. Having lost that Test, wherein a young wrist-spinner, L. Sivarama-krishnan, sprang to fame by taking 12 wickets, they won the Second at Delhi thanks to a headlong Indian collapse on the last day. Smog and rain early in the game at Calcutta made a draw almost a certainty. The crucial victory came at Madras where, after India had been put out relatively cheaply, Fowler and Robinson laid the foundation of a tall score by putting on 178 for the first wicket. Double hundreds by Fowler and Gatting brought England to the highest total ever made in a Test in India. Thereafter India fought hard but unavailingly, and at Kanpur in the last Test England held on to their lead without too much strain.

It is illustrative of the quick turn-over of modern Test sides that only Gatting and Edmonds of the most successful members of the side in India and only four men in all helped England retain the Ashes two years later. The key to the success of the team in India, according to all who took part in or followed the tour, was a remarkable cohesive spirit on the part of all seventeen concerned, a camaraderie for which there is no provision in the scorebook.

ENGLAND v INDIA

Played at Madras, 13, 14, 15, 17, 18 January, 1985.
Result: England won by nine wickets.

India: First innings

S.M. Gavaskar* b Foster		17
K. Srikkanth c Downton b Cowans		0
D.B. Vengsarkar c Lamb b Foster		17
M. Amarnath c Downton b Foster		78
M. Azharuddin b Cowdrey		48
R.J. Shastri c Downton b Foster		2
Kapil Dev c Cowans b Cowdrey		53
S.M.H. Kirmani† not out		30
N.S. Yadav b Foster		2
L. Sivaramakrishnan c Cowdrey b Foster		13
Chetan Sharma c Lamb b Cowans		5
Extras (lb 3, nb 4)		7
Total		272

Fall of Wickets: 1/17, 2/17, 3/45, 4/155, 5/167, 6/167, 7/241, 8/243, 9/263, 10/272.
Bowling: Cowans 12.5-3-39-2, Foster 23-2-104-6, Edmonds 6-1-33-0, Cowdrey 19-1-65-2, Pocock 7-1-28-0.

England: First innings

G. Fowler c Kirmani b Kapil Dev		201
R.T. Robinson c Kirmani b Sivaramakrishnan		74
M.W. Gatting c sub b Shastri		207
A.J. Lamb b Amarnath		62
P.H. Edmonds lbw b Shastri		36
N.A. Foster b Amarnath		5
D.I. Gower* b Kapil Dev		18
C.S. Cowdrey not out		3
P.R. Downton† not out		3
P.I. Pocock } did not bat		
N.G. Cowans		
Extras (b 7, lb 19, nb 17)		43
Total (7 wickets declared)		652

Fall of Wickets: 1/178, 2/419, 3/563, 4/599, 5/604, 6/640, 7/646.
Bowling: Kapil Dev 36-5-131-2, Chetan Sharma 18-0-95-0, Sivaramakrishnan 44-6-145-1, Yadav 23-4-76-0, Shastri 42-7-143-2, Amarnath 12-1-36-2.

India: Second innings

S.M. Gavaskar* c Gatting b Foster		3
K. Srikkanth c Cowdrey b Foster		16
D.B. Vengsarkar c Downton b Foster		2
M. Amarnath c Cowans b Foster		95
M. Azharuddin c Gower b Pocock		105
R.J. Shastri c Cowdrey b Edmonds		33
Kapil Dev c Gatting b Cowans		49
S.M.H. Kirmani† c Lamb b Edmonds		75
N.S. Yadav c Downton b Cowans		5
L. Sivaramarkrishnan lbw b Foster		5
Chetan Sharma not out		17
Extras (b 1, lb 4, nb 2)		7
Total		412

Fall of Wickets: 1/7, 2/19, 3/22, 4/212, 5/259, 6/259, 7/341, 8/350, 9/361, 10/412.
Bowling: Cowans 15-1-73-2, Foster 28-3-59-5, Edmonds 41.5-13-119-2, Cowdrey 5-0-26-0, Pocock 33-8-130-1.

England: Second innings

G. Fowler c Kirmani b Sivaramakrishnan		2
R.T. Robinson not out		21
M.W. Gatting not out		10
A.J. Lamb		
P.H. Edmonds		
N.A. Foster		
D.I. Gower* } did not bat		
C.S. Cowdrey		
P.R. Downton†		
P.I. Pocock		
N.G. Cowans		
Extras (lb 1, w 1)		2
Total (1 wicket)		35

Fall of Wickets: 1/7.
Bowling: Kapil Dev 3-0-20-0, Sivaramakrishnan 4-0-12-1, Shastri 1-0-2-0.

FAR LEFT Gavaskar is bowled by a triumphant Neil Foster – the first of his 11 wickets in the match.
LEFT Fowler and Gatting, who both scored double-hundreds, at the moment when Fowler reaches 200

Champag

ENGLAND v AUSTRALIA

Played at The Oval,
29, 30, 31 August, 2 September 1985.
Result: England won by an innings and 94 runs.

England: First innings

G.A. Gooch c and b McDermott	196
R.T. Robinson b McDermott	3
D.I. Gower* c Bennett b McDermott	157
M.W. Gatting c Border b Bennett	4
J.E. Emburey c Wellham b Lawson	9
A.J. Lamb c McDermott b Lawson	1
I.T. Botham c Phillips b Lawson	12
P.R. Downton† b McDermott	16
R.M. Ellison c Phillips b Gilbert	3
P.H. Edmonds lbw b Lawson	12
L.B. Taylor not out	1
Extras (b 13, lb 11, nb 26)	50
Total	464

Fall of Wickets: 1/20, 2/371, 3/376, 4/403, 5/405, 6/418, 7/425, 8/447, 9/452, 10/464.
Bowling: Lawson 29.2-6-101-4, McDermott 31-2-108-4, Gilbert 21-2-96-1, Bennett 32-8-111-1, Border 2-0-8-0, Wessels 3-0-16-0.

Australia: First innings

G.M. Wood lbw b Botham	22
A.M.J. Hilditch c Gooch b Botham	17
K.C. Wessels b Emburey	12
A.R. Border* b Edmonds	38
D.M. Wellham c Downton b Ellison	13
G.M. Ritchie not out	64
W.B. Phillips† b Edmonds	18
M.J. Bennett c Robinson b Ellison	12
G.F. Lawson c Botham b Taylor	14
C.J. McDermott run out	25
D.R. Gilbert b Botham	1
Extras (lb 3, w 2)	5
Total	241

Fall of Wickets: 1/35, 2/52, 3/56, 4/101, 5/109, 6/144, 7/171, 8/192, 9/235, 10/241.
Bowling: Botham 20-3-64-3, Taylor 13-1-39-1, Ellison 18-5-35-2, Emburey 19-7-48-1, Edmonds 14-2-52-2.

Australia: Second innings

G.M. Wood b Botham	6
A.M.J. Hilditch c Gower b Taylor	9
K.C. Wessels c Downton b Botham	7
A.R. Border* c Botham b Ellison	58
D.M. Wellham lbw b Ellison	5
G.M. Ritchie c Downton b Ellison	6
W.B. Phillips† c Downton b Botham	10
M.J. Bennett c and b Taylor	11
G.F. Lawson c Downton b Ellison	7
C.J. McDermott c Botham b Ellison	2
D.R. Gilbert not out	0
Extras (b 4, nb 4)	8
Total	129

Fall of Wickets: 1/13, 2/16, 3/37, 4/51, 5/71, 6/96, 7/114, 8/127, 9/129, 10/129.
Bowling: Botham 17-3-44-3, Taylor 11.3-1-34-2, Ellison 17-3-46-5, Emburey 1-0-1-0.

RIGHT England's match-winners: Gooch (196) and Gower (157), taking a breather during their magnificent second-wicket partnership of 351.
FAR RIGHT Captain Gower getting the champagne treatment from (LEFT TO RIGHT) Lamb, Gatting, Botham and Downton

ne and Ashes

Daily Mail, 3 September, 1985

AUSTRALIA SURRENDERED the Ashes at The Oval in the Sixth and last Test of the 1985 summer when for the second time running England beat them by an innings. The over-all record of this Australian side, with only four wins in 20 first-class matches, is surely the poorest of any Australian visitors to England, albeit they did win the Test at Lord's where Australia had not lost for half a century.

England went to The Oval 2-1 up in the series, so needed only to avoid defeat to take the honours of the summer, and they insured themselves against that by making 376 for 3 on the first day. Though there was a collapse on the second morning Australia never looked like saving the follow-on. On the last day 15,000 turned up despite Australia being still 161 behind in their second innings with six wickets standing. They saw only 90 minutes' play but enjoyed the traditional Ashes-winning scenes at the finish.

Allan Border was not out, but after holding up his side's uncertain batting all the summer he could muster only 58, so reducing his average over the series to 66. It was an unusual feature that the respective captains were the most successful batsmen. David Gower's 157, made in a stand of 351 for the second wicket with Graham Gooch (196) brought his average to 81. Gatting with three not outs actually averaged 87. Richard Ellison's 17 wickets in the last two Tests at 10 runs each were a decisive factor. For Australia Craig McDermott's 30 wickets in six Tests, average 30, was the outstanding achievement with the ball.

1986

W. Indies humiliated as Pakistan go one up

Daily Telegraph, 30 October, 1986

A NEWSPAPER headline proclaiming the humiliation of the West Indies in a Test Match – against any opposition – has been almost unthinkable for over a decade. As the *Daily Telegraph* report – and more particularly the footnote by the statistics supremo Bill Frindall – goes on to show, their defeat at Faisalabad not only brought a sharp and rare reverse to the West Indies' usual run of fortune but also took them into the record books thanks to their second innings total of 53.

Few people would disagree that the West Indies have lost, for the time being, the position on a lofty pinnacle enjoyed under the captaincy of Clive Lloyd. After leaving Pakistan their subsequent performances in the two one-day competitions in Australia, against the home country, England and – in one – Pakistan showed that they were certainly no longer invincible at that form of cricket either.

By contrast the Pakistan team at Faisalabad revealed a formidable and wideranging depth of attack. They fielded two fast bowlers who could also bat; the first, Imran Khan, acknowledged as one of the world's leading all-rounders and his partner, Wasim Akram, made Man of the Match for his 6 for 91 and his innings of 66. In addition the man who has often been decisive for Pakistan in recent Tests, the leg-spinner Abdul Qadir, came up trumps and effectively bamboozled the West Indians out in their sorry second innings, taking 6 for 16 in under ten overs.

Faisalabad makes history
By Bill Frindall

THE WEST INDIES total of 53, at Faisalabad yesterday, is their lowest in 247 Tests (previously 78 v Pakistan at Dacca in 1958-59), and the lowest in 73 Tests by all countries in Pakistan (previously 70 by New Zealand at Dacca in 1955-56).

There have been only five lower totals in Test cricket since 1946 (772 matches), the world record being New Zealand's 26 v England at Auckland in 1954-55.

PAKISTAN v WEST INDIES
Played at Faisalabad,
24, 26, 27, 28, 29 October, 1986.
Result: Pakistan won by 186 runs.

Pakistan: First innings

Mohsin Khan lbw b Marshall		2
Mudassar Nazar c Richardson b Marshall		26
Ramiz Raja lbw b Marshall		0
Javed Miandad c Dujon b Patterson		1
Qasim Omar hit wkt b Gray		3
Salim Malik retired hurt		21
Imran Khan* c and b Gray		61
Abdul Qadir c and b Patterson		14
Salim Yousuf† lbw b Gray		0
Wasim Akram c Richardson b Gray		0
Tausif Ahmed not out		9
Extras (b 1, lb 11, nb 10)		22
Total		159

Fall of Wickets: 1/12, 2/12, 3/19, 4/37, 5/37, 6/119, 7/120, 8/120, 9/159.
Bowling: Marshall 10-2-48-3, Patterson 12-1-38-2, Gray 11.5-3-39-4, Walsh 5-0-22-0.

West Indies: First innings

C.G. Greenidge lbw b Wasim		10
D.L. Haynes lbw b Imran		40
R.B. Richardson b Tausif		54
H.A. Gomes c sub (Manzoor Elahi) b Qadir		33
P.J.L. Dujon† c Ramiz b Tausif		0
R.A. Harper c Salim Yousuf b Wasim		28
M.D. Marshall c Salim Yousuf b Wasim		5
I.V.A. Richards* c Salim Yousuf b Wasim		33
A.H. Gray not out		12
C.A. Walsh lbw b Wasim		4
B.P. Patterson lbw b Wasim		0
Extras (b 9, lb 8, nb 12)		29
Total		248

Fall of Wickets: 1/12, 2/103, 3/124, 4/124, 5/178, 6/192, 7/223, 8/243, 9/247, 10/248.
Bowling: Wasim 25-3-91-6, Imran 21-8-32-1, Qadir 15-1-58-1, Tausif 22-5-50-2.

Pakistan: Second innings

Mohsin Khan c Haynes b Walsh		40
Mudassar Nazar c Haynes b Marshall		2
Ramiz Raja c Gray b Patterson		13
Javed Miandad (6) c sub (A.L. Logie) b Gray		30
Qasim Omar lbw b Walsh		48
Salim Malik (11) not out		3
Imran Khan* c Harper b Marshall		23
Abdul Qadir lbw b Gray		2
Salim Yousuf† (4) c Greenidge b Harper		61
Wasim Akram (9) st Dujon b Harper		66
Tausif Ahmed (10) b Walsh		8
Extras (b 7, lb 8, w 2, nb 15)		32
Total		328

Fall of Wickets: 1/2, 2/19, 3/113, 4/124, 5/208, 6/218, 7/224, 8/258, 9/296, 10/328.
Bowling: Marshall 26-3-83-2, Patterson 19-3-63-1, Gray 22-4-82-2, Walsh 23-6-49-3, Harper 27.5-9-36-2.

West Indies: Second innings

C.G. Greenidge lbw b Imran		12
D.L. Haynes lbw b Imran		0
R.B. Richardson c Ramiz b Qadir		14
H.A. Gomes b Qadir		2
P.J.L. Dujon† (6) lbw b Imran		0
R.A. Harper (7) c sub (Shoaib Mohd) b Qadir		2
M.D. Marshall (8) c and b Qadir		10
I.V.A. Richards* c Ramiz b Qadir		0
A.H. Gray b Qadir		5
C.A. Walsh b Imran		0
B.P. Patterson not out		6
Extras (lb 2)		2
Total		53

Fall of Wickets: 1/5, 2/16, 3/19, 4/19, 5/20, 6/23, 7/36, 8/42, 9/43, 10/53.
Bowling: Wasim 3-0-5-0, Imran 13-5-30-4, Qadir 9.3-1-16-6.

LEFT Wasim Akram: Imran's partner in a formidable strike attack

Somerset: time to cut the cant

MIKE SELVEY on the cricket row that has divided a county

Observer, 9 November, 1986

THE SOMERSET row which exploded in the autumn of 1986 was one of the most acrimonious in the history of English cricket. Indeed, as one member of the Somerset team wrily remarked at one stage, Somerset had 'out-Yorkshired Yorkshire'. The bomb-shell which started it all was the announcement by the Somerset committee that they would not be renewing the contracts of Vivian Richards and Joel Garner. Instead they would be taking on young Martin Crowe of New Zealand as the county's overseas player following his great summer for the county in 1984. Ian Botham, the third of Somerset's international super-stars immediately proclaimed that he would resign if the two West Indians were not reinstated. Players, the committee, club members and supporters took sides. There ensued weeks of charge and counter-charge, at times nothing better than a slanging match, all under a constant spotlight of publicity.

Eventually the facts of the matter were emphatically resolved on 8 November when the county met at Shepton Mallet and in two separate motions overwhelmingly supported the committee.What could not be resolved so immediately was the damage done to Somerset and to the game of cricket as a whole. Indeed, the county club was fortunate that the unhappy incident blew up in the autumn and winter, when there was not the risk of players' form being affected as would undoubtedly have been the case in the summer, and when they had a few months to put their house in order before the start of the next season.

LEFT Garner, Botham and Richards, the central figures in the Somerset controversy, in happier times for their county

England aglo

England retained the Ashes here yesterday when they won the fourth Test match by an innings and 14 runs with more than two whole days to spare.

Having bowled Australia out in three hours 55 minutes on the first day, they took only 45 minutes longer now, Australia's last six wickets falling for 41 runs in 18.4 overs.

The less said about Australia's batting the better. The omission of Ritchie had left them in the first place with only four front-line batsmen, much to Border's regret and England's delight. England had Botham at No 6 and Australia had Matthews, between whom there is no comparison.

Mike Gatting spoke after the match of a great effort by all his players, and so it was. Not least, England fielded splendidly.

For an England captain, it is a fine moment when he is assured of taking the Ashes home from Australia. In all this century, only Warner, Douglas, Chapman, Jardine, Hutton, Illingworth and Brearley have savoured it. Gatting was not chaired off the field or anything like that, but that was because at the end England had met with such little resistance.

Gatting said that he had not enjoyed every moment of his captaincy (who does?), but he was enjoying yesterday all right. It made a joyful ending to what has been for the most part a depressing year for England.

The Times, 29 December, 1986

RIGHT Chris Broad, England's top scorer of the series, acknowledges applause upon reaching his hundred at Melbourne. It was his third century in succession.

with Ashes triumph

JOHN WOODCOCK'S Fourth Test report from Melbourne on England's retention of the Ashes in the last days of December 1986 eschews rapture – the match was in any case too one-sided for that. The praise and the delight however come through clearly enough, and one knows from experience – a cricketwriter's feeling when a long losing run comes to an end. In England's case it amounted to three series: against West Indies, India and New Zealand, adding

up to 11 Tests without a win. Here, against a hapless Australia, Mike Gatting's side repeated *in three days* their victory in the First Test at Brisbane and so put the Ashes out of Australia's reach.

John must also have taken pleasure from the fact of this being his nineteenth and in all probability last Ashes series as cricket correspondent of *The Times*, an unbroken sequence not bettered nor ever likely to be.

Gatting's 'greatest moment'

AUSTRALIA v ENGLAND
Played at Melbourne, 26, 27, 28 December, 1986.
Result: England won by an innings and 14 runs.

Australia: First innings
G.R. Marsh c Richards b Botham		17
D.C. Boon c Botham b Small		7
D.M. Jones c Gower b Small		59
A.R. Border* c Richards b Botham		15
S.R. Waugh c Botham b Small		10
G.R.J. Matthews c Botham b Small		14
P.R. Sleep c Richards b Small		0
T.J. Zoehrer† b Botham		5
C.J. McDermott c Richards b Botham		0
M.G. Hughes c Richards b Botham		2
B.A. Reid not out		2
Extras (b 1, lb 1, w 1, nb 7)		10
Total		141

Fall of Wickets: 1/16, 2/44, 3/80, 4/108, 5/118, 6/118, 7/129, 8/133, 9/137, 10/141.
Bowling: Small 22.4-7-48-5, DeFreitas 11-1-30-0, Emburey 4-1-16-0, Botham 16-4-41-5, Gatting 1-0-4-0.

England: First innings
B.C. Broad c Zoehrer b Hughes		112
C.W.J. Athey lbw b Reid		21
M.W. Gatting* c Hughes b Reid		40
A.J. Lamb c Zoehrer b Reid		43
D.I. Gower c Matthews b Sleep		7
I.T. Botham c Zoehrer b McDermott		29
C.J. Richards† c Marsh b Reid		3
P.A.J. DeFreitas c Matthews b McDermott		7
J.E. Emburey c and b McDermott		22
P.H. Edmonds lbw b McDermott		19
G.C. Small not out		21
Extras (b 6, lb 7, w 1, nb 11)		25
Total		349

Fall of Wickets: 1/58, 2/163, 3/198, 4/219, 5/251, 6/273, 7/277, 8/289, 9/319, 10/349.
Bowling: McDermott 26.5-4-83-4, Hughes 30-3-94-1, Reid 28-5-78-4, Waugh 8-4-16-0, Sleep 28-4-65-1.

Australia: Second innings
G.R. Marsh (2) run out		60
D.C. Boon (1) c Gatting b Small		8
D.M. Jones c Gatting b DeFreitas		21
A.R. Border* c Emburey b Small		34
S.R. Waugh b Edmonds		49
G.R.J. Matthews b Emburey		0
P.R. Sleep run out		6
T.J. Zoehrer† c Athey b Edmonds		1
C.J. McDermott b Emburey		1
M.G. Hughes c Small b Edmonds		8
B.A. Reid not out		0
Extras (lb 3, w 1, nb 2)		6
Total		194

Fall of Wickets: 1/13, 2/48, 3/113, 4/153, 5/153, 6/175, 7/180, 8/185, 9/189, 10/194.
Bowling: Small 15-3-40-2, DeFreitas 12-1-44-1, Emburey 20-5-43-2, Botham 7-1-19-0, Edmonds 19.4-5-45-3.

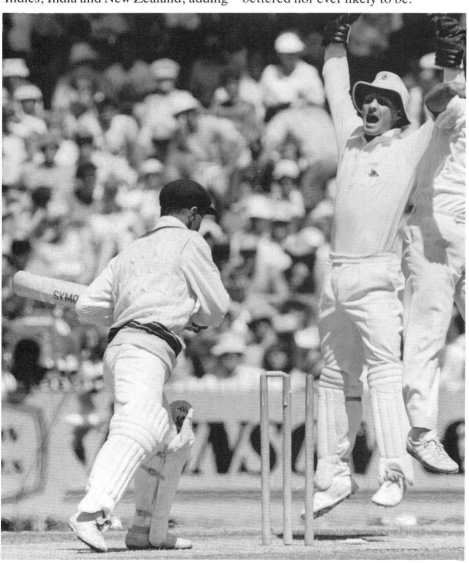

LEFT Matthews is bowled by Emburey for 0 and the Ashes are almost secure

207

1987

Botham delivers a grand slam sign-off

Independent, 12 February, 1987

IT SEEMED fitting, having given extracts elsewhere in this book of the national newspapers which since 1900 have closed down, that the last item, covering the climax of the England tour, should feature the new *Independent*, launched in the autumn of 1986. It is only a pity that its concluding story hardly reflects the *Independent's* general attitude to sport. It was reasonable to accord the headline to Botham since he took three good wickets in this last match. The editorial, though, typified the current media obsession with this dramatic, mercurial cricketer at the expense of a balanced view. This is neither good for his ego nor fair to others.

Did that 'grandest of slammers' perform his 'customary heroics'? After his splendid hundred in the First Test he 'slammed' just two scores of over 50 in 19 completed innings. His three wickets here mentioned brought his bag to seven in the 10-match (so called) World Series, taken at almost four runs an over and at 55 runs apiece.

Conspicuously, Chris Broad with the bat and several with the ball achieved a good deal more.

England's triple success in Australia in 1986-87, in both one-day competitions as well as in the fight for the Ashes, was essentially a victory for team-work, chief credit for which must be divided between Mike Gatting, the captain, and the management combination of Peter Lush and Micky Stewart. What an unexpectedly happy note on which to finish!

ENGLAND v AUSTRALIA
The World Series Cup final
England

B.C. Broad c O'Donnell b Matthews	53
I.T. Botham c Ritchie b O'Donnell	25
C.W.J. Athey c b Matthews	16
D.I. Gower c Wellham b Taylor	17
M.W. Gatting* run out	7
A.J. Lamb c Zoehrer b O'Donnell	35
J.E. Emburey c Zoehrer b Waugh	6
P.A.J. DeFreitas c Jones b Taylor	1
N.A. Foster c Taylor b Davis	7
B.N. French† not out	9
G.R. Dilley not out	6
Extras (lb 4, w 1)	5
Total (for nine wickets, 50 overs)	187

Fall of Wickets: 1/36, 2/73, 3/102, 4/120, 5/121, 6/143, 7/146, 8/170, 9/170.
Bowling: Davis 10-0-44-1, O'Donnell 10-1-37-2, Waugh 10-0-42-1, Matthews 10-1-31-2, Taylor 10-2-29-2.

Australia

G.R. Marsh lbw b Botham	28
A.R. Border* c French b Botham	27
D.M. Jones c and b Emburey	13
G.M. Ritchie c DeFreitas b Botham	4
D.M. Wellham c Gower b DeFreitas	30
S.R. Waugh run out	22
S.P. O'Donnell not out	40
T.J. Zoehrer† lbw b DeFreitas	0
G.R.J. Matthews run out	3
P.L. Taylor not out	3
S.P. Davis did not bat	
Extras (b 1, lb 6, w 2)	9
Total (for eight wickets, 50 overs)	179

Fall of Wickets: 1/55, 2/70, 3/72, 4/80, 5/124, 6/135, 7/135, 8/151.
Bowling: Dilley 10-1-34-0, DeFreitas 10-1-34-2, Botham 10-1-26-3, Foster 10-0-51-0, Emburey 10-2-27-1.

RIGHT Botham the big-hitter

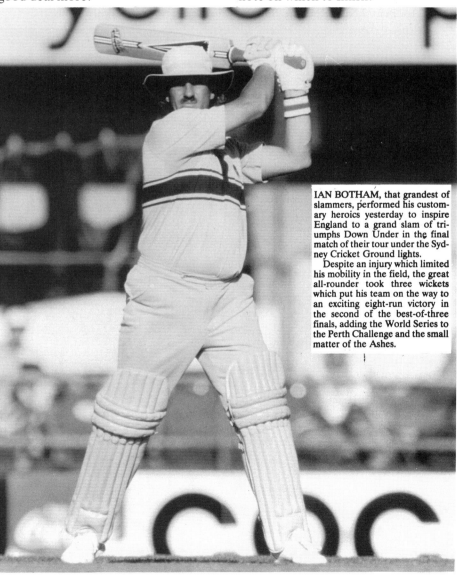

IAN BOTHAM, that grandest of slammers, performed his customary heroics yesterday to inspire England to a grand slam of triumphs Down Under in the final match of their tour under the Sydney Cricket Ground lights.

Despite an injury which limited his mobility in the field, the great all-rounder took three wickets which put his team on the way to an exciting eight-run victory in the second of the best-of-three finals, adding the World Series to the Perth Challenge and the small matter of the Ashes.